THE INSTABILITY OF TRUTH

ALSO BY REBECCA LEMOV

Database of Dreams:
The Lost Quest to Catalog Humanity

World as Laboratory:
Experiments with Mice, Mazes, and Men

The
INSTABILITY
of TRUTH

*Brainwashing, Mind Control,
and Hyper-Persuasion*

REBECCA LEMOV

W. W. Norton & Company
Independent Publishers Since 1923

Copyright © 2025 by Rebecca Lemov

All rights reserved
Printed in the United States of America
First Edition

For information about permission to reproduce selections from this book, write to
Permissions, W. W. Norton & Company, Inc., 500 Fifth Avenue, New York, NY 10110

For information about special discounts for bulk purchases, please contact
W. W. Norton Special Sales at specialsales@wwnorton.com or 800-233-4830

Manufacturing by Lakeside Book Company
Book design by Daniel Lagin
Production manager: Julia Druskin

ISBN 978-1-324-07526-4

W. W. Norton & Company, Inc., 500 Fifth Avenue, New York, NY 10110
www.wwnorton.com

W. W. Norton & Company Ltd., 15 Carlisle Street, London W1D 3BS

10 9 8 7 6 5 4 3 2 1

To my dad, who always asked a question.
Michael Lemov, 1935–2024

*

To my graduate advisor, who taught me to do my own research.
Paul Rabinow, 1944–2021

CONTENTS

Introduction: From Twentieth- to Twenty-first-Century
Mind-Control Techniques   1

PART 1
BRAINWASHING ARRIVES

1. Lima Beans at the Bottom of the Ocean   11
2. The Volleyball Problem   39
3. The Lonesome Friends of Science   67
4. Violence Studies   97

PART 2
BRAINWASHING SPREADS

5. Literal Brain Control   131
6. A Small Uh-Oh Opened Up in My Soul   177
7. I Accommodated My Thoughts to Theirs   207
8. Darksome House of Mortal Clay   241

PART 3

BRAINWASHING EVOLVES

9. How to Look Inside People, Extract Their Intimate Data, and Gently Nudge Emotional States into Being   279

10. On Being Emotionally Chained to Technology—Namely, Your Radio, Television, Internet, Social Media, or Friendly-Yet-Somehow-Predatory Chatbot   305

11. Hopium   339

Conclusion   367

Acknowledgments   377

Note on Sources and Methods   385

Notes   387

Index   435

THE INSTABILITY OF TRUTH

INTRODUCTION

From Twentieth- to Twenty-first-Century Mind-Control Techniques

I seek to create afresh the stages by which the mind gives way to compulsion from without . . .
—Czesław Miłosz, *The Captive Mind*

"That's the brainwashing of brainwashing," my dinner companion said to me. "The fact that it is unrecognized while it is happening." It was summer and we were sitting in the dining facility of a fancy German research institute situated in the woods of Berlin, a city not known for woods but one that is actually full of them. I had been describing my current research, how I was exploring the history of mind-control techniques and was connecting them to the way our increasingly data-driven lives affect our collective and individual senses of reality. And how, despite all this, we seem unable fully to realize what is happening. "*Brainwashing erases itself,*" my friend added.

I almost fell out of my chair at her insight (and also possibly because I had just flown from the US the night before and had been up for thirty-six hours by the time the salad course arrived). When I think about it in my own time zone, though, I still believe that she was correct.

Brainwashing is hard to see. This is because it has a doubling effect, operating both on the world and on the observation of the world, so that you often cannot see it while it is happening. It obscures the one level from the other. Unless, as this book argues, you look really hard for it.

Here is an example to start with: While studying in graduate school in Berkeley, California, in the 1990s, I embarked on an intellectual love affair with a set of fascinating French thinkers. I was looking at their words for ultimate meaning, for a path to enlightened knowledge, for my very own "Key to All Mythologies," to borrow the working title of the never-finished book the terrible husband-scholar in George Eliot's *Middlemarch* labors to write. After a while, reading these charismatic but difficult-to-understand books, my own writing changed, because my thinking had changed. What I was writing shifted on the page, leaning toward inscrutable, showoff-y. It offered something, but then took back its meaning. A reviewer of an article I wrote commented, "The writer writes in a style that is unrecognizable." My professor praised the work for being the best in our class and, possibly, better than her own, because it was so cryptic and hard to understand.

While maybe this is the point of a graduate education—to learn something new, to change yourself—the group dynamics also resulted in cult-like behavior: Some students chose to align themselves with the select group who liked "theory," and some didn't or couldn't. I labored under the impression that I would find a kind of transcendent truth if I could only read the puzzle-like prose of Jacques Lacan or Jacques Derrida carefully enough. I would "nail down" this truth even if the effort to swing the heavy hammer of deconstruction pulled me backward off my feet as in a Hanna-Barbera cartoon.

This may seem a small and trivial example to draw on, since no lives were ruined, only prose. After a couple of years, the spell of this set of ideas wore off, and I thought it would be better to write something that people, including myself, would understand; something to which the reader would bring their own experience. What caused the spell to break? By then I was in my late twenties, and I had gone through some crises, including divorce and broken health. Emerging from them, I started from scratch and began to study the processes of social and human engineering—tracing how social control is played out day-to-day in an almost invisible way, right in front of our faces.

Instead of dizzying theories, I turned to history, asking: How do we know the things we think we know? I found a set of lost actors in the behavioral sciences who had the ultimate ambition to create a perfect technology of human behavior prediction. Their work started in the 1930s and grew in force through the 1950s. In fact, they built what may have been the Largest Filing Cabinet in the World in order to track all forms of human activity across all cultures (or a representative sample), from death rituals to belief in God to the varieties of nose-blowing techniques. They rendered all this information in a codable, transferable form. Although no one but me thought this forgotten data was interesting in the slightest—it was as out of date as anything could be within my field—I loved the idea that you could say something yourself, for yourself, and try to convince others of its strange, if unintentional, poetry.

I recently discovered this fact about Lacan: In the French countryside, one day, when his car was stalled in the muddy road, he requested that several passersby help him get it moving. But instead of lending a hand along with his helpers, he stood by aristocratically and allowed them to move his car for him. This did not surprise me. It's not that the deconstructionists were absolutely wrong, it's just that they stood by the road when others labored to push.

Later, when I thought of these theorists and of my own entrancement, I asked myself: Had I been brainwashed? I was thinking thoughts not quite my own. I was expressing myself in ways foreign to my inclinations. I was even voicing opinions I did not hold. (For example, I remember saying with great conviction, "I hate little dogs!" on seeing one trotting down the street. I had the impression that women such as the type I aspired to be were unsentimentally opposed to small canines. But on reflection I saw that I had nothing against them; in fact, I really like them.)

What does my intellectual affair with the French thinkers and my personal turning points have in common with, say, Patty Hearst in 1974, abducted into a left-wing, militant homegrown terror group, after which she "elected" to stay with the group as a self-described urban guerilla? What can it have in common with an American soldier held on the Chinese–North Korean border in the 1950s, abandoning all hope, betrayed by his own government, and opting to join Communism, becoming a true believer? Or, more recently, with a young actress-entrepreneur such as Sarah Edmondson seeking female empowerment in the NXIVM group only to end up seared near the hipbone with a cattle brand of the cult leader's initials entwined with those of his second lieutenant, and once known primarily as a star of the television show *Smallville*? Or with ourselves collectively, as online browsers, giving away our personal information for a glimpse of acrobatic pleasures or a round of shopping? These may seem to be disparate experiential samples spread across decades and cultures. The common theme is that, whatever the circumstance, we surrender to these influences, which then shape our choices further, in ways we simultaneously understand and neglect fully to understand.

My school experience is just a small example, but it raises the question of how the small relates to the large, the personal to the ideological, the individual to the collective. How the "hard" (of coercion) crosses into to the "soft" (of persuasion). How brainwashing erases itself. I do not ask you to agree with me up front about this truest conclusion; but instead, I urge you to join me in treading this historical path of wild, unlikely, and strangely ordinary experiences. Consider it, then, the going hypothesis: that what we call brainwashing is not rare but common, a potential of all moments, a set of forces that can be activated, and it is not so much what happens to those other people as it is what can happen to anybody, especially anyone who assumes blithely that it has nothing at all to do with themselves. Saying it is something shameful and embarrassing that happens to others ("I heard he was in a cult," "How could anyone fall for that?" "Purple Nike sneakers, really?" "Why didn't she just leave?" "Isn't that a conspiracy theory?") is a way in which we distance ourselves from its commonness.

This is a case for not distancing—and instead for looking closer at a hidden yet constantly activated dimension to people's lives.

....

Many books exist about brainwashing, from different perspectives, with titles such as *The Rape of the Mind* and *The CIA's Control of Candy Jones*. The first title—published in 1956 by the Dutch physician Joost Meerloo—is an example of an influential theory which held that the procedures of thought reform constituted a targeted campaign of forced submission, or menticide. Since that time, many additional theories have been brought to bear on the topic: dual-process theory, game theory, social maximization, cognitive biases, sunk-cost calculations, the agentic shift, and cognitive dissonance among them. There are neuroscientific findings, and there are existential musings. There are books that analyze films about brainwashing (it's surprising how many of these movies there are!) and books that look at literary allusions. The second example—about a New York model who patriotically agreed to undergo hypnotic training from the CIA and (unwittingly) became a "virtual zombie" named Arlene, who was used to test the extent of possible mind control—details first-hand experiences that are, it is appropriate to say, mind blowing. (Such accounts are also, like the events taking place in many clandestine projects for which records have been destroyed or suppressed, difficult to absolutely confirm.)[1]

Where the many definitions and theories about this phenomenon fall short is in capturing the paradoxes brainwashing generates.

(If it were enough to offer an authoritative definition or two of this key term, brainwashing, there would be no need to write a book.)

Likewise, if it were as simple as just communicating that brainwashing exists, the whole matter would have been settled long ago. I would not have wanted to teach a class on it for a decade. Experts would not have needed to fight about it. Legal cases would not have been borne along and then sunk by its effects. The military would not have designed counter-weapons. The public would not have panicked and taken up (in some cases) their own countermeasures, nor would we enjoy the habit of lobbing the insult "brainwashed idiot" at each other or our relatives at Thanksgiving.

....

In more than ten years of teaching the course "Brainwashing and Modern Mind Control Techniques," the most remarkable part is that the topic has become less knowable the longer I've taught it, the more I've tried to fathom it. (Remember that the word *fathom* comes from undersea measurement—and brainwashing would elude exact measurement throughout its history, retaining a murky "Do-I-really-see-this?" quality.)

My field of study is, in fact, measurement: quantification. When I was a teenager, tired of how my dad constantly counted up my exploits in sports or academics (my GPA or half-mile time), I began to refer to him as The Great Quantifier with some resentment. Funny that I would come to study quantification itself. In the words of Ted Porter, the renowned author of the classic text *Trust in Numbers*, "The push for routines of calculation" explains much in the development of bureaucracies and modern life's dullest corridors.

But I also was drawn to those things that cannot be quantified—and here we are suddenly back in the territory of brainwashing. Just because something cannot be measured with a galvanometer or a MMPI or an fMRI—its action pathways cannot be "seen" in the way one can trace the trajectory of a rocket or the movements of someone making a pizza—doesn't mean it does not empirically exist. I ended up in a wonderful specialty called the "History of Science," which was born at Harvard and combines elements of philosophy, sociology, and other fields to understand how science works.[2]

In this book, I use what I like to think of as the two superpowers of my field to make a new argument about brainwashing. The first superpower is the "actor's category," a tricky and beautiful method, not invented by historians of science, but one that is used in an important way by our field. The actor's category, a concept that originally hails from a practice called ethnomethodology in the 1960s, basically states that if you are studying something or someone, you should be sure to try to understand it from the involved person's point of view (the actor) before you rush in (the analyst) to impose your own preexisting assumptions or judgments. Sounds basic, but when applied to science and scientists, it becomes radical.[*] A more recent explanation goes, "Let it be accepted that sociological explanation"—of scientific activity such as studying galvanic waves or making retinopathic diagnoses—"must begin with the perspective of the actor."[3] Only later can there be some feedback between the views of analyst and actor.

A lot of research about the topic of mind control begins with an extensive discussion of terms, theories, and definitions. This is all very well and worth doing. But how do I know that what one person means by "reality" or "cult" or another term is the same as what someone else means? It is refreshing to say, *Let's see how people used it. Let's see what the actors themselves meant.* So, I've done this with brainwashing, which is admittedly a complex task. Yet I found that specific people used it in specific ways, and tracing how this usage varied, and changed over time, sheds new light on the problem of what it is. (Does brainwashing really exist? I'm always asked. The answer is yes.) It also allows us to track how the term has spread across the

---

[*] Radical because scientists are actively in the process of shaping categories in which they also participate, and this seems to contradict some of the stricter definitions of objectivity.

globe, such that a Nigerian woman in the 2010s could use the term *brainwashing* to explain the terrorist activity of Boko Haram to a BBC news crew.[4] When some of those people are the very expert psychiatrists or behavioral scientists whose views would change lives (their actors' categories are also analysts' categories), the stakes are raised. I've tried to capture many forgotten or neglected dramas from the history of brainwashing's courtrooms, secret labs, military schools, cult compounds, and—today—digital sites.

This actor's category may not seem like a superpower, but it is, because it allows the expansion of mind. The actor's category is almost literally mind expanding and time expanding. It requires a rigorous shifting of perspective.

The other superpower is the "second-order observer." This is a term that the German sociologist Niklas Luhmann came up with. Luhmann was a thinker who loved to describe systems from an observer's point of view, but it was a different kind of observer. (He also enjoyed building strange boxes called *Zettelkasten* or slip-boxes where you could keep torn-up scraps of data from your research, and mysteriously he used the contraption to produce thirty-five books, thus solving the problem of scholarly writer's block.)[5] His concept is otherwise defined as "observing observers as observers."[6] It serves as a counterpoint to the actor's category, in other words. Once we have immersed ourselves in the worlds of those who were on hand, on stage, we can take a step back and watch the system itself. In the history of brainwashing, these two superpowers allow me to understand with care what is new and what is real in this paranoiac's dream of a phenomenon.

In what follows, I use these special tools of my field to investigate the past and present, with an eye toward the future.

Against the typical view holding (until recently) that brainwashing is a myth or something ridiculous, I argue that it must be taken seriously. But also, it must be understood in a new way, linked to trauma, its emotional taproot, and grasped dynamically rather than cartoonishly.

PART 1

BRAINWASHING ARRIVES

How an unknown word—*brainwashing*—launched a hundred programs, a thousand diagnoses, a million rumors, and ten ships.

1

Lima Beans at the Bottom of the Ocean

For my PhD, I researched human and social engineering in the mid-twentieth century, spending years peering into leather-bound journals at articles that described rats running through mazes millions of times. These seemed like the least-sought-after things in the library. Making my way along the shelves, I looked into radical behaviorist experiments that were first dreamed up in laboratories before World War II and then streamed into the world (as I argued) after World War II. I titled the resulting dissertation "The Laboratory Imagination."

When I graduated in the spring of 2000, just as a new millennium began, I looked around myself. The dot-com bubble had just burst in the California Bay Area where I lived. The bubble's "irrational exuberance," as then Federal Reserve chairman Alan Greenspan put it around this time, had meant huge tips for my waiter boyfriend who worked at a celebrated place with end-grain wood tables where they made upscale corndogs for the employees in the afterhours.[1]

Suddenly, when the exuberance drained away, so did the outsized gratuities (not to mention the corndogs, which slipped in quality). I had no permanent job and was considering an academic post—my doctoral supervisor had arranged a one-year stint at a private college a few states away—but I felt unequipped for the job, which scared me. I decided instead to dedicate myself to a year of yoga by enrolling in a teacher training program. Studying esoteric practices and working as a (very) part-time legal secretary to support myself felt like a way to address the sterility of a world where social control procedures were proliferating—the way everything was so *managed*, from your Starbucks order to your health insurance (had I been lucky enough to have any).

All around me, I was seeing the experiments I had studied come to life. Some of the most sophisticated of my scientist subjects, the ones whose previously neglected work I had exhumed, called their goal "canalizing." The point of canalizing was to channel people's impulses into desired responses by crafting their outer surroundings and even their inner psychology. (The "transformation of duty into desire," as one put it.) People must be taught to *want* what was best for them. This was human engineering through behavior modification, and it was the opposite of neglected.[2]

Canalizing appeared to be everywhere in the 1990s. Uniqueness was just starting to be mass produced. The slogan for a cell phone company around that time captured the nascent vibe: *"You're a unique individual. This phone is just for you . . . and everyone like you."* Even the Army was recruiting based on scripted individualism rather than social duty in those days, debuting a new slogan, "An Army of One," in 2001. "I am an Army of one," declared a corporal running across the Mojave at dawn while carrying a thirty-five-pound pack in a widely run TV advertisement: "Even though there are 1,045,690 soldiers *just like me*, I am my own force." As in the military, so in the academic world: Aspiring to be a bold free thinker around that time in Berkeley, California, led to quandaries. Aiming to be a "thinker of one" was full of pitfalls. You were unique but simultaneously part of 1,045,690 others who were "just like me." There was an acceptable way to be "different." Norms expanded to incorporate this quirkiness. And so was born, or reborn, the hipster.

I had spent almost half of my twenties studying the long-forgotten records of a huge experiment in inculcating unfreedom. At Yale's Institute of Human Relations, a well-funded program of running rats through mazes, with the objective of establishing a universal science of behavior control, flourished during the 1930s. It featured many scientists announcing breakthroughs in what they described as "the maze that a human must learn" in order to live decently and capably in society. But not every experiment was a success. In a 1934 study by psychologist Neal Miller, one particular small Norwegian rat—an animal that had been "variable throughout," according to its handlers—suddenly refused to run at all after facing myriad electric shocks in an alleyway. The animal's recalcitrance sabotaged the data for the whole experiment, and the umbrage-filled note in the scientific publication—"Unfortunately . . . [t]his [refusal] spoiled the statistical reliability of the outcome"—piqued my interest. Even in a huge program like Yale's, one that sought to apply its animal discoveries to humans, a lone two-ounce creature could derail an experiment. I wondered: How did the past, with its seemingly unrealized stakes, contend with the bigger stakes of the present?[3]

To bridge the gap between past and present, I started to think about brainwashing, a topic I had not covered directly in my dissertation but was implied. Brainwashing was a well-worn term, and certainly everyone could recognize it—yet I found I didn't really know what it meant. It was over-the-top, scandalous, frightening, possibly silly. But it also struck me as possibly the most successful method in history to mold a human being into some new form. It was not just a matter of compelling someone to do something they didn't want to do or breaking a person down. After all, brute force had a long history, a lot longer than brainwashing. Brute force did not really change people's minds and sometimes it actually inspired resistance. Sheer physical punishment ("getting medieval on your ass" was the way the character Marsellus Wallace put it in *Pulp Fiction*) was not reliably successful. The Central Intelligence Agency's MK-ULTRA program would prove this. Even an average man of the late seventeenth century, the priest Urbain Grandier of Loudun, France, managed to resist making a forced confession at the hands of his tormentors as he was burned alive.*

What concerned me were modern methods, in which physical force was involved but was not the primary driver of change. As Czesław Miłosz observed in his 1953 classic, *The Captive Mind*, "We are concerned here with questions more significant than mere force."[4] The scarier thing was people gladly *volunteering* for terrible outcomes—begging for the gallows or sacrificing their previous beliefs and blindly embracing new ones. Observers from Aldous Huxley to a notorious Communist interrogator agreed that whereas it was possible to resist torture, new methods of the mid-twentieth century were close to 100 percent effective in attaining compliance. Just about no one could withstand them. "If God Himself was sitting in that chair we would make him say what we wanted him to say," claimed the interrogator. No one was exempt anymore. Said Huxley in *Brave New World Revisited*: "Government through terror works on the whole less well than government through the non-violent manipulation of the environment and of the thoughts and feelings of individual men, women and children."[5] Breaking the will, *Brave New World* style, was possible using behavioral technologies of modern mind control. Not only pain but a targeted mix of pleasure and pain would ensure adherence. Brainwashing is neither pure persuasion nor sheer coercion but both: coercive persuasion.

---

* In *The Devils of Loudun*, Aldous Huxley made this point, and reflected, "Our ancestors invented the rack and the iron maiden ... but in the subtler arts of breaking the will and reducing the human being to subhumanity, they still had much to learn," Aldous Huxley, *The Devils of Loudun* (New York, Harper & Row, 1952), 228–29.

What was this method? Was it possible that, to have a rate of compliance nearing total, the subject must—on some level, in some way, even subtly, even unwittingly—agree? And what did this all have to do with me and my concerns with being a unique and free individual—like everyone else—at the dawn of the internet age? This was not just a random cell phone campaign or a bohemian style of conformity but hard evidence of an extreme process.

The natural place to begin was during the early Cold War. Any proper discussion of brainwashing, I thought, must commence with its entrance into the English language. And even this was hazy.

....

In late 1949 and early 1950, in technical papers deep in the files of an operative from the Office of Strategic Services (the organization that preceded the Central Intelligence Agency), a new word in English, *brainwashing*, was starting to be used.[6] The first published mentions came soon afterward, first by a French reporter writing in the British *Guardian*, and soon after by an American journalist and OSS (later CIA) operative named Edward Hunter in a 1950 article for the *Miami News*.[7] Hunter was proud of his work bringing this threat to public attention. Brainwashing was a concentrated "mind attack" that made people confess to crimes they had not committed and willingly absorb ideas they did not believe in previously. Hunter quickly followed up with a book in 1951, *Brain-Washing in Red China*, which sold well.

A lot hinged on the words *xǐ nǎo* ("brain-washing"). It was different from the widely known term in Chinese *sīxiǎng gǎizào* ("reeducation"). Hunter wrote, "The plain people of China have coined several revealing colloquialisms for the whole indoctrination process. With their natural faculty for succinct and graphic phrases, they have referred to it as 'brain-washing' and 'brain-changing.'" He favored the first one. I speculate this was because it sounded cooler and more ominous in English. At any rate, Hunter was also interested in establishing provenance, like the owner of a thoroughbred or a famous painting. In the book's second edition in 1962, Hunter claimed his was "the first book to use the word"—back in 1953—and therefore deserved credit for "putting it into our language."[8] He even referred to brainwashing as "the word I gave"[9] to the public, which when you think about it is a pretty grandiose way to describe what elsewhere he presented as common Chinese slang. (Although the characters *xǐ nǎo*, for "wash" and "brain," do represent Chinese words, they were not habitually put together at that time, Chinese scholars and friends have told me, and do not appear in any Chinese dictionaries from the era.)[10]

So brainwashing was not quite a translation, but closer to an invention. A "keen student of propaganda" (in historian Marcia Holmes's description), Hunter, in fact, later was building his own large archive of Communist Chinese persuasion efforts—especially visual campaigns.[11] Basically, he collected cartoons (*liánhuánhuà* or "picture talk-books") from Mainland China as well as Hong Kong, and exactingly translated them. None from the mainland used the Chinese words for brainwash (at least, I could not discover any such use), although other phrases were common. It bears remembering that in the 1940s and 1950s, access to troves of images was not easy to gain; OSINT—open-source intelligence, gleaned from websites and other electronic media—did not yet exist. Value lay not simply in collecting things but in making them available "at your fingertips," and this is in effect what Hunter was doing, first at the OSS and later at the CIA, even as he also worked the Chautauqua lecture circuit and went on book tours.

Digging deeper into Hunter's own documents does offer direct evidence that the cognate term (brain-change) was used *in English* in Hong Kong *before* Hunter or even the OSS put it in print. An anti-Communist comic book, *The Little Boy and the Big Nose*, appeared in Hong Kong in 1949 by a dissident artist named David Loy. It tells the story of Ah Si, a lovely boy born in a small village in China who enjoyed a happy life until Communists, led by "the Big Nose, the

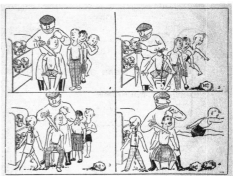

This 1949 comic book was found in the "father of brainwashing" Edward Hunter's collection of political cartoons from China. In it, the main character, the little boy, only barely escapes a gruesome fate of decapitation, euphemistically described as "brain transformation." The little boy depicted here evokes a long-standing tradition in twentieth-century Chinese cartoons, Sanmao. This was a series of adventures featuring a hapless yet feisty urchin with only a few hairs on his head—hence his name, Sanmao, which translates as "Three Hairs"—who was constantly encountering oppression, injustice, poverty, and various scrapes associated with these things. The character always managed to escape dire straits at the last minute. The twist in this tale, published in Hong Kong, is that it is the incoming Communist government that is being criticized rather than greedy capitalists or the nationalist forces. DAVID LOY, *THE LITTLE BOY AND THE BIG NOSE* (HONG KONG: SWEN PUBLICATIONS CO., 1949). AVAILABLE THROUGH THE CENTER FOR RESEARCH LIBRARIES (CRL) IN CHICAGO, ILLINOIS.

aggressor from the north," made existence miserable, and his parents were put to death for resisting. The cartoon tells Ah Si's story by satirically pairing a phrase of Communist propaganda with the contrasting hypocritical reality. "Freedom of Speech," for example, shows the boy being brutally silenced. In the penultimate pair, the "Latest Invention—Brain Transformation" is illustrated gruesomely by a line of dutiful young citizens waiting to have their heads hack-sawed off their bodies. (The heads are placed on a nearby shelf once the operation is complete.) Ah Si, the last in line, is the only one who flees.[12]

It's not clear that Hunter's claim to have heard the word *brainwash* from Chinese "plain people" bears up. The China scholar Mitchell Ryan does find some use of the term in the 1920s and 1930s among educated elites and Chinese people who were eager to embrace modernity, but it did not have its current meaning, did not refer to any particular program of indoctrination or forced change, and instead conveyed "a very general sense of political awakening."¹³ It meant the very opposite of coerced persuasion or forced reeducation. In the meantime, I propose, based on the evidence available, that it *was just beginning to be used* in China as a play on "heart washing"—a Confucian procedure much like the European Christian religious terms for washing the soul.

The Bible's Psalm 51, for example, contains the plea that the Lord "Purge me with hyssop, and I shall be clean: wash me, and I shall be whiter than snow." (Note that *heart* and *brain* in Chinese do not translate exactly in English, and that in Chinese the heart is seen as the seat of what Anglophones would consider mental functions, while the brain appears as the site of emotions.) In English-speaking countries, brainwashing resonated with a longer Christian history of conversion narratives stretching back at least to Paul's conversion on the Road to Damascus, in which God spoke to him and he fell down, blinded. In such narratives of religious ecstasy, both wanted and unwanted, from Elizabethan London to Portuguese Brazil, the life-changing event of conversion was often framed as "sudden, dramatic, and emotional."¹⁴ Not surprisingly the advent of brainwashing as a new word in 1950 generated a strong reaction. The word evoked uncanny feelings among Americans, as Hunter probably intended.

In a paradoxical outcome, the popularized English word—misleadingly asserted to have its roots in a common Chinese phrase—did integrate into spoken Chinese in subsequent decades. Thus, it affirmed a claim that was questionable to begin with, and brainwashing became well known also in China.

·········

Whatever the word's origin, several US businessmen soon unhappily vaulted into the headlines in the early 1950s as textbook cases of this new thing. One was Robert Vogeler, an American executive who was working for the International Telephone & Telegraph company in Budapest, Hungary, when he was arrested, found guilty of espionage, and kept for seventeen months in a solitary cell, where he was subjected to long interrogations, bright lights, ice water dunking, sleep deprivation, and other travails, which he was unable fully to remember on his release. Possibly, he thought, he had been drugged. Returning from Eastern Europe, he was "not himself," broken, twitchy, and unable to speak fluidly. He was somehow unmanned. Photographers swarmed and press reports described him as "back from the dead," though his appearance suggested the morbid state was ongoing.[15] Instead, his sexy wife took the stage. Lucile Vogeler reported that her husband, once notable for his upright posture and square shoulders, was now "sagging all over," barely recognizable as the person he once was.[16] After Vogeler was called away for a couple weeks to recover at the US National Naval Medical Center (now the Walter Reed National Military Medical Center) in Bethesda, Maryland, he emerged with a more coherent story. He was able to talk about his ordeal: "The very body is forced into league against one's personality," he said, thus providing a clue about the true dynamics of brainwashing that would be fatefully ignored for decades to come. And since he had lost his corporate job with ITT, both he and his wife joined some of the most prominent early voices to warn about the new brainwashing hazard, becoming professional speakers on the anti-Communist circuit. They specialized in taking bitter exception to the Cold War liberalism of President Harry Truman and his secretary of state, Dean Acheson.

Another newsreel feature around this time was of Cardinal József Mindszenty, the highest bishop in Hungary and a World War II hero who, after Communist police arrested him in 1948, endured what was (at the time) a new and unknown torture ordeal. Mindszenty's treatment in a Budapest prison was, in fact, much like Vogeler's, though it entailed slightly more status-based humiliation. For example, because he was such a revered figure, the cardinal was made to dress in a lowly clown costume, was jeered at, and had to beg for his food, in addition to suffering relentless interrogation, occasional roughing up, and forced confession. After twenty-eight days, he was publicly tried for forty crimes against the state, to all of which he, broken physically and psychologically, confessed. Through newsreel footage of the trial, he emerged on the world's stage like a propped-up puppet: glassy-eyed, admitting to venal sins against the church, and listlessly mouthing propaganda. (As he famously recalled in a memoir published some years later: *"Without knowing what had happened to me*, I had become a different person."[17] This phrase would keep cropping up in future brainwashing research. It would be invoked again and again by the psychiatrist Louis Jolyon West, among others, as containing the paradoxical kernel of the semi-participatory process.)

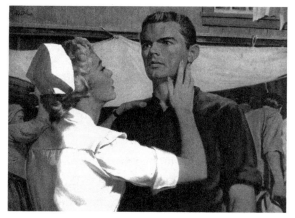

Illustration from a 1955 *Saturday Evening Post* short story exploring the harrowing effects of brainwashing. ILLUSTRATION BY LARRY KRITCHER.

The headline captured brainwashing's specter of loss of self, and of the destabilization of identity. Eventually Johnny does return to his wife.

Becoming someone else was alarming enough, but the nightmarish part was that you had no ability to *recognize* that this had happened. That too had been obliterated.

But it was the prisoners of war in Korea who really brought home brainwashing, gave life to the term, and added a shocking jolt to people's anxieties. When I first read about these men, I was surprised at how much attention their stories had garnered at the time and was taken aback at some of the kitschy responses, such as a chest-heaving story in the *Saturday Evening Post* about a nurse whose "Johnny" was magically converted to Communism and who had to win him (and his vacant, unseeing eyes) back from Chinese loyalty. Over the years, though, as I read more of their stories, my surprise took a new form. These were actual young men to whom something had happened. As a *New York Times* reporter on the Vogeler case put it, "Some terrible thing has taken place behind the scenes."[18] The deeper I went, the more I recognized this behind-the-scenes place.

Yet the "terrible thing" would continue to be a mystery through the succeeding decades. In attempting to unravel it, I came to understand that the dimension of trauma was somehow impossible to recognize during the 1950s in the experiences of the brainwashed, and that this had huge consequences. Because they could not see the dynamics of vulnerability and the way a new reality is stabilized out of an unstable situation, brainwashing turned into a magical, shameful phenomenon. This set off a long line of responses, many of them still reverberating today.*

---

* If the expert response was not to acknowledge trauma (erasing the bodily-emotional dimension of the brainwashing experience), the scholarly response, starting in the 1990s when professors began to write books addressing Cold War mind control, was to treat brainwashing as a hysterical cultural reaction and political cover-up with no real reality to it. Brainwashing became all too real in public and not real at all in academia. This book attempts to learn from both overcorrections. Recent work by scholars of the human and brain sciences has taken stimulating new directions: Andreas Killen, *Nervous Systems: Brain Science in the Early Cold War* (New York: HarperCollins, 2023); Daniel Pick, *Brainwashed* (London: Wellcome Collection, 2020); Joel Dimsdale, *Dark Persuasion: A History of Brainwashing from Pavlov to Social Media* (Yale University Press, 2021), and Marcia Holmes, for example in "Brainwashing the Cybernetic

At first glance, it may seem that trauma was ignored seventy years ago because there were simply not many words for it. Trauma was not understood in the form of post-traumatic stress disorder (PTSD), because the term would not be coined until the 1980s as a diagnostic. The simple word itself—*trauma*—was not widely used on the street or in the home. People did not speak that way, and even psychiatrists were trained to believe that trauma was quite rare: You might practice psychiatry for decades and never see a true case of trauma, or at most only one or two, say, in the instance of a victim severely burned over the surface of his whole body. Other terms said to apply to trauma, such as *war neurosis, soldier's heart, combat fatigue,* and *shell shock*—as well as *gross stress reaction,* a disease category which first entered the *Diagnostic and Statistical Manual of Mental Disorders* (DSM) in 1952—were more accepted. Yet it is a matter of the scientific record that none of these was applied to the brainwashed men, either. (As we will see, only in the 1970s did one psychiatrist start using the word *numbing* in a radical new way, so beginning the process of writing trauma into cases of extreme coercion.)

To put it another way: Trauma was not an "actor's category" in the mid-twentieth century, not even for the specialists. Today, for just about everyone, it is. Why? What does this tell us about the dynamics of what is and isn't possible to see and say at any moment?

It is important for us to examine this writing-out, and subsequent writing-in of trauma, because we face new versions of the same problem today in our engagement with hyper-persuasive media. During our own historical moment, although we seem to see trauma everywhere the workings of internalized pain remain elusive. If someone falls for, say, an online therapy scheme or a cryptocurrency cult leading them to lose their savings, they may be greeted with mockery. (Just as the brainwashed soldiers of the Korean War who "fell

---

Spectator: The Ipcress File, 1960s Cinematic Spectacle and the Sciences of Mind," *History of the Human Sciences* 30 (2017), 3–24. The revival of interest in cults has also brought the role of trauma to the fore.

for" Communism often were.) It would be, it should be, possible to understand properly how each person's own repository of unresolved suffering is key to their recruitment and subsequent psychic dismemberment, but this route is generally not taken even now.

Let's begin by turning to some of the men who were slated to have the "terrible thing" happen to them as prisoners of war.

....

Just as in a dream where you might "find yourself" somewhere that seems both unlikely and foreordained—a particular beach, a train, a rocky black-and-white outcropping—so also have prisoners of war often used the phrase "I found myself" in this or that startling situation. The phrase designates a surreal circumstance often closer to nightmare than reverie. Soldiers in *Remembered Prisoners of a Forgotten War* (an oral history of the Korean War) described how, only days after disembarking in Korea, they found themselves in unreal circumstances. This happened to Morris Wills.

High-school student Morris Wills from Fort Ann in upstate New York was still growing at the age of seventeen when, measuring five feet ten inches in height according to his doctor's physical, he signed up with the United States Army. The summer between his junior and what would have been his senior year, he "wanted more and more to get out of there," as he recalled later.[19] In July 1950, he enrolled to fight in a place he had never heard of, against his father's wishes (his mother had died a few years before). This was before newspapers had even announced the official start of hostilities in Korea. Wills shipped out in the fall.

Funding for this undeclared war in Korea was tight, so the military had repurposed tanks from the previous war's Pacific campaign. DIY prevailed. When blades broke on Naval ships' helos—some of the first helicopters ever used in combat—there were no replacements. "So," recalled Commander Robert A. Close, "we used our hands to smooth the busted [wooden] ribs and fabric back into reasonable aerodynamic shape and bandaged the wound with masking tape." They flew the taped-up rotors for two weeks until supplies came. On the ground, men outfitted with old M1 rifles, their barrels so pitted and scarred that the bullets' trajectories would twist when emerging, confronted North Korean fighters in Russian-made T-34 tanks. Their 2.36-inch bazooka rounds bounced off those tanks, which rolled serenely by the poorly equipped Americans, and sometimes rolled over them.[20]

Told that he would be facing an ill-prepared, poorly trained enemy, Wills, like other soldiers, instead discovered themselves—young Americans in their first sortie since the Second World War, no less—to be the ragtag ones. The outfitting of US troops with obsolete equipment caused many soldiers a sudden onset of demoralization. They were supposed to represent a dominant nation but found themselves unimpressive even in their own eyes.[21] This downturn in image mixed with resentment toward higher-ups to form an emotional brew they continued to carry for decades. Five thousand enemy troops "felt like 50 million," recalled Irv Langell forty years later in his oral history, remembering how the Americans ran out of ammunition and hoisted their out-of-date firearms to no use.[22] Some simply turned tail and ran from battle. Akira Chikami, a GI from California, recalled watching in amazement as his platoon sergeant jettisoned his rifle and ran by him, rearward, right out of the battle. (The same sergeant was next seen getting a Silver Star.)[23]

On paper, the Korean conflict barely qualified to be a war. At first, the Truman administration designated it a "police action" and this non-declaration led to confusion among troops. Some expected they would be engaged in traffic-direction duties. "I thought we were going to patrol the streets or something," recalled Charles Harrison of Virginia. But not long after arriving, "I ... seen the blood pouring from the backs of those trucks."[24] The police action went forward under the auspices of the United Nations, with troops from Turkey, France, Greece, Australia, and elsewhere—including the Republic of Korea—but the intervention was entirely US-led, leading to further confusion for American troops. Later, the United States would officially name it the Korean Conflict and colloquially call it the Korean War. South Koreans mostly dubbed it 625, after the day hostilities began (June 25, 1950); while the Chinese attached to it an official label, The War to Resist America and Assist Korea. In North Korea it was (and remains) the Victorious Fatherland Liberation War or simply the Chosŏn War.

Later, still, this war of many names would be obliterated so efficiently from Americans' memories that its main identifying epithet grew from this wiping away: The Forgotten War became pretty much the standard way of describing it. The death toll of approximately three to four million human beings (depending on which scholar you are reading) makes it perhaps the deadliest Cold War conflict—certainly the deadliest "forgotten" conflict—and one marked by the highest proportion of civilian deaths (between 11 percent and 20 percent *of the entire Korean populations to the south and north of the 38th parallel* are estimated to have perished).[25] Many American fighters never spoke of Korea at all once they came back. Captured soldier Robert MacLean not once in later years as an ironworker mentioned his wartime POW experiences, but he also never stopped thinking about it. He could not work indoors due to "walls closing in," nor could he explain why this peculiarity was the case.

So suppressed were aspects of the war that key documents remained unread even fifty years later. Historians continue to discover archival documents spurring periodical declarations that the Forgotten War is forgotten no more. In 1999, an Associated Press report revealed "startling new documents" testifying to events now known as the "forgotten massacre," in which US soldiers shot hundreds of unarmed villagers at Do Gun Ri (forgotten at least within the American if not the Korean public).[26] Whereas a scholar in the 1990s might justifiably apologize for not sufficiently citing the "large body of Vietnam soldiers' memoirs, oral histories, and testimonies" weighing down many library shelves, there was no comparable number of sources giving voice to the experience of Korean War soldiers until a scattered web of online sites began springing up in the twenty-first century.[27] In 2021, the Chinese blockbuster *The Battle at Lake Changjin* became the second-highest grossing film of that year (the number one Chinese film of all time); it revisited the Korean War as the occasion for a direct boots-on-the-ground confrontation between Chinese and American troops—one that proved the People's Volunteer Army's heroism in the mountains at Sinhung-ni—though most Americans have likely forgotten this confrontation took place.

But let's return to Morris Wills: He soon found himself in a scenario he could not have imagined when he elected to skip his senior year in Fort Ann's high school. To say he was ill-equipped is both literally true and a vast understatement. He arrived in "total confusion" with "not the slightest idea what was going on, what we were supposed to be doing," and found himself readying for battle in inches of early snow, toting tin boxes of ammunition for miles, and digging into foxholes with no idea of the direction from which the enemy might be coming.[28] For the United Nations forces in the initial months after Truman's declaration of a police action, an early September victory at Inchon was followed by a series of defeats as Chinese forces, first sending intelligence corps and later, in November, dispatching military units, entered the conflict to back up the North Korean forces (NKVD). Over the course of one year, 1950–1951, Seoul passed hands no less than four times. However, the entry of Chinese ground troops into the conflict shifted momentum. Facing chaotic circumstances and a strong Chinese-led surge, many US troops surrendered and then found themselves joining a long line of bedraggled prisoners. Christian missionary Larry Zellers was riding a train into Pyongyang when, looking out his window, he saw the straggling lines of marching men coming into the station after four months of mobile captivity. "These ragged, dirty, hollowed-eyed men did not look like any American soldiers that I had ever seen."[29] Many were teenagers. Soon Morris Wills would join them.[30]

....

Soldiers in the Korean War experienced a phenomenon that could be described as *ungrounding*—an interruption in space and time is another way to put it. All their familiar surroundings were upended, as were all their usual activities. (The term *ungrounding* describes the destabilization of the environment and of any sense of continuity or stability someone may once have enjoyed.) Troops lacked proper preparation, full support, adequate equipment, and beyond that were surprised to find themselves technologically as well as mentally outgunned. Clarence Adams, an African American enlistee in a newly desegregated US Army, served in an all-Black howitzer battalion in charge of heavy equipment. When the battle turned, the surrounding white troops—Adams's compatriots, who were tasked with protecting the howitzers—rapidly retreated, leaving his unit unprotected and mired in mud. He was betrayed by his own fellows and would remain convinced, to the end of his life, it was because they were Black that they were expendable. Soon after, he "found himself" in surreal conditions, where he was offered a handful of grain and a confusing hug by the Chinese soldiers as they pulled him out of a hole. An interpreter explained in English that the hug was in sympathy because of his presumed experiences of racism growing up in the United States.

Meanwhile, Wills, who had never been farther than Albany before shipping out, found himself far outside of the United States, and in "just complete confusion. The whole war was like that." The first battle he fought, Operation Killer in March 1951, came with standing orders to take no prisoners and so, as Wills looked on, the sergeant in command deployed a couple of teenaged enlistees to shoot, point blank, the two injured-but-still-ambulatory Chinese soldiers they had captured. One did not die immediately, and Wills walked away shattered by confusion and dishonor as one of the soldiers emptied his whole clip into the prisoner to finish him off. Two months later in a night battle on Hill 755, Wills was taken prisoner. "We all were in *a state of shock.*" He wondered if they would be shot. "This was the beginning of the process by which we would lose all our standards," Wills reflected later.[31] In fact, it was already underway—with the destabilizing effects of physical and moral chaos, and ungrounding.

The phenomenon of ungrounding (the "how did I get here" feeling of disorientation, of finding oneself in a dreamlike circumstance) is probably pronounced in any war, but in Korea it was extreme. Ungrounding is also the dominant prelude to extreme behavior change. Psychiatrist Robert J. Lifton postulated that it is "milieu control"—the heavy monitoring of all information entering and exiting an environment—that is the basis for extreme behavior change. This is borne out by events in Korea. *But before the milieu can be controlled, it must be destabilized.* Ungrounding—and the trauma that often comes in such chaotic situations—set the stage for the great brainwashing crisis that followed. The crisis would break out in the US during the 1950s through early 1960s, though its aftereffects would spread around the world and continue to ramify today.

But before we dive into Wills's experience, itself a case study in something we might call "hard" brainwashing, let's pause for a moment to think about ungrounding in less dramatic context. As unlikely as it may sound, ungrounding—a process of sustaining successive shocks to the point of disorientation—is ever more common in the twenty-first century than it was previously. This modern ungrounding occurs because of rapid technologically driven social change via the digital realm. We may not experience the wartime extremes that Morris Wills did, but our environments are destabilized by small and large shocks nearly daily, hourly. With this in mind, we can use the example of Wills as a foundation to later ask important questions: How does targeted immersion in the digital realm result in a seemingly "soft" and subtle, yet equally profound, ungrounding? And how are the effects of apparently soft brainwashing in fact more confusing than the brutal kind?

....

For months, mobile captivity wore on. Prisoners in the dilapidated remains of their summer uniforms moved northward by foot and rail away from Inchon to Pyongyang and from there north to Manpo as the ground froze. Winter came early that year. The prisoner-soldiers were already hungry and in many cases shoeless and coatless, as these items, especially the smaller sizes, were highly attractive to North Korean guards, who could sell them to the public. A CIA aerial surveillance document from 1952 listed the existing POW temporary camps where the prisoners lay over a night or two, giving brusque summaries of survival odds as measured in per diem rations. At the Kangdong camp, prisoners boarded in caves, "received 600 grams of cereal and salt each day," and were dying at an approximate rate of two men per day from "malnutrition and eruptive typhus"; while at the underground Suan camp (a former mine), "the prisoners received only rice balls for food" and there were no sanitary facilities.[32]

On October 31, North Korean major Chong Myong Sil took over a large contingent of those marching on foot. Nicknamed the Tiger, the commander lent this appellation to the abuse that followed. Prodded by bayonets and rifles, hundreds walked on a precipitous mountainside trail, the sadistic commander's yells accompanying them, watching as in some cases the Tiger pushed weakened soldiers off the cliffside road to their deaths below.[33] Along the way, in what many soon called the Tiger Death March, a group of French, German, and American civilians, many of them Methodist, Anglican, or Orthodox missionaries and their families, merged with the exhausted troops. A US soldier carried an exhausted seventy-six-year-old nun, Mother Beatrix, for some miles, but faced orders to leave her so that she could be taken in a cart purportedly coming up behind them.

However, as the soldiers drew away, they heard shots and Mother Beatrix was never seen again. She was the first civilian to die on the march, followed by many others. The soldiers were in even worse shape, frequently, because they had been malnourished for longer. The death march left only 500 soldier survivors of a total of 845 who began it.[34]

One GI attempted to put the exact quality of the experience into words and recalled in an oral history interview, "We would lay over during the day"—to avoid US aerial strafes—"and every time I got up to march at night, I'd have to bend over and open the cuts on the back of my feet so the blood would flow and I [c]ould move my feet."[35] Extreme conditions—exhaustion to the point of preferring to die and dire malnutrition, among others—were rampant. Some were shot, some fell off the mountain, some were pushed, some froze. Some collapsed mid-step. Simply sank to their knees. Even young men wore out, especially those in shock. When soldiers ran back to try to carry a collapsed man, they, too, were almost certainly lost, or they were simply unable to bring the dying along—for, despite their youth, and despite the lightness of their now-skeletal compatriots, the would-be rescuers themselves lacked the necessary strength and had to leave their fellows heaped where they fell. "We would pass creatures hard to recognize as human, prostrate on the road," recalled captured war correspondent Phillip Deane of the dying dropped by their carriers.[36]

During the marches (the march leading up to the Tiger Death March as well as that death march itself), men and women also risked friendly fire attacks, especially US forces' zealous napalming of the ramshackle structures in which they were given brief hours to sleep. "Even my eyebrows were gone," recalled one soldier of the loss of all hair from own-side napalm drops at night. The combustion agent, designed to be more exact in encouraging fires than simply spraying gasoline, after being used in the Pacific theater in World War II, was deployed again in Korea (the 635,000 tons dropped on Korea exceeded the 503,000 tons released half a decade before).[37] In battles south and eventually north of the 38th parallel, napalm took on a "close air support" role. Experimenting with this new tactic, low-flying planes flame-threw the chemical to light up bombing targets at night or to provide "fire support." Napalm thus shaped the battlegrounds where Morris Wills and others were captured. When carpet bombing started, especially of the north, North Koreans increasingly

Map of POW Camps 1 through 10 where UN forces were held. Spellings of place names reflect mid-twentieth-century English-language equivalents of Korean terms. ARTIST'S RENDERING AFTER "THE PROBLEMS OF US MARINE CORPS PRISONERS OF WAR IN KOREA," BY JAMES ANGUS MACDONALD, FIGURE 9 (1988).

POW Camp 5 along the Yalu River. Hundreds of Americans were buried on the hillside above the camp. COURTESY AUSTRALIAN WAR MEMORIAL.

shifted strategy to move prisoners by foot rather than by railroad, and used improvised billeting in insecure mines, requisitioned peasant huts, and abandoned dwellings. These fratricidal experiences in Korea were a factor in the decision to abandon the use of close air support in the conflict. Getting napalmed by one's own forces also set the scene for a deepening feeling of betrayal among some of the troops, making them in certain cases more sympathetic to Chinese critiques of American values.[38]

At last, on Easter Sunday 1951, a large group of US prisoners arrived at a camp on the bank of the remote and still frozen Yalu River at the northern border of Korea. It was Camp 1, where there was no barbed wire or fence because there was nowhere sufficiently appealing to run to. Prisoners came to call the remote terrain No Name Valley.* Initially, they found living in a permanent camp was not much better than the mobile marches. POW Clarence Adams, the GI from Memphis, arriving at this time, saw many men whose untreated wounds combined with the lack of will to wake up the next day caused them to "just die" overnight. POW Robert MacLean observed a friend who could not stop recalling the hamburgers he had eaten growing up. His mind became so obsessively occupied that he lost appetite for the worm-peppered suet that was provided and simply passed out of this world while "still talking about hamburgers."[39] Others perished from bad water. This was in part because their common latrine was a slit trench with two logs. "One guy fell in, and no one had the strength to pull him out," recalled Adams, who himself was in the process of wasting from 140 to 90 pounds. The indignity of this lack of sanitation (seeing mates die in this or other equally unheroic ways while being unable to help, or, worse, seeing

---

* In later months, once their health improved, some men did attempt escape, managing to live outside the camps for up to two days, but all were recaptured, and the instigators were placed in solitary confinement. Morris Wills, not yet a prisoner, was to arrive at the camp several weeks later.

others take advantage of the dying) was as devastating as the bacterial infections themselves.[40]

Life and death intermeshed. This, too, was part of the ungrounding process, a descent by which prisoners entered a surreal realm of conduct. Without preparation, without warning, they (again) found themselves in a wholly new condition with unrealized basic standards or no rules at all: an upside-down world.

Ironically, prisoners found that social relations deteriorated even further in the permanent camps than during mobile captivity. Cooperation and basic social bonds disintegrated. Morris Wills observed some preying on others; for example, certain prisoners would get hungry men to bet their next day's meal for an extra one today, thus going into food debt. Others became informants. Men fought over a quarter-inch cigarette butt. Each group elected a trusted "spoon man" to divide up their rations fairly during each meal, yet his every hand movement was nonetheless scrutinized, and fights broke out over favoritism. Any sex drive was absent in this period: "A Brigitte Bardot could have walked through the camp, and nobody would have raised an eyebrow."[41] After their emaciated and diminished fellows died during the night—such soldiers often perished in the dark, having held on through the day—prisoners took the corpses and propped them up against the cabin wall so that Korean administrators making a quick head count in the morning might mistake them as alive and the deceased's food rations would keep coming until the mortality was noticed. (In below-zero temperatures, it took a while for the flesh to decay.) When this ploy was discovered, soldiers stripped their fellows' bodies of clothing to salvage some extra layers. Others, more respectful, carried the naked remains up the hill and tried to bury them in frozen ground, but the extra exertion, in at least one case, killed the gravediggers, too. When burying wasn't possible, the newly dead were piled on top of the already dead to wait for softer ground come spring.

A year after the earliest arrivals had been in residence at Camp

1, a total of fourteen camps had been established along the Yalu River and in nearby parts of northern Korea. Chinese staff took over running the Yalu camps from the Korean administrators. With the takeover and the "lenient policy" they introduced, camp life saw increased organization. In the spring, the ice on the Yalu River started breaking up and a boat loaded with rice and millet came through, so POWs got hot food each day for the first time. Chinese administrators redistributed prisoners among the camps, dividing them by nationality and race (along Black and white lines).[42] Over time, physical conditions improved to the point where meat and vegetables were served, a cigarette ration was allotted, and some mail came and went on the boats. Soon, a new vocabulary arose for the Chinese to describe the cooperative and the uncooperative: Progressive and Reactionary, labels that the POWs adopted themselves.

In a 2013 *New Yorker* article tracking down one of the still unaccounted-for prisoners from that era, Brian McKnight, a historian at the University of Virginia, observed, "The POW experience in Korea was worse than any other since the Civil War."[43] This seems indisputable (almost 40 percent of these Korean war prisoners died versus 1 percent of those taken prisoner in Europe during World War II). But what is up for debate is what part of the experience, of the many subpar aspects, qualifies as the worst from a roster of horrors: starvation, poor sanitation, untreated wounds, loneliness, betrayal by country, indignity, racist orders, summary execution and threats thereof, theft, pervasive lice, social-bond deterioration, bunking with corpses, and even "death by hamburger." But not on this list is the cornerstone of the experience, the most distinctive part, the one we have not yet addressed, and that was the application of Maoist struggle procedures—also called reeducation, the Method, or thought reform. This is what would eventually earn the enduring name, in English, of brainwashing. In time, this would become the only thing many Americans knew about the war in Korea.

Ungrounded and unpredictable life circumstances, disturbances of time and space, finding oneself in a surreally horrifying situation are key prerequisites for brainwashing. Add traumas such as suffering from disease and demoralization, and facing, above all, the indignity of dying while going out to relieve oneself in the middle of the night and freezing to death, or finding one's friend in the morning having succumbed in this way, and the stage is set. These humiliations were never named as trauma per se, not by the men themselves nor by the experts who would later study what happened to them, but they were vital factors in what occurred. For those who suffered in the camps, it was part of a new regime of horror alternating with boredom, and would be followed, when Chinese administrators took over, by Maoist reeducation. Comparative research on extreme coercion would confirm that factors such as the degrading removal of autonomous functions including the ability to keep one's body clean, and the witnessing of social decay among one's band of brothers, were quite effective in bringing about radical changes in consciousness. Sometimes these transformations were experienced as a blissful release. But the dynamics of that release, and the trauma that preceded it, would not begin to be understood for twenty years, and arguably their extent and reach are still not fully grasped today.

·········

High-school enlistee Morris Wills's time as a prisoner was also characterized by mental self-torture. Months before, while dispatching to Korea via ship, Wills received C rations that included a can of lima beans and ham—these were not to his taste, he decided. He offered them to others but found no takers. Ham, maybe; lima beans, no. On January 16, as they sailed into port, soldiers received orders to clear everything out of their lockers, which resulted in Wills taking a fateful action: He jettisoned the can from the ship's porthole as they docked. Once taken prisoner, he found himself ruminating on the unopened can, how he had so easily unburdened himself of it, how careless of this treasure he had been, how the beans now lay on the bottom of Pusan Harbor. His mind looped and looped. "I've never regretted anything more in my life," he wrote in his memoir, a sentiment on which he had ample time to reflect in his three years of imprisonment.[44] He regretted it more than he would one day regret his conversion to Chinese Communism (which he was soon to make in the camps), more than his embrace of an anti-capitalist "new self," more than his eventual resolution not to return home. The lima beans had a second and third life inside his consciousness even as they rested on the sea floor.

Fragments of men's and women's stories surface from the past in surprising ways, ways that bear on current conditions. Examining the histories of men and women involved in the great brainwashing crisis of the Korean War makes it clear that a common thread was great suffering. Losing eighty pounds, dying from the memory of hamburgers, or fixating on subaquatic food on the harbor floor, these details don't necessarily conform to the image of how mind control operates. But it is simply the cadence of ordinary and extraordinary events—the quality and type of suffering that leads to brainwashing and proceeds from brainwashing—that has rarely been fully accounted for in the hype-filled responses it frequently occasions.

Morris Wills would eventually return to the United States a decade and a half after his time in the camps. He then measured six feet two inches tall, and was a married, disillusioned man accompanying his Beijing-born wife and their baby daughter home. He had grown four inches since embarking from Fort Ann, New York, and had gained back the weight he lost under starvation conditions. The small family walked across the covered wooden bridge from Mainland China to Hong Kong in 1965 while flashbulbs lit them up in bursts.

Lima Beans at the Bottom of the Ocean

Morris and Kaiyen Wills with their daughter, Linda, arriving in the US, November 4, 1965. AP PHOTO/SAN FRANCISCO CHRONICLE.

The circumstances of this return could not have been anticipated except perhaps by a dystopian novelist such as Arthur Koestler. Instead of a fortuitous slide into civilian life or a dashing welcome to his hometown, he arrived on US soil already famous as a living embodiment of something evil, something nefarious, something untoward: For Morris Wills, it was widely announced in headlines across the country and whispered in military-government circles, had fallen victim to a new superweapon. He was one of twenty-one American soldiers who had refused to return home. He had gone on to spend twelve years living in China. Morris Wills, as unlikely a candidate for brainwashing as might be imagined, seemed to have succumbed to mind control and somehow prevailed to tell the tale.

2

The Volleyball Problem

In her 1951 work, *The Origins of Totalitarianism*, Hannah Arendt painted a horrifying picture of totalitarian camps functioning as Pavlovian experiments where men turned into "ghastly marionettes with human faces." But the strange thing about Chinese Communist brainwashing was that quite a few of its victims seemed pretty cheerful. At least, the twenty-one POWs from the Korean War who refused to be repatriated on American soil did. They did not fit the gulag image at all. Like the occupants of totalitarian camps in Arendt's account, they had ceased "to affirm their identity"—they no longer saw themselves as the same people they were before, no longer shared the same allegiances—but they were rather rosy cheeked in the literal as well as figurative sense.[1]

The ashen faces, the marionette actions, and verbal mimicry, the abject choice of "deciding to live or else you died," as one prisoner put it, had come earlier for most of the POWs of that war. By the time the Chinese-run reeducation program became fully operational, most prisoners—even if they had struggled through two years of starvation, disease, and horror—were receiving at least two meals a day and a cigarette ration, if they were good, plus a sugar ration, if they were very good. There were more vegetables, less millet, and fewer tiny worms to be found in the food. The lice that tormented them in summer and winter came under control as all prisoners were dusted with DDT. To another prisoner it felt at that point like "moving from under a bridge into the Ritz Carlton Hotel," in comparison to earlier conditions.[2]

After a while, once they put on some weight and their skeletons no longer protruded, you couldn't see what had happened. Their trauma was hidden. If you expected the crushing of men's souls to look one way—or if you expected the crushing of men's souls to be captured regularly in AP photographs—you faced a lacuna in expectations. This lacuna caused comment. A newspaper called out the returning POWs for looking "bronzed" and fit. A New York resident commented to a reporter about one of the survivors as she saw him on TV: "He was awfully fat."[3] (By that point, the soldier in question, Morris Wills, had endured much.) Confusing matters further, some of the GIs' letters home had praised the "wonderful treatment" they were receiving in the camps.[4] Even if these sounded suspiciously like bland words forcibly inserted within their correspondence, peoples' responses to such sentiments confirmed one of the strangest known ironies about how propaganda works: even if you knew it might be false, it also had its effect. The letters reassured family members that their loved one had not been subjected to the most brutal treatment, or they wouldn't have been writing letters at all. To military interpreters, these same letters, some twenty-nine thousand of them, became evidence not of torture nor of traumatizing treatment but of active collaboration with the enemy.[5] They also suggested deep character flaws in the men who had been captured.

Appearing to some onlookers to be sleek as seals, the Yalu River camps' survivors wore the vestiges of extreme deprivation and drawn-out trauma in such a way that they were often hidden. I argue that these vestiges were visible if one knew how and where to look, but, for a variety of reasons, they became effectively concealed to most contemporaries. In general, *the experts charged with understanding the brainwashed men, whether psychiatric or military or governmental, did not use the word* traumatized *or the framework of trauma to describe them.* Nor did they apply equivalent terms such as *shell shock* or *war neurosis.* There is a brief adjectival mention of the men's "uniquely traumatizing experience" in a report by psychiatrist Robert J. Lifton (a seed that would bear fruit in decades to come), but this is the only mention I have found.[6] More immediately, the common focus was on the *how* of this strange transformation that was brainwashing. It was not that the behavioral scientists lacked compassion or understanding of the extreme and possibly unique circumstances to which the POWs had been exposed, but trauma was not mobilized in that understanding.

·········

Morris Wills of Fort Ann underwent Mao's method while held in the Yalu River wastelands. One of the most powerful keys to understanding its mysterious effectiveness is to point out that Maoist struggle procedures—sometimes called the Method, and sometimes reeducation or thought reform—was used on the captured US troops (as well as the Greek, Turkish, British, Australian, and South Korean prisoners) in much the same way it was used on Chinese citizens. In part, the camps offered a chance to test whether struggle worked just as well on Westerners, almost like a lab. This was especially of interest for Westerners judged to be the class doubles of Chinese peasants and landlords. (GIs were the equivalent of peasants, class wise, and officers were akin to landholders, loosely speaking, among the Chinese.) After all, the Method was supposed to be universal and to work on everyone— except perhaps the 7 percent of people Mao declared to be incorrigible. Therefore, it followed that in field trials it *had to be universal* to prove its own worth. Running the experiment required a positive outcome. Mao

Zedong saw the power of thought reform as "a spiritual atom bomb" at the heart of global revolution.[7] It would hasten the birth of new souls for a new world.

As the China historian Aminda Smith's groundbreaking study shows, despite its purported universality, the Method was applied differently to different people, depending on whether they were seen as of the exploited or exploiting classes. Chinese prostitutes and petty criminals, thus, experienced leniency. American POWs, especially Black US servicemen, but also those from modest backgrounds or farming families or who were low on the chain of command, also experienced a kind of initial leniency. Higher-ups, the pugnaciously resistant, the ardently religious, and those determined to be from "landlord" or capitalist classes experienced extreme brutality. Yet all of this was subsumed under the Method. Smith argues that Cold War scholars have hugely underestimated the sheer "Maoist-ness" of the brainwashing efforts that were applied to the POWs.[8]

....

During reeducation, Morris had lots of time to consider his background and his native society, to neither of which he had given much thought before. Wills was the product of a long line of farmers who, since the 1600s, had worked the land in upstate New York, periodically fighting wars they were called to fight. (One ancestor defended New London, Connecticut, against Benedict Arnold in the Revolutionary War; five of his uncles fought in World War II.) He signed up with a fellow high-school classmate, both joining the Army because the bad teeth of Jimmy, his friend, ruled out the Air Force. Military service was against his father's wishes for his still-in-high-school son, but he ultimately gave his permission. In the struggle sessions, Wills had acres of time to consider his upbringing—how he was his mother's favorite, how she died when he was twelve. That was the same year he went to work at his uncle's dairy farm milking cows and tending the milking machines.

The Volleyball Problem

(He loved machines of "any sort," and was good at fixing them.) Point blank, early on, Chinese reeducators asked him to defend the American way of life, but he found he could neither defend nor really even define it. Army affidavits from the mid-1950s, recently declassified, reveal that other GI's who knew him in the camps saw Wills as especially young ("appeared to be about seventeen years old at the time"), well brought up ("I got the impression that Wells came from a nice family"), and initially very much avoidant of the Chinese running the camp ("he tried to get out of the meetings by hiding when the instructor came around looking for him" and "appeared to be afraid of the Chinese").[9]

Speaking to his memoirist in his as-told-to autobiography, *Turncoat*, Wills clarified, "Let me clear up one point right here: We Americans toss around the word 'brainwashing' without much idea of what it means. Brainwashing is not done with electrodes stuck to your head; you are not turned into a robot obeying the orders of a Chinese master." (In fact, no one wanted to create a programmed robot, at least not until the CIA stepped into brainwashing research.) A genuine conversion was far more interesting. As Wills clarified, "What we call brainwashing is a *long, horrible process* by which a man slowly—step by step, idea by idea—becomes totally convinced, as I was, that the Chinese communists have unlocked the secret to man's happiness and that the United States is run by rich bankers, McCarthy types, and imperialist aggressors."[10]

There is much to say about the special conditions in which Wills and the other famous "Turncoat POWs" were held and the "long, horrible process" in which they participated. Before the process started, they experienced, many of them, distress beyond imagining, physical bodily torture as well as psychological abandonment. But the "slowly, step by step, idea by idea" procedure—after severe ungrounding—is what stands out. Even though brainwashing eventually became an eye-catching subject of sensationalism and runaway theorizing, the POWs' experiences demonstrate that a genuine *washing of the brain* was indeed happening to some soldiers; true conversions, in other words, could be triggered given the right combination of circumstances.

The "long, horrible process" played out over months and years. As described by Mao himself in the Report to the Supreme Conference of the State (written in 1951 but published in February 1957): *"One cannot force a people* to renounce idealism or force a people to believe in Marxism. To settle ideological problems, one must act through the democratic methods of discussion, criticism, persuasion, and appropriate education."[11] Mao understood that for these captive soldiers, especially the ones from rural backgrounds, the same methods used on Chinese peasants could be made to work. The Method was proof of itself in day-to-day results—and so it was both a demonstration and an experiment. The POWs along the Yalu were its research subjects. (First in Camp 10 as a trial, later in the other camps.) It would be gentle until, as Mao said, it was not.

Boiled down to its simplest formula, the Method involved three steps: "Discussion-Criticism-Unity."[12] Participation was obligatory; otherwise, a soldier would be sent for a stint in the turnip bins (closed, dark spaces under guard watch) for solitary confinement. Sometimes resistors would be forced to hold standing positions for long periods. Beyond the differing degrees of abuse administered, there was variation in how the individual men experienced the Method, whether they found it harsh or mild, for example. Or whether they found it to be boring or not. There was variation, too, in how they spoke of it later—especially to psychiatric evaluators or military interrogators on their return.

In step one of the Method, Discussion, individuals narrated their stories. William Hinton's Maoist classic book, *Fanshen*, described the process, as witnessed by and told to Hinton, who was an English teacher living in China in the spring and summer of 1948. The death of landlordism took place in Peasant Unions across China, through which even the remotest villagers could (indeed, must) participate in the process of *fanshen* or, literally, "the turning over." The specific meaning of turning over was not just about collectivizing land but about collectivizing, in a sense, people's psyches. Even though land reform was the physical goal, a reform of the self was at the heart of it.[13] Originally, such study groups, or study societies, arose in the May Fourth era around 1919 (this movement marked a time of uprising when Chinese people, in the wake of World War I and Japanese territorial incursions, demanded change from long-standing feudal and inward-looking ways) and hosted "genuine debate about the nature of society and solutions to its problems," as the scholar Rana Mitter argues, but by the time of the Korean War they had long since calcified into sites for the imposition of orthodoxy through shame and distress and intense socialization.[14] "Speaking bitterness" was part of the emotional labor of turning over the self. For Chinese peasants, there was a lot of material to draw on: In years of famine, desperate families sometimes sold a girl child for a few bags of rice or donated her to the Catholic church, renting her back, in essence, until maturity, when she was required to pledge herself as a nun; poor boys could be endlessly indentured to pay off debts, and, as one such boy told Hinton, he had never known a single happy day nor enjoyed a full meal in his years after the age of six, laboring for a small landholder.

Far from home, upended in trauma, POWs were likewise encouraged to "speak bitterness"—that is, summon any simmering resentments. They had some. Prisoners described how they had received promises they would be "home for Christmas" but felt abandoned by their country, left to molder in unspeakable conditions, and watch their flesh waste away. Witnessing war crimes their fellow soldiers committed before their eyes, observing themselves fail to help civilians in distress, caused some GIs to doubt that they were the good guys after all. One soldier remembered others in his squad "running down" American leaders and "talking in great detail about MacArthur's personal lifestyle."[15] African American POWs often carried with them a long record of betrayal experiences—both in and out of the war, before and during the fighting. Charles Rangel, who served in the 2nd Infantry and later went on to become a long-standing congressman from New York districts, for example, recalled that despite the official desegregation of the Armed Forces in 1948, there were only two integrated units in Korea. And "integrated" meant all-Black units led by all-white officer corps: "I can assure you by 1952," Rangel emphasized in a recent oral history, Truman's executive order for desegregation "did not get down to the troops *at all*."[16] An African American infantryman who joined up from a Southern state in 1949 recalled that he had anticipated better treatment in the North but that, even fully suited in his uniform, he could not get served breakfast at a diner in New Jersey, causing him to realize the truth of the saying, the Mason-Dixon Line begins at the Canadian border.[17]

Nonetheless, repeating their stories and receiving encouragement to speak was powerful. As in psychoanalysis, the imperative to talk and talk, in this case in front of other members of a group, although a seemingly simple act, bore profound consequences. Although Chinese indoctrination efforts geared up slowly with the showing of clumsy Russian propaganda films and subsequent forced hearing of long lectures in the cold while sitting on little stools ("you could feel yourself freezing" said Morris Wills), the talking discussions were still effective in many cases.[18] For the first time in his life, a soldier such as Morris Wills found himself in something approaching an open environment for self-exploration—oddly, in a prison camp. (Farm boys, even sensitive ones, did not tend to be offered therapy in the 1950s.) It was as if he'd been shipped halfway around the world, had all his values upended, and then, at the very edge of the known Earth, he was asked to participate in psychotherapy. As Morris's family later pointed out, he had always been "bright enough, good-looking enough, likable enough" yet somehow, they felt, he was "ingrown" especially after his mother's death. He

The Volleyball Problem

An example of the diaries that Chinese instructors gave to POWs. At least once a month they wrote an "autobiography" in which they were forced to reflect on their past family lives, as a twenty-year-old GI named Rogers Herndon recalled. PHOTOGRAPH BY UNKNOWN PHOTOGRAPHER FEATURED IN *LIFE* MAGAZINE, MAY 25, 1953, 121: "DIARY REVEALS A STUDENT AT THE 'SATURATION POINT'" IN "VALLEY FORGE GI'S TELL OF BRAINWASHING ORDEAL."

never talked back and never quarreled, his aunt Katherine recalled when she was interviewed after the brainwashing scandal emerged: "If Morris didn't like a thing you wouldn't know it.... Nobody could get to him; he was kind of all by himself. Maybe he was more sensitive than we knew."[19] Here, far from upstate New York, in an environment now restabilized with more plentiful food and with overnight casualties reduced almost to zero, interrogators compelled Morris to speak about himself and to justify his view of life, his country's purpose, his role in the larger sphere of things. Now turning eighteen and then nineteen, he *shared*. They forced him to introspect. They compelled him to write a journal. They required him to scour his memory so as to construct a confession. He got some things out in the open—his love for his mother, his loss of her. His love of his country, his loss of it.

Being a POW, Wills said, "got to me." He brooded over what Chinese instructors were telling him about capitalism and the essential unfairness of US society. Also, "I felt... they"—the US government and military—"didn't care about us."[20] He would stare at a big mountain each day. Thoughts came to him about how they weren't fighting the war right. He felt disgust with his own nation. "You don't even care about going back" after a while. Over a year in which he wrote and rewrote his autobiography (full of self-made lies, at first), he was, you could say, deconditioned.

The youngest of the twenty-one "brainwashed" men, David Hawkins, now in his eighties, was the subject of a 2017 documentary by the British filmmaker Nasheed Qamar Faruqi. Hawkins recalled how he was subjected to five to six hours of lectures a day, the intensive reading of Communist literature, and the repeated writing of his own life history. "It was like being psychoanalyzed," he concluded. Some of the questions prisoners were required to reflect on—reflect, or else suffer punishment or the loss of medical treatment—sound distinctly "journal-y" to the twenty-first-century ear: "In writing the autobiography we were to be guided by two pages of questions entitled, 'Outline of Self-Analyzation,' which had about twenty-five topics on it," recalled Rogers Herndon, a soldier from Jacksonville, Florida. "You had to write everything about your own life from the time you were a kid. You had to tell about your sisters, brothers, mother, father, friends . . . who had the most influence over you. . . . They kept making you write them, about once a month." (A later Army HumRRO report revealed how diligently this requirement for forced introspective journaling was applied: 91 percent of Army prisoners were made to write autobiographies.)[21]

In Maoist terms, Morris Wills was becoming a blank slate. "By the end of 1952, this feeling created a vacuum in my mind." He became a little bit interested in what the Chinese had to say and in turn they became a little bit more friendly. He started reading from a library the camp administrators had set up in a room with a potbellied stove, sometimes featuring, next to it, a tray of warm wheat buns.

In step two of the Method, Criticism, instructors re-narrated, interpreted, criticized the stories prisoners told about themselves. Sometimes the group joined in. An official Communist Party report described the reeducation of Chinese prostitutes in this way. "As internees told their stories," the report observed in a typical formula, they "recognized who *our* true Enemies were, and their minds gradually became clear."[22] The prostitute may have started out engrossed in the petty particulars of her life, but, pushed to see things another way, she could grasp that her tale was one of exploitation by greedy oppressors and revealed a common enemy.

Some, including Morris Wills, had never heard of Marxism before coming to the camp. He consumed books from the library he had never read. Offerings included Mark Twain's *Tom Sawyer* and Charles Dickens's *The Pickwick Papers*—books judged congruent with a class analysis—as well as an array of dialectical materialist tomes. "As far as I can remember, Marx had never been mentioned in our school," Wills insisted in his memoir with some outrage. "He should have been; we ought to have been given a basic idea of his theories. There is absolutely no way of combatting an argument in his favor unless you know something about him."[23] He felt ill-equipped for the Criticism part of thought reform. This entailed being forced to make arguments defending his own system (and life choices), so that his arguments, and he, could be criticized.

In a sense, he ripened perfectly within the education procedures of Maoist praxis, step by step. He turned over. And his reeducators, some of them professors, some of them educated in the US—one was an alumnus of the University of California, Los Angeles—confronted him with damning information about the ills of America: racism ("the Negro problem"), unemployment, poverty, and crime in the US. "I couldn't explain a lot of those things. In the camp this happened constantly with everyone." He fell into a "type of wavering," he recalled years later.[24] Wavering led to more wavering. It was hard to know what to think. A "way forward" through Chinese friendship finally offered itself. China now seemed to him like a better system and clearly America was rotting. He had evidently not been well educated. He was invited for tea.

An equal society, with planning and security for everyone, began to "look pretty nice" to Wills.[25] He moved out of his old hut and formally joined a live-in study group of other progressives to go further with the process. They gradually enacted radical change. Group struggle sessions allowed the process to gain a firmer foothold. As a POW from another camp reported, the Chinese teachers showed them that their history books were "all fixed up" to cover up "how bad we treated the Indians and the Spanish."[26]

In step three of the Method, Unity, a positive replacement was created for what had been "washed away" in the first two steps. (Later, social psychologist Edgar Schein, borrowing from the theories of Kurt Lewin, would label this third step Refreezing—a process in which new beliefs fix themselves into the basic patterning of the individual and so come to feel quite normal.)[27] Questions about the viability of this third step have stuck in some scholars' craws, because it's easier to tear down rather than build up a person's belief system. During the Cold War, the challenge of implanting new ideas would become widely recognized, as the CIA studies called MK-ULTRA would show.[28] Yet Chinese thought reformers appeared to have remarkable success with the "replacement" part, positive indoctrination, even if it did not always last. The evidence tells a compelling story: it did not need to last because it was designed to be perpetually renewed.

Here is where what the philosopher Jacques Ellul calls the theory of the "mold" comes into play most strongly.[29] The point is to press a person in a mold, anchoring him there periodically, to "re-mold him systematically." This work is never finished. It is an ongoing process. The molded entity might start to lose its crisp shape. As Mao himself said, "We ourselves are being placed in the mold every year. . . . I have gone through a remolding of my own thoughts . . . and I must continue." Struggle is never complete. No one is exempt from ongoing criticism and self-criticism. Everyone is coming into form or leaving it, according to doctrine.

The Volleyball Problem

For Morris Wills the shift from step two to step three was gradual. But as disillusionment with his own country set in (made up of personal resentment and a broader bitterness), he became curious about this other place. By December 1953, Wills, now twenty, was a changed man: "I felt I would like to see China, where everything was nice and orderly."[30] (So he had been told.) He admired the discipline of the Communists, faulting himself for his own lack of discipline.

Once the mail started up under the more relaxed policy of the later camp years, Morris's family noticed that the letters that occasionally appeared in their mailboxes came across as phony. They seemed almost to be from another person, a not-Morris. These letters can serve as an outer index to compare with Wills's account of his inner journey. In one letter he wrote, "It is my understanding that there is a peace movement back there, so tell Father that with all my heart I hope he supports the peace movement to his fullest ability in faith that it will bring me back home, quick and safe."[31] The letter went on to mention the family's wheat harvest and their "hired man." Wills, according to his sister Muriel, never referred to their father as anything but Dad, and theirs was a dairy, not wheat, farm where there was no hired man (or, at least, they wouldn't have used that stilted term). When Wills declared himself as one of the twenty-one, he insisted, "There is not a democratic government in the United States as long as McCarthyism and McCarranism are allowed to exist."[32] (McCarranism referred to the Internal Control Act passed in 1950, also called the McCarran Act, requiring all Communists to register with the US government.) Indeed, Wills adopted clichéd language to express himself, a trait that experts would later identify as a classic step in mind control.[33]

Rather than synthesizing these odd details, I am aiming here to paint an empirically driven portrait from more than one point of view: For Wills, lingering trauma and survival needs within a topsy-turvy environment motivated a genuine quest for education. For his family and, later, for the US military evaluators examining the letters for treason, it looked like betrayal of the American way of life. For diagnostic experts soon to be assigned to his "case," it looked like evidence of mental torture and an extreme form of behavior modification. And to President Truman and his secretary of state, it appeared the Communists were in possession of a new superweapon.

....

After so much horror, it may come as a surprise that the POWs in China were eligible to compete in an "Olympics sports" event during their detention.

Far, far north along the Yalu River, nestled in a long string of POW camps (on the outskirts of the fifth camp of fourteen total), was a spot called Pyŏktong, where the summers were buggy, marijuana grew wild on the hillsides, and the winters were interminable. There, the

Volleyball was a popular pursuit in the Yalu River camps once the Chinese administrators took over. Many men played, whether or not they were sympathetic to the reeducation efforts being imposed on them. Morris Wills was a particularly vigorous player, appreciated for his skill and sportsmanship. GETTY IMAGES. SOVFOTO/CONTRIBUTOR.

The Volleyball Problem

Chinese government in November 1952 hosted hundreds of prisoners of war from the US, England, Turkey, Australia, and other United Nations forces to participate in a POW Olympics. As armistice day in the Korean War approached, the captured men, many of whom had survived by that point more than two years in captivity, donned athletic uniforms and engaged in different activities, including tumbling and jousting, in addition to traditional sports. Communist officials in white gloves toasted them with glasses of white wine as the men competed on athletic grounds surrounded by pungent fields of night soil—human waste used as fertilizer. Although it was a mock Olympics not endorsed by the official governing committee of the Olympic Games, it mimicked the event by, among other features, including an inaugural torch carrier lighting a flame. Photographs of the games reveal javelin throwers, gymnasts, footballers, and wrestlers; also appearing were tug-of-war and sack race events, making the scene look a bit like regular summer camp, not prison camp. In basketball, nation faced off against nation, at least in the rare case where sufficient prisoner-athletes existed to make up a team—namely, the Australia versus US basketball games. Finally, there was volleyball, camp against camp, played in sand pits. Aside from the surrealistic elements of the scene, it was hard to understand how the appearance of such enjoyable conditions squared with stories of torture and mind control.

This is the volleyball problem. If the POW experience was one thing, how could it also be another? How to reconcile image and reality, how to make the false and the true lie in their proper spots, so the keen eye can separate one from the other. It is not so simple as to say that the Pyŏktong Olympics was a Potemkin village and behind it lay the reality of coercion and desperation. That's because, first, not all the men, or even most men, participated in the Olympics. Yet a good proportion did: Between November 15 and 27, 1952, over five hundred men from eight countries including the US, South Korea, UK, Philippines, Turkey, France, Holland, and Australia

Fiercely competitive basketball games between representatives of rival nations were some of the best attended events at the POW Olympics at Pyŏktong, which took place in 1952, in Camp 5. The event allowed prisoners from all the camps to mingle (which rarely happened), and offered (temporarily) lavish food. COURTESY: AUSTRALIAN WAR MEMORIAL.

took part.[34] Second, not all who participated had "gone over" to the Communist side, yet some had. So one could not say determinatively that all who played a sport had been indoctrinated. Some were just bored. On the other hand, the image of the Chinese-run Olympics, despite the positive coverage given by the British Communist journalist Alan Winnington, was not a strictly accurate story. It was both distorted and partly accurate. The reality "behind" the POW Olympics was that its significance was in plain sight—its image was its reality. An example was Memphis-born Clarence Adams, who competed in lightweight boxing, and said: "It was great fun and made us forget about where we were for at least a few days."[35] It was no less true that Adams had nearly died of starvation and, due to gangrene from an untreated wound, had two years earlier, on one of his first days in Camp 5, forced himself to amputate several of his own toes at the first joint using a knife improvised from the steel arch support of his boot. As a teen, he had not been allowed to box against non-Black opponents in segregated Memphis; now, boxing without a few toes on an international stage was an outcome of his enlistment he could not have imagined. Was it, then, an unreal event? Some said so, and called Adams and others merely mindless pawns. (Years later, Adams would be called before the House Un-American Activities Committee to explain his defection to China, an enemy of America, and would state simply: "I had the right to go to any country that would honor my quest for freedom, equality, education, and happiness.")[36]

The Inter-Camp Olympics, as Adams and others were likely unaware at the time, took place during armistice negotiations and were publicized to garner world sympathy. Chairman Mao dropped by to attend the event, according to Roosevelt Powell, an Army staff sergeant who was among the prisoners who met with the Chinese leader and who recollected, in an interview for the *Tulsa World* in 2019, that Mao spoke fluent English, answered the POWs' questions, and, while explaining he'd had a long day of traveling to get there, "sat down on the ground as he talked. Then he took a two-hour nap." This retrospective interview occurred recently, when Roosevelt Powell, at the age of ninety-one, was at home in Okmulgee, Oklahoma. Powell explained that the "Olympics" were mostly for show but also that they added a brief infusion of pleasure to his three years of POW life.[37]

Finally, a truce arrived. The prisoners moved to a neutral camp under joint command of UN and Korean forces at Panmunjom and run by Indian UN police—a global village in the DMZ. Here they spent some months, months that turned into a year and a half in the end. During this time, the war took a turn toward theater. Instead of planning for the troops to return automatically to their own home countries (in a wholesale exchange, as mandated by the 1947 Geneva Convention), the US insisted that each POW should exercise a choice—thereby undergoing *voluntary repatriation*, or, as it was otherwise called, nonforcible repatriation, aka, the Fifth Freedom.[38] The Truman administration anticipated that this would be a coup for the Free World and look very bad for Communism. By insisting on a choice, they would wrest a symbolic victory from the obvious lack of military victory in Korea. And indeed some forty-seven thousand North Koreans and Chinese elected not to stay on that side of the 38th parallel. This tally was somewhat misleading as many North Korean fighters had been forcibly garrisoned in the first place and so just wanted to go home; it was not *such* an ideological coup as it may have appeared to many Americans. Still, there were a lot of non-repatriates on that side.

Voluntary for the goose is voluntary for the gander. *All* were required to choose, even those whose choice was presumed; that is, good, homesick American soldiers held in dreadful camps for such a long time.

The May 25, 1953, issue of *Life* magazine featured a photograph—"A General Among Fronds"—depicting the distinguished General Omar Bradley, chairman of the Joint Chiefs of Staff and military head of policy for the Korean war, practicing a speech he was about to deliver to the Women's Press Club in Washington, DC, while concealing himself in a potted fern. This was "Picture of the Week." PHOTO: DOUGLAS CHEVALIER.

The Volleyball Problem

Four of the nonreturners posing with a peace dove en route to their new lives in China. (Morris Wills is second from left.) PHOTO: AP.

And so, the unthinkable happened. In September 1953, all United Nations prisoners had to make their choice. Twenty-three US soldiers elected not to return. Hard on the shocking news came a ninety-day "cooling off period" during which the soldiers' mothers were deputized to try to convince them (by letter) to change their minds and, for a time, the military considered sending all twenty-three moms in person to Panmunjom. (Higher ups ultimately decided this ploy could backfire if Koreans and Chinese sent corps of mothers, too.) Portia Howe of Alden, Minnesota, did try to fly to the DMZ, but she was stopped at the border, blocked by the Pentagon's ad hoc no-travel policy for the men's relatives; however, she made it as far as Tokyo. Her son rejected her appeal. She in turn insisted he was "a victim of brainwashing."[39] During the cooling-off window, the owner of the Cleveland Indians, Myron Wilson, offered the men jobs in his baseball club or private industry if they would relent. The governor of Maryland teamed up with another mother to record an entreaty to her son, assuring the young man, "Regardless of what you may have been told, the United States has no imperialist ambitions," while his mother, her voice breaking, urged, "Jack, please hurry!"[40] The sum of this activity was sufficient to cause two of the twenty-three to reverse their decisions (not Jack).[41] Despite their reversal, these two men found themselves stockaded and court-martialed, one of them sentenced to life in prison, thus deterring any more of the remaining twenty-one to change their minds, should they have contemplated it. The two served three and a half and four and a half years in prison respectively, and neither was hired by the Cleveland Indians.

The remaining twenty-one held firm. They sang the "The Internationale" (the worldwide Communist anthem) for newsreel cameras and chanted a loud riposte to the self-voiced question: "DOES ANYBODY WANT TO GO HOME?" "NO!!!" The pictures were amazing, the film footage even more so. "McCarthyism, McCarranism, and KKKism" was the shorthand they gave for not returning. In fact, it was not completely unknown for US troops to defect—a few had done so in the USSR and East Germany—but these actions had not garnered headlines as they did in 1953–1954, when they threatened to overshadow the whole brutal war, so that it would be defined, ever since and to the extent it was not 100 percent forgotten, by the great and mysterious brainwashing scandal.

Living in Freedom Village (the name given the global village in the DMZ), Wills did not consider himself a defector since the protocols mandated that they be given a legal choice. He told himself he was "help[ing] America in a different way." And anyway, he was still hung up on the fact that his country had "left him there to rot."[42] For the first time, Chinese personnel addressed him as "comrade," which was gratifying. New cycles of criticism and self-criticism were soon to follow

The Volleyball Problem

during Wills's and others of the twenty-one's careers in China, but for now he felt strongly committed to give this new path a try. "Although I did not think so at the time, I suppose you might say I was brainwashed," he commented in his 1968 memoir.[43] Even after all he had gone through, even after what he would go through, Wills—at times—was hesitant to embrace the name for what happened to him: "*I suppose you might say . . . .*" Brainwashing, at least in its common pejorative sense, did not cover the full picture, not really. This is significant.

....

Instead of going directly to Peking to be hailed by parades and celebrations, the twenty-one men found themselves herded onto a train and then a bus to a musty banquet hall in an obscure northern locale. Wills felt they immediately became a liability—perhaps the Chinese had not expected such a yield of converts and, after accruing any possible PR advantages, did not quite know what to do with these foreigners. Each of them was evaluated and dispatched accordingly. Wills, much luckier than those who were sent to work endless no-weekend jobs in truck factories or low-tech chicken farms, was deemed educable and became one of nine Americans who were sent to school. He attended Peking (Beijing) People's University full time.

He and the others continued to take part in thought reform via small study groups, which were mandatory. It was also mandatory to repent with regularity. Repent of what? Of your own actions to the extent you supported or profited from a corrupt system of capitalism. Repentance could be sought for tiny infractions, too. "And you have to criticize everyone—for something," recalled Wills. There was a rhythm to it: On the first day of criticism, you crawl; on the next day, you get angry and they escalate attacks; on the third day you "become like a whipped dog. You don't even want to look at anyone. You have now reached the stage of repentance." It was akin to a brain coating—putting a repellent layer on your mind against temptations of non-Marxism, Wills felt. You learned to stop forbidden thoughts before they crystallized.[44]

A strange effect of the brain coating: just after reaching the stage of utter, hangdog remorse, was a welling up of joy: "*A sense of exhilaration and cleansing follows* as you walk out," recalled Wills. "You feel close [to the others]."[45] Years later, Wills was still in awe of the power of this technique, not only to make a person feel bad but to make him or her feel good. This caused him to conclude, "I don't wish Communists would take over the world. It is what I fear."

Though he arrived in something close to an enchanted state, eager to sample this new society, Morris grew disenchanted. The best times were in university, where he studied Chinese, made genuine friendships, and played basketball. (His height was an asset, and he valued the team feeling.) After graduating, Wills went to work at the Foreign Languages Press in Beijing, where several other expatriates worked. The press, which specialized in translations of Chinese materials into English (propaganda for Westerners, really), increasingly came under heavy-handed Party control. Ironically, it frustrated Wills that the editors refused his suggestions about effective colloquial English and instead used slogan-filled wording that sounded like a child had written it.

Wills lived through the solidification of the Chinese Communist Party in his twelve years there. The Chinese revolution was after all only triumphant in 1949. From 1953 to 1965, he watched as the new state took over old China's remnants and marketplaces. He saw a kind of madness prevail as criticism increased and vindictiveness spread during the early stirrings of the Cultural Revolution. Other POWs, who landed in the countryside with little food and nothing to do aside from rote work, spent their hours glued to Voice of America. They almost instantly wanted to leave but were initially unable to. Some went to jail for insubordination. Some tried to walk out of China and were imprisoned. Later they were allowed to return stateside.* One (Lowell Skinner) negotiated his return to the US and was forced to leave his wife, whom the Chinese Communist Party said they would provide for, but didn't. Another married an Eastern European expatriate (as Chinese officials tended to discourage intermarriage). Clarence Adams from Memphis fell in love with and married a Chinese general's daughter. David Hawkins, the youngest of the twenty-one, attended university and worked as a truck driver during his four years in China. Like several other Americans, he left as famines and paranoia swept the country in the late 1950s.

A couple of times Wills was found to be slipping in his devotion and was sent out to the countryside to be reeducated once more. Rougher treatment came each year from the police. He also noted a precipitous downturn in the term of address officials used with him: From the high point of "comrade" (*tongzhi*) leveling at the lukewarm "friend" (*pengyou*) and finally sinking as low as "mister" (*xiansheng*) meant that his time was now limited within any sort of good graces of the state. Wills saw his "stock going down" fast in the years approaching the Cultural Revolution, when all Westerners came under increasing suspicion. He fell in love and the authorities tried to dissuade his fiancé, Kaiyen, by imprisoning her for some weeks; she persisted and the two were permitted, though grudgingly, to marry. By 1963, only eight of the original twenty-one Americans remained in China.

---

* In China, of the nine former American POWs who attended a university, five completed studies. Morris Wills and William White remained at People's University in Beijing and graduated; Harold Webb and Richard Corden completed their studies in Wuhan with Clarence Adams, all graduating. William Coward, Lewis Griggs, and Otho Bell left the country in summer 1955. By the end of 1958, Richard Corden and several others including Lowell Skinner had also returned to the states. By this time, several years into their stay and under changing political and economic conditions, the Chinese were only too pleased to allow them to go. Harold Webb married a Polish woman he met in Wuhan and moved to Poland; John Dunn moved to Czechoslovakia with his Czech wife. Scott Rush, Morris Wills, and William White married Chinese women and brought them back to America when they returned, as did Adams. James Veneris and Howard Adams married Chinese women and remained in China until their deaths.

One day, late in his sojourn there, he was required to take part in a mass bird killing. All citizens were instructed to bang pots furiously and force any bird to be disturbed from landing, and to die of exhaustion or be stoned on the ground. The authorities intended this to protect the wheat harvest in the face of growing food shortages. It didn't work anyway (it was not the birds that were responsible for low yields), though it did succeed in obliterating one of the great joys of life in Peking, the beauty of the avian life there. Increasingly, native Han Chinese people were afraid to befriend him, Wills found. Further, among his circles of foreign elites, he noted that indoctrination over such a long period of time resulted in a rampant strategic-ness. Even the sincerest and most dedicated became cynical as both the regime changed and they changed. Ultimately Wills was faced with "this hideous system of everyone spying on everyone else," which he found intolerable.[46] He and his wife packed up their infant daughter and left. By the mid-1960s their departure was a mutual decision; the Party wanted them out as much as they wanted to leave.

....

Twelve years earlier, Morris Wills had been on the front page of newspapers as one of the "Twenty-One G.I.'s Who Chose Tyranny," in the words of a 1954 headline, because, at least in the view of some press members and eventually most of the American public, they had betrayed their country by succumbing to propaganda messages.[47] What was then a new "Korean puzzle" emerged in soldiers like Wills who refused to return home, observed the *U.S. News & World Report* in October 1953. Wills, for his part, consistently maintained—in his memoir, to his family, and to the FBI when they came to question him—that he had only exercised his legally granted choice, and never betrayed his country.[48] As public opinion gradually hardened against the men, articles drawing on the US military's views painted them as groveling collaborators; as "rats" who had no loyalty; or as sex addicts who succumbed to Asian women. (One story was about how Morris Wills had "fallen for" a Chinese nurse in the camps, which was said to explain his decision.) Or perhaps some were homosexuals.[49]

Some newspaper reporters had commented on how the men were plump, and thus could not really have suffered. Images of them playing volleyball were effective propaganda, working both ways. They upheld Chinese claims to decent treatment, and they undermined POWs' reality of suffering-unto-death and starvation that preceded the event.

The Chinese press too, as early as 1950, ran with stories of American POWs converting, though in the context of China it played as a positive and effective "thought remolding" (to quote one translation of the Chinese term for it),[50] showing that thought reform worked even on American grunts. A report in the *People's Daily,* the official newspaper of the Chinese Communist Party, obliquely referred to the fact that several of the men were African American, observing that it was "out of the question" for them to return to their homeland due to "McCarthyism, lynchings, and ethnic persecution."[51] Another *People's Daily* piece included the following anecdote about a "Captain Nugent" of "the American Army's 24th division, 52nd battle regiment," who managed a small theater in the US before going to war, and was the highest ranking man in the small group captured with him. "Before he had become conscious," the *Daily*'s reporter remarked, he "only knew that Korean apples were delicious." Through exposure to the Method, he sang a new tune, declaring (as the article quoted him), "We in this group of captives believe that all foreigners should immediately leave Korea and let Korean people solve their own domestic problems."[52] The story is far-fetched, as few Americans, even the educated, would be likely to have an opinion about Korean apples—although perhaps it suggests he was given apples to eat and commented on their extraordinary deliciousness. Nonetheless, such stories were popular in Chinese newspapers, magazines, radio broadcasts, and films throughout the early 1950s.[53]

Meanwhile, hundreds of remaining POWs who were homeward bound received the label "voluntary repatriates." While they were repatriating, they underwent intensive study. Experts diagnosed a preponderance of them, up to 80 percent, as having been at least mildly brainwashed, that is, of succumbing to indoctrination to a concerning degree. That number rose to nearly 100 percent if you counted any sort of cooperative accommodation to the enemy. Three of them, in therapy with a young psychiatrist, cowrote a four-couplet poem on the USS *General John Pope* as they departed Inchon Harbor in late August of 1953. One of the couplets read:

> You ask if I was captured, if I was wounded too,
> Yes, I was badly wounded, but *what does that mean to you?*[54]

Injured, captured, tortured, maimed: These were relevant points of interest to the public and to the military and would sometimes receive sensationalized coverage but, as the men already sensed while sailing home, there would be trouble to come. You could answer questions and still not be understood. Meaning was obfuscated in the telling. The stressed words—*What does that mean to you?*—stood for an impossible gap: Who can ever really know what it was like and beyond that *what it meant* if they were not there?

Over sixty years later, a veteran reflected on what he, as one of the soon-to-be-converted POWs, witnessed in his early months at camp. A seemingly small detail came up in the interview, a detail that suggests all that was left out of the many years of historical and political commentary on these events. One night soon after arrival in the Yalu River camp, a fellow soldier died in his sleep, most likely from starvation, freezing temperatures, and untreated wounds. The soldier had been resting his feet, hours before and through the bitter night, against his

The Volleyball Problem

own to warm them against frostbite—a small act of kindness—but when the young man awoke, he found his compatriot's had turned cold. His eyes welled up at the memory from more than half a century ago and several continents away: "And I didn't even know his name. That's what bothered me."[55] Even those returning home from the camps felt doubtful of ever expressing what had happened and wished to "forget the whole thing" (as the last line of their poem went). Almost all the POWs experienced social derision or public disregard on their return, such that it was best, as one veteran said, to "put everything out of my mind."[56] Or try to. Many had nightmares persisting into old age. Others found their flashbacks worsened *after* they left the workforce as retirees. By the end of the twentieth century the whole war was known by critics as the first of the no-win wars, best forgotten.

It is also a war with no end. No peace treaty to this day has been signed, and in a sense the war continues in that it has never officially ended. What also continues with no end is the persistent half-life of "brainwashing."

3

The Lonesome Friends of Science

Recently, the actress and entrepreneur Gwyneth Paltrow described in an email newsletter for her lifestyle brand Goop the experience of a healing session for early childhood experiences of trauma. "I was gagging, heaving, my whole body was shaking, I was soaking through my clothes," she recounted to her subscriber-only newsletter, a message later sent out more broadly. "Releasing, releasing, releasing." She had put herself in the hands of Lisa Cooney, a healer from Texas, who has a five-step method for locating the precise bodily spots where emotional injuries reside and getting the "pain point" to disperse by recognizing its origin. Please don't think I am making fun of Paltrow or these procedures—aside from the fact that I have done a lot of this kind of thing myself and find it effective, I mention it as a striking cultural symptom of a dawning awareness. Trauma has not only arrived, not only gone mainstream ... it can be considered a new universal in an age where we have very few.

Almost every long-form television saga, it seems, relies on character development through the discovery of a past trauma and how it is driving the action. These cultural signs suggest many people in the second decade of the twenty-first century have been thinking about what happened to them in new ways. As the COVID-19 crisis paused the way things were done, social destabilization and personal disruption caused many to look back at their individual and collective pasts. A growing interest in trauma—the "trauma plot," or "trauma porn" as some called it suspiciously even before the pandemic—heightened further. The idea is that hidden trauma can fuel present-day behavior until it is felt and acknowledged, an idea with enough interest to cause Bessel van der Kolk's book *The Body Keeps the Score* to hover at number one for a remarkable number of months, despite that it was not a new release, as the pandemic morphed into endemic. The book is based on Van der Kolk's, his colleagues', and other researchers' redefinitions of trauma in the early 2000s. (Of course, the history of defining and redefining trauma extends much further back.)

This process had been going on for me as well, both personally and professionally. I had been teaching a class on brainwashing for over a decade, using examples from the brainwashed POWs' stories, and, frankly, I admit that somehow the processes of bodily borne trauma had never occurred to me as being an active component in their transformations. Indeed, for a while, even though I *knew* that the original brainwashed men must have suffered, I mostly saw them as emblems, almost like cartoons. I read what others said about them, but not what they said about themselves. It was as if they were cultural signifiers over people who once had lived and died. Gradually, though, I began to rectify that mistake.

I had come across first-person accounts of the brainwashed POWs (those subjected to Maoist reeducation), but these tellings were rare, written in self-defense during the Cold War or the result of a gotcha story on *The Mike Wallace Interview* television show, filmed in a smoke-filled studio.[1] Recently, that has begun to change. In light of new understandings about the dynamics of dissociation and the way the unspeakable continues to affect the person who encounters it, the experiences of the POWs look different. I began to see how ungrounding, profound destabilization of place and self, set the stage for change in prisoners, for an ideological program to take hold. It was not freakish or weird or "how bizarre!" It was trauma playing out. And yet, when you read what follows, bear in mind that this trauma would not be consistently named by a single expert in all the miles of files gathered on these men during the twentieth century. This lack of mention would be a decisive factor how intensive political indoctrination would be understood to take place.

Some social scientists would treat them as "fascinating natural experiments in attitude change," as if the men were guinea pigs in a wished-for scientific protocol.[2] Many members of the public would see them as fat and lazy, or traitors. Other experts practically drooled over the men as potential models for human engineering. Few would really want to consider what it would be like to go through what the prisoners had gone through (all indications were that actual grifters were not susceptible to brainwashing). The effects of trauma in people like Morris Wills and Clarence Adams, described in the press as dishonorable men who had "renounced their own country, become Turncoats, and disappeared behind Red China's Bamboo curtain," would go from unmentioned to unnecessary to mentioned.[3]

The effects of trauma's hiddenness are equally manifest in equivalent present-day contexts. This is part of why brainwashing is somehow hard to understand correctly, whether in the lingering fog of war (Korea as the Forgotten War), or in confused understandings of how cults work (you'd have to be an idiot to fall for that), or in the near-pornographic fascination with Patricia Hearst's kidnapping (her supposed wild ride), and finally with the ongoing challenges people face in the digital realm when interacting with algorithmic entities that bring up pleasure and pain (you have a problem, not me).

....

By the time the returnees arrived home, suspicion was spreading of any veteran who had been a prisoner. Many POWs were preemptively branded cowards and likely collaborators. They were seen as guilty just for having been captured, effectively. Shame was immense and carelessly applied, as in the case of one returning soldier who went out for a beer in his Midwestern hometown with his uncle, to whom the bartender commented, on learning the nephew was a prisoner in the camps, "Oh, he's one of them cowards." After this, the soldier never spoke of that part of his service again.[4] (The fact that, forty years later, he told a historian the bar story is another indicator of its impact.) In the atmosphere of such Manichean black-and-white categorization, you either had or had not collaborated. You either were or were not a traitor. There was little room for acknowledging the fact that while almost everyone cooperated to some degree (simply to survive), almost everyone also resisted in little or big ways. This was true even of the twenty-one nonreturners.

The returning men received plentiful invitations to share their tales. However, such opportunities often amounted to twofold exercises in not being listened to. On the one hand, relatives and friends exhibited a bit too much eagerness to relish their horrifying stories. On the other, civilians diminished the intensity of horror, rendering the experiences of POWs as simple cowardice or worse—what a PhD dissertation later called "ultimate proof that many American POWs had behaved less than honorably while in captivity."[5] Your own physical survival could be proof of conduct unbecoming.

In the face of incomprehension, soldiers tended to retreat into silence. Responses like this are, of course, typical of trauma as understood today—making it the more remarkable that it was almost universally unrecognized as a tip-off in the Korean War's returning prisoners. Such an about-face appears in a now-classic depiction of trauma, Jonathan Shay's *Achilles in Vietnam*. Although based on the experiences of Vietnam vets, Shay's work applies retroactively to the Korean experiences (no surprise as it traces ancient themes of war injury back to the *Iliad*). People, even well-meaning family members or curious press corps, it seems, wanted to hear only about the easy-to-name horrors, and these were sometimes undone by the details. *Some horrors were simply too horrifying.* Others had to do with seemingly trivial matters, even depictions of the easy life. It was all hard to reconcile.

....

Robert J. Lifton became an expert on the "mind's vulnerability to manipulation and coerced change" by accident, in a way. Answering the American government's call in 1950, at the outset of the Korean War, for a special draft of doctors (there was a shortage in the military), he signed up, completing year two of his psychiatric residency by the summer of 1951 and enlisting in the Air Force (as the alternative was to be drafted as a private into the Army). At first, he served as a psychoanalyst at the Westover AFB near Springfield, Massachusetts, but as the junior unmarried psychiatrist at the base, he was first to be dispatched abroad. He soon became the only Air Force psychiatrist in all of Korea (though the Army had many), and of necessity became a "flying psychiatrist" airlifted to bases to "evaluate anyone who seemed to be in psychiatric trouble" in Korea.[6] This turned out usually to be minor troubles, he averred; anything major would go through higher disciplinary channels. Later, the Air Force had him set up an outpatient clinic in Japan for servicemen.

Around this time, he got married, and his new wife, BJ, a war correspondent, began reporting from Korea during the armistice preparations. As Lifton wrote in his 2011 memoir of this time, "Most Americans, myself included, were unaware of its"—the Korean War's—"dimension of killing and dying, which were to rival those of the later Vietnam War." This admission, *that even the Air Force psychiatrist treating their forces had no idea of the dimensions of the war at the time it was going on*, provides a startling insight into the detachment of just about everyone, even at the time, from the experiences of the captured POWs.[7]

When BJ excitedly informed her husband about the Switch operations underway—sending physically and mentally injured men back stateside, first the most injured in the Little Switch and later a larger group in the Big Switch—and the psychological process that seemed to have contorted the men's views, Dr. Lifton asked to be assigned to the project.

A veritable psychiatric brigade, dozens strong, was gathering to study these seemingly brainwashed POWs. Most of the expert group were young up-and-coming researchers (or relatively young, at least, in their mid to late twenties), almost all were men (with a notable exception), and a preponderance, for reasons I cannot explain, seemed to have come from families of recent Jewish European immigrants to the United States.* Each of the military branches appointed their own team to study the problematic POWs. All these appointees, whether their field was sociology, psychiatry, clinical psychology, or some other specialty, agreed there was no "magic" to brainwashing; and each adopted a decidedly deflationary tone in their work on the brainwashed soldiers. They criticized, for example, the journalistic hysteria on the topic, and they frowned at the talk of a new evil "never before" confronted, as one notorious piece put it.[8] At the height of the frenzy, a friend even jokingly signed a letter to Lifton, "Yours brainwashed." It's not that Lifton and his cohort did not take brainwashing seriously. They did. But they resisted its cartoonization, the "lurid fantasy" aspect of brainwashing that made politicians tend to grab it and make end-run statements about failing American manhood and the nation's faltering soul.[9]

This attitude carried into CIA adaptations of their research, as

---

* Perhaps this interest from the children of Jewish European immigrants was because of the post-atom-bomb rise in prestige among Jewish intellectuals, as my friend, the émigré physicist Maurice Neumann, once told me he had experienced firsthand in the postwar environment of America; it was also the heyday of Freudian analysis, itself associated with the Viennese Jewish society of Freud; and finally, perhaps this reflected an existing tendency in the field itself (who was drawn into the field), as well as an as yet unmade reckoning with the dark human capacities revealed by the Holocaust.

indicated by the first warning placed at the head of a classified CIA report, "Brainwashing from a Psychological Perspective" based on sociologist Albert Biderman and psychologist Herbert Zimmer's Army work completed in 1956: "1. The term brainwashing is used in a very restricted sense. It is an unfortunate term and its uncritical use should be discouraged."[10] *Back off!* in other words, was the implicit message— *This material is just for insiders who have the proper tools to be critical and avoid the temptation to use fear-mongering words.* Yet the problem of brainwashing, and the reports generated, rose to the highest levels of the national-security apparatus.

....

After the mock Olympics ended, after the Freedom Village dispersed, after the twenty-one unreturning soldiers with their chants and (according to one account) their "wild folk dances" boarded a bus going to China, the remaining American prisoners who would head back to the US finally began doing so.[11] Thousands of POWs journeyed home in operations dubbed Little Switch (for the most gravely injured men, 149 sent back in April 1953, of whom 3 were Marines with amputated limbs) and Big Switch (for the rest of the POWs, 3,600 total, who arrived later in the year).[12] In the process, the men became objects of study within the ships' interrogation chambers and in other rooms in Honolulu, San Francisco, and Washington, DC. "We came home on a slow boat from China," joked William Baker, a returning POW, who also remembered how hard it was for them to start eating rich food again and how this augured challenges to come. He continued to struggle for decades with beriberi, a thiamine deficiency resulting from the malnutrition he experienced while incarcerated.[13] Meanwhile, experts homed in on a different kind of malaise: widespread "infection" with indoctrination was discovered. The men's files grew large.[14]

As the disoriented POWs with their thousand-mile looks arrived gloomily stateside, some of them (according to Lifton, one of their attending psychiatrists) not even bothering to appear excited as they docked the medical ship, the USS *Pope*, in San Francisco, they became emblems of brainwashing and brainwashing became an epidemic of fear. Another attending social scientist identified a common "zombie reaction" in the men ("They appeared bland, apathetic, and retarded.")[15] As epidemics will do, it spread. Not the zombie reaction itself—which seemed to pass in a few days—but the extreme startle response when faced with different facets of society at large, which persisted. Likewise, US society had, in effect, its own startle response. As the POWs faced difficulties settling back into normal life, their behavior was not recognized as traumatic response, but rather seen as symptoms of a mysterious brainwashing. Interconnected crises unfolded.

Within three years, the US Senate would hold hearings looking into the "techniques and methods" to which these and other US prisoners had been subjected. Head of the Permanent Subcommittee Committee on Investigations, Senator John McClellan, declared it a new Communist "brainwashing weapon" that aimed to "not only control the land areas of the world, but the minds and souls of the members of the human race."[16] In Americans' minds, this weapon acted to destroy faith in God and love of country. Robert F. Kennedy as attorney general led the questioning of a string of social and medical scientists. This project folded into the incoming Eisenhower administration program on the how-tos of psychological warfare. Charles Douglas "C. D." Jackson had just ascended as Eisenhower's chief advisor for psychological warfare. Jackson was a proud advocate for what he called "democratic propaganda." He invented the Psychological Warfare Board and later Radio Free Europe, drawing from his experience in World War II, when he, like many officials and science administrators, drew on Nazi learnings and techniques (via Operation Paperclip and related actions, which sometimes even imported the ex-Nazi men of science themselves) to repurpose them with the goal of supporting a democratic vision. As a very young man, Jackson had worked with the legendary Edward Bernays, Freud's nephew, who was the founder of the field of public relations. Jackson was a key "psywarrior" and an "invisible architect" of American exceptionalism, who, though largely forgotten today, took personal exception to the behavior displayed by the returning POWs, and called the men "goons,"[17] thus amping a process, slow at first, but accelerating exponentially, of vilifying them in public.

Yet Jackson also wanted experts to study them, for it was a key principle, one to be greatly emphasized in the future studies of mind control, that understanding *how it was done* was as important as how to undo it or fix it or (who knew what might be necessary?) do it yourself. Techniques were techniques, neutral. What mattered was who was using them and for what purpose. This was Jackson's view.

Initially, though, due to worries that this weakness-of-mind contagion would spread within the general population, experts isolated twenty of the worst afflicted from the Little Switch operation as security risks and mandated their quarantine in April 1953. When their

A journalist captured striking portraits of the just-arrived men a few days after they were taken to Valley Forge Army Hospital for isolation and study. Twenty-year-old Rogers Herndon (left), whose right hand had been amputated, learned to write in his reeducation diary, while in captivity, with his left hand.
ALLAN GRANT/THE LIFE PICTURE COLLECTION/SHUTTERSTOCK.

Robert Shaw, at forty-four the oldest of the brainwashed crew depicted in *Life* magazine, a veteran of fourteen years, made a call home from the Valley Forge quarantine site using a pay phone.
ALLAN GRANT/THE LIFE PICTURE COLLECTION/ SHUTTERSTOCK.

plane landed at Travis Air Force Base in California, the twenty men found themselves surrounded by military police with machine guns, an armored car circling in the background. Directly, they transferred to a flight to the Valley Forge Army Hospital in Phoenixille, Pennsylvania, for psychiatric evaluation, treatment, and further interrogation. If there was a contagion it must be isolated, studied. De-brainwashing would be attempted. (Apparently, they were also fed hamburgers as a partial curative; a *Life* magazine profile suggested this had a positive effect. They began to offer reflective statements in wonder at what had happened to them in the camps, as in one GI's statement: "After a while you say things you don't know you're saying.")[18]

Operation Big Switch, which took place later in 1953, was handled differently than Little Switch, with no triage to separate out the most concerning "cases." Paradoxically, this resulted in *all* the men receiving the status of potentially contaminated. (Eventually, all Korean War veterans would feel the taint of brainwashing, as it would be the one thing most people remembered about the war.) This larger group of returning prisoners sailed on a sort of floating laboratory where they met with a psychiatrist at least once and usually took several more meetings with intelligence agents, and in some cases, should investigators deem their actions to have risen to the level of treason, were assigned as well to a criminal investigator. On board, each answered a seventy-seven-page questionnaire and submitted to intelligence tests, emotion-revealing questionnaires, and the Rorschach inkblot diagnostic. Such batteries, containing projective, intelligence, and emotional gauges, were particularly in vogue in the late 1940s and early 1950s and social scientists had administered them to a range of people including Nazis under trial at Nuremberg, Nobel Prize winners, and heroin addicts. In addition, each GI's file included letters, diaries, and "all allegations, favorable and unfavorable" about them. And so, experts amassed for each repatriate a dossier, some of which grew to two feet long.[19] (Later, ambitious psychologists would seek out these records as part of a project to construct a compendious "database of dreams" holding the details of many people's inner lives.)[20]

In the spirit of demystification, each expert group advanced instead a patented theory that ranged from soothing to understatedly exciting, often managing to hit both notes. Army psychologist Major Henry A. Segal was one of the earliest to submit "initial findings" on tactics, techniques, and effectiveness—what had been done, in short, to the Korean returnees—in 1954. Observing the first batch of men as they repatriated, Segal emphasized their odd, startled look (at first), followed by their mild euphoria, followed by their utter confusion. Further study was mandated. Segal chose to frame the Korean returnees in the context of World War II fighters who had experienced a syndrome, informally called rice brain (this was how both fighters and physicians described it), marked by "excessive drinking or spending or both" as well as untoward demands made upon, or isolation from, family and environment. No one really got better and the group "subsequently proved incapable of adjusting to either civil or military life."[21] Segal wrote in the spirit of avoiding this failure to help sufferers readjust to society in the previous war. This was one of the first and last times an expert would portray the Korean vets as suffering from something *like* World War II vets. Soon, the *unusual* would be stressed almost exclusively.

Another set of studies looked at the POWs' Rorschach test results. What had the men said, after eating their burgers (or, perhaps before), when they were shown inkblot images on eight-by-ten-inch cards, in sequence, some black and white and some, later, with bursts of red or pastel colors. These colors, which enter the series beginning with Card 3, were meant to induce in some viewers what Hermann Rorschach called color shock, in which an immediate state of "emotional and associative stupor" took hold.[22] Findings indicated that the returning Korean War POWs were different, not only in expression of color shock. In other ways, compared with veterans of other wars, they were more disturbed.

Walter Reed Army Institute of Research psychologist Margaret Thaler Singer, then a thirty-two-year-old with doctoral training from the University of Denver, headed the analysis of the tests. (Years later she would use the cards to evaluate the kidnapping survivor Patricia Hearst.) She started studying them in 1953. By 1958, with the help of several other psychologists, she had performed a thorough analysis not only of the men's Rorschach test responses but also their results in another projective test (the Thematic Apperception Test), as well as their answers to the Sentence Completion Test.[23] The team found, to put it bluntly, that the men were messed up. There was widespread impairment of judgment and evidence of extreme emotional distress. At least 46 percent of them (a proportion especially pronounced in the Big

The Lonesome Friends of Science

A photo essay in *Life* magazine on October 7, 1946, led with this depiction of four "successful young New Yorkers"—a lawyer, a composer, a procurer, and an executive—"studying an inkblot intently to see what images it suggests." ALLAN GRANT/THE LIFE PICTURE COLLECTION/SHUTTERSTOCK.

Switch sample) displayed "apathy and pseudo apathy." Pseudo apathy meant that although the men's results might appear to indicate that they were affectless blanks lacking in strong emotion, there was indication of hostile aggressive undercurrents, too.

What did the returning prisoners, having been through so much, have to say when, lying in a hospital bed or sailing on a ship across the Pacific, they were shown inky pictures on cardboard and asked to tell what they saw? Among the general population the most common answers to Card 3 were two waiters in tuxedos or two drummers drumming. Yet when one unnamed POW saw this card, he described, "A couple of guys pulling the heart out of another man, pulling the other man's chest open. They have the insides of his body pulling it apart."[24] This type of disturbance was prevalent among the returnees.

Next in the Walter Reed study, Singer compared two sets of replies to the deliberately disturbing drawings in the Thematic Apperception Test, a visual test, often considered the number-two test to the Rorschach's number-one in this era. It was said to act as an "x-ray of the inner life."[25] The returnees' responses, when looked at against those of World War II veterans of a similar age who had been tested in 1947–1948, revealed persistent distress. When shown Card 8, the World War II vets had spoken of death or illness of a parent, whereas the Korean POWs tended toward *"Thinking of a frightening or unpleasant event which could not be erased from memory."*[26] Another card in the series depicted a man leaning against a lamppost in what the test language characterized as "a hazy atmosphere." When shown this card, Singer reported, the Korean POWs' responses came out more disturbed than the other POWs. While the normative group of veterans saw the man as the potential victim of attack, "Repatriates saw the man as sad and lonely, plotting an aggressive act." [27] As an external "check" on their findings, the scholars sent twenty randomly selected tests "blind" to several outside psychologists who confirmed the original findings (emotional impoverishment and latent hostility). What Singer called "the apathetic . . . records" were thus double-checked. The men were, in fact, apathetic.

They also studied resisters versus collaborators: Was there an X factor that led to better outcomes (that is, an ability to resist the enemy)? Possibly yes, Singer suggested. Yet her positive conclusion demanded that you be able to tell resisters from collaborators. As one of the lead authors of another POW study, Army psychologist Edgar Schein, wrote in 1960, the very definition of collaboration within the foggy morass of the camp environment was so ambiguous that "these statistics"—about the degree of collaboration among the men—"become meaningless."[28] If you couldn't reliably define collaboration, you couldn't find out what factors made a collaborator. Still, the obsession with who was a collaborator allowed experts to sidestep evidence of trauma. The drama of who withstood brainwashing, and who did not, ignored a much more complex web of suffering in which all prisoners were caught and, as a result, changed, at least to some degree.

Perhaps not surprisingly, due to the difficulty of defining collaboration, the Rorschach and Thematic Apperception Test studies of the men faded away quickly, but other research programs did not. One of the most lasting was a social model. Schein (Singer's colleague at Walter Reed) advocated a model of "coercive persuasion," one that worked by activating social bonds. In fact, for Schein the whole phenomenon of so-called brainwashing was *social, not psychological*. (Schein was on to a key understanding, largely sidestepped today, that what we call brainwashing is not about one mind so much as an outgrowth of many minds and bodies interacting in a complex situation.)

Schein felt that there was no inner conversion happening in the men, merely behavioral manifestations of coercion. "The problem which confronted the West with the POWs," he explained, "was not so much their ideological conversion, of which there was virtually none, but rather a variety of collaborative behaviors (such as making radio broadcasts praising the CCP [Chinese Communist Party], signing 'peace' petitions, asking others to cooperate with the enemy, serving on 'peace' committees, making germ warfare confessions, and so on) which the Communists used skillfully to embarrass the United States in particular during the Korean episode."[29] The problem, thus, was embarrassing behavior rather than an actual existential "conversion" or turning over of self. Schein basically *behaviorized* the crisis—redefined it in terms of actions seen as problematic, so that the core issue effectively disappeared. The POWs' brainwashing experiences were mostly significant as "fascinating natural experiments in attitude change" rather than as a society-level threat, he concluded—except in China, where the use of these same techniques on the whole population was worth watching.[30]

A second influential take was that of Army-trained Air Force psychiatrist Dr. Louis Jolyon West who studied a group of thirty-six Air Force pilots who had—shockingly, to some—confessed, after being captured, held, and brutally reeducated, to flying bacteriological warfare missions over China. One of the most famous of these men was Colonel Frank Schwable, a highly respected military pilot and four-time awardee of the Distinguished Flying Cross, who never recovered either from the demoralization of his captivity in North Korea or the humiliation of his threatened court martial in America (although the action was ultimately dropped). West and his team were the first to examine this group, who tended to be of a much higher military rank than the other returnees.

West discerned complex behavioral conditioning at work, and developed what would become a much-cited frame he called DDD: debility, dependency, and dread.[31] "Debility" meant the subject was run down physically (wounds not treated, care not given), but not too far. "Dependency" was created by the need to turn to captors for every need, including food and toilet, and every comfort. (This explains in part why many POWs displayed hyper concern over bodily functions after they were released, fixations sometimes lasting decades.) "Dread" was the imposition of looming threats—that you would be executed, that your family would be tormented, that unknown horrors might arrive at some unspecified date. (If a prisoner saw these things happening occasionally, it made the dread more real.) Isolation, darkness, and a rapid-fire interrogation process intensified the effects of DDD, which resulted in a zeroing out of the person—or "ultimate demoralization," as West and his researchers put it: a disastrous loss of orientation to self and personality. Margaret Singer, who would become Dr. West's associate a few years after she left Walter Reed in the late 1950s, studied the pilots too, at Lackland Air Force Base, where West by that time was working as lead psychiatrist.

A third lasting study belonged to Albert Biderman, a social

scientist with the Air Force, who created what is known today as "Biderman's Chart of Coercion," as well as a 1956 edited collection about the prisoners, *The Manipulation of Human Behavior*—with a focus on the interrogation of the unwilling, noncooperative prisoner.[32] Biderman's work was adopted in the mid-1960s as the basis of Army Field Manual 32–54, "Intelligence Interrogation"[33] and a contributing source to the CIA manual called KUBARK, on the interrogation of compliant and resistant subjects. (KUBARK was a cryptonym for the CIA itself; once highly protected, this manual, which has since been made accessible under the Freedom of Information Act (FOIA), is now available in a popular edition and sells at Walmart.)[34] It presented brainwashing research more in a "how-to" mode than an interior account. If the arc of many POW studies bent toward an external analysis of outcome, a focus on visible manifestations, and the abandonment of an attempt to access the inner feel of what it meant to be brainwashed, this arc did not describe Lifton's work.

....

Robert and BJ Lifton went to Hong Kong as part of celebratory globe-hopping travels after he was decommissioned from the Air Force. By this time, in 1954,[35] all the returning POWs had gone home, their files had been amassed, interviews conducted, research formulated, and publications were underway from the other military branch's experts. Yet Lifton became obsessed during their stop in Hong Kong when he got the chance to interview people who were just being released across the covered bridge from Mainland China. These were civilians who had gone through intense thought reform procedures. Refugee conduits put him in contact with some of them. Other times Lifton would scan the *South China Morning Post* where lists of recently deported Westerners appeared and invite them to meet with him.

Instead of returning to Boston to start a civilian career or traveling around the world on a fellowship to study psychological education,

Lifton stayed in Hong Kong to interview fifty Europeans who had lived in China (for example, the daughter of an American Midwestern missionary and a French clergyman), and fifteen members of the Chinese educated class (university students and urban intellectuals). Lifton felt he needed to modify his training to promote more decisively "the human encounter" at the heart of the meeting, combined with "disciplined research probing." He recognized, more than he had with the POWs, that "I was working with vulnerable people who should not be pushed too far," people who had been broken, truly. Surprisingly, some seemed to be still "confessing"—even to him. They feared that he was a plant or a secret spy for the CCP, or else they could not shake their deep training to obey any figure who resembled an interrogator. In his recent memoir, *Witness to an Extreme Century*, Lifton described these subjects as traumatized, something that was almost never done in the mid-twentieth century, when experts considered trauma to be exceptionally rare and the post-traumatic stress disorder (PTSD) had yet to be defined diagnostically, much less conceptualized as nearly ubiquitous, as it is today with complex trauma (CPTSD). (These ongoing changes would have to wait for their initiation with the return of Vietnam veterans, the recognition of battered woman syndrome in the 1970s, and the investigations of somatic storage of trauma reactions in the 1980s and 1990s. Lifton himself would be instrumental in introducing some of these diagnostic changes.)[36] In short, Lifton could not yet put into words in 1954 what he could in 2011: "They had been put through a traumatic procedure that could leave them confused about what had been done to them." Although "well aware that I was not and should not be their formal therapist," he felt that possibly he could help while advancing his research.[37]

Perhaps most clearly among the multitudinous American experts called to comment on the brainwashing phenomenon, Lifton saw that the brainwashing of US prisoners was an "export version" of the program that millions of Chinese people were undergoing, a "compulsory movement of purification and renewal" dominating an entire vast society: Mao Zedong Thought, as many Chinese called it.[38] A 1951 program had targeted intellectuals and students, especially. Later, Lifton would describe it as apocalypticism. In contrast to the chart-making (of Biderman) and the "behavioralizing" (of Schein), the psychometrics (of Singer) and the CIA-readiness (of West), was Lifton's take, eventually published as *Thought Reform and the Psychology of Totalism*. If I had to reduce this work to one adjective, almost a cliché of the postwar years, it would be "existentialist." One reason is that Lifton admits a large debt to Camus. And besides, there is the sense of a dark backdrop against which figures are stuck in a struggle between meaning and meaninglessness.

....

In the process of doing interviews, Lifton encountered a French physician named Charles Vincent, in his early fifties, who had arrived in Hong Kong just five days earlier. On meeting with Lifton, Dr. Vincent suspected that this young American psychiatrist might be pursuing professional gain, using Vincent's story to advance his own career. (In fact, many experts did advance their careers based on research with brainwashed troops or civilians.) In effect, he suspected his questioner of being a bourgeois spy. "It was clear to me that he was still . . . deeply confused" about what he had been through, observed Lifton.[39] In the moment, worried the fragile doctor would simply break off the interview and leave, Lifton reassured him that he was from the non-Communist world but was curious about the other, and this satisfied the physician sufficiently for him to continue.

Dr. Vincent's backstory—his life before he experienced three years of brutal thought reform—gave Lifton further perspective on Vincent's two-sided paranoia. Vincent was born and brought up in southern France in a pious, middle-class family. His father was a painter of Catholic religious art. Sent to a strict boarding school between the ages of ten and seventeen, Vincent did well in studies but, in his phrase, "recognized no rules," was rebellious, and kept emotionally aloof. So much did he enjoy ecstatically romping around in the woods that his father at some point physically chained the adolescent to their house (which may say more about the father than the son). Dr. Vincent described himself to Lifton as a sort of wild child. Medicine became his way of connecting socially with people, and his passion about the subject consumed his intellect and emotions. Thus, despite his idiosyncratic comportment, he was able to graduate at the top of his class at age twenty-six. After this he married a woman he appreciated mainly for leaving him alone and departed with her for China on their wedding day, excited by the challenges of medical practice there.

In China he started a private clinic, which he combined with part-time employment for European governments. He made broad bacteriological surveys for the French. He treated Chinese and foreigners of all walks of life, all the while scrupulously avoiding intimate personal relationships with anyone including his family. Other expatriate Westerners in Shanghai disliked him, viewing him as strange and "somehow evil" (Lifton's phrase), but the doctor believed he was useful to the patients he had and felt himself entirely happy once he moved his practice to the countryside after World War II, and could be close to nature again.[40] He kept three separate clinics and traveled among them by motorcycle, horse cart, and mule, while the Chinese civil war waged on. He hunted and fished in the morning, painted in the afternoons, and was an overachiever in the healing arts. "There was no man as happy as I," he said in recollection of that time.

Just before the Communist takeover in 1948, his family—his wife and children—left for Europe without him. As his services were in demand in the city, in 1949 he moved there rather than returning to France; anyway he was not terribly attached to his wife and children.

To put it simply (Lifton says), he was a man unable to love. Some of his patients were Communist officials, and the doctor thought he had good relations with them, good enough to avoid arrest at least. Although warnings came from the French embassy that he was in peril of imminent detention, he disregarded them. Sometimes he made reservations to leave but he canceled them. One day, walking in the streets of Shanghai, five men with revolvers confronted him; showing him a warrant for his arrest, they took him to a "re-education center."

Placed in a small, eight-by-twelve-foot bare cell with eight other prisoners, all Chinese, who had been residing there for some time, he found the cell-chief addressing him by his prison number. (Receiving a number or a symbol instead of a name was and remains an important part of thought reform, no matter the context.) He sat at the center of the cell with the others ranged around him and heard them all shout invectives such as "Spy!" and "Imperialist!" at him. They demanded that he confess. To his protests, they answered, "The government has all the proof. They have arrested you and the government never makes a mistake. You have not been arrested for nothing." This would not be the first time he heard the refrain that his guilt was a foregone conclusion and that only the details of his crimes remained to be discovered. (In fact, this was another ironclad rule of Communist reeducation whether Soviet or Chinese, or even versions used in previous centuries: The government only arrests the guilty. Hence, the prisoner in question's guilt is assumed and must only be demonstrated, not proven.)

Dr. Vincent's first interrogation took place in another small room with an interrogator, an interpreter, and a secretary present. Vague accusations came from the interrogator (here, Judge), along with an emphatic demand that he come clean about his crimes. Again, he protested his innocence. Each protestation was met with an implacable assertion of his guilt:

Judge: You have committed crimes against the people, and you must now confess everything.

Judge: The government never arrests an innocent man.

Judge *(continuing to question him about his activities and hinting at a threat or promise of lenience)*: The government knows all about your crimes. That is why we arrested you. It is now up to you to confess everything to us, and in this way your case can be quickly solved and you will soon be released.

(Dr. Vincent's unavailing insistences on his innocence interspersed the judge's pronouncements.)

Over the next ten hours, Dr. Vincent faced questions that focused more and more on his alleged connections with the French embassy; American government officials; and Catholic, Japanese, and Nationalist Chinese agencies. The session, ending at 6 a.m., had produced much information, though Dr. Vincent was still asserting his innocence and denying he was a spy. He still did not understand his arrest. The judge, angry at this, ordered handcuffs applied to Vincent's wrists behind his back and told him to think over his crimes.

Ten minutes later, when Vincent still could not see his crimes, the judge became further incensed. Chains were put on his ankles, and he was sent back to the cell.

At this point struggle sessions started in earnest with his cellmates. "They start 'struggling' to 'help' you," Dr. Vincent recalled. He spent all his time in chains, standing in the cell, rejected for his insufficient zeal to reform himself by his cellmates, who themselves had been through similar struggle after their own arrests. "You eat as a dog does, with your mouth and teeth. You arrange the cup and bowl with your nose to try to absorb broth twice a day. If you have to make water, they open your trousers and you make water in a little tin in the corner. . . . You are never out of the chains. . . . Nobody washes you." If he would only confess, he learned, things would improve. The degradation had strong effects—as a CIA report on brainwashing would soon describe, under this general plan of treatment (the Soviet model differing from the Chinese mainly in its lack of a group component), 99 percent of all prisoners will yield and become utterly demoralized, no longer caring for themselves bodily (to the extent they might have been able to), and even desisting from trying to clear their names. All this occurs—reliably, regularly—without the need to inflict direct physical blows.[41] Vincent's chains caused pain, but they were in a sense passive tormentors. If a judge were to resort to ordering violent blows or harsh beatings, this would break rules adopted against such crude methods. And, in fact, it had been found that beatings caused the prisoner to activate their spirit of resistance, whereas these other methods when systematically applied were not recognized as torture—neither by the men nor by the interrogators. They were the rightful consequences of being in the wrong. They inexorably led to utter demoralization.

Next, Dr. Vincent conceived of a "wild confession"—anything, as he later said, to get them to remove the chains, for they had come to dominate his thoughts. For a night and a day, he bragged he was a master spy, a big criminal. Surely this would satisfy them. He was part of an American ring. But his claims lacked convincing detail and did not satisfy his interrogator. On the third night, he changed tactics again. He became a pointillist, very empirical, recalling every detail of every conversation with friends and associates over twenty years spent in China. What would produce the desired effect on these interrogators? Vincent engaged in a trial-and-error procedure. Giving lots of minutiae seemed to be the right direction if his goal was to have the chains taken off his wrists and ankles.

Things seemed to speed up now, as he had stopped claiming to be either innocent or a bigwig. More demanding interrogations ensued. These interspersed with rapid walks in chains. A scribe took daytime dictations, writing down everything he said or did. After each session, he signed with his thumbprint. (Signing this way was due to the sores on his wrists that made it impossible to write, but it also served to downgrade him to the status of an illiterate.)

Eight days and nights passed with no sleep in this manner. Interrogations alternated with group struggle sessions. "He found himself in a Kafka-like maze of vague and yet damning accusations. He could not understand what he was guilty of and could not convince them of his innocence," Lifton commented. The only way out was to hang details on top of the skeleton form of his putative guilt. As the CIA report would point out, this self-hanging process can begin as a strategy to exonerate oneself—*if I tell them everything, they will see that I have done nothing wrong*—but rapidly turns into its opposite, self-incrimination. "Many men divulge all they can remember about themselves because they feel quite sure that they have done nothing which may be regarded as criminal," commented the brainwashing expert Albert Biderman in a report for the CIA.[42] In the end it is precisely this detailed information that condemns them, sometimes (as in the Moscow Show Trials under Stalin in the late 1930s) to actual hanging. Arthur Koestler's 1940 allegorical novel *Darkness at Noon* depicted the fate of a loyal revolutionary named Rubashov, now a man late in his career, as he proceeds step by step to descend, through three successive interrogation hearings, into avid self-denunciation and the willing embrace of his own execution, even in the absence of having committed any of the named crimes.

About ten days into this process, overwhelmed, Dr. Vincent ceased all resistance. This moment was pivotal. "You are annihilated," Dr. Vincent told Dr. Lifton. In fact, almost 100 percent of those subjected to this method of indoctrination mixed with interrogation did cease to resist—or so bragged a Soviet interrogator in a 1951 public trial in Hungary, as confirmed by US research. Even God could be made to confess, the interrogator claimed. One could be so broken down by the sheer routine that an animal response took over.

The Lonesome Friends of Science

....

Dr. Vincent's crime began to emerge in more detail, though it still had wild elements. Each night he signed with his thumbprint. After three weeks, he found he must report on others. The long histories he detailed, the addresses he provided, his exhaustive lists, all initially half-truths in his mind, now became denunciations.

Clamoring followed him as his cellmates urged him on further: "Confess! . . . Confess all! . . . You must be frank! . . . You must show your faith in the government! . . . Come clear! . . . Be sincere! . . . Recognize your crimes!" An example of a "crime" to be confessed was Dr. Vincent's conversation with a man who was friendly with an American military attaché. During what had seemed a casual conversation, "I told him the price of shoes [in China] and that I couldn't buy gasoline for my car." During interrogation, he had already agreed that this exchange constituted economic intelligence. But this admission was not enough: Dr. Vincent had to say further that his intelligence mission was received directly from the American military, that it was all witting and willing. "This was the people's standpoint." In this way, "*Your invention becomes a reality.*"[43]

Two months after his arrest, Dr. Vincent was now considered ready for a beginning "recognition" of his crimes. He was progressing. He had to learn to look at himself continuously from "the people's viewpoint." He was dazed, compliant, unenthusiastic, when, suddenly, a remarkable improvement in his status occurred. Handcuffs and chains disappeared. Study opportunities were offered. A comfortable seat was permitted in talking with the judge, and Dr. Vincent found himself addressed in friendly tones. He had entered the phase of leniency. Of this "friendly phase," the CIA analyst commented—judging from Soviet enactment of exactly this tactic—"Prisoners find this sudden friendship and release of pressure almost irresistible."[44] It is startlingly effective, the report observed, even though it would seem from the outside to be so obviously calculated (tea, cigarettes, a kind tone).

Yet the body in self-inflicted pain attunes to a different rhetoric—that is, when the pain source is removed and when balm is applied. A small kindness can be irresistibly comforting. As Morris Wills had found, warm baked goods offered in a well-heated library had an eloquence of their own.

On Dr. Vincent, too, the friendly turn had a profound effect, especially when he was allowed to sleep at last for eight hours in a row. "For the first time he had been treated with human consideration, the chains were gone, there was hope for the future," Lifton related. But if he resisted even slightly, the chains reappeared, and the sleep allotment disappeared.

Group study followed. Dr. Vincent joined in a regular cell routine. There were two daily excursions to toilets, during which everyone ran, with their heads down, to the latrine and back. There was poor but adequate food. The sores from the chains were treated. He was now an active participant in a reeducation program. Group study went on for ten to sixteen hours per day. They read from books or newspapers and added Marxist critique.

Included in the ensuing long period of struggle was the requirement for Daily Life Criticisms. These consisted of self-examination practices. He learned that "under the cloak of medicine," he was nothing but a representative of European "exploitation," an imperialist agent, a lifelong spy, an enemy of the people. It was necessary to "examine himself over and over again." What seemed innocent was reframed as culpable. If he took up too much room while sleeping, this was considered "imperialist expansion," and he had to modify the way he slept.

The true twist came after weeks and months, when he began more actively to apply these judgments to himself. It was no longer a mask he wore and could take off, but his true face, as it were. "You talk and talk," he recalled. Marxist theory was not only spoken but absorbed so that it became automatic. Ironically Dr. Vincent had to learn to express himself "spontaneously" in this exact prescribed manner, so that it was as if coming directly from his heart and soul, and after a while it was. In other words, he must always produce real "wrong thoughts" and must always correct them.

Finally, after more than a year, he reached advanced standing, in which privileges now consisted of one hour's worth of outdoor exercise a day, some additional recreation in the cell, and permission to give French lessons to other prisoners and to conduct medical classes. He by this time believed and accepted his guilt, "although not in a simple manner." For moments, though, not all the time, "You think they are right." "It is a special kind of belief" is what Dr. Vincent said. By this he meant, a belief you don't really believe but have been made to really believe. It was a belief beyond critical judgment.

The unimaginable had happened. He had been reeducated. Finally, the Chinese authorities declared him cured of imperialism. Because of his crimes, he would be banished—forced to leave the country, never to return. When Lifton asked him about his experience, shortly after his release and relocation to Hong Kong, Dr. Vincent was so dazed that he could only say it is was unimaginably horrible, with no more detail forthcoming at first. Flawed recall like this, a CIA report detailed in parallel, was true for recovered schizophrenics as well as the Korean War POWs.[45]

Let's look to a moment when Dr. Vincent suspected Lifton of being a bourgeois spy. At the start of their interview, Dr. Vincent asked Lifton, point blank: "Are you standing on the people's side or on the imperialists' side?"[46] Reeducation, as the legitimately paranoid Dr. Vincent correctly pointed out, meant something totally different depending on where you were standing. From the so-called imperialistic, capitalist side, "re-education is a kind of compulsion," it was cruel coercion, and he, as a doctor, had had something bad happen to him. But from the "people's side" (as he put it), reeducation "is to die and be born again."[47] It was full of meaning. He could be grateful. The physician was saying that he had experienced something close to a religious conversion. And then, according to a sunk-cost logic, if he gave up the "people's side" as a way to see what had happened to him, he would forfeit the status of "enlightened comrade" for that of a victimized ex-doctor who failed to resist, who was a broken man, who had experienced a catastrophe. His own existential guilt, family traumas, and personal shortcomings became weapons to be used against him.

He could keep the significance of his experience if he held to his tormentors' definitions of it. Only if he shifted to European mores did his fate change its meaning into coercive injustice. Of all the studies, Lifton's was the best at capturing the inner stakes and the bodily toll, as in Dr. Vincent's experience. He tended to paint these in existential terms. Yet, again, he did not report Vincent or any soldier or re-educatee to have been traumatized. None of the military's or government's experts would.

....

Brainwashing—whether this term or some substitute was used—was the issue du jour as the early Cold War set in. Two high-up brothers, Secretary of State John Foster Dulles and CIA Director Allen Dulles, met with their deputies and received briefings. Policy changes resulted. Courts-martial proceeded. The military branches instituted their Code of Conduct as a direct result of the men's seeming failure to observe the "name, rank, and serial number" limiting protocol. Anti-brainwashing training for enlistees developed—which news articles of the time characterized as the US Army's "Schools for Sadists."

At this point, the trail of the great brainwashing crisis's effects went underground and took a veer toward the surreal. Further investigations continued through clandestine research, namely, MK-ULTRA, experiments in active interrogation combined with drugging, hypnosis, sleep deprivation, occasional brutality, simulated drowning, and canceling the capacity to dream. There were published (unclassified) and unpublished (classified) versions of most research from here forward.

The volleyball problem—the mismatch between image and reality, the struggle to identify suffering—was not solved but absorbed. It contributed to the invisibility of trauma, the persistence of addiction. Experimentation and simulation came next.

4

Violence Studies

Glenn Petersen was a radar operator who flew seventy combat missions during the Vietnam War as part of a naval flight crew on an E-1B surveillance and reconnaissance aircraft. He first came to visit my class on brainwashing around 2012, after I discovered a 2009 op-ed he had written. In the *Nation* and the *New York Times*, Petersen, now an anthropologist, addressed the topic of the trauma he had suffered (and then forgotten) as a flight-team trainee. Petersen mentioned that the damaging techniques that had been used on him were repurposed for use in Iraq, Afghanistan, and the Guantanamo Bay detention camp—GITMO—in Cuba. During the twenty-first century's first decade, many people were reckoning with the aftermath of the Bush regime's use of "enhanced interrogation techniques," sometimes also known as soft torture, on prisoners held at a detention facility in the Bagram military base in Afghanistan and GITMO, and Petersen felt he had a personal stake. Specifically, accompanying a 2009 report to the Senate Intelligence Committee was the release of hundreds of photographs documenting the ritualized humiliation and torture of prisoners captured and held as suspected Isis fighters, and this looked entirely familiar to him.

On receiving my invitation, Petersen wrote back to accept:

> Rebecca—I go through periods when I can talk and write about the war and periods when I can't. I'm actively writing about it these days and would very much enjoy an opportunity to talk to a group with a professional interest in this topic. For a field ethnographer it would be like turning the tables on myself, becoming the informant. So, yes, I'd be happy to come to Cambridge and speak to your class in March.[1]

This would be the first of several visits over almost a decade, each one—as Petersen promised—an occasion in which he essentially became an informant on himself. Students gathered around a table that spring for his guest lecture, directing their gazes to the slim, resiliently dark haired, mustachioed professor as he launched into his military story. We had already spent several weeks on the topic of mental manipulation during the Cold War (which, for the college students, tended to seem like a long time ago). Now we had a real person describing one of the pivotal experiences of his life: Undergoing "survival training" designed to protect him against indoctrination via mind control should he ever find himself shot down in missions over North Vietnam. What had been meant to protect him nearly destroyed him. It also paradoxically gave him strength.

Under the influence of Petersen's words, it was as if everything we had studied so far, including firsthand stories and scientific articles and other guests—had been merely theoretical. This was riveting reality. Petersen took students into the "what it was like" of, among other things, being brought to the point of breakdown by one's own superiors.

Violence Studies

"I'm going to die in here . . . Let me out!!" The year was 1966 and Glenn Petersen was locked in a dark wooden box that sat baking in the sun at 3,366 feet of elevation somewhere in the Cleveland National Forest in a remote area northeast of San Diego, California.[2] The box was far too small for his body, even rolled up, as he was, in the fetal position. With rising panic and the sure knowledge that he would not survive, Petersen screamed mentally but did not make a sound. As his limbs lost feeling, *he also lost track of the fact that he was in a simulation.* It was a Navy training program meant to mimic the brutality he might suffer in captivity. The box was too small by design and was meant to restrict the occupant's ability to breathe and to regulate body temperature. Variously called the Syrian box, the sweat box, or the hot box—though Petersen did not know any of these names—the device, in the prototypical form of a vertical coffin, had a checkered history in the United States where it was used in the Revolutionary War on both Tory and Native American prisoners, and later to break the will of enslaved people on plantations. (After the 1877 riots at the State Reform School for Boys in Westborough, Massachusetts, the sweat box torture of boys made newspapers.)[3] In the present case, its occupant retained one hope: That though he might die, he would not be broken.[4] Later he would reflect that he had been training to arrive at that point all his life.

Two years before, in 1964, Petersen had been a sixteen-year-old, Vespa-riding runaway working on an assembly line making telephones in Santa Barbara, California, when he elected for a more exciting path and joined the military just after he turned seventeen. A few days later, the Navy assigned him to train as a radar intercept controller and flight technician—an essential part of the role was to spot, via radar simulators, any intruding attack planes, or "bogeys," and direct jet fighters to shoot them down—as part of a flight crew flying off aircraft carriers. (This assignment, for which he earned his gold aircrew wings and under circumstances where, as he later put it, "success... was the only acceptable option," was unusual for an enlistee who had barely completed tenth grade, but Petersen was precocious.)[5] Not long after that, he began about two years of electronics and avionics instruction. He did well. But before he shipped with his crew to the Gulf of Tonkin, he faced the final necessary step of undergoing POW training in the high desert northeast of San Diego at the Navy's school for SERE, which stands for survival, evasion, resistance, and escape. (Survival school or Warner Springs was how everyone involved referred to it then, though it became more commonly known as SERE, pronounced "seer," in the 1980s.) The biggest lesson of the curriculum was the R (for resistance), which entailed learning to endure forceful interrogation, or (its synonym) brainwashing. Specially intended for air crews and river boat crews deemed in high risk of capture, the school artfully created the experience of finding oneself at the mercy of a brutal enemy. It was, in the words of SERE materials posted on a Special Operations website not long ago, designed to be "as realistic as possible"—to place volunteers in "a realistic captivity scenario."[6] It was a simulation, in other words, of abusive prisoner conditions, but it generated (to use language common today) *in real life and real time* a set of intense emotional and physiological responses that were undoubtedly genuine.

The course began when the trainees were released into the spare conditions around the Warner Springs area of the national forest and told to live off the land for several days, though there was hardly anything to live off, with no weapons and little equipment provided. Soon weak from hunger, they crawled through fields strung with concertina wire and swept by machine gun fire. (Today, most versions of the training include tracker-dog evasion but no concertina wire.) They slept on the ground wrapped in parachutes. Thus "suitably weakened," as Petersen put it in his memoir, they entered stage two, a fully equipped mock POW camp constructed to mimic such confinements with rudimentary toilets, bleak surroundings, and rifle-bearing tower guards. There, the "prisoners" (Petersen and other Navy personnel about to ship off) hauled heavy stones back and forth across the compound for hours each day, while the "guards" (Navy survival instructors) punched them and, once they landed on the ground, kicked them until they stood up. Petersen saw that guards took several of his co-trainees to be waterboarded, while they forced others to watch their comrades suffer, paying for some mistake attributed to the trainee. Legally granted the right to inflict harm on the trainees, guards were skilled at it. Even today, deep in the YouTube comments sections, one can discover tales of legendary harshness. In response to an official US Navy video promoting the SERE training, @newfoundlandknight wrote, *"My dad was the head SERE instructor at Warner Springs in the early 1970s. Betcha there are still men who hates [sic] his guts. . . . He waterboarded men all day long, beat you, starved you, put you in a box that caused cramping in minutes and you would stay there for hours."*[7]

But @newfoundlandknight did not mention that the guards in the simulation training intended for men going to East Asia play-acted in a different geography: "The guards were well-trained to act entirely in the role of foreign, generically eastern European soldiers," Petersen recalled. Even post-Korea, during the Vietnam War, and continuing through the 1990s, the dominant Cold War demand for brute "realism" dictated that East European rather than East Asian surroundings would be best for instilling the necessary feeling of fear and subsequent (hopefully) resistance.[8] Thirty years later, a 1995 Marine Corps trainee encountered SERE instructors "who wore Warsaw Pact-style uniforms and spoke with thick Slavic accents"; and his mind's ability to reassure himself that he was in a simulation "rapidly deteriorated."[9] At some point, possibly around 2005 or 2015 (depending on the training location) the generic Eastern European milieu was replaced by Arabic accents, jihadi garb, and a faux-Ramadi-like urban setting.

At one point, the guards deliberately "broke" one trainee in front of the rest of the group, first reducing him to "bawling tears," so that he sobbingly agreed to anything they demanded. They then seated him in the shade beside his comrades laboring in the sun, and gave him food and water. This man symbolized the Korean War traitors a decade before, whose weaknesses spurred the training they were currently undergoing. Petersen and the others were told the broken man would be made to sign papers confessing that the US was engaged in biological and chemical warfare in Vietnam, a dishonor that would reside permanently on his record. "It was a distressing, disturbing sight, seeing him there, I was deeply afraid the same thing would be done to me."[10] The fear of a contaminated personnel file was particularly frightening. (It is possible the trainee was an actor, Petersen sometimes considers, but it was fully convincing to him at the time, and to this day he feels the man really was broken in their presence.)

After a day or two of brutality, a guard singled Petersen out, marched him through the gate into the open area surrounding the camp, and then guided him toward some black boxes resting on the ground at a 30-degree angle. The guard swung open the lid and motioned for Petersen to climb in. He did, and as he stepped in the guard "crammed me down" into a fetal position and closed the lid. In the stifling heat inside the box, with the sun hammering overhead, he could not move. This was when his unvoiced scream began. The near total desperation also marked a turning point. Realizing he could not know how long he might be in the box, he relaxed, just a bit. This little bit was enough to help him recognize that though he might die, he wasn't going to do so in the next second. It would take some time. He told himself that if he could focus on anything else, he could momentarily keep from thinking about how painful his position was, how difficult it was to breathe, how hot the interior of the box was, how long his stay might be. Again, panic rose and again he fought to relax just enough to let it pass by. Petersen estimates he lost consciousness a couple of times, perhaps from lack of oxygen, the heat, the panic, or insufficient blood circulation.

It was useless to remind himself this "wasn't for real," that it was a mock camp, that the guards with accents were Navy men, and that his government was unlikely to let him die. Perhaps he had died already. At any rate, "The notion that this wasn't for real did nothing to alleviate the fear, the pain, the sense that I wasn't going to make it."[11] Shifting focus enough to unwind tension, and relaxing enough to shift focus, was what allowed him to hang on until, finally, a guard returned to haul him out of confinement, drag him into an interrogation chamber (he couldn't walk), and push him stumbling onto the floor of the dark room.

At a table was an interrogator and two or three guards behind him. He faced toward the table. Powerful lights shone in his eyes, but his glasses were so dirty they blocked out some of the glare. Questions came at him from the table, and he gave nothing but name, rank, serial number, and date of birth. On orders, the guards began punching and kicking him, then bending him over backward into an awkward position, where they strapped him into place for a time. He does not remember this part much (the box was seemingly the pivotal experience for Petersen). Then came more questioning. He gave up some inconsequential information but refused to speak more and, at last, was ordered back to the box torture. Outside again, a guard steered him toward it. He was sure he wouldn't last long, and he again came to a pivotal resolution: "I made up my mind to endure as long as I could before I began screaming to be let out." He knew he would crack eventually, but vowed to keep on, one second to another second, stringing together as many as he could.

At that point, the guard guided him up to the boxes, and then past them, stopping at the compound entryway, where he shoved Petersen to the ground. This kiss-the-dirt moment was one of the happiest of his life. By then, he was eighteen. In a paradoxical way, as he described in his recent memoir, he learned from the experience but also was deeply damaged by it. His visits to my class were breathtaking—students hung on his words, unlike their usual behavior when I was lecturing.

Almost forty years later, on March 31, 2002, a thirty-one-year-old Palestinian associate of Osama bin Laden, captured three days earlier in a US raid on a Faisalabad, Pakistan, safe house (and gravely injured in the process), became the CIA's prisoner number one in the Global War on Terror. Abu Zubaydah (his full name is Zayn al-Abidin Muhammad Husayn) also became likely the first prisoner to undergo enhanced interrogation techniques following "rendition," that is, clandestine transfer to an unofficial non-US environment not subject to laws or protections—in his case, to a black site (secret prison) in Thailand. There, among other treatments over about nine months, he periodically endured hours in a small box to force him to reveal information. (Zubaydah, who has never been criminally charged, remains a near permanent prisoner at the detention facility in Guantanamo Bay, though by 2006 the CIA conceded he "was not a member of Al Qaeda" nor linked to the events of 9/11. I say near permanent because, after a quarter century, negotiations began, but stalled, in 2024 to have him released to an unnamed country where he would be perpetually surveilled.)[12] Abu Zubaydah's sketch of where he was held—the eighth of forty sketches he made depicting his enhanced interrogation experiences—is startlingly familiar. It depicts a naked, shackled man curled up in a box that, in his words, would "barely fit a medium size dog." Inside he felt "the bondage of my extremities with my organs," difficulty breathing, and the pain of his head being twisted and contorted inside the box.[13] Long hours in this container sometimes caused him to black out from agony.

The techniques Petersen experienced via the simulation (being boxed; deprived of sleep; subjected to beatings, humiliations, interrogations, held positions, and simulated drowning or the witnessing of others undergoing such drowning) were applied to detainees suspected of terrorism—first Abu Zubaydah, then others—by two Air Force psychologists coming from a long lineage of Air Force psychologists formed by SERE training.

The fact that Petersen, an eighteen-year-old Naval enlistee for flight crews in Vietnam, and Abu Zubaydah, a thirty-one-year-old Palestinian Saudi Arabian, shared the experience of "confinement in a small space" some four decades apart shows the persistence of a method that promised and delivered human breakdown over time, but without guaranteeing that accurate information would be revealed. Though neither was subject to struggle procedures—reeducation, the Method, or thought reform—they did experience the pressure to confess, and to release empirically exact intelligence. This would seal their fate. For half a century since survival school, Petersen told my class, what mattered to him "wasn't the physical so much as the emotional, moral, spiritual, and neurological things that happened, with effects that rolled down through the years."[14] Despite that the box was essentially the same box, one was considered mock (training against brainwashing) and the other real (technique to extract information). Both methods emerged from the great brainwashing crisis. The way the training turned into a regular military ritual, later to spawn a new form of twenty-first-century interrogation, says something about American history. Loosely speaking, it conveys much about our capacity to respond to (unacknowledged) trauma by enacting it on ourselves and others.

·········

In 1955, eleven years before Petersen was placed in the box in the Cleveland National Forest, the military debuted its experimental Survival School (the earliest version of SERE) before the nation. The newspaper corps were invited to observe them. Incidentally or not, they got *terrible* press.

Military histories often incorrectly date the original such camps to the immediate aftermath of the Vietnam War. Many sources hail

Colonel James "Nick" Rowe as the inventor of SERE training, crediting him—entirely incorrectly—with formulating it in 1981. Rowe was a Vietnam POW who survived sixty-two months of torture and imprisonment in the "Forest of Darkness," including many hours in a bamboo cage and the infliction of unspeakable suffering, described at length in his memoir, *Five Years to Freedom*. A military-oriented website's 2017 article relates how, "after returning to the United States, Rowe developed the Army's SERE (Survival, Evasion, Resistance, and Escape) School and training at Ft. Bragg, North Carolina, largely based on his experiences."[15] This origin is widely accepted in military circles, or is, at least, widely circulated to trainees about to undergo SERE. Although Rowe himself never claimed to have invented the training, the deceased servicemember still receives credit for inventing it, perhaps because he fills an idealized role, someone who himself suffered agony on agony, and still triumphed.[16]

In fact, it was a corps of behavioral scientists—sociologists and psychologists and one or two pivotal psychiatrists, sometimes jokingly referred to in other contexts as the military's "chairborne divisions"—who developed this training. Mostly, it was based on studies of the Korean conflict's returning brainwashed men and on further experiments with animal and human subjects.

One man best represented this turn to experiment. He was psychiatrist and US Air Force Lieutenant (later Major) Louis "Jolly" Jolyon West. Dr. West was "willing to work the dark side," to invoke an archetype spelled out years later by Vice President Dick Cheney.* West worked not only the shadows but the surreal. In one still little-known project, as an alternative to the commonly used interrogation technique of sleep deprivation, he developed a way to deprive subjects of their ability to dream: dream deprivation. Although this never became

---

* Or, it might be better to say that Cheney's "work the dark side" archetype came from precisely these kinds of Cold Warriors, which after all was exactly the world from which he came.

a popular counterintelligence method, it does communicate West's willingness to try out almost any experimental variation.

The original blueprint for a military training with emphasis on gritty survival emerged just before Korea, in 1949, when General Curtis LeMay authorized it. LeMay is much better known for implementing the night bombing campaigns on Japanese cities during World War II, especially the Tokyo firebombing, in which a hundred thousand civilians perished. He drew on the existence, during the war, of certain local survival schools that were already training men in the hard conditions of tundra or extreme heat.[17] At Camp Carson in Colorado, LeMay had the Air Force create its first major survival training program (which relocated to the Nevada desert near Reno's Stead AFB in 1952). At first it was designed by psychologists such as Paul Torrance to put men in difficult situations where they would be forced to kill desert creatures, make ad hoc shelters, and withstand discomfort of many kinds to survive. A seventeen-day course solidified. This would become the S (survival) in SERE. The remaining letters—E for escape and evasion, and R for resistance—would soon accrue.

....

Louis Jolyon West's star rose from an initially unprepossessing start as a college dropout after one year at the University of Wisconsin. He had grown up poor in Madison in a Jewish immigrant family from Ukraine. "My father was born in a shtetl somewhere between Odessa and Kiev," West said in a commencement address he gave at Hebrew Union College in the 1990s, though he did not broadcast this origin story much in his early career.[18] His father anglicized the family name during the First World War. At eighteen, West enlisted, eager to serve, but, as he told it, "was sent by the military" to the University of Iowa and later the University of Minnesota for medical school training under the aegis of a program to build up the corps of medical doctors. (A much earlier document, dated 1955, details that his service in the Second World War initially was in the 94th infantry and eventually included military police work, but no overseas duties.)[19] In 1944 at the university hospital in Iowa City, he performed what he vaguely but ominously described as a "controlled study of two men receiving emergency circumcisions." Foregoing anesthesia, he used only hypnosis for pain control in one subject, he recalled in a 1953 Air Force talk, neglecting to clarify how an emergency circumcision—implying urgent, unstructured, nonexperimental conditions—was consistent with a "controlled study." Still, West's results (the hypnotized man fared better) boded well for the future of hypnosis as a mode of interrogation, which became one of his central research preoccupations.[20]

During his three years as an enlisted man, West met and befriended a not-yet-famous Charlton Heston when both were in their early twenties. West rose in the Air Force to the rank of lieutenant colonel, only completing his residency years later, in 1952, at Payne Whitney Psychiatric Clinic of The New York Hospital (now known as Weill Cornell Medical) in New York City. He would remain close friends with Heston for the rest of his life, including a period when both were civil rights activists in segregated Oklahoma City, and a later period when they lived near each other in stately homes high in the Santa Monica mountains.

By happenstance or not, Cornell University Medical College, of which the Payne Whitney facility was a part, also was the spot where two of the most prominent CIA-funded brainwashing experts had their faculty posts: Doctors Lawrence Hinkle and Harold Wolff. As a young resident, West trained under them in 1950–1952. Researcher John Marks's classic study, included in his book *The Search for the "Manchurian Candidate,"* indicates that Cornell University Medical College was soon to host experiments in mind control of live human subjects (often, captured military prisoners) in response to the POW crisis, starting in 1953. West, who would leave for Lackland in 1952, a year before that project started, began a parallel path embarking on CIA research. Though some have pointed out that he worked with Wolff and Hinkle on their mind and behavior control studies—"When he got out [of the war]," investigative journalist Tom O'Neill writes, West "researched methods of controlling human behavior at Cornell University [Medical College]"—it appears he decided to pursue his own program (which became a CIA "sub-project" on drugs, hypnosis, and the creation of dissociative states). West liked to be the lead man, the one designing the research. His residency, which prepared him for this future, was, to say the least, not typical medical training.[21]

"Research" is a word that covers myriad things, potentially, and is thus usefully vague yet encompassing. The liaison between the highly connected Dr. Wolff (a neurologist who worked with the OSS during World War II, was consultant to the secretary of defense's Advisory Committee on Prisoners of War, and treated CIA head Allen Dulles's son after he sustained a debilitating head injury in Korea) with the up-and-coming Dr. West continued through the 1950s. Dr. Wolff would visit Dr. West for a week at the University of Oklahoma medical school in February 1957 when West headed a newly formed department. According to the *Daily Oklahoman*'s description, Wolff was an expert on bodily stress and the effects of pain: "Dr. Wolff's investigations of pain led to the belief that it is not pain itself so much as how you feel about pain as you experience it that causes discomfort" (the very lesson Glenn Petersen learned in the sweat box).[22]

Wolff specialized in the pain-fear-pain cycle, is how one might put it today.

....

Around this time, in a speech to Princeton University alumni, a public display of candor occurred when, in early April 1953, CIA Director Allen Dulles warned that Communist spies could turn the American mind into "a phonograph playing a disc put on its spindle by an outside genius."[23] Free will could be dissolved, the target reduced to parrot-like mimicry and robotic obedience. Dulles voiced the fear of a Manchurian Candidate before the term *Manchurian Candidate* had been coined. It referred to the main character of an eponymous 1959 novel in which a fictional Korean War unit is ambushed by Chinese troops and taken behind the 38th parallel. There they are hypnotized and mentally tinkered with, and then rereleased into society with "programming" to destroy their own government. The novel was adapted as the 1962 film *The Manchurian Candidate*, starring Frank Sinatra as a lieutenant doing a good deal of sweating while he realizes the recurring brainwashing nightmare he has been having is actually a flashback. Declaring that this type of control was now possible, Dulles's warning marked a pivotal moment: Afterward, much of the government's brainwashing-inspired activity would go underground. Days after his Princeton remarks, on April 13, Dulles officially but secretly set Project MK-ULTRA in motion. (MK-ULTRA was a clandestine program within the CIA's Technical Services Division that ran from 1953 through the early 1960s and was designed to investigate every possible lead—including hypnosis, drugs, and interrogation on witting and unwitting subjects—in the quest for operative mind and behavior control. I mention the "early 1960s" as its end date because 1963 was the year the CIA's own legal department discovered it, conducted an audit, and deemed it massively, criminally unethical; but it is not clear exactly when it disbanded.)

Almost immediately, in June 1953, West, newly arrived in Texas at the air force base, wrote to the head of the ultrasecret program offering his services. How exactly he first gained access to the pseudonymous address of a chemical company "front" that led to MK-ULTRA's head, the psychologist Sidney Gottlieb, is unclear, but his mentor Harold Wolff was likely his connector to those shadow worlds. In his introductory letter to the pseudonymous Sherman Grifford—"S. G." for Sidney Gottlieb—of the nonexistent Chemrophyl Associates, West proposed nine experiments exploring ways of shaping the subjective states or warping the will of a human subject.

Letter from Louis Jolyon West to the head of CIA's MK-ULTRA program, Sidney Gottlieb, under the pseudonym of S. G. or Sherman Grifford. S. G. wrote to West under the front, "Chemrophyl Associates." Here, West is writing back from his quarters at Lackland Air Force Base, proposing his clandestine experimental program. UCLA LIBRARY SPECIAL COLLECTIONS, CHARLES E. YOUNG RESEARCH LIBRARY, UNIVERSITY OF CALIFORNIA, LOS ANGELES.

Gottlieb (as S. G.) wrote back in early July 1953 to "My Good Friend," Major Louis J. West at Lackland Village, "Frankly, I had been wondering whether your apparent rapid and comprehensive grasp of our problems could possibly be real. A considerable portion of your letter"—West was always fulsome in the spoken and written word—"indicated that you have indeed developed an admirably accurate picture of exactly what we are after."[24] What they were after was what West would soon build: a free zone of experimentation in a clandestine laboratory where various incapacitating agents (such as, but not limited to, LSD) and incapacitating procedures (such as, but not limited to, hypnosis) could be applied, in various combinations, to human subjects. S. G. ended by complimenting West for being "quite an asset" and assured him of "a separate sum of money to be given to you personally for such matters," thus making West's funding pipeline doubly illicit.

We should note that any operations the CIA undertook within the United States were against its charter, which permitted only international activity. This may explain the on-again, off-again queasiness Gottlieb expressed concerning West's military affiliation.[25] The two soon tentatively devised a medium-term plan to move West out of Air Force auspices—and into the comparatively freer precincts of the University of Oklahoma—for precisely two reasons: There was already resistance at the base, which threatened West's operations, and there were constitutional implications of the setup.

Amid these negotiations, West expressed that he had no desire to leave the Air Force (despite S. G.'s warnings), as he was now happily settled in the middle of the country, this time Texas, with an array of heady responsibilities. "I gather from your letter that you do not look with favor on attempt to have you maneuvered out of the Air Force very soon," Gottlieb wrote to West in July 1953, early in their relationship, and not long after he had settled in.[26] And no wonder Lt. Major West was ensconced. Suddenly at the age of twenty-four, this fledgling physician with no apparent clinical experience gained the high-level station of chief psychiatric officer at Lackland Air Force Base. His job was to study, first, the returning Air Force pilots who had been marked as "bw" (for brainwashed and biological weapons) twice over—airmen who were deemed both (1) false confessors to dropping infected spores, rats, and chicken feathers on Communist territory, and (2) victims of mental manipulation. (In a confluence of abbreviations, both referents to bw appear in Air Force documents.)

Amid accusations of widespread bio-weapons drops on their soil, the Chinese "broke" thirty-six of a total fifty-nine pilots captured. The men had been sent back to Lackland. When West and the team at Lackland questioned these men, some of them cried uncontrollably, he reported. (At other times, West claimed to have studied eighty-three prisoners of war, fifty-six of whom had been forced to make false confessions.)[27] Almost all displayed an inability, for weeks, "to give a coherent account of what had happened to them."[28] Working with Margaret Singer, who came over from Walter Reed Army Institute of Research to Lackland, he got the men to revert and admit there had been no bw of the germ-warfare kind, and that bw of the second type no longer affected them—overall, a sort of deprogramming. West and Singer helped them with the recovery of memories and with getting straight on the nonexistence of US biological warfare flights.[29]

West's work marked a pivotal point for brainwashing in 1953–1954. Basically, he turned research into experiments when he applied the basic understandings from the POW studies to operationalize and find surefire techniques for altering human belief and behavior. West spoke of the need for guinea pigs. Likely candidates could include volunteers and non-volunteers (both informed and uninformed). He was drawn to "certain patients requiring hypnosis in therapy, or suffering from dissociative disorders (trances, fugues, amnesias, etc.) [who] might lend themselves to our experiments."[30] This was a time when there was a great lack of clarity (some call it "slippage") between who was a "patient" and who was an "experimental subject."

West, though very young, had the temerity to ask the CIA for "some sort of carte blanche," as he put it.[31] And he seems to have received it. Jolly (an adaptation of his middle name, Jolyon) West was researching ways to cause "dissociative states" in subjects and was reporting back to Gottlieb on his promising leads (including with sensory deprivation). As a result of Gottlieb's urging him further, he devised Sub-project 43 of MK-ULTRA. This was designed to test what West called "the actions of a variety of new drugs which alter the state of psychological functioning." At least some of these tests he would conduct in a "unique laboratory [with] a special chamber in which all psychologically significant aspects of the environment can be controlled.... In this setting the various hypnotic, pharmacologic, and sensory-environmental variables will be manipulated in a controlled fashion."[32] Clandestinely, the CIA was to pay $20,000 to build this lab for West at Lackland Air Force Base (this was the "money to be given to you personally" that Gottlieb had promised in their opening epistolary exchange).

The money was ready, West was ready, and some higher ups among the Air Force were ready to inaugurate what West was calling his Air Force Psychosomatic Laboratory, and what Brigadier General H. H. Twitchell (Air Force) referred to as "your special project." But there was a stumbling block. It seems that some at Lackland's medical corps and others occupying higher levels of the Air Force objected to West using the base for his classified research. General Twitchell, a friend of the project, wrote to West to describe meeting with several other Air Force personnel, who all agreed that "it seemed ill advised to establish the Air Force Psychosomatic Laboratory either at Lackland or an Air Force base in Oklahoma only to have to abandon the project upon your release from the service twenty months from now. Therefore, General Powell, Major Hughes, Major Kollar, and myself conferred to discuss the best way to get your special research project underway on a continuing basis."[33] Head-scratching ensued. "Major West's case is a peculiar one," wrote Major General Joe Kelly, "and the first of its kind encountered since the inception of the Air Force Medical Services."[34] Soon a solution emerged.

That the CIA was involved—though not necessarily the decisive voice—in these maneuverings became clear by the fall of 1954, when S. G. wrote again to West describing the Air Force's ultimate "nay" vote. S. G. was not willing to put their objections into writing, and Gottlieb was circumspect. "Actually there are justifications, which I will elaborate when I see you, that are logical from the service's viewpoint," Gottlieb wrote on in September. "Although this rather adequately stops our present effort," he continued, "it does not erase the need for research in the field."[35] He would be in the San Antonio area within the month and would stop by.

Almost immediately, a generous job offer materialized from the University of Oklahoma medical school, which announced it was starting a new department of psychiatry and neuroscience. West would be the ideal man to set it up. In accepting, West sotto voce assured various correspondents that he had the full backing of the university to continue working with the CIA—indeed, this was the condition of his employment. He specified, "My acceptance of the professorship was predicated upon full support of these very experiments"—that is, his "special research assignment"—"without explanations being required. The Medical School agreed, and has since promised to supply laboratory space, technical assistance, and equipment as soon as I might be able to begin."[36] In turn, the university insisted on a structure of plausible deniability. (Twenty-three years later, the university's president, Paul F. Sharp, would declare himself surprised to discover—when informed by the CIA—that they had been used in this way. President Sharp, from his desk at the university, and Dr. West, contacted by reporters at his post in California, assured the public that no human subjects had been experimented on, only animals—by implication, the elephant Dr. West injected with LSD in 1962 at the Oklahoma Zoo—and that mostly it had been in the 1960s. Neither of these claims was true.)[37]

Let's explore for a moment the world of the CIA "cutout," a term used to describe the movement of illicit funds through cover organizations acting as conduits.* There was a good deal of what I'll call

---

* West was less diligent than the CIA in destroying records related to MK-ULTRA experiments. The West archives contain no classified files (these must have been destroyed, removed, or filed elsewhere), yet careful combing reveals many lost details within the correspondence, research, and teaching files that remain. Through these traces, I have pieced together how this "double conduit" worked, and some further insights into how the military, CIA, university, and nonprofit entities interacted. (Although Freedom of Information Act requests to the CIA did produce MK-ULTRA's financial records, which functionaries

conduiting involved in getting the money for clandestine, sub-legal research, into West's orbit. Across its various projects, MK-ULTRA employed such arms as the Geschickter Foundation (housed at Georgetown University in Washington, DC), the Josiah Macy Foundation (located in New York City), and the Human Ecology Foundation (stationed at the Cornell Weill medical center under Dr. Wolff) to facilitate the hidden funneling of CIA funds without naming them as such. This was done for at least three reasons: (1) Not all researchers would be willing to accept such a source of support, and these men and women, who were dubbed "unwitting," could simply be fooled by a false name, (2) Even those researchers who were happy to work for the CIA and saw it as patriotic science might not want the banner waving for all to see. And most of all, (3) Key personnel felt it better to fly under the radar, because the research was classified, even from large parts of the Agency itself. West's Sub-project 43 was effectively the beneficiary of two conduits, the architecture of which I recently unearthed and am revealing here for the first time. The first ferried money out of the Geschickter Fund (initially, the $20,000 S. G. promised). CIA documents reveal that this cutout received a 4 percent "service fee" for all monies conveyed, a fee the Agency paid.[38] The second—since West was not allowed to receive payment directly at the university—operated out of an organization called the Oklahoma Medical Research Foundation, which received it and disbursed it to West.

This second cutout, a private nonprofit, originated in 1946 with (as their own PR put it) no money, but "great hope." Specifically, that hope was to support experimental medical research in the southwest and make Oklahoma a thriving center of such research. By 1953, they had a million dollar a year enterprise going, with laboratories, a wing for animal research, "beds" for patients undergoing

---

neglected to destroy when purging the files, these internal papers do not reveal all the twists and turns of disbursement.)

experimental treatments, administrative suites, and a lavish foyer in an $850,000 building. While it is not clear what all their sources of funding were, several local groups contributed small donations (for example, from the Oklahoma City dentists' association) and lent a hand via the activities of their wives in hanging curtains and furnishing the rooms for the patients, who were also subjects. Bigger donations came from a range of federal and private sources. As it happened, an old friend of West's from Cornell Weill, Stewart G. Wolf, who had moved to the University of Oklahoma to chair the medical school, also headed up the neurology unit at the foundation. No doubt, Stewart Wolf (not to be confused with his colleague and coauthor Harold Wolff, together known as the "Drs. Wolf and Wolff") was instrumental in finding a place for West in the medical school.[39]

West asked, initially, merely for one room at the foundation, in addition to their receipt and conveyance of his funds in present and future. And "it will be necessary for me to acquire some official standing" at the foundation to be able to receive money there (hence the room) to circumvent the university's staunch refusal to take in checks, even from a cutout.[40] West also recommended a psychiatry wing be formed around himself. (This did not happen, though he did get the room.) To both intermediaries West expressed that he was confident of receiving money over many coming years; this was just the beginning of their arrangement.

So it was that West's personal project with MK-ULTRA was officially if clandestinely underway by fiscal year 1955. Despite the delay in implementing his vision—caused by some combination of administrative hiccup, collegial umbrage, moral objection, and constitutional concern at Lackland—West's enterprise was duly installed in Oklahoma City. His liaisons would be Robert Lashbrook (the deputy director of MK-ULTRA), James "Trapper" Drum (the head of the CIA's TSS [Technical Services Staff]), and Gottlieb (head of MK-ULTRA). As it happened, this same triumvirate of Lashbrook,

Drum, and Gottlieb also oversaw the dosing, death, and subsequent coverup of Frank Olson, a CIA biochemist colleague with expertise in the other bw, biological warfare. (Lashbrook secretly dropped a strong dose of LSD into Olson's drink one day in the late autumn of 1953 at a remote retreat gathering in Maryland, without his foreknowledge. Post-trip, the biochemist evidenced paranoia and self-doubt, new personality traits that turned him into an overnight liability to the CIA, for he was involved in highly sensitive research. An early operative of MK-ULTRA, Olson had traveled to prisons across Europe where he saw the interrogation-to-extinction of enemy Soviet agents deemed expendable or rendered so traumatized that they died in the process. According to his children, by the time he imbibed the secretly dosed drink on November 19, 1953, he already was beset by ethical qualms and had quit his toxicology job, maintaining only a CIA position at that point. A few days later, on November 28, 1953, tragically, Olson jumped, or was pushed, out of the window of the Statler Hotel in New York.) West would continue to work with these three as his minders.

The fact that an underground tunnel joined the Oklahoma Medical Research Foundation to the university's medical school appears today not only convenient but symbolic.

At times, West represented the power of "forceful indoctrination" (his more technical term for brainwashing) as lying primarily in prolonged sleep deprivation, seemingly a nontechnical technique. "What we found enabled us to rule out drugs, hypnosis or other mysterious trickery," he said. "It was just one device used to confuse, bewilder, and torment our men until they were ready to confess to anything. That device was prolonged, chronic loss of sleep."[41] Still, at the same time as he pursued sleep deprivation research and made such nothing-to-see-here announcements, he also worked in the "mysterious trickery" domain.

Sleep was one prominent avenue, although he also, as mentioned, pursued others. In the Oklahoma facility and in other locations—including, at one point, the South Pole, where he "also had a laboratory" to investigate how six-month-long nights caused profound changes in sleep and personality architectonics—West tested what happened under extreme conditions of sleeplessness.[42] There was, for example, the case of Peter Tripp, a disc jockey who volunteered for sleep denial as an on-air charity stunt in January 1959. After several days of living mainly in an Armed Forces chrome-and-glass recruiting booth in Times Square and garrulously broadcasting updates on his state of mind, he began to believe he was a simulation of Peter Tripp.[43] Paranoia and open-eyed hallucinations descended as West and a psychologist from Walter Reed observed the DJ deteriorate, and helped him prolong his stunt after the fifth day by injecting him with drugs and removing him to the Astor Hotel for tests intermittently. His stretch of eight days (201 hours) was the longest without sleep ever recorded. West wrote that subjects rarely crossed the 100-hour threshold. (Tripp may or may not have fully recovered, and over the years apparently continued at times to think he was merely an impersonator of himself.)

West and colleagues also supervised two sleep-deprivation marathons in Oklahoma City in 1957, during which participants made it past the 100-hour mark with his help. They noted a "fifth-day turning point" in Tripp and the Oklahoma City marathoners at which point stark biochemical and physiological changes became evident. "During periods of greater alertness there is a hollow-eyed, suspicious stare, so typical that we have dubbed it 'the Mindzenti [sic] look,'" he wrote.[44] The reference is to Cardinal József Mindszenty, the World War II resistance hero and beloved Catholic priest in his native Hungary, who was arrested in 1948 by Communist police and subjected to a schedule of physical and psychological humiliations, after which—a shattered man—he made bizarre confessions on camera, claiming he had stolen the Crown of St. Stephen from the church, had betrayed his country, and was plotting World War III. West and other brainwashing experts considered Mindszenty's to be the "classic" brainwashing case pre-Korea. One could call it induced psychosis, externally precipitated self-alienation, or brainwashing.

Press accounts have described the stunt as Tripp's idea. The so-described "doctors" monitoring him were there simply to make sure he was all right, and "tried to argue him out of" his plan. "Medical doctors and psychologists agreed to stay with him during the event to make sure he was safe," as a courseware internet site recently put it—this is a nice way to think of what happened, perhaps, but it's pablum.[45] Oddly, it was never explained why a CIA-funded University of Oklahoma specialist in brainwashing happened to be called to Times Square to monitor the diurnal health of a shock jock. Published accounts confirm that Dr. West was *injecting him* with stimulants to *keep him awake past the fifth day*, not simply hovering over a self-motivated publicity hound. West was looking at whether sleep deprivation could induce a psychotic break or permanent structural change to the personality, as he indicated in published and unpublished work.

In other experiments from the time, West (according to the CIA's remaining files) seems to have infiltrated a teenage gang with the aim of "mass conversion" to new forms of behavior, and to have explored how to implant an "inception" memory of having committed a crime, but this one is unclear, as the records have been destroyed.*

---

* West conducted a project in Oklahoma City to infiltrate teenage gangs for the purpose of changing their members' behavior. Labeled "Mass Conversion," this project was funded by Sidney Gottlieb. There was also the case of Jimmy Shaver, a twenty-nine-year-old Lackland airman who, in the summer of 1954, abducted a three-year-old girl from the parking lot of a local bar where her parents had left her in the car with her brother. Shaver then raped and killed her, but had no memory of doing so, amnesia that persisted for months. This garnered the headline in the *San Antonio News* on July 5, 1954, "Thrice-Wed Man Held in Death of Tiny Girl." Dr. West, as head psychiatrist on the Lackland base, hypnotized Shaver and administered sodium amytal so as to extract a confession after the murder (and may have treated him before it occurred). There is no record that this was related to West's ongoing CIA-funded experiments, but some suggest it may have been (see O'Neill and Pieperbring, *Chaos*, 370–74). My own research reveals that West intended to write a book about the case, though he never did.

Anywhere the spooky met the hallucinogenic in the broader territory carved out by violent violation, West landed with seemingly unerring accuracy. Along the way, the CIA's "conduit" or "cutout" funding apparatuses faded to invisibility when investigated, as these supports were intended to do. Turning to what might be called the even more "applied" and "practical" side of things, West in 1956 reported back to the CIA that the experiments he'd begun in 1953 had at last come to fruition.[46]

In 1957 (the year the DDD [debility, dependency, and dread]study was published, though it was conducted earlier), he received additional military funding to study brainwashing; and it seems more clandestine CIA money as well. He reported better and better ways to create altered personalities. He was close to quantifying how you could make someone dissociate through sensory deprivation, stimulating or disorienting drugs, and hypnosis.

Around this time the English novelist and relocated Los Angeles hill dweller Aldous Huxley befriended Dr. West—"an extremely able young man, I think," was how the older man described the younger in the summer of 1957.[47] By this time, West was deep into LSD research. Huxley was interested in the mysteries of art as described in a scientific idiom—his own family tradition ever since his grandfather T. H. Huxley served as Darwin's Bulldog. It was not only mysteries West was after, though Huxley could not have known that. As Dr. West put it more vaguely in a speech to a group of civil defense experts, "The maladaptive behavioral response, and the psychological basis for it, have recently come into the field of experimentation."[48] Presciently, West saw all phenomena in the behavioral realm as part of a churning and changing information system "all of which [responses] are definable in terms of information processing."[49] He described his project as a psychopathological reactions lab that undertook research on how "reality-testing behavior" was affected in a subject who was given drugs, deprived of sleep or food, pushed into ill health, confined in sensory deprivation chambers, overloaded with information input, or even denied the ability to dream. He also looked at how a person under hypnosis could, instead of anesthesia (the blocking of pain), be made to experience hyperesthesia (the multiplying of pain) where there was no physical cause—including, as West described it, "blisters of the skin, elevations of blood pressure, increased secretions of gastric acid" and many "mental and emotional aberrations."[50] Nightmares made real, and reality made nightmarish, in short.

Here we can pause to appreciate what exactly Gottlieb meant by "our problems" and "exactly what we are after," and why he did salute West, after scarce acquaintance, as "My Good Friend."

....

The Fort Stead experiment (as the *Saturday Evening Post* dubbed it) was a trial-and-error approach to inoculating fighters against the new threat of brainwashing. Yet there was a fine line, constantly crossed to the point of erasing it, between protecting against brainwashing and actively brainwashing the men. The goal was no longer just the empirical study *of* the men. It was no longer adding to their files. It was figuring out an action plan to protect future fighters against this virus and to weaponize it, when necessary, against enemies. The Air Force Personnel and Training Research Center called it reality practice.[51]

But something was lacking, as the "shock" of returning Korean War POWs revealed. While the Marine Corps' experts issued a large report declaring their personnel had fared incredibly well, all considering, the Air Force made no such claim. In fact, the Air Force was particularly alarmed due to the high-profile, upper-rank airmen's confessions. A component of "resistance" should be added to the survivalist mandate, was the consensus, and a new iterative program began to be tested. Experts on mind control converged on the Stead AFB area, as well as a few other Air Force sites.

West was one of them, called in to help devise resistance training. This became the R in what evolved into SERE. The S and E were already developed (from LeMay). West's DDD team used their research to devise a training program to help soldiers understand the mechanics of extreme conditioning to some degree. For even if brainwashing in the pop-culture sense did not really exist—there were, as West and the other experts all insisted, no evil scientists from the Pavlov Institute hatching plots and polishing their scientific instruments—there certainly was such a thing as forceful indoctrination, which through the step-by-step application of DDD produced remarkable transformations. The program was designed to dispel the dread, disability, and despair components of DDD.

Nearly thirty thousand men ran through arduous training (to test its efficacy), as described in one 1955 newspaper account: "Herded behind barbed wire for a 36-hour interrogation period, the 'prisoners' are subjected to electrical shocks, crammed into an upright box where they can neither sit nor stand, forced to stand shoulder deep in water for hours of darkness, fed a mixture of raw spinach and uncooked spaghetti, made to stand naked before their captors, and to listen to slanderous talk about their wives."[52] It was standardized through these trials.

The Stead training center opened for pilots and other high-risk military in 1955. Simultaneously it opened for press coverage, probably to publicize the military's actions not only in developing the Code of Conduct but the training to uphold the Code. (A uniform Code of Conduct, adopted in 1955, maintained six responses, especially including that the soldiers give no more information than name, rank, serial number, and date of birth to guarantee that they return with honor.) The invited press did not hail what they saw. Outraged reporters dubbed the training "Schools for Sadists," where young men were not only taught about brainwashing but subjected to it.

Other scandalized writers spoke disapprovingly of "training by torture."[53] "Marines 'Torture' Each Other," reported the *New York Times* while *Newsweek*'s first dispatch stressed the "Ordeal in the Desert."[54] As reporters waxed indignant about the irony of training soldiers by means of the very thing the authorities deplored—"At Fort Stead, Nevada, the trainees are not merely instructed about brainwashing; they *are* brainwashed," observed the *Saturday Evening Post*—a further irony accrued.[55] Since all reporters received special access, access the military need not have granted them, it is reasonable to assume that the military *wanted* its tactics known. The Air Force *wanted* to be known for being hard. And so, too, did the Marines, Army, and Navy, all of which developed soon afterward (and in communication with the Air Force) their own nearly identical versions of the Stead experiments.

At Camp Pendleton in California, Marine reserve pilots were dropped six miles outside of camp and, on attempting to crawl into a "safe spot," found themselves tortured by sixty amphibious corps regulars lurking in the hills, the *New York Times* reported in August 1955. This coincided almost to the day with Eisenhower's release of the Code, which the *Times* also mentioned. The article revealed that although placed in hot cages and pits too shallow for standing, denied food and water, the men did not die and moreover that, fortunately, "none of them cracked."[56] The apparently critical coverage was, in effect, PR. Were the men being punished or prepared? It was hard to tell.

....

Over the next fifty years, survival training scaled, spread, and standardized. Certain modifications came about: accents changed to Middle Eastern, boxes made of metal not wood, loud music added, psychological-medical-dental screening required, and a limited amount of supplies (which as of 2019 apparently included "a parachute and a few simple tools, like a Buck knife and an unlubricated condom," which, "in a pinch . . . can help gather water or administer first aid").[57]

What the brainwashing experts devised extended during the Vietnam War (from 1959, when the first US soldiers were killed in South Vietnam, through its fall in 1975) to the Army Special Forces, Navy, and Marines.* In the 1960s, West answered a call to return and in tandem with another hypnosis expert, Dr. Martin Orne, redesigned the program to avoid crushing soldiers' psyches in irreversible ways. Still, in 1976, scandals about abusive SERE exploits resulted in further revisions. In 1984, the Resistance part of SERE was designated as Level C (the highest of three levels). Level C training is today's version of Petersen's Warner Springs experience. (Some evidence suggests there may be higher levels than C, instances where SERE specialists are given remit to "torture" students at the rank of general, but these trainings are not spoken of.)

Today SERE training continues across all branches, as well as the DoD and CIA, with three levels of intensity available depending on how high the risk of capture is deemed to be. Offered ten times per year, the Marines' Full Spectrum Level C SERE training lasts eighteen days. The descriptive language has changed—simulation exercises are now called "vicarious learning evolutions" and consist of Academic Role-Play Laboratories (ARL), field survival exercise, an evasion exercise, experiential Resistance Training Laboratories (RTL), an urban movement phase, and a course debrief—but a central goal remains to adhere to the Code of Conduct and prepare to

---

* The Navy's SERE school opened in the late 1950s. Regional centers specialized in harsh conditions such as the cold camp in Alaska, the jungle camps in Okinawa and the Philippines, swim training in Florida, and other spots featuring additional microclimates or elemental challenges, some of which went back much longer in prepping soldiers. These centers, under separate command from SERE, also grew during the Cold War; but they did not carry out the Code of Conduct part of the training. Some centers did have preexisting resistance training, but it was not yet systematized; see Robert Genter, "Understanding the POW Experience: Stress Research and the Implementation of the 1955 U.S. Armed Forces Code of Conduct," *Journal of the History of the Behavioral Sciences*, 51 (2015), 141–63.

return with honor.[58] The 2008 Senate hearings (the "torture hearings") discussed SERE's waterboarding and provided ample evidence that not much had changed in the early twenty-first century except for the need, before training, to screen, and after training, to guarantee some sort of well-being. "Extreme care," according to Dr. Jerald Ogrisseg, former head of Psychological Services of SERE, was taken with psychological screening before admitting students.[59] During pandemic conditions, all participants showed proof of COVID-19 vaccination and a negative PCR test.

By the 2010s, SERE would become so well established, and such a rite of passage, that you could buy SERE-insignia-emblazoned spittoons, aprons, patches, and other gear. Researchers studied it, too, as an extreme stress event: They reported that stress levels reached during SERE exceeded skydiving, Ranger training, and major surgery (however, childbirth levels were not part of the comparison). When trainees' adrenaline was measured twenty-four hours after SERE was over, the levels of Special Forces soldiers registered at normal proportions. But adrenaline levels in non–Special Forces soldiers remained depleted. Women began taking SERE training at Level C when they started being eligible for risky combat and Special Forces positions.

Civilians such as corporate representatives who feel they are at high risk of kidnapping or abduction can pay for unofficial SERE training with former SERE instructors. Some challenge-seekers even travel to such sites to take it for the experience of learning to resist forceful interrogation. Thus, civilian for-profit versions proliferate, along with YouTube videos of woodsy interrogations. For a time, after GITMO abuse revelations, people's SERE experiences were much written about online, although the military added a stringent Fight Club–like oath around the 2010s: One of the first rules of SERE is no talking about SERE. There are some mandated outlets, though. The US Navy's official YouTube video, "Surviving SERE," features a tough-looking and tough-talking SERE instructor, who declares, "We train the best for the worst . . . and that's it." Instead of his name, "Name Withheld" features prominently on the screen's corner, emphasizing the video's underground "challenge" feel.

The military branches keep SERE going, despite reams of documented abuses, because of a conviction that it works. It is not torture to no purpose; it is torture *to* a purpose. "It's intended to be arduous and stressful," says Rich Van Winkle, a former SERE instructor, "and it is." Testimonials confirm this, of pilots shot down who used the techniques and the insights they gained. They allow a captive a more realistic sense of options, and their pilot instructions (including which local plants in a particular area can be safely eaten, should they be shot down) are updated frequently in refresher courses or lectures. (As mentioned, even Glenn Petersen feels he learned about himself from the experience despite, or in addition to, the lasting trauma.) Still, studies in the early 2000s showed that, as Yale medical researcher Charles Morgan testified, "nearly everyone" going through SERE school will experience some PTSD effects along a "spectrum of impairment."[60] This didn't mean the training wasn't valuable in preparing students for stressful situations.

However, the ramifying effects of self-torture do not stay within this lineage or just within the intended outcome. They spread, and this spread is part of the prism of their effects.

....

A surprising outgrowth of SERE and the techniques that reverberated like a pinball (or several pinballs) through the decades was the rise to household-name status of waterboarding—controlled drowning—and the national debate over whether this technique constituted torture. This led to a spate of voluntary "let's-see-for-ourselves" waterboardings around the late 2000s.

Perhaps oddly but perhaps not, the only qualified people around to conduct such waterboardings were former or current SERE specialists. Under the sponsorship of *Vanity Fair*, the essayist Christopher Hitchens, skeptical that just water could constitute torture, had several trainers abduct and waterboard him in 2008 to judge for himself . . . garnering for his troubles over 5.3 million views and a rich thread of YouTube comments: 10,929 as of last time I taught this video but, as of September 2023, down to 9,550, curiously. (Hitchens died in 2011.) Of the experience, he wrote in an article titled, "Believe Me, It's Torture":

> I have to be opaque about exactly where I was later that day, but there came a moment when, sitting on a porch outside a remote house at the end of a winding country road, I was very gently yet firmly grabbed from behind, pulled to my feet, pinioned by my wrists (which were then cuffed to a belt), and cut off from the sunlight by having a black hood pulled over my face. I was then turned around a few times, I presume to assist in disorienting me, and led over some crunchy gravel into a darkened room. Well, mainly darkened: there were some oddly spaced bright lights that came as pinpoints through my hood. And some weird music assaulted my ears. (I'm no judge of these things, but I wouldn't have expected former Special Forces types to be so fond of New Age techno-disco.) The outside world seemed very suddenly very distant indeed.[61]

He almost immediately called off the procedure, using the agreed-upon safe word, a "make it stop" option not available to trainees or detainees. As one viewer commented, "Imagine what it's like when the people doing it don't like you."[62] Some months later conservative talk show host Mancow conducted a waterboarding "experiment." His stunt followed loosely along the same lines, though without the aid of a genuine SERE waterboarder, just a Marine sergeant. Both Hitchens and Mancow concluded that waterboarding, and therefore the enhanced interrogation techniques, were without a doubt torture.

PART 2

BRAINWASHING SPREADS

So far, we have followed brainwashing techniques as they played out in remote prisons, in special wards, on ships filled with psychiatrists, and in military survival training. "Brainwashing" faltered when it was used to describe as a permanent state of being, as if its victims became forever not themselves. The process was not quite so irreversible, though it could be dramatic. Investigations revealed that vast changes in attitude, self, and spirit can and do take place in a controlled, coercive environment.

What would happen when those procedures scaled? Or when they appeared in special research wards as well as cults?

5

Literal Brain Control

Leonard Kille was raving in a Southern California shopping mall parking lot sometime in the summer of 1969. The youngish-looking middle-aged man told those passersby inclined to listen how two doctors in Massachusetts had implanted electrodes in his brain and caused him endless suffering. He had driven across the country to flee their influence, but to no avail. Microwaves pursued him, directed by certain operatives from MIT and Harvard, and they were murdering him slowly over time. Local police picked him up and delivered him to an emergency-room psychiatrist, who felt sorry for him. Still agitated, Leonard Kille might have then insisted—although we have no verbatim notes available from the encounter—that he was an important inventor of new technologies. Naturally his interlocutors that night would have found the idea of sustained cognitive brilliance coming from such a disheveled source unlikely. Soon afterward, he received a diagnosis of paranoid schizophrenia and was dispatched to a Veterans Administration hospital in Long Beach near where his mother lived.

Had anyone checked or been capable of running a quick internet search that day, they would have substantiated most of what Kille spoke about. His tone and circumstances made the claims sound outlandish, as if he were the crazy one, yet the United States patent register by that time included four of his co-inventions, among them the Radio Transmitter for Use with Flash Photography, No. 3153195 (A), filed October 13, 1964, and the Electronic Flash Apparatus, No. 3187170 (A), filed June 1, 1965. Both were components of Polaroid's legendary line of self-developing Land Cameras—the first instant cameras. His résumé, had it been available, would have revealed a long upward path across Cold War engineering firms including Douglas Aircraft, Honeywell, and Block Engineering.[1] Further, Kille was correct in reporting his doctors had used a "new and experimental procedure" to install electrodes in his brain and map his responses to stimuli.[2] As a follow-up, the limbic portion of his brain, through what his doctors would congratulate themselves on as "delicate" notches made in the deep tissue using electronic searing strokes, was essentially destroyed. The aim of the procedure, from a therapeutic point of view, was to quell the patient's difficult temper. From an experimental point of view, it was to see if remote stimulation of the brain would work. From a political point of view, it was to test broad-scale social control procedures on a particular individual seen as violently dangerous. And from Leonard's point of view, it was to save his marriage.

A preliminary conclusion to be drawn from the transpired incident, now half a century ago, is that, under some circumstances, quasi-philosophical stoner bromides can literally come true: *"Just because you're paranoid doesn't mean they're not after you"* is not just a cynic's throwaway line.

But the man lost in the parking lot was wrong in one respect. His Boston doctors, psychiatrist Frank Ervin and neurosurgeon Vernon Mark, both associate professors at Harvard Medical School and up-and-coming brain specialists at Massachusetts General Hospital,

Literal Brain Control

were no longer "after him." They did not even take particular interest in him anymore. As Kille moved in and out of hospitals over the next few years, they published an encouraging account, in 1970, of the case (anonymized) to celebrate their initial success in curing him of his problems. (Leonard's problems included a troubled marriage and history of angry outbursts maybe, or maybe not, stemming from epilepsy. Whatever its etiology, Leonard's case related to brainwashing in an almost literal way: It became a project of direct brain control to achieve behavior control. The scientific pair attempted to render the desired behavior changes first through implanted electrodes and, next, through brain alteration.) After that, the two moved on to more pressing matters in their research agenda: solving the problem of violence in the world. Around this time, one of his doctors did in fact leave Massachusetts for California, *as if pursuing Kille*, to accept a job alongside the brainwashing specialist Louis "Jolly" Jolyon West.

We can accordingly update our preliminary observation as follows: *"Just because you're paranoid—and even if you're probably right to be—doesn't mean they are still after you."* The mix of regard and disregard Kille experienced would be characteristic of an emerging program for social control of aggression through behavior-management technologies, a program that technically, even spectacularly, failed but in some senses has only grown.

....

Leonard Kille was born in 1933 in the Cambridge City Hospital, which still sits just off a two-lane street running south from the nearby Science Center. As a child Leonard lived in the Massachusetts city known for its largest landowner, Harvard University, but was raised in a neighborhood far away, not in distance but in prospects, from its ivory towers, or more accurately, its colonial brick redoubts. In a Pleasant Street apartment, the Kille family dwelled in some tumult, as the father was a chronically out-of-work stonemason who (according to at least one account) on the odd occasions when he was unavoidably home, abused his wife. The family, which also included an older sibling, attended the local Catholic church. Cambridge at the time supported a working class in its own parishes (no longer the case), and Pleasant Street, which runs from Central Square to the Charles River, lay on the edge of a neighborhood called Cambridgeport, full of small houses, duplexes, and other congeries pressed together in an even more puzzle-pieced manner than the rest of the old city. Today, a large Whole Foods resides near where they once lived.

After a brief move to Schenectady, New York, to find mason work yielded nothing, the family returned, again setting up in the cheaper parts of town. At some point, Leonard's father departed for good, leaving his wife to work such long hours at a machine shop and part-time at a coffee shop to support the two boys that she enrolled them in a church-run boarding school, which they nicknamed "the orphan asylum" for its atmosphere. Aside from special attention from teachers, because he was smart, Leonard received particular focus from one of the priests at the school, who took an interest in him possibly for grooming reasons—it is a matter of record, and relevant to later events, that several priests teaching there would be revealed as abusers of children. Leonard, despite this, excelled, first at the boarding school and subsequently, when allowed to move back home, at Rindge Technical High School, where he especially focused on engineering. When he was sixteen, in 1948, Kille dropped out and joined the Air Force. While training for Korea at a ballistic missile defense radar monitor stationed in Portland, Oregon, he suffered a collapse, perhaps due to a peptic ulcer and infection, from which he lost blood and remained in a coma for several days. Medically mustered, he returned home and went back to high school while working as an electrician's helper. He and his high school girlfriend, Janice, married once he turned eighteen (she was a year younger).[3]

Literal Brain Control

From his working-class roots, he became a highly sought-after engineer. For a time, the young couple, now with a newborn, joined his mother and new stepfather in Southern California, where Leonard worked at the Douglas Aircraft plant in Santa Monica as a photographic instrumentation engineer, and meanwhile a second child arrived (1955). Around the birth of their third (1958), they returned to the Boston area, finding a house in lower-rent Somerville, during which period Leonard began work as a draftsman for Polaroid. A promotion allowed them to move north of Cambridge, and he rose in status again, to assistant engineer. This was the period when he coinvented several key technologies for Polaroid's Land Camera, notable because of its elegant design and because it was instant (self-developing). Despite his success there, and personal mentorship from Edwin Land, he resigned from Polaroid to start at an MIT spinoff of Edgerton, Germeshausen and Grier (EG&G), a thriving national-defense contractor started by Harold Edgerton, the pioneer of high-speed photography. (If you've ever seen the gleaming milk drops in mid-splash, icons of photography that capture the epic in the ordinary, you've seen Edgerton's work.) At the time, Kille was doing classified government-contract work on a flash-activated trigger, which he later described as a "government blind seeing rod," used in Operation Dominic, a series of thirty-six nuclear test blasts on and over the island of Kiribati and surrounding atolls of the mid-Pacific in 1962.[4] Kille's trigger was one of many experimental devices tried out over several days.[5] He did not stay long at EG&G, though, and with his skills had no trouble landing another job. Eventually the couple had seven children. Self-made and educated mainly hands-on, Kille labored amid armies of PhDs. To call him a gifted engineer, as not only his employers but his doctors eventually would, was only fair, perhaps even understated.

The marriage, however, was deteriorating. While Kille rose through various firms, his homelife was marked by discord. As later described in the case study his doctors penned, Leonard's "chief problem" was "his violent rage." This took the form of spells of mounting anger that could build for hours until reaching a climax. "He was very paranoid, and harbored grudges which eventually produced an explosion of anger," wrote Drs. Mark and Ervin. He would stare, brood, and, in many cases, become obsessed with "some innocuous remark" his wife had made, which he took to indicate that she no longer loved him.[6] Her denials of having insulted him caused him to ruminate further. During the peak of his outbursts, Kille would "throw objects" in the room, according to his own psychiatrist and subsequent hospital records, though not directly at his wife, and he never injured anyone.[7] Janice Kille sought a restraining order in 1961, but they reconciled. In the fall of 1964, Leonard began seeing a psychiatrist, Dr. Michael Curtis of Medford, who was also treating his wife. Dr. Curtis appeared, from his later testimony, to have been dubious of Leonard's claims to engineering prowess: "There were many times when he mentioned patents he had devised. They were difficult to understand. He had periods of depression."[8] As conflict in the Kille home continued, their psychiatrist viewed Leonard's anger as the root of the problem and presumed it to be based in the biology of his brain. (The orientation of the shared psychiatrist was neurobiological, rather than, say, Freudian.)

A 1966 rear-ending traffic accident left Kille with a concussion that only exacerbated his combined worries over a large mortgage, a change of jobs, and a family of young children. The arrival of anxiety attacks intensified marital chaos. Leonard had come to believe a fellow church member, who was boarding in the top floor of their home and had integrated into their family life, was having an affair with his wife. (The boarder and Janice Kille would later marry.)* Around this time,

---

* Kille's grandchildren would know only the (former) boarder as their grandfather. For many of Leonard's seven children, not understanding what really happened to him was and remains difficult; they were told bits and pieces, and occasionally taken to visit him at the VA hospital. Some years ago, two of Leonard's daughters contacted Stephen Chorover at MIT—an expert witness at the trial—to begin to assemble documents, and several

Literal Brain Control

Janice and Leonard's psychiatrist referred him—fatefully—to Dr. Ervin, director of an experimental ward at Massachusetts General Hospital. Ervin, along with the neurosurgeon Dr. Mark, were working to prove their hypothesis that violent behavior "is an expression of the functioning brain."[9] They specialized in patients like Kille, who seemed literally "triggerable," transforming from normal to rageful at the drop of a hat. The singlemindedness with which they searched for "brain triggers" made their work unique. (As it happens, this was not unrelated to the phenomenon Louis Jolyon West was investigating when, in 1962, he administered LSD to a male elephant at the Tulsa, Oklahoma, zoo, seeking to understand what would set off the "musth" phenomenon, which is a burst of rage in an otherwise placid animal.) Many of their colleagues avoided taking on violent patients, as the work was so often "disagreeable and personally threatening"[10] that one might easily justify another area of medical focus. Mark and Ervin were among the few who did not.

When outbursts in aggressive patients occurred, it was likely the result, Mark and Ervin believed, of abnormal brain activity previously undiagnosed. The resulting violent spells, which they labeled "dyscontrol episodes," could be stopped, they posited, by skillfully destroying pinpoint brain regions. (They claimed considerable success in this experimental treatment, and even claimed Leonard Kille as one of their proofs of efficacy, but this is a doubtful estimation of the results to say the least, and it relies on mis-reporting; Mark and Ervin admitted later they did not hew to strict accuracy in their portrait of "Thomas R.")

Brain-based explanations for why people do what they do, including having colossally uncontrollable fits, constituted a rising theory in the mid-1960s, but one with deep roots in the late 1800s. Those who favored these explanations would say that outbursts such as Leonard's

---

grandchildren now are involved in the ongoing family effort to reconstruct events leading to the tragedy.

were due to pathologies in localized parts of the cerebral structure (rather than, say, the social or environmental conditions surrounding the violent episode). When it came to fixing these outbursts, or other unwanted behavior, doctors were focused on a specific, walnut-sized part of the thalamic brain, the amygdala—since the 1920s considered the seat of violent lashing out. So it was that around the world, surgeons from Japan to India to Denmark to Thailand, Argentina, and Czechoslovakia began carrying out psychosurgeries (amygdalectomies) with the explicit purpose of controlling the behavior of difficult or incipiently violent individuals.[11] The prominent Japanese neurosurgeon Dr. Hirataro Narabayashi of the Neurological Clinic in Tokyo helped to establish the resurgent method along more sophisticated lines. "Amelioration of the hyperactive or destructive behavioral pattern" was the goal, Narabayashi wrote; he started operating on epileptics and other patients deemed feebleminded (often very young) in 1951. He kept up a pace of about ten patients a year between 1958–1972, including some with hyperkinesis, reporting "calming and taming effects" on these children.[12] With its global reach, a second sweep of psychosurgery started up in these years—the "return of the lobotomy" as some critics put it.

Kille's doctors—sometimes called the Sweet group after their mentor, Harvard Medical School professor William H. Sweet, the "dean" of neurosurgery in Boston with an international reputation—were key players in this movement. Although they were not the most experienced in the number of surgeries undertaken (ultimately they would do twelve), they distinguished themselves in two ways: first by their near obsessive focus on trigger points in the brain, and second by their bent for writing wake-up-call essays with titles such as "The Role of Brain Disease in Riots and Urban Violence,"[13] published just after the Watts rebellion in Los Angeles. For Mark and Ervin, what was even more important than answering age-old questions about the relative weight of biological or social explanations of things was adopting a functional, can-do approach: It didn't matter if the brain

Literal Brain Control

was more biologically or behaviorally shaped; surely both were at work, and what mattered was where the patient found himself and what could be changed (ideally through targeted, electrode-guided surgery, if pharmaceuticals failed to work) at any moment. Mark and Ervin's work at the Stanley Cobb Laboratory for Psychiatric Research took place under the supervision of Dr. Sweet. Officially admitted to Mass General, Leonard became not only a patient but arguably an experimental subject there when he entered a locked-down ward in April 1966.[14]

....

In August of the same year a former Marine named Charles Whitman stationed himself at a tower mid-campus at the University of Texas at Austin and used a high-powered rifle to pick off scores of people below—forty-four shot, fourteen to death—in an event now seen as inaugural in the rise of mass shootings. Leonard Kille's doctors were called to examine the brain of the shooter, who was killed on the spot. The three specialists, Ervin, Mark, and their senior mentor, Sweet, joined a team that found (controversially) that Whitman had a nickel-sized tumor in his thalamus that pressed on additional brain tissue which, in turn, compressed his amygdala, causing him to spring into violent action—a sequence of actions quite a bit like what they (also controversially) would soon believe they found in Leonard Kille's brain.[15] (In fact, the cases were quite different, as Kille was a chronically stressed out temperamental husband whereas Whitman meticulously planned his crime, down to writing in his journal for several weeks details such as which outfit he would wear while firing his rifle from the tower.)[16] Some years later, on another forensic exam, this one of a high-profile airline hijacker who attempted, but failed, to force a passenger plane to dive into the sea, they again discovered abnormalities. This occasioned Dr. Mark's observation at an academic conference that at the deepest level, the abnormal brain itself was the causative agent. Any political aims were secondary.

He had "found clear symptoms of brain damage" in the man, an article in the *New York Times* reported not long after, as Mark's view made news.[17]

The link between brain injuries and reactively violent behavior is no longer controversial. We live at a time when many of the broad ideas that Drs. Mark, Ervin, and Sweet purveyed are accepted and acceptable, despite the early pushback they received, the controversies they generated (especially Ervin, as we will see), and the outrage that accompanied some of their programs. Traumatic brain injuries, for example, are understood to change the structure of the brain and potentially to cause aggressive behavior.[18] The two protégés, Mark and Ervin, were, in essence, pioneers of a bio-psycho-social view of the mind-brain—they were not strict determinists at all—a view that, after everything was said and done, looped back to prioritize the brain (acknowledging that it is ever changing) as the driver of behavior. In their ambitious coauthored book, *Violence and the Brain*, Mark and Ervin at times described their approach as "a new and biologically oriented" take on "the problem of human violence," but at other times nodded to the complex, multicausal nature of such violence (while still calling it "potentially solvable").[19] With the return of hopes for direct intervention on the brain, surgically oriented psychiatrists altogether could be seen as conflating mind control as brain control. Some have called such views the triumph of an extreme biologization of the brain—do we not look to the brain to explain just about every single twitch, turn, or tic?—but in fact, their vision was closer to a brain as a data-processing center that is constantly incorporating input from experiences, family patterns, social life, cultural constructs, within its organic structure.[20] We are making our brains every moment merely by living.

Nonetheless, it was arguably politics and not biology that led to trouble for the doctors, particularly one of the pair, Frank Ervin, and their patient Leonard Kille.

Amid the team of Mark and Ervin's prominent forensic examinations of wayward brains, the national spectacle of catastrophic assassinations continued. By June 1968, *Life* magazine weighed in with a front-page piece suiting the dirge-filled moment. Against a dark backdrop, two small portraits, one of Martin Luther King Jr.'s assassin (James Earl Ray), and the other of Robert F. Kennedy's assassin (Sirhan Sirhan), appeared as if out of the blackness, along with the words, "The Two Accused." Underneath unfurled a simple heading, implying a solution: "The Psycho-biology of Violence." The article celebrated the work of the three doctors, Mark, Ervin, and Sweet, for offering hopes that "brain control" of disturbed people within the wider population was within reach, if only the right approach were grasped.[21] The medical profession, in Sweet's words, could now start to make a "special contribution to the prevention of violence."[22] Their "episodic dyscontrol syndrome" (they laid claim to its discovery) was an urgent problem for the nation and the globe. In a letter published in *Science* the following year, they estimated ten to twenty million Americans likely suffered from some form of the disorder.[23] In light of the brain damage that almost always lay at the root of violence, especially "senseless" violence and what the *Life* article called "deviant behavior," the most direct response was to home in on the aberrant cerebral tissues. While the three acknowledged that, in the case of presidents shot down, airplanes taken over, cities burned, and innocents slain, there were additional downstream factors and complex social conditions that at some point came into play, they stressed that the likelihood that these terrible things flowed from defective brains (structure and function) was too often ignored. They proposed a remedy for a worried society. Their remedy was technological. Their remedy was, more specifically, electrosurgical.

New kinds of psychosurgery could resolve some of the most

resistant cases of aggressive behavioral dysfunction, the two believed. Set aside your misgivings, Dr. Ervin assured reporters when asked: These were not the bad-old-days, "blind-cut" type of hatchet lobotomy, which by the 1950s bore a heavy stigma and spawned films such as *One Flew Over the Cuckoo's Nest*. Instead, they would make use, in the 1960s and 1970s, of new, less invasive, more exact, even futuristic techniques, some derived from astronauts. (A reporter visiting Ervin at his lab described him as markedly self-possessed: "Dr. Ervin, a giant of a man with a luxuriant blond beard, leaned back in his chair, puffed on his pipe, and tried to explain the team's work. A photograph of Einstein and the white, pickled brain of a hydrocephalic kitten stared at him as he spoke."[24])

Highly assured, the doctors felt their high-tech interventions were the only way to find the "stopping mechanisms" and the "starting mechanisms" of the brain. And why should they not be assured? Medical colleagues reviewing their work in established journals hailed Mark and Ervin's "vast clinical knowledge of violent persons," and congratulated them for putting to rest the "either-or morass between 'environmentalists' and 'biological determinists.'" The *Journal of Psychosomatic Medicine* noted respectfully Mark and Ervin's fifteen-year experience in the stereotactic implantation of subcortical electrodes. Likewise, the *British Journal of Psychiatry* foregrounded the doctors' having "successfully treated" three cases at the heart of their book.[25] (Granted, one of those cases was a pseudonymous Leonard Kille's, concerning which a declaration of "success" perhaps did not fit the bill; nonetheless, they claimed it.)* In other words, the

---

* Mark and Ervin do misrepresent—or overoptimistically present—the case of Kille, and its outcome, in their book. In addition, the two likely overstated that Kille, whom they call "Thomas R.," had "clear cut brain damage." Other experts disagreed on this point. It should be noted that Mark and Ervin's program of using sophisticated cuts in the brain to cure violence before it took place was, after extensive review, rejected by three committees of Mark's and Ervin's peers four years after Leonard's operation, when the two applied to create a Unit for the Study of Violent, Assaultive Behavior that would have specialized in scaling up the procedure used on Kille to broader populations.

Literal Brain Control

Life magazine's profile of the violence unit at Mass General, where Leonard Kille received psychosurgery, featured photo stills of a nineteen-year-old co-patient, "Julia," who was the first patient to live with the remote-control device called the stimoceiver. PHOTO: ELEK TOTH.

Seeking a cure in the brain of a frenzied girl

 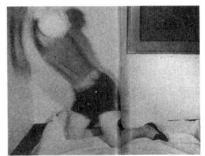

When certain areas of her brain were stimulated remotely, "Julia" flew into uncontrollable rages. PHOTOS: ELEK TOTH.

pair was respected by peers for their hands-on experiences with difficult patients. (Criticism, when it came for them, would issue from other quarters than the academic journals.) And Mark and Ervin saw themselves as rather conservative in their approach to surgery, lowering the damage to the brain tissue by 90 percent over previous lobotomy procedures. No doubt in the future it could be done even less destructively.

So it was that Leonard Kille, intermittently consenting to an experimental treatment—though some, including his mother, would later question whether they had been informed of exactly how experimental the treatment was—began "pretreatment testing" in April and, later, October 1966. Sedated and locally anaesthetized, his head was shaved and fixed in a stereotaxic instrument (a new device that essentially nailed the skull into stability). His doctors then employed another innovation: Polaroid X-ray film. With its rapid development capability, this technology allowed them to visualize Kille's brain landmarks instantaneously and create "plotting charts" for where electrodes would be embedded. (Considering Kille's role in the Polaroid camera, its use in surveying his own brain was ironic.) Through an opening in the back of his skull, Dr. Mark, as the surgeon of the team (Dr. Ervin was not a surgeon, but a neurophysiologist and psychiatrist), planted fingerlike arrays called stranded electrodes in his brain bilaterally, their tips along the amygdalae, their tails trailing out through a tiny second hole a bit above the larger entry point. After a brief recovery period from the surgery, Kille participated in a series of trials over nine months. In a film of these tests, the viewer can see him, wires protruding from the back of his head, the top of his skull swathed in bandages, responding

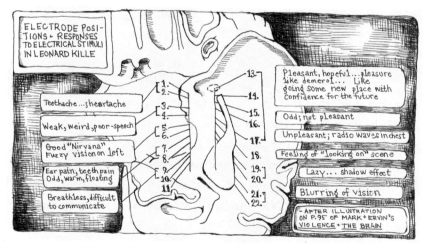

Map of Leonard Kille's "subjective verbal response" while having his brain electrically stimulated. This artist's rendition highlights key verbatim responses from Kille displayed or uttered while the embedded electrodes in particular areas of his amygdala were undergoing stimulation. ARTIST'S RENDERING BY AUTHOR OF FIGURE 16 IN *VIOLENCE AND THE BRAIN* BY VERNON H. MARK AND FRANK R. ERVIN (1970).

Literal Brain Control

to different targeted stimulations. At one moment, as a surge reached a special area of his brain, Kille said he felt euphoric, describing his state as one of "detachment and relaxation." When another area received current, he reported a painful "feeling of being backwards."[26] Occasionally, a rush of pleasure "like Demerol" suffused him.[27] Meanwhile, monkeys in Ervin's lab that received the same implants were given the capacity to self-deliver current. The creatures would stimulate the pleasure-giving spot over and over, neglecting to eat.

Correlating Leonard Kille's descriptive words with the area they were activating when he uttered them, his doctors drew a sort of push-button subjective map of his brain. One site interested them particularly, a spot where Leonard, on the delivery of electrical current, experienced muscle spasms, which his doctors labeled "psychomotor seizures"—and which MIT neuropsychologist Stephan Chorover, a prominent critic of the method, would later call "alleged seizures." It may be tempting in retrospect to see Kille's doctors simply as mad scientists push-button-hacking the brain of a mild-mannered man. They would assert that Kille had epilepsy (as Ervin reported in an interview for a popular 1974 book called *The Brain Changers*, in a published case report, and later in court).[28] And while it may seem strange to our ears to hear it alleged that a middle-aged patient had suddenly been found to have a condition that to the average person would seem to be flagrantly obvious in its presentation, epilepsy has a long history of difficulty in diagnosis.

Even a cursory reading of Owsei Temkin's classic *The Falling Sickness*, which tells the history of epilepsy from the ancient Greeks to the inception of modern neuroscience, may render one amazed that exact diagnosis has prevailed at all, such a hodgepodge of mysticism and materiality did the condition continue to be for centuries. Hellenistic society regarded epilepsy as a "sacred disease," full of meaning, providing evidence of visitation from the spirits, and due to nosological features such as the sensory aura and the curious feeling of déjà vu that precede an incoming seizure, it has remained a portentous disease, consistently woven into literary works such as Dostoyevsky's *The Idiot*, which opens with an account of the start of an epileptic seizure with all its mystical and even metaphysical implications—"He fell to thinking that in his attacks of epilepsy there was a pause just before the fit itself . . . when suddenly in the midst of sadness, spiritual darkness, and a feeling of oppression, there were instants when it seemed his brain was on fire, and in an extraordinary surge all his vital forces would be intensified. . . . His mind and heart were flooded with extraordinary light," the epileptic hero Prince Myshkin feels. There continue to be cryptogenic forms of epilepsy—such as Dostoyevsky's own, it seems—where the disease has an unclear origin and may co-occur with life stresses or alcohol consumption. Only in the late nineteenth century did physician John Hughlings Jackson make a compelling case for the neurological origin of most forms of epilepsy.[29] And still, diagnostic exactitude and medical agreement were far away. As Oliver Wendell Holmes once said, "If I wished to show a student the difficulties of getting at truth from medical experience, I would give him the history of epilepsy to read."[30]

By the 1960s, of course, medical men and women were much more assured in their diagnoses, but assurance is a moving target. Mark and Ervin wrote of epilepsy not as a disease but "a symptom of brain dysfunction and electrical disorganization."[31] For them, it was a signifier of things to come. It resulted from a confluence of factors that in turn, although not always, led to violence. Whether or not Leonard Kille suffered from full-blown epileptic fits or a cryptogenic epilepsy or no epilepsy at all (the doctors mention "lip smacking" having been observed, and to this day, one of the treating residents, Dr. George Bach-y-Rita, is convinced Kille certainly did have the disorder), these symptoms were key to the eventual diagnosis and treatment, for according to Mark and Ervin's methodology they indicated (a) some sort of existing brain dysfunction and led the way to (b) the

Literal Brain Control

precise portion of the brain that needed to be destroyed. This was in-line with some of the most forward-looking medical thinking at the time (although it did have its critics). The diagnosis also happened to advance a larger program exploring the surgical control of violent behavior.

Part of this story is about how radically forward-looking medical treatments can shift. Lobotomy is the perfect example of a procedure once hailed as modern and high-tech but later relegated to ghoulish. Most people are likely unaware there was a second wave of lobotomies in the United States, Norway, Japan, and other technologically advanced countries post Ken Kesey's *One Flew Over the Cuckoo's Nest*. Yet there was. This second wave in the late 1960s and early 1970s used a new name for lobotomy, deployed innovative techniques, and made new claims for the social ills it could address. It is not simply that some sort of sadistic delusion dropped from the sky and entrapped these eminent practitioners, causing them to begin lobotomizing patients again. Rather, such shared cognitive systems are how medicine works. Consider that only eighty or so years before Mark and Ervin at Massachusetts General Hospital in Boston undertook the brain stimulation and searing amygdalectomy of Leonard Kille, bloodletting was still practiced there.[32] Granted, bloodletting was on its way out in the late 1800s, along with cupping and leeches; but it is useful to see how plastic standards are, and how radically they are shaped by medical exigency and social needs, as well as the role of the often underestimated force of professional backslapping.

Kille's electrodes were implanted in October 1966. Then came nine months of pretreatment stimulation, after which Kille's doctors recommended surgery in the form of a double amygdalectomy to burn away the problematic portions of his brain, though they put it more delicately. Kille's wife told him that she would divorce him unless he underwent the operation. Though desperate to repair his marriage, Kille was not enthusiastic until, experiencing one of the electrode-delivered "highs," he did sign a consent form. But again, once the exhilaration wore off, he opposed the intervention. In fact, his doctors, frustrated at the return of Kille's "wild and unmanageable" resistance to the prospect of having destructive lesions made in his brain, redoubled their efforts to skirt what they deemed his pathological paranoia so that, after much suasion, they once again induced him to agree to surgery. Dr. Mark then moved into the final phase of treatment, which the two presented as a far more high-tech and less damaging procedure than the old lobotomies: stereotactic surgery, compared with lobectomy, destroyed less than a tenth of the amount of brain tissue.[33] Furthermore, their technique of running weak current through implanted electrodes to identify specific brain responses, and transmit them back, constituted a "unique opportunity to learn about the relationships between brain mechanisms and violent behavior."[34]

During a further period of intensive experimental brain stimulation, the left amygdala was seared (via microwave) between January and February of 1967, the right at the end of a period between February and May. Via the indwelling electrodes, Dr. Mark delivered high-frequency currents into limbic loci on the parts of the amygdala he would then target. The presumed problematic tissue was destroyed (burned away) along with an additional several millimeters of the amygdala. As many critics would observe in antipsychosurgery protests that would soon arise around the country, this kind of brain alteration, unlike the effects of electroconvulsive therapy (ECT) and most psychotropic drugs, cannot be reversed. Nonetheless, it should be remembered that from the physicians' point of view, as from that of Lennie's wife and the couple's shared psychologist, Kille's situation was a desperate one, and dangerous for the family. It is true that up to this point, hospital records described him as "meek and docile"—with his only outburst occurring when the physicians suggested operating on his brain, but how someone acts in an institution does not necessarily describe how they act at

Literal Brain Control

home. It is up for dispute exactly how wrathful Kille could become, and whether or to what extent he had ever physically struck his wife and children; or if he had repeatedly frightened them with his temper and irascibility.[35]

At points during his months at Mass General, Leonard began to worry he might have become the subject of a "science-fiction" plot, as he wrote to his mother—and indeed his travails did inspire the 1972 thriller *The Terminal Man* by a young Harvard medical student named Michael Crichton, who was observing Kille's treatment. In the bestseller, doctors Mark and Ervin become doctors Morris and Ellis, while the experimental patient, presented as a computer programmer rather than an engineer, is described as "a meek, pudgy 34-year-old man, with a sort of permanently bewildered air about him" and, later, as someone who transforms alarmingly from asking careful questions about the hospital accommodations (Would there be a view? Just how comfortable are the beds?) to a human experiment gone awry: a raging thing that must in the end be "put down." A young Crichton, having not yet abandoned medical training for full-time novel writing, shared his superiors' fears about the rising tide of violence in the United States, and the book lays out a nightmare scenario, exploring the unwelcome truth that some human beings, with the flick of a switch or the glance of an eye, can become murderous monsters: "I've always wanted to rewrite Frankenstein," the author announced about the book modeled on Kille's case, "and this is it."[36]

Eventually Kille's mother would sue Drs. Mark and Ervin on her son's behalf in a high-profile, lavishly lawyered $2 million malpractice action claiming the two had not secured adequate consent, had not informed Kille or his family of the risk, had treated Kille as an experimental research subject rather than a clinical patient, and had rendered him, permanently, a near vegetable. The suit would allege that Mark and Ervin, who were not only clinicians but researchers of the effects of brain surgery on violent behavior, and who spoke of increasingly "justifiable" cases on which to practice, had leapt at the chance to try out their novel procedure and attributed epilepsy to Kille when he had none. (This question, as discussed previously, is far from settled, even today.) Dr. Mark would insist that Kille was receiving proper medical treatment for epileptic seizures. Around the time of his mother's 1973 filing, the National Institute of Mental Health and US Justice Department would grant Kille's doctors a further $500,000 [plus] for the violence research unit they were running at Mass General. They were pushing a plan—a sort of "early warning system"—to screen people for neurological irregularities that might lead to "assaultiveness." Additional monies were to come from the Department of Housing Urban Development. Evaluators in Massachusetts, however, pulled support at the last minute.[37]

As protests mounted, Kille's doctors and other prominent psychosurgeons found it hard to navigate the conferences they attended and the labs they ran. Demonstrators gathered at the Elizabeth Hotel in Colorado for a professional society meeting and physically pushed Mark offstage. Then, demanding he speak, they made a circle and (as he later recalled) "began hissing at me like a gaggle of geese."[38] Elite professional opinion, which had generally supported the esteemed colleagues, began to teeter. The eminent neurosurgeon Elliot Valenstein wrote that good intentions were all very well, but these programs were *unthought-through*: "I have every reason to believe that this group of clinicians is seriously concerned about violence and they have no desire to violate guaranteed freedoms, but it appears that they have not given sufficient thought to the ramifications of their proposed solutions. The possibility of developing a means to detect persons with poor control over dangerous impulses may be 'appealing' when considered in a social vacuum, but there is a very dangerous precedent inherent in the suggestion of combating 'the violent-triggering mechanisms of the brain of the non-diseased.'"[39] Shortly afterward, the two doctors ceased working together, and

Literal Brain Control

never again collaborated clinically. Dr. Ervin decamped for what was slated to become a well-funded violence research center at the University of California, Los Angeles. To say he disagreed with the considered criticisms of his colleagues and the loud chants of his opponents is an understatement.

His new colleague was Louis "Jolly" Jolyon West, the newly converted violence expert.

....

By most measures, Dr. West's visible career as of 1970 traced success upon success. His exploits in Oklahoma City revealed him as not only an energetic principal investigator but also a prime example of what used to be flatteringly phrased as a Big Man. (Such personnel are still found to be very useful at universities in boosting the stature of a department, but they are not called big men anymore.) West near-single-handedly built up from scratch the Department of Psychiatry and Neuroscience at the College of Medicine of the University of Oklahoma, despite the difficulty of recruiting high-profile talent to that part of the country, and even though he began the task at the untested age of twenty-nine. One of West's recruiting letters to a medical researcher who expressed reluctance to uproot himself gives a sense of Jolly's pitch: "Bob Bird, that well-known dapper bachelor about town in New York, expected to retire from the human race when he got to Oklahoma," wrote West to a prominent Payne Whitney Clinic clinician. "Yet Bob is much happier than he ever was in New York, and twice as busy socially."[40] He often wooed recruits in this way.

Nor did West himself retire from humankind in Oklahoma; he continued to play an active role in the MK-ULTRA program. Fresh from the Air Force and still working for the CIA in the form of various shell organizations, he seemed to manage several jobs, with an additional challenge of keeping secret his CIA work, and another of hiding his extensive and perhaps compulsive extramarital liaisons, which his wife, the psychologist Kay West, detailed in recalling that period.[41] He was carrying out free-form investigations in sleep deprivation, in hypnotic programming, in drug dosing, in violence inculcation, and combinations of all of these. He was learning, he reported to his CIA handlers, to produce "dissociated states" in almost anyone, anytime using hypnosis, sensory alterations (flooding or deprivation), and drugs. Next year, in 1956–57, he planned to employ a purpose-built "special chamber in which all psychologically significant aspects of the environment can be controlled," and where he could adjust all variables so as to produce quantitative data on the changes that subjects were undergoing. (A CIA operative noted under the word *dissociated*, "definition not clear," but West meant by it to secure the building blocks of brainwashing: Dissociation was the necessary beginning to breaking down a person's sense of self under pressure.)[42]

Here the archival trail runs aground. These experiments may always remain shrouded; the historical record, obscured by the destruction of documents and mandates of secrecy, may never reveal the exact parameters constituting West's work, but it is clear he had relatively unobstructed rein.

Alongside his MK-ULTRA involvement, West dove into further psychological and psychoanalytic training in the growing ambit of the emerging behavioral sciences. According to his CV, released in a FOIA request from the CIA's files, he underwent personal psychoanalysis at the Topeka Psychoanalytic Institute in 1958 and 1962. And he sought further training at the Tavistock/A.K. Rice Institute in England intermittently from 1965–1975. Topping off the trifecta of forward-looking behavioral science juggernauts, West became a fellow at the Center for Advanced Study in the Behavioral Sciences in 1966–67 at Stanford University, a retreat center located in a bucolic setting in the hills of Palo Alto. How might all this training have shifted his focus, if at all?[43] For his sabbatical he moved deeper into the study of psychotropic drug effects via the counterculture. He spent the year in the San Francisco Bay Area. He was rarely in residence in Palo Alto where his fellowship was located, but instead spent much of his time at an open-ended experiment in what he called his "hippie laboratory" in the Haight-Ashbury district of San Francisco.

The lab was in a rented six-room apartment where he had three graduate and three undergraduate students conduct participant observation, taking extensive notes on the doings of drugs by various runaways and scenesters. "As participant observers of the scene our efforts included turning 'bad trips' into good ones in the back rooms of the Haight-Ashbury Free Medical Clinic, helping 'Plastic Man' and other members of 'The Diggers' to feed hungry people in the park, conducting group therapy for some of those pilgrims who wanted and needed it the most, weaning a few drug users from their chemical crutches, steering some runaways in the right direction, and otherwise being helpful in our fashion. The acceptance won in this fashion made it easier to gather large amounts of interesting data on the life and times of the hippies," wrote West and his co-investigator Dr. James Allen, a psychiatrist with Harvard affiliations. West recorded his upset emotions when Dr. Allen spoke to the press and referred to *his* pad as the "Harvard crash pad," staffed by a "Harvard Team." Sometimes the researchers dubbed it the "Psychepad," West noted in his diary, continuing, "I have made almost no effort to 'keep my distance' from the people whom I have been hired to study."[44]

Several articles resulted, speculating on youth culture and brainwashing, but one on-site PhD student reported an odd "scene" not so much of youth but of the middle aged: West himself, along with some of his friends, in costume and getting high on the sofa.[45]

The hippie project extended into the early 1970s, long after his sabbatical year ended. The infrastructure through which it continued (I hesitate to call it a "cutout," but it did function like a cover organization) was the Haight-Ashbury Free Medical Clinic.

Dr. David Elgin Smith founded this legendary treatment center in June 1967 and gave West an office in it during the second half of West's stint in the Bay Area, starting the very month of its inception. The clinic was a nonjudgmental source of gratis medical care aimed at shoeless hippies and others who struggled—"those weirdos," Smith's malpractice insurer called them, on the occasion of refusing to continue insuring him.[46] Kids came in with complaints such as "VD . . . colds, caved in veins from shooting barbiturates; and pregnancy," wrote one of West's student observers in his diary.[47] The free clinic's facility at 558 Clayton Street served as a supplementary locale, and recruiting spot, to pipeline people to West's apartment lab not far away on 335 Frederick Street. Befitting his sabbatical mode, West wrote some fiction (unpublished, but atmospheric), and his team was making a film.

Once he went back to the academic world in 1968, West continued to be a sort of off-site principal investigator to a new enterprise called the Amphetamine Research Project, under which some of the personnel from his Haight-Ashbury lab continued close study of various hippie families, using both the pad on Frederick and the clinic on Clayton, and taking field trips farther afield to visit communes. As Dr. Smith recalled recently in a podcast interview, "We had gotten a grant for an amphetamine project . . . because we were the ones that were on the front lines treating methamphetamine addiction and he"—Jolly West—"was the head of it."[48] Jolly was a big name, after all. It made sense to position him as the lead scientist even if he was not there very much after 1967. Under West's aegis operated a panoply of behavioral scientists and medical researchers, including project director Roger Smith (not related to David Smith, the clinic's founder), who was a criminologist, drug researcher, and, as it happens, Charles Manson's not-very-effective parole officer. Working for West were, in addition, Alan Rose (a research assistant who went rogue and lived with the Manson Family for four months), several graduate students (more or less enthusiastic about joining the hippies, but trained to observe

Literal Brain Control

them), and a disaffected undergraduate named Kathy, who wrote bitterly about West in her notebooks.

Some have claimed that this project was a CIA front, and that Charles Manson in this period may have been one of their experiments, on whom they employed West's triad of hypnosis, drugs, and environmental engineering to derange him or teach him to derange his followers, but I have not found evidence either proving the first claim (of direct CIA involvement), nor the second (of direct contact sustained between West and Manson). The documents in West's files point to the National Institute of Mental Health (NIMH) as the primary source of financial support. (Meanwhile, claims of CIA backing have caused a certain defensiveness among surviving personnel in light of the compelling research published in O'Neill and Piepenbring's recent bestselling book, *Chaos*.) Though I have not found a surefire CIA document trail, this lack of evidence does not mean evidence of lack, as they say. The CIA's mode was, of course, clandestine, and they were known to destroy or obscure records. Looking at the early MK-ULTRA documents, one finds ample evidence of the almost obsessive i-dotting and t-crossing care with which they approached even trivial communications. We saw previously how West's Oklahoma subproject entailed not one but two cover organizations.

It is indisputable that Charles Manson and his family were connected, at times intimately, to this maze of projects (the ARP, the HARP, the Psychepad, the HAFMC itself). Manson and his women were required to complete parole check-ins at the free clinic, and they also received medical care there. By some accounts the Manson Family appeared relatively sane compared to others walking around the Haight. Researchers came to know them well and even may have engaged with them in a version of "The Game" (a popular cult tactic pioneered by the group Synanon around this time). However, further links are elusive as the relevant files of the amphetamine project strangely disappeared from Clayton Street the night Manson's and his family members' arrests were announced. As the forensic psychologist then in administrative charge of the research project (and second in command to West), Dr. Stephen Pittel, insisted in an interview: "They were absolutely stolen." His colleague, Dr. Ernest Dernburg, a prominent San Francisco psychiatrist affiliated with the free clinic, agreed: "It was a considerable amount of research—the premier amphetamine research conducted at a street level. It would have been very important to the clinic . . . and it disappeared. Call David. Ask Roger if he has the files or knows where they are."[49] Both Smiths (David and Roger) deny this theft took place. Nor are those records found in West's archives.

The year in California was a turning point for West personally. Soon afterward, in 1969, he accepted a newly created position in Los Angeles heading the new Neuropsychiatric Institute (NPI) at UCLA. Taking his elevated reputation and growing family, he settled in the hills above Westwood in a large home near the estate of Charlton Heston, his old friend. Still known by the moniker "Jolly," and appropriate to the mien he generally wore, West's institution-building energies made him an attractive candidate for the UCLA job, and hopes were surely high that he would help another fledgling institution grow. He was ambitious. The advantages of Oklahoma City notwithstanding, West came west permanently.

As his opening foray, he aimed to do no less than revolutionize the behavioral sciences in the direction of making them more powerful and more predictive. The vessel for this change was an enterprise called the Center for the Study and Reduction of Violence, sometimes also known by more cumbersome names such as the Center for the Long-Term Study of Life-Threatening Behavior, but, in time, simply as the Violence Center. Despite the fanfare, West's initial project at his new California position brought unexpected challenges. His first hire was Dr. Frank Ervin, who was relatively fresh from the experimental treatment of Leonard Kille in Boston. Events did not go smoothly.

The Violence Center, as West informed the *Los Angeles Times*, would house an array of studies looking at "human beings, rodents, and primates to determine what causes aggressive tendencies."[50] According to his panoramic vision, it would serve as a "base of operations" for studies of incipient violence—twenty-four categories were identified as of the initial project draft released in 1971, and eventually twenty-nine were unfurled for the final draft in 1973.[51] Most of the projects would focus on *potentially dangerous people*. This was based on the concept of "dangerousness," which West hoped to quantify and further define. Abused children, menstruating women, prisoners, epileptics, hyperactive kids, all were categorized as potentially "violence-predispos[ed]" due to nonorganic brain disorders. (Within a bio-psycho-social approach such as West advocated, nonorganic disorders were, by definition, altering the brain because of the way it assimilated external information and pressures. Here West joined a longer tradition in the history of medicine of seeing nonorganic disorders as incipient organic ones.) In the 1930s and 1940s this was the rationale behind what were then considered "advanced" types of blind-cut lobotomy—that pathological habits could eventually harden in neural tissue. Thus, one could operate on the brain to change existing negative behaviors in what some of its practitioners were by the 1960s calling sedative neurosurgery.[52]

West had a gift (or perhaps a curse) for showmanship, and for making his views into news. He sent out several press releases about the new center. From rats on LSD (Would they fight more?) to violent veterans (Did they have brain disorders to begin with?) to battered children (Would they have brain disorders going forward?), to Black urban residents who rioted (Was there structural or functional brain damage there, too?), the scheme aimed at a "complete and integrated" understanding of what causes person-on-person violence, as West's second-in-command, Dr. Robert Litman, stated around this time.[53]

The underlying idea of the Violence Center was the hope for social control enacted through technology. Two dreams fueled this pursuit: push-button exactitude and predictiveness. The first dream, push-button control over consciousness, was a fantasy where consciousness could be defined as (reduced to) brain activity. To understand how to achieve this control, you could start by studying dangerous people, or people deemed to be potentially dangerous. Ultimately, this work would serve as a bridge to behavior prediction of all kinds.

The second dream was predictiveness, a concept akin to Philip K. Dick's sci-fi notion of "pre-crime." If ten to twenty million Americans, according to Mark and Ervin's estimate, should be considered pre-violent—that is, they were predisposed to episodic dyscontrol due to brain disease, whether organic or nonorganic—then the problem was huge, amounting to 5 to 10 percent of the entire American population, including all those restless children. No wonder West planned a full-court-press effort to uncover "brain-triggers" in many possible sources of brain problems that led to violence. The approach was quite a bit ahead of its time in its distinct brain-centrism—what historians of medicine Fernando Vidal and Francisco Ortega call "the belief that 'we *are* our brains,'" and what other scholars have described as part of the large-scale biomedical reduction of disease.[54] Such advocates did not deny that other factors existed, but they put the brain's function and structure at the heart of it all, and so with a single stroke thus made "brain" equivalent to "mind" and "self" in all important ways. Although West would commit over his long career to a multivariable, ecological, holistic approach to understanding the mysteries of human functioning (and although he would come to regret putting his hopes for psychosurgery down on paper), his plan for the Violence Center nonetheless frequently stressed the search for biochemical root understandings of the brain, with cultural and social domains portrayed as realms where effects subsequently played out or variants could be registered or data could be gathered.[55] It may seem strange that a self-described bio-psycho-social psychiatrist would gravitate toward such a seemingly brain-centered approach, but it makes sense when you consider the commonly held view in these circles that a person's external environmental cues and experiences actively wove themselves into the fabric of the brain moment by moment.

While at UCLA, Kille's former doctor, Ervin, was set to head a program to implant deep-brain electrodes in patients "whose outbursts of uncontrolled rage are linked to abnormal electrical activity in the brain."[56] So far, this was just mimicking what had been done to Kille (using human subjects sourced externally at prisons or mental hospitals or even local emergency rooms). Yet the new Ervin lab was intended to take things one step beyond this. As West declared, a remote-control device called a stimoceiver, invented by Jose Delgado, a professor of neurophysiology at Yale, was key to the proposed setup: The initial stage (indwelling implants like Kille's) would be followed by a "possible experimental program" that would allow "freely moving subjects" whose brains contained those implants to be remotely monitored, so that the subject, on displaying incipient violent patterns, could receive a shock or other corrective intervention or likewise a pleasure-boosting reward. All this, West announced in his blueprint for the Violence Center, was possible. Later, due to storms of controversy, Ervin's name would be removed from the proposal.

Like many fans of automats and other modern conveniences, Mark and Ervin were fascinated by the promises of technological innovations to control behavior, and Delgado's stimoceiver, in particular, offered the possibility of a remote control, on-off switch. Mark and Ervin described the "brain triggers and brakes" their electrode experiments revealed.[57] They worked directly with Delgado, who was willing to lend them his stimoceivers to try out on patients in their unit at Mass General. Previously, Ervin had demonstrated that a cat implanted with electrodes and stimulated in a particular area (limbic system) would "learn to seek objects to attack," would be highly motivated to do so, and would be willing to "run mazes, open doors, and climb barriers" to act out his aggression. However, the cat's start switch could be moderated by other areas, "stop points," which seemed to tranquilize the animal and make her suddenly eat or groom or purr.[58] So, too, in humans could violence triggers be turned on and off, Ervin and Mark suggested. As Dr. William Sweet wrote in the preface to their book, *Violence and the Brain,* their collective method held hope for identifying the *"violence-triggering mechanisms* in the brains of the non-diseased."[59] Importantly, this covered not only those they deemed to be organically brain damaged but all people who behaved poorly and in a senseless manner. In this way, the doctors revealed that the quest for engineering the brain—turning its operation into a "technical problem" that was therefore "solvable"—not merely theorizing about it, was their key motivator.[60]

....

The center-to-be was already full up with federal and state monies before West had yet produced the final blueprint for its existence. By 1972 it had full first-year funding from the California State Department of Mental Hygiene and the California Council on Criminal Justice, with $1.5 million pledged and a further $2.5 million in grants expected from federal sources (namely, the federal LEAA, or Law Enforcement Assistance Administration, which had already funded Mark and Ervin's violence unit in Boston by this time). Additional nongovernmental support for its initial two years was expected to grow for "there is a great interest in the project on the part of a number of private foundations," as a prominent researcher observed in a press release.[61]

Around this time, a twist of fate placed West in an encounter while

Literal Brain Control

standing next to Governor Ronald Reagan (perhaps at a cocktail party) and, making use of his gift for suasion, West was able to spark the governor's personal interest. Or perhaps (another story goes) the 1972 shooting of segregationist Dixiecrat presidential candidate George Wallace at a shopping mall in Laurel, Maryland, was the catalyst for Reagan to take action and fund the Violence Center.[62] Either way, Governor Reagan in his January 1973 "State of the State" speech endorsed West's brainchild as a way of curbing violence, especially crime that afflicted middle-class white Californians.

Financially, at least, the Violence Center was ready to go. Institutionally, at least, it was beyond reproach. Ethically, however, concerns arose from the start.

Arriving in Los Angeles from Boston, the personage of Frank Ervin served as a kerosene-soaked rag to stoke national and local protest movements. When West's draft plan leaked (or was foolhardily released?), a poster urging "FIRE ERVIN!" soon appeared on campus kiosks: *"As a partner in the Mark-Ervin psychosurgery team at Mass. Gen. Hospital, [Ervin made] numerous decisions to destroy peoples' lives and turn them into vegetables. A case in point is former engineer Leonard J. Kille, whose mother has filed a $2 million suit against Mark and Ervin."* Ervin took umbrage—even the prospect of appearing before these students to defend his research, as they were asking him to do, meant giving in to their irrational hysteria. As he became persona non grata at his new academic home—students burned him in effigy on the UCLA campus around this time—Ervin opined that the important task was to "clarify the complex issues concerning the center . . . especially [in light of] the cloud of emotions and general public misinformation extant." He had been awaiting a summons from Jolly West to serve as a resource for the new center, but the knock on his door never came.[63] People's feelings were blocking a clear rational view of what science could do.

In an interview given during the early 1970s just before he left

Boston, Ervin argued that surgeries such as Kille's were the best science could do at the present time: "As I see the importance of our surgical cases, it is that during this limited historical period, when we have no better means for coping with these people's problem, they provide us with the only detailed insight we can get into the neural mechanism of the human brain."[64] Perhaps chemical implants or pharmaceuticals in the future would replace the surgical cuts, he suggested (displaying a certain prescience). Yet Ervin also betrayed the contradictory logic of his position: Were the surgeries helping Kille cope with his problem or were they making use of his problem for experimental insight into the workings of the neural brain? Could these two imperatives coexist? Perhaps, but only if acknowledged and consented to. (The history of neuroscience, where treatment has often overlapped with research, offers notable examples of such coexistence, to the detriment of neither.)[65] The team of Mark, Ervin, and Sweet offered non-acknowledgment and non-consent, many argued.

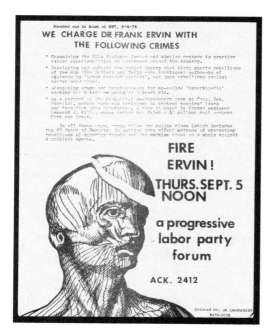

"Fire Ervin!" pamphlet appeared on UCLA kiosks at the time Ervin arrived to take up his new job. LOUIS JOLYON WEST PAPERS SERIES, UCLA LIBRARY SPECIAL COLLECTIONS, CHARLES E. YOUNG RESEARCH LIBRARY, UNIVERSITY OF CALIFORNIA, LOS ANGELES.

Literal Brain Control

Yet from their point of view, the "surprising virulence" of attacks against them was due to critics' irrational inability to see that experimentation and desperate last-ditch treatment were, or should be, essentially the same.[66]

Meanwhile, virulence only continued to mount in what was turning into a perfect PR storm for West's venture. A national movement to oppose the growing use of psychotechnologies to solve the problem of violent crime now turned against the UCLA project. Here, let's review a key definition: Psychosurgery was universally understood to be elective surgery on the brain to *bring about behavioral and emotional changes*. That is, it mainly targeted normal brain tissue and was therefore not the same as neurosurgery, which was brain surgery to address an organic disease.[67] Yet (as mentioned) Mark, Ervin, Sweet and others operated teeteringly close to the boundary between organic and nonorganic disease by their deployment of the diagnosis of epilepsy, a condition they claimed to find in a range of people, and which was widely considered a trigger to extreme violence. Recall that they did not consider epilepsy a disease per se but rather a symptom. Epilepsy, or epileptic-like activity, or psychomotor fits, or episodic dyscontrol, thus formed a bridge legitimating experimental treatments by blurring the lines between psychosurgery and neurosurgery. (Later, Mark would publicly draw a firm ethical line against operating on a nonorganically damaged brain to modify abnormal behavior, while Ervin would not.)[68]

Nearly single-handedly at first, a young psychiatrist named Peter Breggin drew attention to the alarming resurgence of brain-altering surgeries. In the first wave of psychosurgery between 1936 and 1955, an estimated fifty thousand lobotomies took place. By the late 1960s and early 1970s, a second wave had seen thousands of electronic "searing" or scalpel-driven surgeries (an estimated five hundred to one thousand per year) in which normal tissue was destroyed for behavioral change—so that the patient or prisoner would be less of a problem. By the early 1970s, a range of psychiatrists, neurologists, and medical ethicists joined Breggin to criticize the spread of psychosurgery in the US and around the world. As Breggin pointed out, follow-up studies of these patients frequently showed how they "were ruined to one degree or another, depending on the degree of the cuts that were made into their heads. They had loss of abstract reasoning and loss of their emotional vitality, they had apathy, memory defects and quite often they developed epilepsy as a result of their brain disease."[69] The technology of psychosurgery *caused* the problem it was purportedly designed to solve. The story of Kille, the program of West, the epistolary manifestos of Ervin, all suggest this approach was not entirely about diseased people but about a method of instilling fear in those with normal or normal-enough brains—*this could happen to you*. This, at least, was their opponents' argument. Actually it oversimplifies matters: Psychosurgery was about both. It was the search for a surgical solution to the complex social problem of violence and an accelerator of that problem, for it seemed to prove that skeptics' paranoia was justified.

Nonetheless, the abuse narrative fed existing fears. One *Ebony* magazine reader, responding to debates over Ervin's practice of psychosurgery, wrote, "It seems as if stealing us from our homeland, enslaving us for 400 years, destroying our culture and even denying our basic human rights, is not enough. Now we are threatened with the loss of the most vital part of our brains!"[70] Was this far-fetched? Would psychosurgery target African Americans? Initially, at least, statistics showed that over two-thirds of completed operations were performed on middle-aged white women. Yet this was not the whole story. Following along the winding research paths as West laid them out, an inchoate project emerged into view and began to take solid shape. This project was the *merging* of mind control and brain control. Such programs might become racially targeted. They might begin with incarcerated men deemed likely to become violent, a disproportion of whom were Black. Indeed, a leaked 1971 "letter of intent" from the head of the California Department of Corrections notified prison administrators

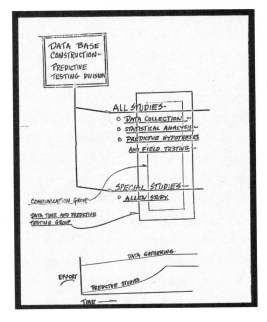

Plans for "Data Base Construction–Predictive Testing Division," which was to be at the heart of Jolly West's Violence Center. UCLA LIBRARY SPECIAL COLLECTIONS, A1713, CHARLES E. YOUNG RESEARCH LIBRARY, UNIVERSITY OF CALIFORNIA, LOS ANGELES.

that a series of these surgeries—just like Leonard Kille's, starting with the implantation of electrodes to diagnose proto-violent areas of the brain followed by surgery to cut out those "cerebral foci"—was about to be undertaken on inmates who were deemed difficult and potentially assaultive.[71] Public outcry blocked this particular series of psychosurgeries from happening.

West set up the Violence Center's infrastructure as a one-way passage made of a series of conduits. Since the Violence Center, with its physical location in the Neuropsychiatric Institute, lacked the equipment to host beds, wards, or labs of its own for all the planned experimentation, it would partner with hospitals (such as Atascadero State Hospital, Camarillo State Hospital, Langley Porter Neuropsychiatric Institute) and prisons (such as the California Medical Facility in Vacaville), as well as other adjunct sites. In one letter to his key benefactor, the director of health at the California Council on Criminal Justice, Dr. James M. Stubblebine, West suggested that a recently abandoned Nike missile encampment was an ideal site for such studies, as it was close enough to UCLA for an easy commute yet bounded by, essentially, barbed wire and beyond that the bobcat-filled relative wilderness of the Santa Monica hills: "Comparative studies could be carried out there, in an isolated but convenient location, of experimental or model programs for the alteration of undesirable behavior," West informed Stubblebine.[72] Experimental studies, some of them using Black and Hispanic junior high school students who were deemed pre-criminal, would explore whether violent crime could be stopped before the youth in question had even entertained it. (Later, when demands for clarification and retraction arose, West said the Nike center would be used only for animal studies.) Such sites would allow relatively free experimentation but would not be directly under the aegis of the Violence Center—would not be fully traceable back, as in a one-way bridge—thus guaranteeing them latitude of operations.

One of the cooperating facilities was at the aforementioned prison in Vacaville, where its medical facility was already a thriving venue for drug experiments on prisoners. It was also a place where highly speculative surgeries along the lines strategized by Mark and Ervin had already gone forward: Three "violent prisoners" received psychosurgeries, out of twelve total performed on California prisoners, to diminish their aggressiveness. (The state of California was not alone: In Michigan, twenty-four sexual offenders received such operations.) Running in tandem, the drug-testing program constituted "a brisk traffic in human subjects for drug company experimentation," as Jessica Mitford reported in the *Atlantic*. This was far more widespread at Vacaville than surgeries. Depending on the number of studies underway at any given time, up to two-thirds of the fifteen hundred residents were taking part in tests of new and often unpleasant drugs.[73] Vacaville also received funneled support from the CIA's operation CHAOS and earlier operations MK-ULTRA and MK-SEARCH.*

---

* This was only publicly revealed several years later, in 1977, when the then superintendent

In 2017 a psychiatrist who worked closely on the case when he was a young medical resident, Dr. George Bach-y-Rita, offered retrospective commentary on their approach: Kille's treatment was not standard but rather was "an experimental procedure . . . the cutting edge."[74] Dr. Bach-y-Rita hastened to add that Kille in his view certainly had epilepsy, though Bach-y-Rita admittedly never met or examined Kille until after the amygdalotomy. "He didn't entirely need that procedure," Bach-y-Rita said, as it was not standard for epilepsy, or for any condition, at the time. (Testifying at trial some years earlier, expert witness Dr. Robert Grimm declared that "under no circumstances" should Kille have been diagnosed with epilepsy either before or after the surgery.)[75] Though we may like to pretend a firm separation, the history of clinical medicine is inseparable from the history of experimenting with new techniques. This is how we have the smallpox vaccine, for example (eighteenth-century doctors self-experimenting and using volunteers wishing to be variolated, as well as orphans sometimes serving as unwitting subjects). These crossovers can be uncomfortable to scrutinize, and they can also shift one's perspective by taking seriously the previously described actor's category.

The historian of science Katharine Park's groundbreaking *The Secrets of Women* demonstrates that in medieval and Renaissance Italy (fourteenth and fifteenth centuries), contrary to common belief, prominent families would give the remains of their daughters who died in

---

of Vacaville, Dr. T. Lawrence Clanon, spoke at a press conference about his "distress" at discovering that between 1953 and 1973 the CIA sponsored experiments [on] "truth serum" drugs at California's medical prison (that is, Vacaville). Clanon, who took over in 1973, assured the public that as of 1977 only aspirin and low-risk drugs were used on "inmate volunteers." He further said that after searching prison files, he could find no evidence of any harm accruing from these experiments; indeed, only a single case of poison oak in 1962 indicated harm to a prisoner (making one suspect the files were less than diligently maintained). As the Associated Press reported, Clanon announced that medical experiments were "carried on using the university as a cover." Bob Egelko for AP, "CIA Drug Tests . . . State Official Sites Memo on Medical Prison Acts," *The Sacramento Bee*, March 2, 1977.

childbirth or of disease over to physicians to explore the "secrets of women" hidden within those bodies. Park argues that this willing dismemberment of female cadavers (previously, historians believed most dissected cadavers were of men) demonstrates a hitherto unknown willingness to explore the mysteries of where babies came from and other urgent topics. The viewpoint of these early practitioners was neither entirely religious nor entirely scientific.[76] With the emergence of modern medicine, efforts to distinguish between experimentation and (mere) observation began with Claude Bernard in 1865, who specified that the motive or intent of the physician in designing the procedure was what made something qualify as a medical experiment or not. Nonetheless, "physicians make therapeutic experiments daily on their patients," he admitted. This murkiness of definition continued into the twentieth century, until 1966–67 when Kille's amygdalotomy took place.[77]

Yet starting in the 1960s, too, experiments began to undergo a new sort of ethical scrutiny in America. (You'd think it would have happened earlier, due to the Nuremberg Code in the aftermath of the Nazi medical war crimes, but it didn't. Many US researchers believed the code applied only to those with ill intent, not themselves.)[78] The pivotal "moment" occurred when Massachusetts General Hospital anesthesiologist and Harvard professor Henry Beecher published his 1966 whistleblowing report on twenty-two unnecessarily risky research experiments presented as treatment. All were conducted at prominent institutions. None were flagged by ethicists or peer review. Some involved newborn babies. Beecher himself was a veteran of CIA-sponsored truth-drug research, which was in part what spurred his subsequent misgivings. In the 1970s, attention to other abusive experiments, many of them conducted on inmate or orphan populations, grew, and in the 1980s Robert J. Lifton's writings on the Nazi doctors who committed atrocities on human subjects in the name of research further aroused sensitivity to the possibility of

Literal Brain Control

experimental exploitation.[79] With hindsight (in our example of Kille), complex historical factors wrangling over the definition of medical experiment and the proper conditions of consent were all in flux. It may be tempting to say a given procedure was an experiment and only an experiment—not a treatment—but in the exigent moment and immersed in the vanishing standards of a distinct time, it can look different.

....

Meanwhile student opposition to the enterprise grew, fed by the public hiring of Ervin and the actions of activists such as Breggin as well as several young psychiatrists doing their residencies at UCLA. Some stationed themselves in front of the NPI's classrooms handing out flyers (to be duly collected in West's capacious archives; he never met a receipt he did not want to save, it seems). They chained themselves to its front doors. They staged protest plays. They wrote eloquent rebuttals. Partly West was taken aback because his collaborators, like he himself, were generally Cold War–era liberals despising Communism with its limits of free expression, valuing civil liberties for patients and their right to self-determination, and promoting equality of opportunity for all races. These were their stated values. He had been a pioneer in the civil rights movement, protesting the all-white restaurants in Tulsa in the late 1950s, when he walked arm in arm with his colleague, psychiatrist Dr. Chester Pierce (who was the first to describe the dynamics of microaggressions and who became one of the first tenured African American professors at Harvard), and his lifelong best friend, actor Charlton Heston (who was then, like West, a Cold War liberal with progressive views on race). Ervin, too, was proud of his previous record as an activist for civil rights. West himself had faced down threats against his family and experienced middle-of-the-night rocks through his window in response to his actions. How could he possibly be racist?

And then, to have his own institute targeted as reductionist (biomedically reductionist, that is) by critics who were, in his view, themselves extreme reductionists (morally reductionist, in West's view), was alarming and—again—entirely surprising to the institution builders. From West's point of view, the critics seemed unhinged, lacking in rationality, unfair, even unkind. They attributed all sorts of plots and conspiracies to him when in fact he was guilty of nothing (his own view) or of ham-handed naivete (the view of colleagues). All administrators at UCLA continued to support him, at least for the time being. When West, against all advice, tried to talk to his opponents—ushering several student activists into his office—they did not *get* him. Surprised by so much criticism, West defended the Violence Center as a progressive alternative, or a seedbed for many progressive alternatives, to heavy-handed policing practices. "If we don't get [the available state block grant money]," West observed, confident in the rectitude of his project, "then it will go into more vans, police cars, dogs, and tear gas."[80] Without intending to, West confirmed the view of the journalist B. J. Mason, who wrote in *Ebony* magazine that the UCLA center was designed to be an "early-warning system for riot control."[81] Secure in his own positive record of civil rights activism, secure in his view about the causes for the historical rise of violence, West did not anticipate opposition and certainly not on the grounds of racism.

Called to testify before an increasingly skeptical California State Legislature, West gave a definitive statement that was anything but reassuringly solid: "The question whether there would or wouldn't be any psychosurgery done at UCLA is a discussible question. My view is that there will not be any, and this has to do with the definition of psychosurgery, a word that is used very loosely."[82] A direct predecessor to "it depends what your definition of 'is' is," his statement did not inspire confidence in the state senators.

By 1973 and 1974, things—events, people, movements—were

Literal Brain Control

consolidating to constitute a new point of view. An important inflection point was the release of a US Senate study in 1974, which, culminating a two-year investigation, concluded that behavioral technologies including psychosurgery, behavioral regimes of reward and punishment, and forced drug dosing of patients for behavior change constituted "impermissible tinkering with mental processes."[83] The federal government should not be funding these interventions, argued the 1974 study's authors to the Senate Subcommittee on Constitutional Rights, especially without adequate protections and protocols in place. It was a pivotal time for West, too. The annoying "psychosurgery flap" (as West called it, relegating it to the status of a silly misunderstanding) only escalated, interfering with the institute he thought was good to go. Hastening to correct his blueprint, which had made so many people angry, he released at least eight revised versions, each strenuously designed to deflect critics' charges yet ineffective in accomplishing that dissuasive mission. Finally, it came to a vote. A campus-wide tally rejected the Violence Center. (However, according to a *Daily Bruin* article, 133 UCLA faculty members maintained their support and only "three shrill opponents" on the faculty—one of them said to be a lowly specialist on snail behavior—were against it.)[84] Around the same time, following the Senate subcommittee's lead, the LEAA (Law Enforcement Assistance Administration) in Washington banned funding any medical or behavioral research that involved physical or psychological risk to the patient, effectively scuttling West's project by 1974. West also lost his bid that year to become president of the American Psychological Association.

As a disgruntled researcher whose own violence center at another university was refused funding due to the contretemps at UCLA complained, "This could be a lesson on how not to write a proposal and how not to deal effectively with public pressure. It is all most unfortunate." In fact, West's Violence Center did go on to become a what-not-to-do case study of clumsy messaging some years later at the Hastings Law School at the University of California, San Francisco. Yet as a key opponent, the young UCLA psychiatrist Terry Kupers saw it, the key takeaway was not one of failed public relations, nor that Jolly had personally handled things badly; rather, the Violence Center's approach itself was "destructively iatrogenic"—meaning, its method for fixing the violence problem was itself part of the violence problem. The cure contributed to the cause.[85]

....

Despite considering the experience as the greatest defeat of his career, West stayed on as head of the NPI for the rest of his professional life. In 1976, two years after the Violence Center defeat, he surfaced as the lead defense expert witness in the media-circus trial of Patty Hearst, his aura undiminished. Oddly, one of the Vacaville drug-test prisoners, Cinque, designed and carried out her kidnapping. The Hearst trial would revolve around the allegations that Cinque and his revolutionary army had carried out a sophisticated brain-control operation on Miss Hearst.

In succeeding years, the social and political agenda Ervin, West, Delgado, and others held for brain technologies—that they be used for snuffing out urban violence and imposing a minimal standard of managed behavioral conformity society-wide—have, seemingly, dropped away, at least in their crude 1970s iteration. The term *psychosurgery* has gone massively out of date. But their undergirding in techno-solutionist hopes have not. (This is why I have tried here to contextualize their actions as meaningful in their time, not simply horrifying in our own.)

First, the hopes are reborn as budding technologies, though none are yet fully active. For example, there is Elon Musk's Neuralink implant for brain-interfacing. It features 1,034 electrodes (rather than a mere 12), sleekly locked into the brain tissue using a sophisticated

Literal Brain Control

robot-driven method for embedding the device. In an early feasibility trial in January 2024, the first human volunteer, Noland Arbaugh, underwent surgery to receive a Neuralink implant, which then allowed his mind to interface with a computer through thought alone. A second volunteer, Alex, followed Arbaugh in the summer of 2024, and was playing video games with his mind and designing accessories for his computer stand within half a day of the operation. In contrast to Kille's implant, it should be said, this one is to assist with a spinal injury (not to correct a behavioral shortfall) and is controlled by the patient, not the doctor. If Neuralink were to become widespread, however, it could work on modifying a variety of psychological or psychosocial conditions—Musk has named obesity, autism, and schizophrenia as targets—and would also be vulnerable to hacking or the assertion of external control.[86] There are, too, the ongoing Harvard Medical School studies of deep brain stimulation, techniques carried

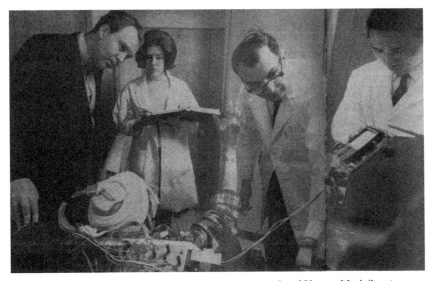

Newspaper photograph of Frank Ervin (leaning over, in suit) and Vernon Mark (leaning forward, in white coat) along with additional members of the research unit, observing a patient in Boston. PHOTO: IVAN MASSAR.

out by some of Delgado's own students. And there are the blockchain-based Web3 dreams of enacting behavioral "token" reward systems across a hive-mind-like collective to incentivize and optimize social molding. Legal scholar Nita Farahany's *The Battle for Your Brain* is a cautionary encyclopedia of neurotechnologies that can track and gather up our thought patterns—ways to "tap directly into our minds, deciphering the emotions, sentiments, and even unuttered speech that they detect."[87]

Second, one can argue that the program succeeded far beyond its forebears' fantasies. While some of its specific "asks" dissipated or (as in the case of the Violence Center at UCLA) never came into being, and others went out of vogue (ADHD is not treated by surgery), the program's behavior-control logic did not die along with West's Violence Center, with Ervin's public shaming, or with the drying up of the supply of human subjects in prisons.

The imperative to seek behavior control (for the social good) through brain implants preexisted, could be tracked, and it continued. Call it the disposability agenda: Some things (including animals treated as models and people treated as experiments) need to be made disposable for an elect or select larger group to thrive, or even for social thriving overall, so the logic goes. This social argument based on disposability is part of a larger mandate of efficiency arm-linked to efficacy.

....

During the years Ervin was settling in at UCLA, Leonard Kille's stays in the hospital grew longer and more frequent. Just after the operation and the divorce (which took place while Kille was in the hospital), Leonard wrote to his mother that he hoped to move to California to be near her, and to work at Douglas Aircraft again. He envisioned his kids visiting him in the summers. However, he never was able to get another job, and he soon went on full disability. Though notes from his presurgery medical records in 1965 described him as a "bright,

Literal Brain Control

creative engineer" who "has never hurt anyone," and his medical records presurgery had no diagnosis more serious than "pattern personality disorder," a string of postoperative observations in California traced a contrast soon afterward.[88] By 1972, he was so worried about his brain being invaded by electrodes that, as his mother described it, "he sits in one corner with a cap on to keep the electrodes from burning his brain so much."[89] Notes from the Long Beach VA hospital spelled out "the patient is not employable" . . . "the patient is not competent . . . " (1974). Later reports had him as "delusional, unshaven, unkempt, actively hallucinating," and with rotting teeth (1975). In the same year, he received Prolixin injections and was at times "pleasant, alert" but with "remarkably little eye-eye contact" (1975). In December that same year, he returned to the Long Beach VA hospital poorly nourished and given to "uncontrolled seizures and outbursts of rage." He insisted he had "invented polaroid camera; government blind seeing rod." The next year, in August, he was quoted as saying, " 'I'm Jesus Christ'; 'I'm a doctor' . . . and many other grandiose illusions" (1976). In December the patient spoke of "UCLA, Yale, Harvard" and said, "My heart is bleeding." When asked about his lifestyle he said, in 1976, "Trying to stay alive."

His son and daughter moved him to the New Bedford, Massachusetts, VA hospital, where he appeared in notes as "disheveled, pre-occupied, dirty, sits head hanging down." He was returned to the hospital when "found wandering in old neighborhood" (1977). A psychological report described him as a "disheveled middle-aged [man who] appears older than [his years]." He claimed he had "5 PhDs by age 9." He said, "I am dead inside" (1977). In October through February, he stayed in the renowned McLean Hospital in Cambridge, the city where he was born, where he noted, "They're murdering me in my brain" (1977–78). Returned to the New Bedford VA, he presented a plan to kill himself using a razor blade, with depression, and with the report: "My brain is burning" (February 1978).

Recently Leonard Kille's grandson made his papers available to me; among the highlights were to glimpse at his résumé, revealing him to have been in his last two jobs, literally, a rocket scientist ("responsible for writing environmental specifications to meet Mil. Specs for space vehicles," and "designing optical devices for re-entry vehicles"). An ebullient letter to his mother, written on the Pan American international "In-flight Jet Clipper" stationery at "midnight Eastern time flying over Greenland on the way to England" on his way back from the South Pacific—from above the clouds, Kille crowed that Douglas Aircraft just doubled his salary—testifies to the thrill a young man raised in the straitened parts of Cambridge felt in arriving: "Somehow God has been good to me and I have been highly rewarded for my work."[90]

·········

The malpractice case of Mark and Ervin reached an end in the winter of 1979, a full six years after its original filing, delayed by the trove of research that had been required. The trial itself lasted six weeks. It was much watched in the Boston press and surrounding medical communities. It was much worried about in circles devoted to psychosurgery's hopes. Some felt the Kille case had been used to politicize and demonize neurosurgical treatments of all sorts, closing down what were otherwise promising avenues. As late as 2013, a neo-psychosurgery enthusiast bemoaned the "unwelcome attention" the case had brought and assessed that Mark and Ervin "were pilloried."[91] One of Kille's grandchildren would go on to write a play based on his grandfather's experience, which continues to haunt the family. In a contemporary letter, his mother wondered whether to reveal that they believe Mark and Ervin received CIA funding for their work, connecting this link at trial.

Nonetheless, at the time of the verdict in 1979, a wave of relief came, for some, when the two doctors received full exoneration.

6

A Small Uh-Oh Opened Up in My Soul

So far, we have followed brainwashing's developing story as it played out in remote POW prisons, federal forests, Cuban holding cells, and special violence wards. Our investigations revealed that vast changes can take place in almost anyone when they are placed in a controlled, coercive environment. (Even if, as it would seem later, the changes were not so much to beliefs as to behavior, the techniques of coercion held steady with a remarkable persistence until conditions changed.) The brainwashing we have seen took place in unique, small-scale pressure-cooker places. The next logical question is: What would happen when that "scaled" and many new communities became hotbeds of seemingly similar processes? In the 1970s, high-demand groups popularly known as cults were labs—not only, as they thought, for enlightenment, but also for brainwashing, and for the experts, now in middle age, to be called off the sidelines.

....

During the 1960s and 1970s, young people were joining cults around the world, from US college towns to Italian hilltop villages, from

Indian settlements to redoubts in Mexico, Brazil, Thailand, Japan, Canada, Australia, and Morocco. Sometimes these groups were native-born and sometimes branches of a conglomerate cult. Once new recruits were there, on average, they stayed about two and a half years.[1] Yet if you judged by press photographs of swirly dancing and joyful faces, many such members looked unlikely ever to leave. During World War II and the postwar period, such alternative religious or political groups had been rare, but after 1965's relaxation of laws restricting immigration, a "flood of South Asian gurus and their followers" settled in the United States.[2] Not all, or even most, elective groups were abusive, and many offered a welcome revolution in thinking and acting. Thousands of communal sects sprouted up endogenously, embracing ideologies that ranged from the Twin Oaks Intentional Community, which sold homemade hammocks and ran itself in central Virginia and Sonora, Mexico, according to B. F. Skinner's behaviorism principles—at first glance, an approach unlikely to occasion a back-to-the-land movement—to the large-vegetable-growing outcrop of Findhorn, a Scottish ecovillage where many young Americans flocked.

At first, the new groups experienced little pushback. Congregations of colorful devotees were a veritable hallmark of the hippie lifestyle in the mid- to late-1960s. They drew their converts from white-collar-society runaways ("lost" or "searching" young people) who gathered at Haight and Ashbury Streets in San Francisco, or at least comported themselves as if they were on their way there. Upper-middle-class families waited for wayward offspring to extricate themselves. Small, religiously experimental groups preached peace and love, which was more annoying than threatening from the point of view of what the renegades would describe as the straight world. The guiding ethos flowed easily into Pepsi ads of the day, some of which borrowed followers' expressions of undiluted ecstasy. A writer could file a what's-it-really-like puff piece for *Time* or the *New York Times Sunday Magazine*, playing on the public's fascination for back-to-the-land dropouts, with accompanying, titillating photos of youths in overalls preparing pea patches or rolling cigarettes.[3] (After all, one person's manipulative cult is another's utopian intentional community.) If anything, it was the more overtly political and civil rights arenas that appeared more disruptive to dominant power relations in the 1960s—not gauzily dressed cult members.

I'll pause to admit that *cult* can be a misleading word as I've been using it here. Its simplest definition is of a small religious group of any type, anywhere, at any time—smallness being what makes it a cult. But the aura of this word has come to include danger, abuse, or unfair coercion. Even in this sense—of manipulation and awestruckness—cults were not new to the mid-twentieth century. We know that the ancient Greek Eleusinian mystery cult regularly drew in followers eager to participate in its rituals, and one can speculate about prehistoric psychedelic sects—as Werner Herzog does in his dizzying night-vision film *Cave of Forgotten Dreams*—who practiced in the Chauvet caves of southern France some thirty-two thousand years ago. What was new in the 1960s was that cults became embedded in the religious, spiritual, and political aspirations of that precise moment. They represented, in some ways, the highest hopes of young people that life could be different from what their families' expectations laid out for them. Psychedelic colors were not just an effect of hallucinations but an expression of joy and possibility in lines broken down and swirling. As Robert Hunter, lyricist for the Grateful Dead, wrote: "There is a road, no simple highway / Between the dawn and the dark of night." When many others were choosing to live differently, paths might converge among people who felt similarly. Communes and back-to-the-land experiments abounded, with philosophies from neo-Platonism to whirling dervish-ism.

But as the 1960s turned into the 1970s, the Manson Family murders and their connection to brainwashing upended any vague

The July 1969 cover of *Life* magazine showed a fascination with off-the-grid living. Hippie back-to-the-land movements sometimes overlapped with cultism and abuse, but this concern was not much expressed before the Manson turning point.
JOHN OLSON/THE LIFE PICTURE COLLECTION/SHUTTERSTOCK.

swatting at cults as just an irritation. The hippie dress took on a new ominousness.

....

During the 1970–71 trial for the Tate-LaBianca murders—the infamous slaughter of nine people that took place over two nights in greater Los Angeles in 1969—the author Joan Didion famously went shopping at I. Magnin department store for a dress to be worn by witness-for-the-prosecution and former Manson Family member Linda Kasabian. (I say famously not because Didion was so well known as to be identified while sizing up dresses but because she wrote about it ten years later in her book of essays, *The White Album*.) Kasabian had been a lookout on the first night of killings and had left with Charles Manson on the second night, later driving a getaway car. She had not physically taken part in the murders (though neither, it should be said, had Manson), and eventually won exemption from being prosecuted by her role in the case. The dress was for Kasabian to wear on her first

A Small Uh-Oh Opened Up in My Soul

of eighteen days of testimony. While in a holding cell, Kasabian met with Didion and gave her some details about what she had in mind: The dress could be emerald green or gold, it should be velvet if possible. Or it could be in a Mexican style, a peasant dress with a smock, possibly embroidered. Size 9 petite. The one firm stipulation from the twenty-one-year-old, according to Didion, was just that it be "mini but not too mini" because too short would signify low morals while too long would signify "culty." Kasabian's estranged husband, Bob, who was not associated with the Manson Family but was a hippie-type musician, was clad in just such robes, all white, long to the floor (again according to Didion, describing him standing outside the Los Angeles courtroom).

The writer was doing her errand at the behest of Kasabian's lawyer, a friend of hers, and out of professional writerly interest, as she anticipated the Manson murderers would people her next book. This was a thought she later repented of, saying she had mistaken them for interesting barometers of cultural change at the end of the '60s, but they turned out not to be. Why she dropped the project may have to do with its brainwashing elements, but we will discuss that another time. This is the way cults became a part of American history that lacked mystery—just naming something a cult or cultish was to claim it was clearly understood. Or seemed to be. Most people *think we know* what happens when someone joins a cult—especially at that moment it becomes clear the group really is a cult and not just some meditation circle or a breathing app—because it means they handed over mastery of themselves.

Here, it is the dress, and the length of the dress specifically, that is of interest. Almost overnight, a dress could be seen as too counterculture. This would not stop the 1970s from being full of longish dresses, and it would not stop the definition of a cultlike dress from changing. (The fashion returned in the 2020s, and a recent customer review described a dress of this style on the J.Crew website as "too sister-wife.") Nor would it stop 1970s directors from making use of them in films from the *Stepford Wives* to *Nashville*. Nonetheless it is a sartorial Rubicon.

The prosecution's lead lawyer successfully presented Kasabian, who did appear in a peasant dress, as a "little hippie girl" with a conscience, and thus someone who stood out from the three "bloodthirsty robots" on trial—the three young women who killed on instructions from Manson: Patricia Krenwinkel, Susan Atkins, and Leslie Van Houten. All three were brainwashed, programmed by a "Mephistophelean guru who raped and bastardized the minds of all those who gave themselves so totally to him."[4] What could be called the Great Brainwashing Offense by the prosecution worked in the Manson trial when, on the day the verdict was read, all four were convicted—Manson for the idea of killing, and the women for carrying it out.* As would be true in most trials, the concept, even when it stood up in court, did not exculpate anyone but pushed in the direction of further guilt for the people deemed brainwashed.

....

During the sentencing phase of the trial, three women with long hair took the stand to testify that although they were followers of Charles Manson they were *not* under the control of Charles Manson and if anything, it was he who was under their control. Or perhaps that they were all marching to their own drummer.

---

* The events of the "Manson murder trial" implicated not only Charles Manson, but three other defendants, his female followers. The challenge of the case was to try four people for culpability in the grotesque happenings of Cielo Drive and Waverly Drive, when one of them (Manson) had not actually struck any blows or taken any direct physical action, nor been present on either scene. The prosecution's argument was that three of them acted under the sway of one, and thus that the three had abdicated their rational decision-making capabilities—*but had not abdicated so far as to be deemed insane or held nonresponsible.* There was a middle ground where the women were legally pinned. According to the DA's line of argument, the Manson girls were mentally tractable yet physically culpable. Manson was morally and mentally responsible if physically absent. Van Houten, Krenwinkel, and Atkins had been brainwashed into obedience and yet tuned themselves cogently, even creatively, to the deadly task at hand. The state won its case, and all four were found guilty of first-degree murder and conspiracy to commit murder.

This small parade of women—almost always called "girls" or the "Manson girls"—frequently cited his "magical powers" and acts such as breathing life back into a dead bird in the desert, yelling and having a window break, petting a rattlesnake, and causing animals such as deer and coyote to come to him, as if he were St. Francis of Assisi. He had surely, all the Manson Family believed, caused the earthquake at 6:01 a.m. on February 9, 1971, just before the trial's proceedings were to get underway for the day, which measured 6.5 on the Richter scale, and during which sixty-five died in Los Angeles. The trial was not impeded or postponed by even half a day, though municipal traffic did slow.

On the stand, Manson's followers claimed they did not always think that his powers made him their overlord. Yes, he could make the earth shake, but so could they. One of the Family members taking the stand to offer a benign view of their group dynamics was Lynette "Squeaky" Fromme, who grew up in Redondo Beach as the daughter of an aeronautics engineer and had joined the group when she was twenty-two, after her father kicked her out of the house.

Fitzgerald [Krenwinkel's **attorney**]**:** Did you have a leader?

Squeaky Fromme: No, we were riding on the wind.[5]

Brainwashing, if that's what it was, empowered them to be empowered by him. On cross-examination, Fromme admitted, "I have entertained the thought that he was Christ. I don't know. Could be. If he is, wow. My goodness!"[6] Others testified that they would die for Manson or be willing to walk to Mexico to get him a coconut, as he once ordered a follower to do.

....

The women went down in cultural memory and literary prose as robots. Manson "converted intelligent, middle-class kids into putty-like zombies," ABC's *20/20* news show put it in 2017.[7] "You don't even have to say a word out loud, they get it all by ESP," Thomas Pynchon described them in his 2009 book *Inherent Vice*. But this wasn't quite correct, even if it seemed to fascinate people (while incidentally forming a throughline to the entire work of Thomas Pynchon and his views about the subjectivity of women). Their robotic obedience is still evoked in current explorations of female AI sex slaves such as Ava in the film *Ex Machina* or the fembots in the television series *Westworld*.

In fact, their seeming empowerment through self-abandonment was more shocking and interesting than their similarity to robots. If these girls were poster children for brainwashing, then brainwashing seemed to *give them* powers even as it took them away. Both, simultaneously, it seemed. The women appeared to be extensions of his will, yet they radiated a "level of self-confidence and dynamism that was pretty amazing," an observer noted, some quality akin to charisma. "They could walk into stores and get checks cashed without ID."[8]

Cult brainwashing turned out to be more complicated than the simple "deletion" of the person who is under the leader's control. It was a paradox: In losing the self they gained a new self, and in the process, they often felt and acted reborn. That person received all sorts of benefits and powers, at least for a time. They felt they belonged somewhere, and this should never be underestimated as the dangerous heart of what brainwashing is and how it works. This is perhaps why so many high-demand groups call themselves variations of "Family."

In the 1970s, after the Manson trial and the prosecution's success of its Great Brainwashing Offense in court, the potential danger of cults in middle-class American life came under a spotlight of attention, and in this way the question of mind control once again began to take up mental space in the public commons after having fallen into decline and a dusty irrelevance during the previous decade.

A Small Uh-Oh Opened Up in My Soul

....

Over the next thirty to forty years, according to an estimate by the International Cultic Studies Association, 2,500,000 individuals would join cultic groups, with more than five thousand such groups operating in the US and Canada by the start of the twenty-first century.[9] Other estimates were lower. The number of members in each group might range from five to millions. It is hard to estimate and provide accurate data because several components are difficult to define consensually— for example, the abusive cultic group itself. And so, anti-cult organizations in the past two decades have foresworn making lists of which organization is, and which is not, a cult, simply because this always entails an element of non-replicable human judgment. Consensus among those who study cults is that they are widespread if difficult to measure. According to a recent paper in the journal *Psychology of Religion and Spirituality*, such groups, more neutrally known as groups of psychological abuse (GPAs), directly involve *1 percent of the global population*.[10] "Involve" could mean anything from having a loved one in a cult to being briefly recruited by one at a bus stop to falling into a long-term, no-exit, dirge-filled followership. The implications of this extraordinary pervasiveness have yet to be explored. For one thing, it tends to undermine the shock and distancing people go through when exposed to a cult.

In the early 1970s, as countercultural lifestyles experienced a dramatic reputational downturn, the cult phenomenon was cast in a different light. "The Manson murders sounded the death knell for hippies and all they symbolically represented," prosecutor Vincent Bugliosi, author of the book *Helter Skelter*, told the London *Observer* a decade or so in retrospect. "They closed an era. The 60s, the decade of love, ended on that night, on 9 August 1969."[11] That night not just the hippie drug of choice for tripping but the whole philosophy and trappings of hippie communes reached, to put it mildly, a point of inflection. (Although LSD went unmentioned at trial, in later interviews Leslie Van Houten recollected how, for weeks at a time, she and other of Manson's most enthusiastic followers vied with each other to drop acid so continuously that they would never come down. Many cults would go on to harness the disorientating and category-bending effects of LSD for depersonalization and psychic entraining.)

Yet one of the CIA's main experimenters working on the topics of brainwashing, LSD, and hypnosis, Dr. Louis J. West, would reappear in the middle of the cult surge, mid-stage in the drama as it were. After taking the helm of a new Neuropsychiatric Institute at UCLA, West would, in 1976, serve as the pivotal expert witness in the Great Brainwashing Defense of Patricia Hearst (which would fail).

Meanwhile his research partner, the psychometrician Margaret Singer, would become perhaps the leading voice of the afflicted ex-cult members and the distressed parents of lost current members. Singer at times partnered with West, as she always had. Yet increasingly she worked on her own in cult recovery circles, where she rose to prominence using her studies of Cold War brainwashing to conceptualize the workings of cult abuse.

·········

High-demand cults that enthusiastically drained their followers' resources, such as the Hare Krishnas (International Society of Krishna Consciousness or ISKCON), The Love Family, The Love Israel Family, The Family (with many variants and offshoots), and the Children of God, might at one point, pre-Manson, occasioned profiles in trendy magazines but, post-murder, they began to set off genuine alarm. Articles circulated stressing their coercive recruiting techniques. By 1976 a Ballantine pocketbook, *Let Our Children Go!*, the work of prominent cult deprogrammer, Ted Patrick, aimed to warn (and also perhaps titillate) a mass readership with its descriptive copy summarizing the dire situation:

> Most of them are college students, young, white and middle class. They vanish overnight, without a trace, only to surface months later with their personalities changed beyond recognition—disciples of the scores of pseudo-religious groups that have spread across the nation. They sign over their lives and property, duped by scores of false messiahs. They beg in the streets to enrich their masters, live on garbage, revile their parents as devils.[12]

Parents banded together to commiserate about lost children, loose networks formed to share which groups posed dangers, and suddenly the literature on the Korean War POWs began to look terribly relevant to the situation and was to be applied to the new cults. Partly, families of the recruited—fathers, mothers, siblings—were grasping at straws to explain the inexplicable. The scholarship, which had ebbed in popularity, suddenly became compulsively relevant again. With a sense of recognition, people pored over Robert J. Lifton's work, especially chapter 22 of his thought reform book, as Lifton recalled: "I was drawn into the national conversation." The brainwashing experts, including West (with his DDD paper), Schein (with his "coercive persuasion" argument), and Biderman (with his Army study)—were a lifeline for desperate parents, as well as for cult members beginning to realize they were stuck in hellish no-exit cycles of extractive demands (stuck in what one cult member would call a "dark . . . hamster wheel of joylessness"), and for still others looking to make sense of what appeared to be a fraying if not rending of the social fabric. Young and not-entirely young people were disappearing into the maws of coercive organizations, snared by forces little understood and against which there was almost no recourse if your child or family member was older than seventeen.

The parents of Kathy Crampton, a teenager recruited into the Love Israel cult, despaired: "We . . . found that there is no law against destroying a person's mind, i.e., Charles Manson was tried only for murder, not for destroying the minds of his followers."[13] Kathy's mother was explaining in a press release why she and her husband resorted to hiring a specialist to abduct Kathy out of the cult and forcibly deprogram her back to consensual mainstream mores. (The deprogramming industry, which Henrietta Crampton helped to start, formed almost immediately after the Manson trial in the early 1970s.) The fact that many of the young recruits came from high social strata, or as one observer put it of the families involved, "They knew their congressmen, they knew their Senator, they knew their newspaper editor, they might interact with them. In fact, some of these kids who joined the Moonies and Hare Krishna were sons and daughters of newspaper editors and politicians" added attentional octane to the warning stories.[14]

Initially, the concept of trauma did not come up often in the anticult movement, because (among other reasons) the classic brainwashing sources did not ever mention it. Just as women's and children's experiences of intensely personal, intrafamily abuse were "written out" of the understanding of trauma for a long time, so too, in a parallel and related way, were the intimate aspects of cult brainwashing unacknowledged and pushed away. Whole slices of experience were (arguably) not to be found in Lifton's eight principles. (The Lifton principles reassured readers that ultimately a rational orderliness can prevail over the troubling experience, rather than offering an understanding of how disorder slinks into the decision-making process, bidden and unbidden, and sometimes, almost always, is even invited.) Lifton's book was not a guide to how cults harm the participant in stigmatizing them even to themselves. Yet, as we'll soon discover, during precisely these years of cults' rise, at an obscure retreat in Wellfleet, Massachusetts, Lifton was struggling to put into

A Small Uh-Oh Opened Up in My Soul

words the peculiar dynamics of this problem, which he would call numbing—and numbing would ultimately open the door to trauma's modern understanding.

Paradoxically, Lifton and his wife had visited Vietnam—then French Indochina—in 1954 as a peaceful respite from the brainwashing research he was doing in Hong Kong. As the United States was taking over from the French, several on-the-ground correspondents warned him that the Americans would make the same mistakes the French did. For his part, Lifton could not conceive that America would fall into any such trap. "The prediction seemed absurd. It was late in the day for colonialism, and besides, that was European stuff."[15] Yet, over a decade later, the war in Vietnam escalated into a morass dividing the US. Soldiers were returning from Vietnam, and Lifton happened to read an account of the My Lai Massacre in the newspaper. He interviewed the veterans, and wrote his *Home from the War* to draw attention to the terrible psychic consequences soldiers were experiencing after their involvement in a brutal and, he had come to feel, unnecessary war. (It would be another twenty-five years before a similar massacre would be revealed from the Korean War.) "I cannot say that I underwent the same transformation as the Vietnam veterans I describe," he wrote in the book's prologue, "but I did not emerge from this study unchanged."[16] Lifton emerged as an out-and-out critic of military psychiatry, with its claims to having almost zero "psychiatric casualties," because (Lifton argued) they were uninterested in the men, and the delay often seen in their responses, except to return them to the battlefield. Clearly, his views had significantly shifted from the time of the Korean War to the Vietnam War.

Recently I visited Lifton's archives at the New York Public Library, where I found a trove of cassette tapes recorded over decades. In a series titled *The Wellfleet Seminar*, one tape, perhaps unlistened to since it was recorded, holds undiscovered value for the evolving understanding of trauma, suffering, and brainwashing and the mystery of their often being at cross-purposes. The seminar was part of a series of gatherings of the Group for the Study of Psychohistory, which Lifton hosted annually near his beach house in Wellfleet on Cape Cod from the late 1960s through the early 1980s. Invited guests from his circle included Lifton's sometime mentor Erik Erikson; his Cape Cod neighbor, Harvard historian of science Gerald Holton; and the sociologist Richard Sennett, among others. In late summer 1973, Lifton presented a paper in progress likely inspired by his just published work on Vietnam vets who had committed atrocities as well as his forthcoming project on Nazi doctors, in which he was finding that a doubling of the self had occurred among physicians. He was beginning, he said, "to make coherent what a lot of people have noticed is a little incoherent about some of my work, because [we] were developing ideas that . . . were not familiar ones."[17] He was speaking about the formative processes that make up the self, and how an easy-to-miss but ubiquitous factor—*numbing*—is omnipresent in the constituting of consciousness. (It's neither instinct theory nor standard Freudianism, he explained to the group, preparing them, for many of them were deep into Freud.) As he went on with his remarks, little outcries could be heard from the room at his audacity—because he was abandoning a strict or as-he-was-trained psychoanalytic view of how repression and many other things work. Following the philosopher Susanne Langer, he defined feeling as part of cognition, drawing from her book *Mind: An Essay on Human Feeling*: "The entire psychological field—including the human conception, responsible action, rationality, knowledge—is a vast and branching development of feeling."[18] Someone in the audience joked: "I feel therefore I am!" and a ripple of amusement moved through the assembly. They were with him, at least so far.

There are nine categories of numbing or narcotization, he went on to explain, which range from (1) acute numbing, a complete psychic closing off (as seen in survivors of Hiroshima's atomic bombing), (2)

A Small Uh-Oh Opened Up in My Soul

chronic, traumatic desensitization (being in a Nazi death camp over a period of time), (3) brutalization (being a GI in Vietnam and having to kill to feel alive), (4) technological distancing (techno-bureaucratic numbing in carrying out orders, governance), (5) power and hierarchy numbing, (6) image overload and lost ritual, (7) normal or ordinary numbing (here, there need be no external pressure: "Let's call it the numbing of ordinary adulthood," Lifton explained), (8) numbing of ideas and idea systems (a type that is both ideological and professional; this "concerns us all really acutely"), and (9) the numbing of difference (how one becomes inured to other people to the extent we perceive them as different from ourself).

What was this all about? What were the stakes? Simply: he was talking about the "most extreme possibility of suffering," where "special mental protective devices are brought into operation." A Jew awaiting a pogrom, a peasant during the Thirty Years War, a victim of the Inquisition. Such experiential extremities are rare, and yet, all of us feel numbing, at least partially, he argued. The room was shifting, not sure of Lifton's drift. The audience wondered—What of the Holocaust? How can that be compared to job burnout? How can unhinged soldiers who massacre civilians compare to sufferers of ordinary unhappiness in a family system? Yet Lifton insisted that the extreme connects with the everyday. Numbing is adaptive, and we all need to adapt. Even in the Holocaust, people's responses were extreme but not pathological. "The mind [and feelings] had to become deadened, go dead, in order for the mind to stay alive." The emotional became polarized from the intellectual. In Hiroshima or the Holocaust, "death, pity, at that moment" were cut off. Only later did a reckoning come. Lifton told his audience they should suspend disbelief (they laughed) and should realize all this was taking place outside of awareness (or at what Freud would call the unconscious level). But Lifton was discarding any strict Freudianism. He was not yet using the word *trauma* much. The numbing he was talking about was outside of awareness but not unconscious. Such things as death, pity, and grief are stored as in a reservoir.

It was a highly specialized audience who were exposed to these inchoate yet powerful ideas. Today they may seem intuitively correct or self-evident; indeed, they were prescient. But they were hard for a group of eminent experts to understand—or, more accurately, to accept—in 1973. Well into a new century, the fact that these are graspable by many now accustomed to thinking about bodily storage of suffering is a testament to the process by which we make our ideas real, and they become graspable. We stand on the other side of the commonsensification of trauma, you could say.

For the next several years, from the early to mid-1970s, Lifton teamed up with others in the New England area—psychiatrist Chaim Shatan (a psychiatrist who saw "delayed massive trauma" in soldiers), Jack Smith (a veteran and activist), Sarah Haley (a psychiatric social worker)—to identify something Shatan, in a *New York Times* op-ed in 1972, first called post-Vietnam syndrome. Lifton's assistant in this work was a young man named Eric Olson, who also helped in the new synthesis of views on trauma. Eric Olson was the son of Frank Olson, an Army chemist who famously received an unwitting dose of acid from MK-ULTRA personnel, and who died mysteriously as the sequel to his bad trip by, the claim was, jettisoning himself out of a New York City hotel window. However, investigative reporting suggests that the senior Olson had developed conscientious objections to the chemical weapons he was testing at Edgewater Arsenal in Maryland; and that these second thoughts, crystallized in his LSD experience and subsequent interrogation, precipitated what some allege was his murder.[19] This family trauma must have drawn Eric Olson to Dr. Lifton and his research on numbing like a moth to a lantern.

The working group with Lifton, growing to include members with other specialties, such as Arthur Egendorf (a veteran who hosted the first rap groups in New York with fellow vets), Mardi Horowitz (an expert on stress response systems), Nancy Andreasen (a psychiatrist who specialized in patients with severe burns), would eventually

A Small Uh-Oh Opened Up in My Soul

succeed in renaming it "post-traumatic stress disorder," or PTSD, thus opening the door, finally, to adding this category to the *Diagnostic and Statistical Manual of Mental Disorders*. (The closest diagnosis up to this point in the manual was "gross stress reaction.") In January 1978 the working group submitted its proposal for PTSD, and in 1980 it appeared in the section on anxiety disorders.[20]

One point stands out strongly in retrospect: how this cohort used the words *grief* or *haunting* or *undigested* to describe soldiers' and other trauma sufferers' experiences, terms rarely if ever applied to the brainwashed POWs of the Korean War, who were often seen as oddities or freaks or weaklings—nor for that matter are such terms commonly applied to social media "addicts" or confused cult members.[21] Such social media users, as I will show, are unknowingly embroiled in a technology that is fueled from the data of traumatic or unresolved emotional experiences.

For our purposes, Lifton's own struggle to understand numbing in a much more capacious way is of pivotal importance. How would understandings of trauma ultimately carry and not carry over into cult abuse and (later) the information overload characteristic of hyperpersuasive social media?

....

The experience of suffering that is particular to such cultic abuse was poorly understood at that time. Because this suffering wasn't clearly seen, cults were hard to understand in terms of their spiritual-social dynamics. Such misunderstandings continue to this day. This problem came to a head in the revelations brought about through the cult recruits' own offspring, whose voices, when they began to be heard, precipitated the second-generation abuse (SGA) crisis. Because an estimated 5 percent of people in cults stay long enough to bear children, the impact of those progeny's voices, once they came of age and if they were able and inclined to speak out, added an unignorable insight that had been, somehow, ignored.[22] Simply put, the community of individuals "born and raised" in cults—people native to cults—which comprised some 125,000 people, brought attention to this trauma. They would by the late twentieth and early twenty-first centuries, with considerable eloquence, point out that they were not just footnotes to their boomer parents' existential crises, and that their trauma, in the absence of the chance to live a previous life outside of the cult, had a different texture and persistence.

Thus applications of the 1950s literature in the 1970s lacked an understanding of trauma, a grasp of the subjective bodily experience trauma pointed to, and, for that matter, a sense of the dynamics of violence and how "at the core of traumatic stress is a breakdown in the capacity to regulate internal states."[23] As one of the founding voices in modern trauma, Judith Herman, argues in *Truth and Repair*, the disorder in PTSD is more than an individual's problem but stems from a social crisis, a crisis of lack of support, a crisis of credibility and incredulity; most of all, a crisis in how violence is not seen. All of this was missing from the early Cold War-Korean War literature on brainwashing, so that when this literature was brought forward suddenly for a new purpose, what might have been somewhat simple became mysteriously complex.

In the spring of 1970, twenty-year-old Ray Connolly, raised Catholic in a New Jersey township, was not enjoying himself at Holy Cross College, where he had already spent two years looking for something that engaged him, that pulled him out of the low-level depressed state in which he felt stuck. As he later recalled, his attempts to pry himself into a more energetic frame included a brief try at leftist radicalism, spawned in part by the fact that you could get "a good deal on a Mao jacket." Yet his constant searching left him feeling "vague"— adrift without much purpose in what he suspected might be a world without further dimensions than the unencouraging ones that presented themselves, equally brutally and boringly, in front of him. He found himself stringing bunches of words together to express the common complaint of the time, mouthing that he felt lost, disconnected from others, as if separated from them and from the world itself by some sort of artificial barrier, as if the world were a couch covered by a plastic shield and one could never quite get to sit directly on the cushions—feeling an allover sense of "the time is out of joint" and so am I. Sociologists of the day often labeled this feeling anomie or normlessness. Their diagnosis was that commonly accepted social norms and forms had fallen away or been wrenched apart in the 1960s for revolutionary and evolutionary reasons. Yet as a young person, Connolly felt the confusion acutely, personally, as he wandered in a "mist of strawberry scented, New Age vagueness." By that spring, battling more intense depression, he began to yearn for something he could unabashedly believe in, something possibly involving Jesus. He had been primed by his Catholic surroundings growing up, and when sometimes Christ crossed his mind, or a line evoked him in a song, Ray felt "glimpses . . . like refreshing breezes." He wanted to be born again yet he wasn't sure what that meant and had no idea, practically speaking, of how to go about it.

After the breakup of a three-year romance, he dropped out of college, hitchhiked across the country, and ended up in Santa Barbara. There—feeling a series of "intimations" at the beach one morning and begging for a sign from the universe—he went to a political event, during which a crowd of disruptive Jesus freaks wearing floor-length robes paraded through, their solemnity and out-of-this-world quality suggesting to him somehow that Charles Manson had sent them. (The event took place around the time of the Manson trial, a media happening almost no one could ignore.) Still, despite the whiff of danger, despite his repulsion toward cultishness, he was also attracted to these berobed characters. He went over to chat with them at the back of the event, where they were acting in a more approachable manner and eating sandwiches. One of the group members, after a bit of conversation, asked Ray whether he would like to recite the Sinner's prayer and Ray said, yes, he would. Invited to know Jesus, he kneeled, recited the words he was told, and "When I opened my eyes again, it seemed to me that someone had taken the polyethylene wrapper off the world."

Ironically, the group that he joined, which many others had and would soon join, was itself a coercively designed sect that thrived, as the years went by, on using children for sexual enjoyment under the guise of what its leader, David Berg, otherwise known as Mo, called the Law of Love. (This was a cult into which many SGAs would be born and raised. Among them are some well-known individuals, such as River Phoenix and his siblings, and Rose McGowan.) This law stipulated that anything was permissible if carried out in the name of love. The group's doctrine was part apocalypticism, part social critique, part so-called Christianity, and stamped overall by the peregrinations of Berg, whose three thousand "Mo Letters" elaborated on these topics and constituted the only literature adherents were permitted to read. Gradually and then suddenly during the 1970s, the Mo Letters steered toward equating sexuality with love, and love with sexuality, condoned in all expressions (if the behavior was not evidently violent) and among children as young as babies. Connolly was unaware of this, as the Law of Love had not yet been written in 1970, when he knelt in the back of the Santa Barbara stadium. Connolly's story, as captured in his memoir, details how long he was unaware of the abuse once it started, and how he made sure to keep himself unaware, so that, when the evidence finally became too difficult to ignore, and he had a large family of his own, he was so deeply wedded to the organization that he felt he could only acquiesce, at least for a few more years or decades until finally he was able to leave.

But that afternoon in Santa Barbara when Ray recited the Sinner's prayer and was saved, he didn't know the identity of the group. What was this group? He wasn't aware if they were "selling something" (as it turned out, they were); it just seemed to him that they were intent on his salvation, and that he was getting a lot more eye contact than usual. As it started to dawn on him that this was some sort of organized group, "something rather specific," as he put it in his memoir, a small "uh-oh" began "to arise in my spirit."[24] Mysteriously, it proved difficult for him to pull out of this not-yet-cemented commitment to a group whose name he did not know, even on the first day before he had even joined. This tells us something about how very quickly we can form binding narratives ("I was saved . . . so this group, where it happened, must be valuable"), and how they do catch us up, almost instantaneously. It thus demonstrates the point Lifton was making (unknown to Ray or many others at the time) about how thinking and feeling are the same.

Around this time the POW brainwashing expert Margaret Singer entered the field of cult research and rescue. She had this to say about groups such as the one Connolly was in the process of joining: "I have found, as have others, a striking resemblance between the methods of recruitment and control used by the cults and that used on some of the [Korean] prisoners of war, including the clergy. More particularly I have found that the recruitment and indoctrination methods employed"—by such groups—"are tremendously sophisticated. The recruiters engage in systematic manipulation of the social influences surrounding the potential recruit to the extent that the recruit, in fact, *loses the capacity to exercise his own free will and judgment.*"[25] To Singer, recruitment (such as what Ray Connolly experienced) meant that the recruit's rational capabilities had been dismantled, his free will rendered null. Singer's position proved controversial. Legally, her position had no teeth and would never stand up in any courtroom, though she would testify in dozens of them. Aside from the doubtful legal dimension was the personal: Not all former cult members, even those deeply damaged by the experience of high-demand abusive cults, would agree that they had lost their capacity to exercise free will on making what would assuredly appear later as a manifestly bad decision. It raises the question, to which we will return, of what abuse is, and why people end up in abusive conditions that they seem to choose (whether fully informed from the outset or not), and how—this is the delicate part—they may sometimes collaborate in their own oppression and downfall. Choosing is also feeling.

In 1983, Singer offered a definition of what makes a cult a cult. Her seven-point description still circulates widely in the literature of cultic studies. Several notable features must be displayed: (a) the organization must be life-encompassing; (b) the group must have a God-appointed leader who proclaims supernal, exceptional powers; (c) members must devote time, energy, and devotion to their leader and group; (d) members are expected to lose contact with or be separate from the outside world; (e) members are taught they are part of a special or elite group; (f) members experience emotional, physical, or social harm or a combination of these in the group; and (g) each member is expected to spend time daily with other group members.[26]

Still, even Singer and other cult-critical voices would eventually be forced to back away from making an absolute list of which groups were and were not cults. It was simply too subjective in the range of experiences different people might have and how they might interpret them (subjectively speaking, a cult for me might not be a cult for you),* and the boundary between "cult" and "not a cult," despite seemingly

---

* Another way to put it is that one man's cult is another's salvation, and even those assessments are subject to change. What may be a cult for one person is not necessarily a cult for everyone else, in part because they are exposed to different conditions—celebrities, for instance, who join Scientology are typically shielded from glimpsing the extreme abuse that others might suffer within its church—and in part because the claims of enlightened behavior are so murky.

A Small Uh-Oh Opened Up in My Soul

firm definitions, grows hazy on inspection. Throwing the word *cult* at an organization also could get you in a lot of legal hot water, as they would discover. When done with vigor and followed up with decisive action such as physically dragging family members out of groups they had joined, such allegations could get you called a cult yourself, as deprogrammers experienced. All this was to come.

Nonetheless, Margaret Singer's features (a) through (g) form decent "good enough" heuristics to identify something we would call a cult. Life-encompassing. Guided by a purportedly God-given leader. Devoted members losing touch with friends, family, and other resources. Elite status within the group. Rampant abuse unevenly distributed. The requirement to enter a community of others. Connolly did not yet know these features would guide his life for several decades.

....

From the first seconds of his involvement, whenever Ray Connolly hesitated, balancing on the brink of backing out, other members pulled him in. That afternoon in 1970, when he asked if he could go talk with his ex-girlfriend (who was still his best friend), if he might go call her and rejoin the group in another few days, the answer was no. The time was now, else his soul might be lost again. (They reminded him of the promise he had made to God earlier in the day.) A few hours later, having grabbed his belongings from the place he'd been staying, he showed up with his backpack to board the group's bus *still not knowing the name of the organization*. Once they pulled out onto the road, people were passing around a microphone and when it arrived in his hand it fell to him to tell his conversion story, to give some sort of encouragement to others, to testify. To this he responded by mumbling into the microphone that he had, prior to his amazing salvation experience, "thought Jesus was a character in a J. D. Salinger novel."[27] This meta–Holden Caulfield was not quite the testimony desired. He was met by puzzled stares at his literary reference and Josh, his liaison, quickly struck up a "I have decided to follow Jesus" group chorus to mask the awkwardness. Soon, Ray and other new recruits encountered "good cop" messages (welcoming and congratulating them) that alternated with "bad cop" warnings (dire concerns that they would be "crucifying the Son of God afresh" if they turned their backs on Him). Some did slink off, but Ray stayed.

He discovered that this organization was called the Children of God. Ex-bikers and hippies congregated. Mo, the leader—David Berg—claimed spiritual enlightenment as of 1968, dreamed of goddesses and aliens, and left empty sherry bottles around, though his personal alcoholism was never clear to most group members. Accounts indicate he was a compelling preacher, and his flock entered ecstatic throes when in his presence. He would frequently renew and refresh his teachings based on the words of Christ, with further messages received in deep contemplation, which amounted supposedly to a return to the true roots of Christianity. Not long after Ray joined the group, Mo announced the debut of a new technique to be used for recruiting, which he called flirty fishing. Nubile young women received orders to go out and lure men into proximity to the group, after which they would be set upon by more scriptural and group-dynamic tactics. These were the "wild early years," as Ray characterized them in retrospect, during which many people were personally introduced to Jesus through the leveraging of the Bible.

Ray almost immediately found himself immersed in an upside-down world where "it seemed like everything was permanently set on volume 10." Intensive teachings began, and although he tried to walk out on the first day of instruction—missing his girlfriend, Ginny, wondering what she would think of all this, and wanting someone with whom he could "share all this input"—he allowed other members to cajole him back in. He trained in "thought stopping" (though it was labeled single-minded devotion to Jesus). Thought stopping is a technique of diverting oneself with a repetitious prescribed phrase whenever doubts or forbidden thoughts pop up in one's mind. The repetition produced a soothing distraction, and sometimes, when done long or hard enough, an altered state of consciousness. The process of memorizing scripture could indeed serve to block dangerous thoughts, he found: Ray received the phrase, "Trust in the Lord with all thine heart, and lean not into thine own understanding" (Proverbs 3:5), as well as "Delight thyself also in the Lord, and He shall give thee the desires of thine heart" (Psalm 37:4). These did delight him, and assuage his doubts, so that he did not reflect (also he lacked the experience to reflect) on how the practices of the group in front of him might differ from Christian teachings. Deeper and deeper the organized entity drew him in, and he surrendered to it.

He stayed for twenty years, fathering seventeen children with two women. He followed the group's encouragement to embrace the Old Testament practice of welcoming a sister wife, though his first wife (they were assigned to each other in the early days when both had recently joined the group) was not quite on board with the addition of the second. However, by then, "Most of us had long since mastered the art of managing cognitive dissonance," he recalled.

During middle age, the early joys retreated, and the "dark hamster-wheel" feeling set in as he sank his efforts and time into working for the Lord, which translated as working for the advancement of the Children of God. He watched but did not quite track the emergence in himself of a "cult self." This was, in his experience, a kind of internal subletting to an alt-occupant who acts on autopilot so that the effective landlord—Ray—was no longer responding directly to the situations in which he found himself. Psychologists identify the cult self or pseudo self as a primary outgrowth of cultic involvement, and it is accompanied by a "secret self" hidden away from the overseeing function and from the diurnal management of identity. Clinician Cyndi Matthews studied fifteen ex-cult members and found that the formation of such a cult self—with its seeming takeover of day-to-day functioning—was nearly universal. "Most participants reported that they had two identities, one that was constructed in the cult and one secret self that was not known to the cult. Participants felt torn between their two identities." While coming out of the cult, one participant remembered, "I had to find and recognize an inner voice. At first I ignored it in the cult. I wasn't allowed to and I couldn't follow my gut. I am trying to learn to recognize it now. I feel it in my gut."[28] In a way, it was like funneling one's activities into the avatar in a video game, but letting the avatar take over. Since the self was in effect automating its own functioning, or as Lifton might have put it, numbing to the point of creating a nonfeeling self, the results were generally less than heroic. Connolly rose relatively high in the organization, not exactly to the inner circles but swiftly to middle management.

·········

The *pseudo self* evokes a concept the psychologist Stanley Milgram called the agentic shift, which he identified as operating in his famous studies at Yale's Interaction Laboratory in 1961–63.[29] In them, a volunteer enters a psychological experiment and draws lots with another participant (actually, a plant), so that other participant becomes the learner, and the volunteer becomes the teacher. Should the learner fail to deliver the correct answer to a set of word pairings, the teacher is given the task of electrically shocking the learner—always a genial middle-aged man with a paunch who obligingly goes into a back room and, as the teacher watches, has electrodes attached to his bare arm after he rolls up a shirtsleeve. As the shocks the teacher gives escalate, the teacher hears banging and cries of distress from the other room, the learner begging to be let out in no uncertain terms. If the teacher questions the procedure, the attending scientist says, "Please continue, teacher," or a variant of four other polite orders, including "The experiment requires that you continue" and "You have no choice but to continue." Although

A Small Uh-Oh Opened Up in My Soul

most professional psychologists estimated that a negligible percentage of participants would continue delivering shocks to someone displaying such distress, in fact two-thirds continued after objections were raised, and most broke off only after the learner ceased responding at all. Some never ceased following orders given by the attending scientist. Milgram made a film, *Obedience*, in 1962, that etched the dramaturgy of the experiments in the minds of many generations of college students and others. (Although it has never been available on YouTube or other easy-to-access sources except in small snatches, it is worth watching all the way through.)

Perhaps, today, most people feel they have watched the Milgram experiments even if they haven't, so thoroughly have they entered psychological folklore. In recovery, after he left the cult, Ray Connolly watched a clip of the experiments, which struck him strongly and "certainly call[ed] into question just how independent-minded most people really are."[30]

....

Because the Milgram experiments are so arresting, they seem to explain themselves, or at least seem not to require an immediate theoretical explanation aside from "a shocking side of human nature is revealed." People who discuss the experiments do not often mention Milgram's own analysis, in his 1974 book *Obedience to Authority*, of what he believed happened when he placed people at the far end of a shock machine and asked them to issue disabling electric shocks up to 450 volts. Milgram felt this situation caused an offloading of their own agency and that it was part of the human capacity to flick a switch, so to speak, to allow themselves to carry out orders they found noxious or would not otherwise ordinarily have taken the trouble to carry out. Ordinary Germans had done as much during the Holocaust. Often derided as the least satisfying part of Milgram's experiments, the theory of the agentic shift postulated the lightning-quick construction of an automated self, one that is numb to the emotional situation while able to carry out the dictated task. Watching this automated self appear before one's eyes, watching as the participant handed off the decision-making function to that "agent," is the key (in my view) to the uncomfortableness of the study. For it was uncomfortable. Much as it brought Milgram fame, it also brought him inchoate suspicion in the highest circles of the academic world. Indeed, he did not win tenure at Yale, despite his renown, ending up in The City College of New York to continue his creative play-making eschatology in the name of experiment. Although the study continues to be used for all sorts of purposes, in fact it is little understood. Its discomfiting nature is little grasped. Why *did* it destabilize assumptions, beyond the fact it revealed that some people are jerks?

The reason is that the agentic shift is not a simple thing that happens to those other people over there. For years I have taught Milgram's film masterpiece in my classes. Often there is laughter from the audience as the shocks escalate and as the camera pans slowly across the generator, the shock levels rising from mild to medium to severe, followed simply by XXX. (This was in fact a fake machine labelled "Shock Generator Type ZLB," said to be built by Dyson Instrument Company of Waltham, Massachusetts, but really made by a shop in nearby Bridgewater, Connecticut.) Why do they (we) laugh? For a stretch of years, there was always a good deal of chuckling, although in recent times it has subsided, I've observed. Milgram himself noted this phenomenon in his graduate students and research assistants, who sat behind a one-way glass window observing the proceedings and guffawing. In the film, sometimes those delivering shocks laugh, too. It is uneasy laughter—surely there was something funny, at first, about the escalating commands the participant is subject to, the being caught in a nightmare, the nice man going "Ooof!" when he was shocked. To the "teacher" in the experiment, there was sometimes something funny, at first, about the "learner" crying, "Get me out of here, I can't take any more," and thumping the walls, if only because it was so surreal to find themself on an ordinary afternoon in New Haven apparently causing such pain in another human being in a room down the hall. And from the point of view of the observer, whether the assistant behind the one-way mirror or the viewer in front of the film screen decades later, there is something funny, awkward, horrifying about watching a person carry out commands he or she mostly does not want to carry out. You cannot quite believe it, so you (some portion of the audience) will often laugh.

Here is the hidden-in-plain-sight core of the experiment, though. In most participants, it rather economically and beautifully fused three of Lifton's forms of psychic numbing—#3 (brutalization), #7 (ordinary numbing), and #8 (numbing of ideas)—even as we observe, mesmerized, unaware it is happening, looking at something else. There *is* someone really being tortured, and we are watching it, but it is not the person we thought it was. Over the years, the film has entertained audiences by means of a bait and switch—I realized, after countless viewings, that I was watching someone in agony in front of my eyes, but it was not the man pretending to have a heart attack in the back room over and over, and it was not the theoretical-at-the-moment Holocaust victims implied by the study. It was the purported torturer, the teacher, the man in shirt sleeves sitting in front of the camera, mildly hunched, flinching— the man following orders. He *thinks* he is delivering shocks, but he is experiencing them. At the end of the experiment, when it is revealed that he himself was the subject of study, not a helper, that he turned out to embody "ordinary evil," like an Adolf Eichmann managing the Holocaust, it is a palpable shock to his system. The subject is stripped bare in all his limitations in that moment. "I observed a mature and initially poised businessman enter the laboratory smiling and confident," recalled Milgram. "Within 20 minutes he was reduced to a twitching, stuttering wreck, rapidly approaching a point of nervous collapse."[31] We say, just as Milgram insisted, the participant should have been ready for this, he signed up for this. He had his moment and failed. Like the character J. Alfred Prufrock, the undynamic antihero in T. S. Eliot's epic poem, who, in his own love song, worries "Do I dare disturb the universe?" and who perseverates about the "bald spot in the middle of my hair"—but worse—Milgram's experimental subject could not seize the moment and instead simply accepted it. He saw the eternal footman hold his coat and snicker. Who was Milgram to have summoned New Havenites to this moment? Who was he to judge? Who are we? All the discomfort of the experiment comes from this displacement, this dissociation, in which we all participate, from Milgram on down the line. Refusing to see, we cannot see it correctly. We cannot identify a man being tortured in front of our eyes and our own eagerness to collaborate.

Cults are like this: They are judgment machines for onlookers. They are congratulatory devices for not getting your hands dirty. Among many things, it is quite humiliating to come out of one, because this means foregoing all of one's investments. These added up to so much, a whole life of sunk costs in some cases. You had already put in so much, you could only recoup by doubling down. Otherwise, you would have to admit your judgment failed to function properly. It would mean, I was not only a cad, but I was also "had." Anyone associated with this downfall would also be tarnished.

7

I Accommodated My Thoughts to Theirs

During the 1930s, the German Jewish sociologist Norbert Elias completed a scholarly study of, among other topics, nose blowing through the ages. He looked at how German and French people developed standards around what to do on the inevitable occasions when the need arose to clear one's nasal cavities. One etiquette manual from the fifteenth century, *Ein spruch der ze tische kêrt*, warned, "It is unseemly to blow your nose into the tablecloth," while a French manual from a bit later specified, "Do not blow your nose with the same hand that you use to hold the meat."[1] As time went by, Elias noted, less and less was spelled out in these manuals. More was assumed. Advice that adults once had to be told was now directed only at children—for it was taken for granted, by the eighteenth century or so, that no grown person (aside from a peasant) would blow snot into the palm of the hand and "examine it."

The threshold of what Western Europeans found disgusting was changing. Elias noticed that whatever rules there were in the medieval period existed only out of consideration for others. (Do not hold the meat with the hand you have just nose-blown into.) It was not simply that handkerchiefs became more widespread and less ornate. Beyond the technology change was a shift of consciousness. Gradually, rules became internal—even if you were alone, you should not blow onto the ground or relieve yourself in the corners of your lodgings, as used to be done. By the modern twentieth century even a person's inner thoughts were deeply suffused with these guidelines, and "The distasteful feeling [is] frequently aroused today *by the mere thought* of soiling the fingers in this way," Elias commented in 1939.[2]

Personally, I could relate to Elias, an author who came highly recommended by my advisor in graduate school. Academic training meant going through a somewhat similar process in altering human functions and setting new thresholds of disgust or shame, it seemed to me. Maybe a first-year graduate student came with a big, crude question such as: *How are human beings shaped by culture?* Part of the training was to internalize that question and to be taught a minute etiquette of how to ask it. Within a semester or two, a student learned to ask a new question: *How did the Durkheimian school ask that question and how was it modified by the Boasians in the twentieth century, and later by French theorists?* And on and on, so that after a while you might forget what the original question was. You might even begin to question the question itself: *Was culture even a thing that existed?* A student also learned never to say (as I once overheard): *I think that idea comes from one of those H philosophers, was it Heidegger or Hegel or Husserl?* You had to be a bit more sophisticated about how you put things (even if we all struggle with distinguishing the H philosophers). After a while, I came to think that graduate school was about absorbing the training, getting the benefits, but somehow keeping your original big question alive.

For his part, Elias took his observations about nose blowing, how and where to scratch oneself, and the exciting birth of pajamas to build up his own theory of how human beings come to consider themselves civilized, and how this is a changing standard that also deeply changes people. Most pressingly, things and processes we would describe as training for normal behavior (how to hold a fork, how to burp politely, how to wipe your hands at the table, to urinate, to spit, to have sex, and to defecate) become embedded profoundly in our bodies and minds. So profoundly, in fact, that they arouse an automatic distaste, disgust, or revulsion at the visceral level if violated.

We'll leave Elias and his strange histories here for the moment—though his theories of sociogenesis and psychogenesis will prove useful later in our story—but merely pause to make the point of how deeply human reactions, even instinctive behaviors such as sneezes or breathing in and out, are capable of being shaped under pressure. This happens in all childhoods, and it can be mimicked in later life. (This is not the same as brainwashing, but it is—shall we say—the infrastructure on which brainwashing is constructed.) We are all shaped, all the time, by our circumstances, in ways we hardly recognize until or unless we step out of the process—say, by traveling, by a shocking event, or by an interruption of another kind. This explains, to go back to Lifton's 1973 seminar on Cape Cod, how "normal or ordinary numbing" is built into life. The little and big collisions, shocks, susurrations cause us to adapt, sometimes creatively and sometimes pathologically. To enter a cult—or, as in Patricia Hearst's case, to be kidnapped into one—entails an intensive socio- and psychogenesis. Because the processes are so ordinary, the transformation is often unremarked and even unbelievable.

The story of Patricia Hearst's kidnapping in 1974 shows how quickly the shaping process can happen. The story of her trial two years later—the Great Brainwashing Defense of 1976—shows how hard it is for modern audiences to believe in its reality.

....

Patricia Campbell Hearst's narrative has been told and told again. A pair of San Francisco beat reporters recounted it in a mass market paperback released in 1975 before the verdict in her case was even announced (*Patty/Tania* by Jerry Belcher and Don West), a star journalist told it again in 1976 (*Anyone's Daughter* by Shana Alexander), many professors took their turn (among them the Americanist William Graebner, the legal expert Janice Schuetz, the historian Nancy Isenberg, and the "Famous Trials" scholar who tends to a website featuring notable trials going back to Socrates). Several pornographers produced their own versions, and recently the well-known legal writer Jeffrey Toobin offered an authoritative retelling in a 2016 bestseller, *American Heiress*.[3] Aside from Hearst herself, who published her own account, *Every Secret Thing*, most of the people who told and continue to tell her story cannot stop from seeing it as strange or even titillating. It was "the most bizarre kidnap story of the century," according to the 1975 book. In the current century, the story continues to attract similar descriptions, as in the 2016 contribution, which is subtitled, *The Wild Saga of the Kidnapping, Crimes and Trial of Patty Hearst*. Recent podcast episodes feature grab lines such as "One Crazy Summer" (from *Just the Gist* podcast). A naive person might not know from these titular takes that Hearst was the target of her kidnapping rather than its groovy mastermind.

In 2018, in the wake of the #MeToo movement and spurred more immediately by a new film slated to start production, Hearst objected to these portrayals. She wrote in a statement that the filmmakers romanticized her rape, abduction, and torture. She called out the Toobin book and the film being made from it as especially exploitative.[4] Such accounts played up the "rollicking adventure" angle of her story, yet they tended to conclude by turning suddenly stern and invoking with high dudgeon the demand that she pay for her sins and be "held accountable," as Toobin urged not long ago to Renee Montagne on NPR. Hearst reminded audiences that as a nineteen-year-old she was "destroyed inside and outside" by the trauma of her brutal abduction, and that as a sixty-four-year-old it continued to be painful to encounter sources that presented these experiences as somehow fun. On Twitter in 2018, her daughter, Lydia, called Toobin's projects "disgusting exploitation of a rape victim."[5] Although the tweet subsequently disappeared, so too did the film project, which Fox 2000 cancelled around this time. (All this occurred before the word *Toobin* became a verb following the author's flashing incident during a quarantine-era Zoom call.)

The perennial stress on the "strange" nature of the Patricia Hearst case—which, as I will argue was not strange at all, though it was full of horrors—is itself worth considering. It points to a catch-22 at the heart of mind control. Even today, looking back, this displaced strangeness is hard to glimpse. Her trauma remains largely invisible, both legally and personally, even though the (arguably) most powerful legal team in history attempted to establish it. From that point of view, it is we who are strange, not her.

....

In 1973, members of a revolutionary underground group in the Bay Area of California saw a newspaper announcement that nineteen-year-old Patricia Hearst, granddaughter of William Randolph Hearst, was shortly to be married. A member of the group wrote down on a notepad "UC Berkeley art history, junior" and "that daughter of Hearst"—jottings later admitted to trial.[6] (In fact, she was a sophomore not a junior and was the granddaughter not the daughter of the most famous Hearst, William Randolph, the one who founded the media empire.) The nuptials notice appeared fortuitous to the group, who called themselves the Symbionese Liberation Army (SLA), and who in the FBI's words "wanted nothing less than to incite a guerrilla war against the U.S. government and destroy what they called the 'capitalist state.'"[7] Its members had been brainstorming about targeting a person connected to a legendary capitalist family. Such a political action would be a symbolic protest against the economic and racial divide in

America—would demonstrate in a big way their commitments against "pig fascists." Hearst fit the bill and happened to live conveniently nearby in Berkeley (unlike her three sisters, say, or other young scions of privilege), so they pursued what they called a righteous arrest of the sophomore heiress.[8]

On a February night in 1974 three revolutionaries knocked at her door, beat her fiancé with a wine bottle, and pushed her, clad in a bathrobe, into the trunk of a stolen blue 1963 Chevrolet. Firing a machine gun, they sprayed the street as they sped off followed by another two SLA vehicles. After this, wearing a blindfold, Hearst lived for fifty-nine days in a closet, never seeing the light. The SLA group holding her was made up of eight, mostly upper-middle class, mainly white, almost all female former students. Their leader was a Black man named Donald DeFreeze who had recently escaped from

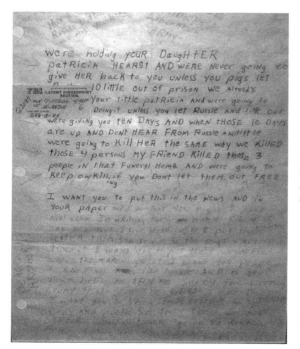

Ransom note from the Symbionese Liberation Army, Western Division
COURTESY: FBI.

the state prison in Soledad, California. DeFreeze preferred to be addressed as Field Marshall General Cinque, or Cinque, pronounced "sin-kay," for short. Taking turns, SLA members joined Hearst in the closet under a rigged-up light and read out loud their Code of War and other tracts, mainly by Chairman Mao and Karl Marx, as she sat in the dark listening.

In fact, there were two closets. For the first week or two, Hearst inhabited one in an apartment in Daly City at 37 Northridge Drive, and later—after being pushed into a trash can that was then deposited in the trunk of the SLA's car—she dwelled in another closet on 1827 Golden Gate Avenue, Apt. 6 in San Francisco. There, the group's head, Cinque, forced Hearst to make the first of a series of cassette tape recordings, which the group disseminated to the media. During Hearst's trial a few years later, the entire jury would take a field trip and examine both closets. On that day, February 16, 1976, the lead expert witness for the defense Louis Jolyon West would note in his papers, "Court Visit to Closets."[9] The Manson murders were only half a decade removed from these events, and they functioned as a sort of discordant symphonic score for the Hearst affair, as it would soon be called, in the sense that her experience would be interpreted as act two of "Hippies Gone Wrong" and Hearst herself would soon be seen by most of the general public as one of those crazy counterculturalists.

The kidnappers did not demand a traditional ransom but instead stipulated that all four million Californians receiving welfare should be given $70 in groceries four times at intervals. Governor Ronald Reagan predicted people would not accept this food since it was extorted as part of a kidnapping, but he was proven wrong when people swarmed the grocery trucks that Hearst's father supplied in desperation, hoping to free his daughter. A television clip showed an Oakland resident sympathetically telling a reporter, "I hate to take advantage of what could happen to the young lady. But my children need food, just like anybody else's kids."[10]

Dr. West's slides of the chronology of Hearst's ordeal, including the two rapes, prepared for the trial and later the book he planned to publish. UCLA LIBRARY SPECIAL COLLECTIONS, A1713 CHARLES E. YOUNG RESEARCH LIBRARY, UNIVERSITY OF CALIFORNIA, LOS ANGELES.

After fifty-nine days of abuse—during the first confinement she was bound, gagged, and required to request to go to the bathroom under escort, while during the second she was almost constantly blindfolded, threatened with death due to her wealthy family, and occasionally permitted exposure to light in order to read political tracts—she displayed disorientation. "*They got nicer everyday they didn't kill me*," she commented (italics added) in a 2003 interview, describing what some would inaccurately call Stockholm syndrome but what she would call a strategy to survive. During the period of stay in the second closet, the SLA told her it would be "uncomradely" to deny sexual relations with two of the group's male members. Due to terror, Hearst had been unable to eat or defecate for the first ten days after abduction. At this point, around forty days into captivity, she was unwashed and bruised. They bathed her in anticipation of William Wolfe (named Cujo) coming in to rape her in the closet, which he did. Three days later, the group's leader did the same.

In springtime, the revolutionaries assembled to ask her whether she wished to join them or go free. These were her torturers but

I Accommodated My Thoughts to Theirs

also her constant companions over the past months, and the request induced a fraught moment. They paused for her to choose; she watched them waiting for her answer. There was no real choice, though. If she didn't join them, she knew they would otherwise kill her, for they liked to brag about shooting the Oakland public school superintendent execution-style in a parking lot not long before, and they had threatened to shoot her, too. They referenced their supply of cyanide-tipped bullets and made a show of loading and reloading their weapons. Finally, they made it clear to her that they would take her rejection of them as a personal as well as political slap in the face, for the personal was political, and the political personal. She then agreed to join the cause, resulting in the ceremonious final removal of her blindfold and much rejoicing. She was one of them now! Hearst's joy had to appear—and in a sense, *had to be*—as genuine as that of the rest of the group in order not to trigger suspicion. Next came a forced ongoing sexual relationship with Wolfe, forced participation in a bank heist during which she carried an M1 carbine (and was captured on security video doing so), as well as many other forced involvements in the revolutionary cause.

After the robbery, images of a trench-coated Hearst holding the automatic weapon became popular posters bedecking college dorm rooms, especially around UC Berkeley. In the photos, some taken from security footage, she looked extremely thin and possibly glamorous. (Her captivity caused her to lose weight, and she was thin to begin with.) Leftists embraced her as a born-again revolutionary. Older and mainstream Americans, after the pictures circulated of her apparently committing a crime, held her in deep suspicion, cementing a public attitude of distrust that was remarkably persistent over decades.

The SLA was by now on the run, and they decamped with a large amount of ordnance from the Bay Area to a rented house in South Central Los Angeles. As an underground group of young white men and (mostly) women following a Black revolutionary, their reception among longer-term residents ranged from protection to resentment, and it was eventually a local grandmother, an exemplar of the latter view, who tipped off the police. Not long afterward, an early SWAT team arrived on the scene. The Los Angeles Police Department had recently devised these teams as a tactical response to the rebellions of the mid and late '60s, especially in Watts, and in response to armed conflicts, too, with the United Farm Workers in Delano, California, outside of Los Angeles, around this time. SWAT stands for "Special Weapons and Tactics," although its inventor, Daryl Gates, who would run the operation against the SLA revolutionaries that day, admitted it originally stood for "Special Weapons Attack Team." (He changed the moniker to mellow out the overly aggressive sound of the word *attack*.)[11] Gates was gaining a name for himself in these years as a "jet-setting . . . law enforcement guru" by pushing a policy of order maintenance that was explicitly based on counterinsurgency tactics tried in Vietnam and transferred to Los Angeles's streets—first with the Black Panther shootout of December 1969, when teargas was deployed for the first time in domestic civilian settings despite being banned by the Geneva conventions. An air of experimentation surrounded SWAT, as the sociologist Stuart Schrader shows.[12] Now SWAT took part in something bigger.

As the heavily armed SLA group refused to surrender, on May 17, 1974, a shootout ensued—estimated (even today) to be the largest in California history—when between approximately 4:00 and 7:00 p.m. some six thousand rounds of ammunition were exchanged (around five thousand by the SWAT teams, FBI, and police; and up to a thousand by the heavily armed SLA, according to estimates.)[13] Special incendiaries—likely a Flite-Rite tear gas canister law enforcement threw through a broken window—lit up the house and the bodies of six of the group. They burned in real time on television as "thousands of spectators" watched the fire from behind police lines, surging against barricades to get closer but falling back when buffeted by tear gas.* The immolation was another first: It marked "the TV networks' inaugural use of 'minicam' (portable videotape) technology to broadcast news live across the whole country."[14] By this time, the FBI was classing Hearst as a fugitive not a kidnap victim. Authorities assumed she was among the dead.

The public airing of the raid reinforced the growing impression among audiences that Hearst was a spoiled heiress having self-indulgent fun. It thus marked the birth of the "spree" narrative. The following year, in 1975, ABC debuted the surprise hit television show *S.W.A.T.* Like millions of others, this show shaped my childish impression of what daring police raids were like. Vans screeching up and disgorging personnel clad in unmarked uniforms and bulletproof vests. Arduous repelling from ropes down urban facades. Raised eyebrows in alleyways. In retrospect, the show's tactical vehicles—Metro delivery vans painted dark blue—look strikingly unmilitarized, as if the tactical team had just deputized the local milkman.

Live TV coverage of early SWAT action was both more and less dramatic than the Hollywood show. As the embers of the firebombing cooled, a Schrödinger's Cat situation reigned, in the sense that Hearst was both dead and alive. In the press photographs, one can see forensic experts scanning the charred field where the house had stood as they examined each of the corpses (including the skeleton of a cat unsuccessfully shielded from the fire by the remains of SLA member Camilla Hall). Cinque was counted among the dead, but they determined that the heiress was not.

In fact, Hearst had gone to run errands with two married members of the group, aptly described by a newspaper columnist as "the always quarreling Harrises."[15] That mission went awry, and itself

---

* At 6:40 two canisters of riot gas were sent in and the house caught on fire as a neighbor, Christine Johnson, stumbled out from her house and was taken to safety. "Live television cameras were on her when the SWAT officer put his boot in the middle of her back to keep her down" (Belcher and West, *Patty/Tania*, 284–86). She went to the hospital later.

ended up in a shootout, but a nonfatal one. The three had left the South Central hideout to pick up camping items at a sporting goods store in a local shopping mall on South Crenshaw Boulevard, in Ingleside, with William Taylor ("Bill") Harris driving a red-and-white Volkswagen van and his wife, Emily, and Hearst as passengers. Bill was a former chess champion from a middle-class family in Bloomington, Indiana, who served as a Marine in Vietnam and came back "so embittered he would not talk about it [the war]."[16] Emily also came from Indiana, where she had been an English literature major and Chi Omega sorority sister at the University of Indiana. Moving to the California Bay Area in 1972 to become teachers, both were radicalized, joined Cinque's group, and continued their rocky relationship within it. By the time fate placed them with Hearst on this mundane errand amid imminent apocalypse, the Harrises had been with the group for almost three years. (Bill had been instrumental in kidnapping Hearst, and to this day he semi-brags about throwing her in the trunk of a car, as in a recent interview on CNN.)[17] The day before the coming firestorm, May 16, they set forth in the VW van heavily armed; it was perhaps excessive just to go buy camping gear (for the SLA planned to go hide in the mountains), but they were, in their minds and in reality, under siege. On orders, Hearst stayed in the van as lookout.

Entering Mel's Sporting Goods Store, the Harrises selected $31.50 worth of heavy-duty outdoor gear, for which Emily paid in cash. Realizing they had forgotten something, Bill elected, instead of paying, to pocket a pair of socks—or was it a canvas ammo pouch that looked like socks, as Harris later maintained, attempting perhaps to sound more radical?—and on being challenged for shoplifting while leaving, he grabbed for his .38 pistol (in his waistband) while the store clerk lunged at him, managing to wrap handcuffs around one of his wrists while Harris wriggled free. (This was evidently a time when shoplifters were pursued much more vigorously than today.) Seeing the struggle, Hearst, stationed in the van, and having been trained

I Accommodated My Thoughts to Theirs

repeatedly for such emergencies, picked up and began to fire her automatic carbine rifle—the rounds of which, thirty-three shots, miraculously hit only the storefront—and as the Harrises tumbled into the van, Hearst, at the wheel, pulled away. During their escape, pursued by the intrepid store clerk (!), who had also called the police, they abandoned the now "hot" van and commandeered a Pontiac, forcing out the owners. When that car stalled, the three took another car, and eventually, a third.

This last was a light blue Chevy station wagon, occasioning a heist that included the physical person of its owner, a mellow eighteen-year-old named Thomas Matthews, who had been trying to sell it when the revolutionaries came along. (Matthews would later report that the Harrises introduced themselves with the sentences "We're from the SLA!" and "This is Tania," using Hearst's revolutionary name. She told him, yes, she was Patty Hearst, and that yes, she had joined the SLA out of her free will. Eventually they went to a drive-in movie.) Once they found yet another car to steal, they left Matthews in his, telling him to stay there for a while. Meanwhile, the abandoned VW van yielded an unpaid three-day-old parking ticket, which within around sixteen hours led police to an earlier SLA hideout and, within a few more hours, with the help of a tip-off to the FBI, to the demise of the other six members of their army.

Later it would be noted that, at the time of the errant shopping trip and robbery, Hearst did not take the opportunity to run away, even when she was left alone for a time in the group's van with the keys in the ignition. Instead of driving off, or otherwise fleeing, she defended her jailers and shot up the front of Mel's store. She did not seem to have been forced to stay, by that point. "Why did I do it?" Patricia Hearst said in an interview with Larry King, discussing the crimes she committed. "By the time they had finished with me I was, in fact, a soldier in the Symbionese Liberation Army."[18] It was a true transformation.

Her story recalls an Old Testament chronicle in which, after defeating a great enemy, King David comes out to meet "the mighty men, helpers of the war" and basically asks these men if he can trust them. The would-be recruits must prove themselves loyal, and one of them goes into a trancelike state to access such a pledge. "Then the spirit came upon Amasai, who was chief of the captains, and he said, Thine are we, David, and on thy side, thou son of Jesse: peace, peace be unto thee, and peace be to thine helpers; for thy God helpeth thee. Then David received them, and made them captains of the band."[19] To survive, Patricia Hearst had to say, in effect, "Thine am I." In fact, she did say something close to this to Cinque and the SLA. Frequently she had to convince them that she was not brainwashed but was a true believer. "You're not brainwashed, are you?," Cinque periodically asked her in response to media speculation that this was the case. In this he shared a common misconception about brainwashing, that it was a type of fakery. For the most part, her kidnappers were convinced enough. But to make her devotion clearer (both to herself and to them), she had to burn her bridges with polite society. She had to become a real SLA soldier.

The incineration of the SLA house in South Central accomplished this, even as it killed most of those she had been at pains to convince. The firestorm also confirmed to Hearst what her kidnappers had been telling her, that they were only the Western arm of a vast revolutionary organization with members spread in cells across the United States, one demanding respect if only because the government poured so much effort into annihilating them. Attorney General William Saxbe declared her no longer a crime victim but a criminal herself—a "common criminal" was how he described her, incidentally using a term derived from *commoner* to indicate loss of royalty status.[20] It was logical then for Hearst to go on the lam. For a year and a half, she was ferried about by sympathetic figures in an informal revolutionary underground. During that time she was hiding out; reading revolutionary books; participating in another heist; weathering beatings by her original kidnapper,

Bill Harris, who in her estimate gave her four black eyes over the ensuing weeks; and drafting a confessional autobiography about her bourgeois upbringing—all before police finally discovered her living in an apartment in the Outer Mission district of San Francisco. Police captured her on September 18, 1975, and booked her on twenty-two counts for the 1974 bank robbery. So thoroughly had she absorbed her pseudo self that she gave her occupation on the intake form in jail as "urban guerilla" and offered a Black power salute during intake.

The repetition of the word *forced* to describe each of Hearst's criminal activities struck many onlookers as improbably soft on Hearst: To many she seemed, like other youth in the 1970s, to adopt the ways of the hippies and the posturing left, and from a surface point of view, if one were to ignore her kidnapping and torture, this was exactly what she did.

·········

World-renowned experts assembled to testify in the Patricia Hearst case. She was one of the three surviving members of the bank-robbery crew (recall that most of the group died in the firebombing-shootout with the LAPD, including Cinque, their leader), but she was the only one charged.

As for the trial itself, four of the country's most eminent experts in brainwashing, three of whom cut their teeth in the Korean brainwashing crisis, joined her defense team. Patricia Hearst's trial featured over two hundred hours of testimony from these psychological experts and thousands of pages of their evaluations. The experts collectively made the case that Hearst had been brainwashed. As part of this, they described how she was coerced, was suffering from traumatic neurosis, had dissociated for a long spell of time—in short, she was operating under the SLA's mind control, and thus was not guilty of the bank robbery for which she was being tried.

All the defense experts agreed: The resonances of Patricia Hearst

Patty Hearst's dream defense legal team of psychiatrists in San Francisco, 1976. From left to right: Dr. Lifton, attorney F. Lee Bailey, Dr. Orne, Dr. Singer, and Dr. West. GETTY IMAGES. LAWRENCE SCHILLER/CONTRIBUTOR.

with the brainwashed POWs and with the broken Air Force survival trainees was *striking*. In strategic discussions before the trial, they said the evocation of what Korean War veterans (and Vietnam War veterans) had endured was compelling to them, and would undoubtedly be so to a judge and jury. If hardened soldiers had not been able to resist coercive persuasion, surely a nineteen-year-old college student could not be expected to emerge unscathed. Specifically, Dr. Louis Jolyon West, the former CIA MK-ULTRA experimenter, and current head of UCLA's Neuropsychiatric Institute, felt called to participate. He could not ignore the parallels. They already had a study of violence running at the Neuropsychiatric Institute (NPI) that accounted for Hearst as a "supervictim" of violence.[21]

West pulled in Robert J. Lifton (the former Air Force expert on Chinese thought reform), Margaret Singer (his erstwhile partner in studying the Korean POWs), and Martin Orne (a prominent researcher on hypnosis). The result was perhaps the deepest "field" of brainwashing knowledge ever assembled, a kind of psychiatric Dream Team. Photographs of their meetings at the Courtyard Union Square Hotel suggest ample amounts of bonhomie circulating in the room, where the four experts strategized with F. Lee Bailey, the lead defense attorney. They were lower in elevation but close in distance from the Fairmont Hotel, where Hearst's parents were staying to prepare for the trial.

The lightbulb moment for West came one day when he turned on the radio and heard the "Patty/Tania Tapes"—a series of recordings Hearst was forced to make while she was held captive in the closets. These sessions occurred long before Hearst was caught and put to trial. Already, while she was on the run, West imagined that he and his cohort would be well equipped to defend her. Thus, it behooves us to ask: What were these tapes exactly and why did they act as a kind of homing beacon for West?

The cassette tapes recorded in the closets where Hearst was held conveyed a transformation. They are a record, almost an archive, of change. In these recordings—a trail of first-person statements made, mailed, and broadcast as a sequential stream of updates on February 12, February 16, April 3, April 18, and June 6 that galvanized public attention as events unfolded—Hearst's case came alive in relationship to the POWs. The SLA demanded they be played over local radio stations. The tapes drew the experts to her, and, in a dramaturgical twist akin to Greek theater, sealed her fate. Via the recordings, ordinary listeners as well as officialdom could hear her transform, hear her proclaim that she was literally renamed as a revolutionary, hear her say that, of course, she wasn't brainwashed. They played an ongoing role in shaping opinions about Hearst beyond the public to the judge himself. The "apparent sincerity of her revolutionary messages" while in SLA hands, according to Judge William Orrick, who took over sentencing in the case after Judge Oliver Carter dropped out (actually, dropped dead) near the end of the trial, justified her long prison sentence should there be any doubt that the jury had erred in finding her guilty.[22] The recordings—for she did them "well" (she had to, she did them to be sure to survive)—cemented the likelihood her story would end up with the adjectives it has: bizarre, strange, mysterious.

A highlight reel assembled by Joan Didion—who at one time hoped to write a book about Hearst—captured the narrative arc:

> *Mom, Dad. I'm OK. I had a few scrapes and stuff, but they washed them up.... I just hope you'll do what they say, Dad.... If you can get the food thing organized before the nineteenth then that's OK.... Whatever you come up with is basically OK, it was never intended that you feed the whole state.... I am here because I am a member of a ruling-class family and I think you can begin to see the analogy.... People should stop acting like I'm dead, Mom should get out of her black dress, that doesn't help at all.... Mom, Dad... I don't believe you're doing all you can... Mom, Dad... I'm starting to think that no one is concerned about me anymore....* And then: *Greetings to the people. This is Tania.*[23]

Didion originally pursued writing about Hearst because she thought her experiences "had some meaning for me," and she imagined Patty Hearst as a girl growing up in California, sitting in her room listening to an album of the musical *Carousel*, like a younger version of Didion herself. But this—her ability to identify with Hearst's story and trial—"didn't turn out to be true."[24] What happened to Hearst was more complicated, more traumatic than that. The soundtrack is arguably less Rodgers and Hammerstein and more Dead Kennedys.

The recordings were a key component (in no small part because they were documentations) in thumbnailing parallels to the POWs' experiences. Contrast Hearst's words in her letter with a broadcast of an American prisoner by the name of Edward P. Dickenson some twenty years before. Dickenson's broadcast began similarly with the most average, letter-from-camp salutation, but one made strange by the fact that it was being projected into a huge global scrum: *"Dear Mom and Dad."* Locating himself in the POW camps, he described what had happened just after his Sunday, November 5, 1950, capture by Chinese troops who had a month earlier entered the war. *"I thought they were going to kill me, but instead a Chinese volunteer shook hands and gave me the last drink of water he had in his canteen. Then he gave me a cigarette."* Under US airstrikes, he said, the Chinese sheltered them against their own government's aggression, fed them pork and rice, and gave them tobacco. Once in the camps, they got toothbrushes and tooth powder, summer and winter clothes, and medical care. *"Six months later, I have been amazed at the treatment they have given to me. . . . We couldn't find better friends anywhere in the universe. I thought they were enemies to us, but I was very much wrong. Some of the American people are asleep to what is really going on in the world today."* (Italics added.) Dickenson decided he would defect to China and adopt a new identity there, but he changed his mind at the last minute, perhaps to his regret, for once he stepped out of the airplane onto American tarmac, he received a court martial, imprisonment, and a heavy sentence, with no excuses for the effects of brainwashing.

The comparison was explicit: As West observed under cross-examination in the trial, "I would compare them"—the tapes—"with the propaganda broadcasts that were made by the American Prisoners of War and the statements they signed and the petitions that were circulated all over the world. And some of the phrases are so reminiscent that it sounds like they were copied out of the same book." Perhaps they were, since SLA member Gelina (her given name was Angela Atwood), the author of these transcripts from which Hearst was made to read, was an enthusiastic student of Communist texts such as Mao's "Little Red Book." West added under cross-examination, "And those were books that I assure you did not enter into the formation of Patricia Hearst's personality up to the time of her kidnapping."[25] She was not a secret fan of Mao's writings, a sleeper cell waiting to be "activated," was his point.

The experts testified, too, that there were other commonalities with the POWs' treatment. These included sleep deprivation, removal of sensory stimuli, endless haranguing questions asked over and over, threats of execution, threats to kill her parents, a forcibly extracted confession, loss of bodily autonomy, and a coercive post-closet project to write a tell-all autobiography purporting to be Patty Hearst's true tale for the masses, a "confession" called the Tania Interview on which she worked with her kidnappers. Lifton commented on the cogent parallelism. In it, Hearst declared herself reborn as Tania, a name chosen to honor Che Guevara's lover and co-revolutionary, and with the help of her kidnapper "interviewers," she laid out how she transitioned from "Patty," a privileged granddaughter of a capitalist media empire to "Tania," a genuine urban guerilla advocating for the oppressed. Her kidnapping had, ironically, been a gift in facilitating this advocacy. As Lifton testified of the Tania Interview under cross-examination, "I consider it a classic document of the kind I have come across many times in regard to thought reform.... What this document represents, Mr. Bancroft, is—and this is very routine for thought reform practice—there is an effort and need on the part of the reformers to take the coercion out of the process and they collude on a document with the victim, the person put through the process, in which they seek a kernel of truth—and there are some factual details in this document about the closet and so on—and then build a, an apparently convincing story in which the coercion is minimal, because a basic aspect of the thought reform process is a reinterpretation of how one ostensibly came to that new truth in a natural way, rather than through the coercion which actually happened."[26] Lifton was probably thinking of Dr. Vincent's narrative, so painstakingly co-crafted with his Chinese interrogators. Coercion was sometimes, in the moment, hard to see.

Around the time these experts took the stand during the winter and spring of 1976, the armed services advised any ex-POWs from the Korean War or Vietnam War still serving to avoid commenting on the trial.[27] Unlike Hearst's defense team, the military did not necessarily want any comparisons expounded in public once more. They had learned from the brainwashing debacles of the 1950s. Dr. West, however, had other ideas. Comparisons were one thing. But key questions remained for his team to answer: How Maoist was the Maoism? If there *was* brainwashing, how deliberate was it? All the SLA-led actions were deemed by the experts as "clumsy" in terms of a coordinated plan to reeducate Patty Hearst. Yet, somehow, they amounted to a coherent program. Sometimes these two claims were at loggerheads: Were the SLA clownish fools or disciplined Maoists? What West and Orne emphasized was—as their classified research on Vietnam War–era survival trainees had shown—how easily the self could fall apart, whether this was a deliberate aim of a program or not. If 25 percent of hardened servicemen (airmen with combat experience) had broken down while being harangued and sleep deprived in a controlled POW training experiment by their own government in the California desert in 1966, why would a young woman held in the dark for so long and forced to condemn every element of the bourgeois life she had been raised in (her private school, for example, as "training grounds for future fascists, capitalistic values, and individualism, competition, classism and racism," herself as "a daughter of a super fascist ruling class family") not also break down?[28] It did not matter, from a certain point of view, whether the revolutionaries had brainwashed her wittingly or unwittingly, intentionally or not.

Each of the expert witnesses for the defense in the trial made the Korean War POW parallel, drew conclusions, and described why and how they came to see her as brainwashed. If she was found to be brainwashed, the argument went, she was not responsible for her crimes.

Coming as the prime expert witness, the jury's "our man," Dr. West reveled in the attention, and his testimony lasted several days. Still, he seemed to lose the case for Hearst in his first substantive answer regarding the term *brainwashing*. His time on the stand began with a long back and forth about his qualifications, including his twenty-nine professional appointments in the preceding twenty years (with highlights listed); his many degrees; his hospital positions; his university posts; his military experience; and "Doctor, have you been the recipient of any professional honors for work accomplishments?" prompted the lead attorney for the defense, F. Lee Bailey. "A few," was West's short reply. He could afford to be ostentatious in his modesty, his manner conveyed. West's curriculum vitae numbered articles in the hundreds.

Bailey continued. Did he publish any books? Yes, West answered, "One, called *Prisoners of War*." Or so he said on the stand, while sworn to tell the truth. And yet, when looked for in 2023, there was no trace of such a book in library catalogs. No such work exists. In other words, this lavishly accomplished man lied within minutes of taking the stand, claiming one further laurel beyond the many he already wore, and though most people assumed that such a learned figure was, as Patricia Hearst characterized him in her memoir, the "author of books and studies on prisoners of war, an internationally recognized expert in his field," he never did finish a book. Experiments, yes. Reports, yes. Articles, yes. Secret protocols, yes. But books, no. (No one has uncovered this before, making my research the first to reveal it some fifty years later, so seamless was his lie and seemingly unchallengeable was the man himself.)

That West perjured himself in such an important case at a pivotal moment does appear significant, for if someone will lie over a small matter on a high-stakes stage, it is hard to imagine what he won't dissemble about, even, or especially, to himself. Since West was one of the top experts on brainwashing in the twentieth century, this fact, which

I Accommodated My Thoughts to Theirs

my research reveals here for the first time despite the many tomes written on Hearst and her trial, has knock-on effects in the way we assess the scientific status of brainwashing.*

The trial moved on. Once his astounding credentials had been established, West's testimony then tackled the main topic. Pivotally, when Bailey asked West what brainwashing was, West fumbled:

Q: Doctor, have you ever heard of the term "brainwashing"?

A: Yes, I have.

The Court: What was the term?

Bailey: Brainwashing.

West immediately opined that this was not a term of "any medical significance." It was true that professionals might occasionally "drop into the vernacular and might use the term 'brainwashing' in a loose way." Yet, he clarified, "coercive persuasion" was the preferred way to describe this forceful kind of interrogation:

A: "Yes, coercive persuasion is usually oriented to someone who has to be coerced in order to get him [into] the position where his behavior or attitudes can be persuaded, whereas the thought reform process can take place even with cooperative people so it isn't necessarily—

The Court: Doctor, so the jury will understand you, are you now

---

* Further credentialing of West took place during the testimony at this point; Bailey had West briefly review his work for the military including the fifty-nine returning captured pilots whom he examined, the research on the POWs, and finally the discovery of DDD (debility, despondency, and dread), the trifecta West and two other researchers identified in 1957 as capable of breaking down almost any human being systematically subjected to them.

attempting to give a definition of that term "brainwashing" by using other terms to describe it? What are you trying to do?

The Witness: Your Honor, what I think I am trying to do is to explain that brainwashing is a term that has become a sort of a grab bag to describe any kind of influence exerted by a captor over a captive, but that isn't very accurate from a scientific or the medical point of view.[29]

So it was that West, the lead expert witness in a trial hinging on a historic brainwashing defense, began by arguing that brainwashing had neither scientific nor medical credibility. One might be forgiven, half a century later, for reflecting something like: "You just lost the case right there, Dr. West." If your brainwashing defense depended on something called brainwashing to exist in some definable way within medical and legal worlds, and the key expert witness for the defense could not really define it or its technical substitute, then you were probably going to be in trouble.

Even Hearst herself found the expert testimony terribly boring, and it went on for weeks. However, she later reported finding the process of working with them—as healers, at least—a helpful one: "But it was only after my arrest and the hours spent with the psychiatrists that I had come to understand just how cruel and inhuman they had been to me, beyond any political or revolutionary theory."[30] The experts were hired to evaluate her, not to heal her, but simply recounting her travails did help. (She found West's voice creepy and hypnotic.)[31] Margaret Singer spent the most hours talking with Hearst: "She remarked ... that this did help her 'get her head back together,'" Singer wrote—she had been allowed in Hearst's jail to reintegrate a narrative structure to what had happened to her.[32] This sense of only retrospectively glimpsing the true violation inherent in what one has endured resonates with the reported experiences of many people exposed to Soviet or Chinese thought reform's cruelties, which become somehow invisible while the process is going on. What happened to them is not seen as torture until later. It is also true of abused children.

During the period after her arrest while awaiting trial, Hearst wrestled with despair, and while in jail she passed the time crocheting. While waiting for her sentence, her right lung spontaneously collapsed, and her heart moved precipitously toward the other lung. Her weight fell to eighty-seven pounds. By then she believed she could be convicted of just about any crime anywhere in California just for being Patty Hearst.

....

The third psychiatrist to testify, Dr. Martin Orne, came across as the most reliable of the expert witnesses friendly to Hearst. The jury, according to posttrial interviews, found him with his cuddly figure and Viennese accent to be like a teddy bear: adorable. Also, he made a clear point and said clearly how he came to it. Orne was a student of the psychologist Henry Murray at Harvard, where he met soon-to-be brainwashing expert Edgar Schein, a classmate, and they discovered they had many interests in common. Schein seems to have introduced Orne to West. After getting his PhD and MD, Orne joined with West to redesign resistance training for the Air Force, coming on in 1966 as a consultant to evaluate the Stead Air Force Base program and the Navy's Survival, Evasion, Resistance, and Escape (SERE) program. Up to one-third of those military men exposed to the counter-brainwashing were breaking down in the training, and Orne was hired to help modify it to be less destructive. Perhaps most significantly, Orne received from the CIA MK-ULTRA program (designated Sub-project 84) for work on hypnosis and the efficacy of "demand characteristics." The latter were factors extraneous to an experiment that may affect the outcome of the experiment and skew or determine results. People may want to please the hypnotist, for example. Orne's specialty was *simulation*, or lying, a question at the heart of Hearst's trial: How could anyone know for sure if she was using brainwashing as an excuse to duck responsibility for her crimes?

A key moment occurred during the Orne testimony on Thursday, February 26, 1976, at 10:05 in the morning. The topic turned to Orne's specialty. He described to Bailey how he repeatedly tested Hearst's sincerity by asking her leading questions, along the lines of (for example), *It must have felt scary to be robbing the bank especially with Cinque standing behind you with a gun. Wasn't it terribly frightening?* A liar or dissimulator would answer in the positive, falling into Orne's trap, but Hearst did not:

> **Orne:** And to [my leading question] again someone simulating would say, "Yes, I was terribly scared," because that's the appropriate response. I mean, at least I would be scared under those situations, and someone expects somebody to be, too, and this is where I was so puzzled because all I could get was the answer, "I don't remember how I felt. It was like a dream." Which struck me as something very different from what I would have gotten from somebody simulating.
>
> **Bailey:** Uh-huh.[33]

In other words, when Orne interviewed Hearst, she could not even say she felt scared during the bank robbery. She had become a stranger to herself.[34] The prosecution would later argue, based on video footage from the Hibernia Bank, that Hearst appeared so "agile" in her movements as she moved through the lobby holding her gun, that she could hardly have been in fear or in a fugue state but must have been an enthusiastic participant. This, of course—alert, responsive, a soldier for the cause, an urban guerilla—was what she had to make herself be.

At certain moments, the word *trauma* began to creep gingerly into the way Hearst was being described in and out of the courtroom. Dr. Orne spoke about Hearst's condition of "traumatic neurosis"—which, he clarified, was "fortunately not something we see in civilian life"—and thereby reaffirmed the point the defense was making throughout: Trauma was something an ordinary person would not experience, and Hearst's travails were more akin to a soldier's taken captive. Trauma was, in a real sense, *elsewhere*. (Likewise, Dr. West, in an interview with a reporter, described how at the NPI "We were reopening the whole trauma story of the victims of violence" and wondered whether Hearst's story would fit there.)[35] Soon after, Robert Jay Lifton took the stand as the fourth psychiatric witness. In his characteristic bow tie, expressing himself with a mix of compassion and scholarly exactitude, he came across as the most intellectual of the defense voices. (In contrast, a reporter described West, at a husky six-foot-four, as "certainly an eye-filling witness" who "looked like a veteran pro linebacker.")[36] In his testimony, Lifton assured the prosecution that anyone could be broken down. And he speculated that perhaps she "had it worse" than the POWs at the Yalu camps, thus engaging, at the behest of the legal team, in a parlor game of sorts: Who had the most hellish experience? In response, certain veteran soldiers (quoted in a *Time* magazine article) repudiated the claim that Hearst had been through the equivalent of the brutality POWs endured, one calling her experience "only a miniature, a sample."[37] Lifton confirmed the diagnosis of traumatic neurosis, which, if anything, made her less sympathetic. Here the defense strategy was backfiring: True trauma was still seen as something only grown men in duress experienced, and even entering the comparison reinforced that in a sense she had no right to claim it.

The fifth expert witness, Margaret Singer, was limited to testifying about what the psychological and other tests revealed, especially and most strikingly that Patricia Hearst had lost dozens of points of IQ in

The second closet in which Hearst was held (bathroom is on left, small closet on right). "I might as well have been in an underground coffin," Hearst wrote in her memoir of her initial impression of the closet.

Another view of the closet in which Hearst was held for most of the fifty-seven days of her confinement (photographed during 1976 trial). SAN FRANCISCO CHRONICLE/HEARST NEWSPAPERS VIA GETTY IMAGES/CONTRIBUTOR.

the process of her traumatizing experience and was only recently starting to gain them back. At one point, she referred to Hearst, just after her capture, as a "low-IQ . . . zombie."

. . . .

In contrast to these heavy hitters of the brainwashing world, the government called as their main expert witness a non-psychologist physician named Joel Fort who was hostile to expertise itself. Dr. Fort, "a tall, firm-voiced man with a shaved scalp," according to the *New York*

I Accommodated My Thoughts to Theirs

Times reporter at the trial, stated of his own evaluation that "It was my hope that there would be no expert testimony, because the jury is capable of deciding this question for itself without a lot of testimony from so-called experts."[38] Hearst had not said she was raped in the closet, Dr. Fort reported of his interview with her, she had only told how she had intercourse with Willie Wolfe to save her life. She had agreed. So it wasn't rape. Soon afterward, in his view, she came to like her abductors, and fell in love with Wolfe. She was a "willing bandit," Dr. Fort argued. She enjoyed herself.*

Dr. Fort woke everyone up after the sleepiness induced by the long testimonies of the brainwashing experts. A cartoon by Joe Papin from the time just before Fort's arrival on the stand showed everyone in the courtroom sleeping, including the eagle on the Great Seal of California hanging above Judge Carter's head, and a lawyer for the prosecution was heard to jibe, "We'll wake him up if we need him." Dr. Fort, according to Hearst, grabbed everyone's attention by calling Hearst the "queen of the SLA," not its victim. Late in the trial, the government's expert witness spoke of the abductee's relatively comfortable detention closets which came equipped, he said, with mattresses, and "friendly contacts" with her kidnappers, as it seemed to him.[39] He compared these closets unfavorably with the POW and concentration camp settings he had visited in his life: Auschwitz, he detailed, had captives undergoing fifty mile marches, dysentery, starvation, and freezing, filthy, cramped quarters; they were transported in cattle cars, herded with whips and dogs, forced to strip naked and to smell burning flesh, he elaborated. "In Patty's case," Fort pointed out, "there was

---

* "What she told me in my interviews," the witness said, "she indicated at some point that it was brought up whether or not she would like to have intercourse with Willie Wolfe. She described to me agreeing to do that, giving as among other reasons, 'I thought it would save my life.' She did not say that he forced himself upon her," Dr. Fort said. "She did not describe it as rape." Wallace Turner, "Doctor Calls Miss Hearst Willing Bandit," *The New York Times*, March 9, 1976.

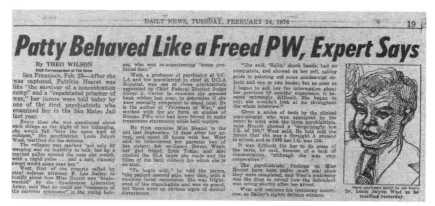

Clipping covering the "Trial of the Century," with a Joe Papin courtroom sketch of Dr. West testifying. COURTESY OF THE NEW YORK DAILY NEWS.

no evidence of sleep deprivation, no starvation."[40] She was converted through poor character and lack of spine, not coercion. Simultaneously, the conversion occurred through personal affection, through desire, through her love for Willie Wolfe: "Nothing magical or brutal was done to convert her," was the summary of the case against her. Simply, she admired her new comrades. As the legal writer Jeffrey Toobin would echo forty years later, approvingly quoting the prosecution's experts: "She was ripe for the plucking."[41]

Fort's attacks on Hearst and his hostility toward the impressively credentialed did succeed. They revealed an incoherence at the heart of the brainwashing defense team's legal reasoning. By their logic, either she was mentally unchanged and lying ("getting away with it") or she had been permanently changed ("converted" for good), which raised the question of how she had snapped back and why she hadn't done that earlier, for example, during long stretches on the lam in the Pennsylvania countryside in the summer of 1975. Believing in the brainwashing of Patricia Hearst seemed to demand that you embrace the paradoxical logic trap in which she was caught, and the jury simply could not take this step, finding Hearst guilty on the count of armed robbery.[42] She served almost two years of a seven-year sentence until President Jimmy

Carter commuted it to "time served" in 1979, and President Bill Clinton pardoned her in 2001.[43]

....

Hearst's kidnapping and trial led to the discovery that brainwashing was almost impossible to deploy as a legal exculpatory framework. It also pointed to the shaky epistemological foundations of trauma, which appeared in the trial occasionally but was not pursued medically as exculpatory or even explanatory.

Evidence of this is seen in the fact that the defense expert witnesses kept calling Hearst "the patient," while the prosecution's expert witnesses never did. In her memoir, Hearst recalled how, faced with horrors during her weeks in the closets, she adapted herself and, as she explained, "*I accommodated my thoughts to coincide with theirs.*"[44] This is, as it happens, a very good definition of brainwashing. Having accommodated her thoughts, the choice to leave or stay and fight was a non-choice. She had already decided to try to live. But it was hard to translate this into something that would stand up in court, especially as Dr. Lifton and others were preoccupied with proving that Hearst never was converted at all, never truly believed in radical feminism or militant anti-capitalism. (She was only compliant, never converted, they insisted.)

Hearst wrote in her memoir that she felt dismayed during the trial. "I tried to respond to the questions"—about why she had not just walked away when she had the chance—"but I had the distinct feeling that here in court no one could understand or wanted to understand the situation I had been in. They had not been there. The crux of it was my state of mind at the time, what I had been thinking, my intent, and only I could know that."[45] Like the POWs, she despaired of being understood by anyone who was not there or had not experienced something like it.

She was right. Most Americans continue to believe her guilty, according to polls up to 2014 and judging by the perennial "wild spree" narrative that pops up in podcasts and clickbait offerings. Almost forty-five years later, the NPR interviewer David Bianculli posed the defense's question—tellingly—once more: "The question was always, was she coerced, or did she become a believer?"[46]

However, at the heart of it, an understanding of brainwashing and mind control is not found with an either-or question. Hearst was coerced into becoming a true believer, and so it was both. Once she was safe, it was neither.

....

The persistent confusion in response to the Great Brainwashing Defense and the process of coercive persuasion in general comes from the assumption that this process must somehow result in a permanent change, or else it is not real. In fact, even Mao Zedong understood that thought reform required frequent renewal, not excepting his own! Conversions by their nature are not fixed, as any study of millenarianism will show. They ebb and flow. Over time, Patricia Hearst Shaw—her married name, taken after she wed police officer Bernard Shaw, who was sent to guard her after Jimmy Carter released her from prison—did seem to return to herself. That is, she re-embraced her socioeconomic milieu and reintegrated into her family. She also continued to change: She engaged in a lot of processing over the years, wrote her own autobiography, participated intermittently in fashion events and John Waters films (the two are longtime friends), and enthusiastically showed her French bulldogs at the Westminster Kennel Club Dog Shows. She was, in 2017, a double winner, with her Tuggy awarded best of breed, and Rubi awarded second prize as best of opposite sex.

Inconsistencies in the brainwashing defense crop up again and again in discussions of Stockholm syndrome. In fact, Hearst is sometimes presented as a sort of poster child for Stockholm syndrome (despite its debunking) and the term continues to be linked to her in both professional journals and popular articles. Even as Swedish and other researchers increasingly question its scientific and ethical viability, the concept of Stockholm syndrome persists as something like folklore, making it a mysterious truth that someone would come to "love" their captor in order to survive. The evidence demonstrates that this is not strange at all: Countless cases of battered women and abducted children show this to be a viable and logical survival strategy, not a bizarre response. Women such as Jaycee Dugard, who have experienced childhood abduction and long-term captivity, deeply contest this additional attribution of "weirdness" to their myriad sufferings.[47]

What the Hearst kidnapping and its aftermath show in painful detail is that it *is* possible to become another person while under distressing conditions. Fortunately, in her case, this was not permanent.* It is wrong to say there are no do-overs in American life (or any life), for we are doing-over ourselves all the time, ceaselessly and ceaselessly. This poses the possibility of harm but also healing. Only in accepting this is there some way forward.

---

* According to the entry for "Brainwashing Debate," in the second edition of the *Encyclopedia of Religion*, brainwashing when defined as "an overpowering psychotechnology that produced lasting transformation of beliefs and attitudes" never has existed in modern life and is akin, according to some scholars who study religious movements, to a conspiracy theory that arises in periods of sociocultural tension. This is accurate in some ways but misleading. The question of "lasting" is at play here. The presumption that transformation, to be real, must be lasting is not only an error but a flaw in philosophy, in experience, and in epistemology—in modern life and in the modern self.

8

....

Darksome House of Mortal Clay

In November 2019, I flew from Boston to Santa Fe to attend a meeting of the International Cultic Studies Association slated to explore the topic of healing sexual abuse in individuals who had left or escaped cults. I checked into the La Fonda on the Plaza hotel, and found myself startlingly upgraded to the wedding suite because they were out of regular rooms. Aside from the palatial scale, view of the historic cathedral, and massive jacuzzi, the room turned out to be strangely appropriate for hosting experiences that would soon resemble, in a way, a marital union—a new beginning, at least for my own understanding of how cults work. I settled into my suite, experiencing the little dislocation shocks usual for a Massachusetts to New Mexico traverse. It's not so much jet lag but that the quality of air and light and space are so different that it constitutes a displacement of self. Before the meeting's first session began, I introduced myself to a few other attendees as a researcher and a professor. But I noticed a pattern. Quickly there came a searching glance and a request for more detail. Was there some more personal reason I was here, an unnamed trauma of some sort? Was I an ex-member of a cult? I would think about it, answer in different ways as I searched my life experiences. Maybe so?

Standing outside in a hallway bedecked with southwestern art, I contemplated this unexpected direction of questioning. Did I look more like an ex-cult member than an Ivy League professor? Was there necessarily a difference—can professors be lured into cults or ex-cult members become professors? Of course. They can and do. Mental acuity has nothing to do with susceptibility or—according to some accounts—it actively makes someone more prone to joining up. (It is not rationality but emotionality that is the weak point of most people.) Yet my querying continued irrationally: Is it because of how I hold myself, dress, or speak? Would a male academic get the same questions? I wondered. Taking a break, I continued down the street where, after dropping in at a circular labyrinth in front of the St. Francis church, the one I could see from my suite, and walking its twists to its center, then stopping by the tiny cathedral store to buy some postcards of saints, I turned the corner to encounter a man carrying a tray heaped with baked goods, little plump loaves of plastic-wrapped pumpkin bread.

Would I like one? I declined, but he was very friendly. He put down his tray and we fell into a conversation that rapidly turned into a probe of the state of my soul. Had it been saved? I confess I always pretty much feel like, yeah, it has—because of my personal metaphysical quest in life or what I sometimes call my agnostic-mystical inquiries in this area. But he was more denominationally exact: Had I surrendered specifically to Jesus? I had to admit this had not happened. His testimony to having left drugs and gang life in Albuquerque behind was riveting, and it was difficult for me to extricate myself, not because I wanted to fall on my knees, but because he was so conversational.

Back at the conference, the unspoken or spoken questions continued. I'm not one to stand on ceremony and perhaps I don't fit the stereotype of a graying, elbow-patched academic. (For full disclosure I should mention that I regularly wear out the elbows of my cardigans, though I do not patch them, nor do I wear tweedy jackets.) Furthermore, I have some bad and painful experiences in my past, so this inkling, this scrutiny, was not totally wrong. In fact . . . Why did I not get this line of inquiry more often?

Stepping back, I could see that my inner dialogue was premised on the idea that there is a particular way a sexually abused cult survivor should look. As in, necessarily not like a professionally put-together person. As in, they should be somehow marked. Easily identified and just as easily stigmatized. And then I thought: If I unintentionally harbor these preconceptions and presumptions after many years of research, after many years of life, what hope is there for understanding from the "general population"? I continued to wonder about this as I attended a session that featured two ex-members of the Children of God, one a father of seventeen children, Ray Connolly, and the other a now grown woman born into the cult (but not his child). It was riveting to hear their joint points of view.

Second generation cult members, sometimes called the "born intos," pose new questions about how brainwashing works. Those who are born into cults do not "decide" to join but have the decision made for them. They are genuinely coerced, persuaded, trained, and imbued in a totalizing designed-to-be-inescapable thought system. They are trained to see the world in a certain way. They start out in what the sociologist Erving Goffman called total institutions. They have not left behind an old, dissatisfying way of life to seek a new one free of middle class or other constraints. Second or third generation adults (SGAs, TGAs) in cults were often abused as children, often sexually trafficked (frequently it is family trafficking), and, if they do manage to exit, or if they were rescued by the FBI in a raid (as several of the Santa Fe attendees had been), they would be released facing a different set of challenges than their elders who entered such groups.

Hope Bastine, a psychologist who grew up in the Children of God, wrote recently in the *Times* of London about the twelve years during which she was forced to live with her childhood rapist, whom she was instructed to treat as a father figure: "Unlike our parents, who made decisions to leave their former lives behind, my brothers, sisters and I had not chosen this way of life and had no way out. We were controlled by fear of all outside systems, including government, police, doctors, and social workers."[1]

The question of the forging of the pseudo-identity within a total institution, which is at the core of how brainwashing works within cults, transforms when the perspective is shifted to the experiences of the children born into them, and their children's children. I hadn't realized this before I went to Santa Fe. I hadn't realized, either, that people's questions for me were not really about what I was wearing or how I seemed, but about vulnerability and fear, and whether I was trustworthy. Walking outside and thinking about all of this, I went back to the labyrinth.

....

The East Bay of San Francisco during the mid to late 1970s was home base for what could anachronistically be called peak cult. Margaret Singer, who cut her teeth as a psychometrician on the cases of the brainwashed POWs in the 1950s, now middle-aged and characterized by one journalist as a "tall Mary Poppins figure" with a "den mother" personality, was living with her husband, a physicist at the university, in the Berkeley Hills where they were raising two children.[2] Teaching as an adjunct professor in the Department of Psychology at the University of California, Berkeley, she was surrounded, in the campus environs, by recruitment activities and cult fallout. Students recounted tales of abuse and narrow escape. Parents of recruited children came to her as clients.

"I started hearing from families who had missing members, many of them being young kids on our campus or others, and they all would describe the same sorts of things," Singer recalled in an interview with the San Francisco newspaper *SFGate*. What things? Their children had started talking differently, had changed their circle of friends, had altered their personalities. They seemed as if they were someone else. They were developing pseudoidentities. "And bingo," she saw the parallel: "It was the same sort of thing as with the Korean War prisoners," Singer said, looking back at her moment of insight.[3] Other colleagues from those days were having the same epiphany. She gradually built up a new occupation, with herself as its foremost practitioner—the cult expert consultant.

Starting in 1972, and gathering momentum through the next three decades, Singer met with over four thousand people, by her estimate, who had negative experiences with high-demand cults, "therapy groups," or large-group awareness training such as EST or Landmark.[4] All of them she analogized to the original "brainwashed" POWs involved in thought reform. After testifying in the trial of Patricia Hearst in 1976, she began appearing widely in courtrooms, where she expounded her view that such super-controlling cults operated by criminally bypassing the targeted person's rational faculties, and that people entranced in this way were therefore not responsible for what happened to them nor what they did under the disproportionate influence of a cultic group (for example, giving away all their money to the group).[5] Innocent or vulnerable recruits had been deceived into paralyzing their own rational processing system, their own critical thinking abilities.

Singer's basic point was that, in a real sense, cult members were cognitively disabled by contact with the cult. This view initially held up quite well in the California civil courts, garnering some legal victories. In one major case, *George v. International Society for Krishna Consciousness*, the group (widely known as the Hare Krishnas) was held responsible and initially ordered to pay $32.5 million in civil damages to Robin George and her mother, Marcia, largely on the basis of Singer's testimony that the daughter (who was fourteen years old during the events in question) had been brainwashed into running away to live in the group's temple during the summer of 1974 and remaining with them for some time. Effectively, "her will was overcome," even though she was *not physically restrained* from leaving and in fact asserted at the time that she wanted to stay.[6] (The 1977 award amount was reduced to around $10 million by the court, and was later reduced again.)[*] Singer's view was that cults (the manipulative ones) were perfidious. Such groups and the individuals who made them up did not deserve the traditional legal protections accorded to religions—for example, the American common-law doctrine of charitable immunity, which had held from the nineteenth until around the mid-twentieth century, that churches were not susceptible to lawsuits for damages. Singer herself was an observant Catholic, and she drew a firm line between established religions and cults. As she put it in the more informal language redolent of her 1930s-era upbringing, the recruited students were lured in by "flim-flam men, pimps, sharpsters" and "there are always sharpies around who want to hornswoggle people."[7] She began to receive large fees that came with legal success. This livelihood was supplemented by her other work as a guest lecturer at various University of California campuses.

Even though, at first, she was not the best-known expositor of mind-control theories, Singer came to prominence as the go-to expert on this topic in the late twentieth century (that is, until her reputation came to ruin due to a calculated and fairly vicious campaign by her professional enemies). For one thing, the other contenders had disincentives

---

[*] *George v. International Society for Krishna Consciousness* was initially tried in 1977 and included charges of false imprisonment of the fourteen- (then fifteen-) year-old, intentional infliction of emotional distress on child and mother, and libel. The case continued to be litigated through 1983, when the original judgment was made, and legal wrangling continued well into the 1990s. Eventually the brainwashing portion (arguing that physical coercion was not necessary for this to have been disabling of the will) was reversed; damages of $5 million were reduced to $2.9 million for emotional distress and libel.

Darksome House of Mortal Clay 247

that dissuaded them from embracing the role of number-one anti-cult expert, especially when it came to courtrooms. Robert J. Lifton, teaching at Yale and The City College of New York, declined to testify in court cases after the negative watershed of the Hearst trial (after all, they lost). As his 1962 work became a touchstone, he was drawn into cult issues, but was torn, as his interests ranged more broadly in psychohistory.[8] Edgar Schein repositioned himself from brainwashing to the field of educational dynamics and won a tenured spot at MIT. Meanwhile Dr. West, who had in 1971 assumed leadership of UCLA's Neuropsychiatric Institute, became august enough to look quite bad if he were to take payment to testify. On the stand in the Hearst trial, he reiterated that he had not received any compensation—the $2,000 payment was for the evaluation report with Singer—and later told a journalist he had never intended to serve as a witness.[9] (He had the air of one who had just wandered into the role.) Despite his protestations, his prominent stance earned him negative press, and he was accused of ambulance-chasing and headline-chasing by some reporters. To be too close to cults, pro or con, was to risk reputational damage oneself, no matter one's bona fides.

Brainwashing, when presented as a scientific theory in legal settings, seemed to lure professionals into its tangles where, perhaps unsurprisingly, they found themselves entangled. As the lawyer Peter Georgiades, who successfully prosecuted many abusive cults between 1980 and 1995, commented on the difficulty of trying to find an expert: "It's the extraordinary individual who will testify."[10] After fifteen years Georgiades gave up such work. His medical experts could be threatened, followed, impugned, their trash searched through. In one famous and non-apocryphal case, cultists left a rattlesnake in their antagonist lawyer's mailbox, with its rattle removed, so that the hand gathering the mail received a disabling bite.[11] Hired experts learned to be vigilant against such attacks, and Singer claimed she had a rifle at the ready against incursions. Like a pothole full of dirty water that sprays the person trying to guide passersby around it, brainwashing tended to splash back on the cult researcher pointing out the danger.

It fell to Singer to become the ex-cultists' bulldog. She was fierce, exacting, protective, and didn't back down. She was paid well, if not lavishly, for testifying and for counseling. She was a female academic in an era when it was much harder for women to gain tenured positions. Though compensation was likely not her primary motivation, it was also not *not* her motivation, as she said later, after all the attacks against her had left their mark and she was no longer welcome in courtrooms. Her rate for consultation, which would become a flashpoint in the coming cult wars, was $350 per hour, in 1980—a factoid that would become a liability.[12] (But she didn't charge ex-members anything, according to her own account.) Since cults often targeted the children of the wealthy, and since the parents of dazzle-eyed children tended to be desperate—and furthermore since experts tended to feel with some justification that there were few others possessed of their specific expertise—high fees were a possibility.

But as the 1970s turned into the 1980s, the momentum Singer and other experts garnered was checked in its steps by one of the least known yet most vicious scholarly skirmishes of recent times—the cult wars of the 1980s and 1990s (sometimes also called the anti-cult movement), which had at their heart disputes about brainwashing, and in particular the person of Margaret Singer, who had thoroughly identified herself with the concept of anti-cultism and the argument about the disablement of the rational will. Some would point out that her view was a distinctive, evolving, and extreme interpretation. Others would say the opposite, that she was the only one who really understood how cults work. Whatever the case, the dispute does show—thirty years later—how difficult it is to map the territory of mind control, and how much your cartographic efforts will be influenced by where you are standing while securing your data points. Understanding brainwashing was much more akin to a Borges story about trying to nail down a paradoxical domain, or an Escher lithograph, than a simple geological survey.

....

Meanwhile, the slow pace and uncertain outcome of legal recourse led many desperate family members whose children had donned robes, given away their inheritances, alienated their families, disappeared into cults, or were last seen selling flowers out of the back of a Moonie van, to resort to reverse-brainwashing their "lost" kin through a process called deprogramming. As defined in the *American Journal of Psychiatry*, the "intriguing" procedure was usually initiated by a parent attempting to recover their adult-age or near-adult-age child from the controls of a cult. Deprogramming "may range from gentle rap sessions to sleep deprivation and sensory overload, with marathon-type encounters that feature shouting, repetitious derogations of the cult, isolation of the person from former associates, moving the deprogramee from place to place within a period of days, and, occasionally, use of physical force in the event that he or she tries to leave or escape."[13] A 1979 study of fifty cult members (some of whom remained in the group, some of whom were deprogrammed and then left permanently, some of whom were deprogrammed and came back, and some of whom left voluntarily) found contrasting responses. Those who were currently *in* cults tended to dissemble—to themselves and others, as measured by use of personality tests and other metrics—about the practices of their group; whereas those who were "out" tilted to paranoia, schizophrenic response, and psychasthenia, according to the study.[14] Depending on whether you were in or out, you had very different opinions not only about the cult, but also about deprogrammers, needless to say. For the latter, deprogrammers were heroes who had rescued them. For the former, they were the very devil.

The first prominent deprogrammer—the coiner of the term—was

a forty-five-year-old African American California native named Theodore "Ted" Roosevelt Patrick Jr., whose fourteen-year-old son, Michael, was walking with friends along the San Diego beachfront on the Fourth of July holiday in 1971 when he nearly found himself swept into the open-doored bus of the Children of God (the same group Ray Connolly and the soon-to-be parents of River, Joaquin, Rain, Liberty, and Summer Phoenix joined). Patrick's son got away, but his near escape planted a seed in the father. As a businessman and Air Force veteran with a strong Christian upbringing, Patrick was alarmed at the wagering of biblical text for the purpose of manipulating the young and rudderless.

A few days later, Patrick presented himself at the spot where his son had been recruited and soon boarded the bus with the intention to investigate by subjecting himself to initiatory procedures. For two days, he lived at the recruiting center where he underwent a "mental and psychological blitzing" process that entailed sleep deprivation (over forty-four hours, he had a total of three hours of sleep, all of it toe to head with strangers), the loud and near constant playing of recordings of Bible verses; sermons criticizing American society (which, as Patrick pointed out, were confusing because you "sort of agree with some of it"—as in, "There *were* things wrong with America"), insistent hugging from other members, and probing questions about one's bank account and financial status, all happening at once. Throughout, surveillance was so intense he never had a moment alone to collect his thoughts. Within a day, he began to come close to succumbing, in his telling: "In spite of all my precautions, I was getting worn down ... one does not use his powers of concentration or critical ability in a normal way" and after a while "you often don't really know what you are doing or saying."[15] It's not—Patrick realized—that you forget how to *think* (rationally) but that you forget how to *feel* about what you think.[16]

As detailed in his as-told-to memoir *Let Our Children Go!*, Ted Patrick was neither the typical cult recruit nor the typical parent of a cult member. Middle aged with a small pot belly, a speech impediment, a discreet Afro, and owlish horn rim glasses, giving the impression of a short-sleeves-and-tie-wearing bureaucrat, he nonetheless gained the nom de guerre "Black Lightning" among the anti-cultists for the speed at which he abducted followers back into their families. This was also a reference to his race, for he stood out in a field largely dominated by the affluent white upper-middle class. *People* magazine in 1976 elaborated that he was "Known as 'Black Lightning' to those in awe of his swift abductions, and as 'Black Satan' to those he had failed to deprogram."[17] Like the experts Singer and Lifton, he analogized cult members to POWs from the Korean conflict. "The way they get them is by on-the-spot hypnosis. Once they get them, they brainwash them. The technique is the same as the North Koreans used on our prisoners of war."[18]

Patrick's mention of "on-the-spot hypnosis," too, was throwback to an earlier era in the Cold War. It is no coincidence that one of the most prominent hypnosis experts in the world (Martin Orne), as well as one of the more audacious hypnosis researchers (Louis Jolyon West), were deeply enmeshed in the world of brainwashing from its inception in the United States. Essentially, hypnosis was interesting to all sorts of people in political and military circles because it quickly could put someone in a dissociated state—a trance or "trance-like state." (West used these terms analogously.) In fact, we've seen how West spotlighted himself to the CIA and military by talking up his accomplishments in hypnosis research (including his controlled study giving two men "emergency circumcisions" using hypnosis as pain control, the detail-sparse reference that may have served to suggest there was no limit to what West was willing to do). With its spooky and ill-understood ways of working, hypnosis entwined, as we've seen, with LSD and interrogation research, and was one of the big three or four areas of dark investigations into getting people, apparently willingly, to do things at the bidding of another—maneuvering them to unburden themselves of timely information, or even of their fundamental concept of self. Cold War researchers wanted badly to know how far it could go. But how did it—how does it—work exactly?

Cold War research on hypnosis sought to make it—as West informed his handlers at the CIA—something that you could quantify, manipulate, and combine. In his "unpublished studies," he showed how hypnosis interacted with other inputs such as drugs and sensory deprivation or flooding. In short, West brought hypnosis into the laboratory—he redefined it as something *belonging to the lab*. (As he wrote to MK-ULTRA head Sidney Gottlieb in a secret report, "Hypnosis may be considered to be a pure-culture, laboratory-controlled dissociative reaction.")[19] One advantage of living in our own historical moment is that the laboratory now includes many more measuring machines; there is ample capability to perform brain scans, for example. Hypnotic trance can be studied with functional magnetic resonance (fMRI) imaging, thus allowing (as in a recent 2016 Stanford medical school study) researchers to understand which areas of the brain are active at time of entrancement.* Imaging the brains of fifty-seven people who ranged from high hypnotizability to low revealed that the brain of a deeply hypnotized person is associated with engagement of the DFM (default mode network)—that is, the activation of several interconnected midline brain structures, with the result that stressful and strategic

---

* The researchers, after scanning fifty-seven subjects undergoing hypnotherapy, defined hypnosis this way: "[Hypnosis] involves highly focused attention, referred to as absorption, coupled with dissociation, the compartmentalization of experience . . . suggestibility, [and] nonjudgmental behavioral responsiveness to instructions from others." Heidi Jiang, Matthew P. White, Michael D. Greicius, Lynn C. Waelde, and David Spiegel, "Brain Activity and Functional Connectivity Associated with Hypnosis," *Cerebral Cortex* 27 (2017), 4083–93; 4083.

activities are laid aside. Those with "high hypnotizability" tended to have decreased brain activity in certain areas associated with worry and vigilance as well as greater brain connectivity (across the executive function and salience networks associated with somatic surveillance and self-regulation), whereas those with "low hypnotizability" did not show these changes. (Hypnotizability is a well-established and measurable trait, gauged by the Harvard Group Scale for Hypnotic Susceptibility.) Still, given how much faith we tend to put in the magic of magnetic imaging, it is perhaps surprising that knowing which brain areas are activated does not at all result in knowing how hypnosis works, nor exactly what it is. "Despite a growing appreciation of the clinical potential of hypnosis . . . little is known about how it works at a physiological level."[20] And even today, the mere act of specializing in hypnosis may impugn respectability, as Dr. David Spiegel of the Stanford medical school observes: "Hypnosis is the oldest Western form of psychotherapy, but it's been tarred with the brush of dangling watches and purple capes." Twenty-first-century hypnosis research usually stresses its therapeutic potential, not its freedom-cancelling abilities. This tended to be true in the mid-twentieth century, too, making West's approach (or the clandestine work he was called to do) an outlier then and now. Recall that West noted he could use hypnosis to increase or create pain, too.

Ted Patrick's deprogramming method borrowed from the forced-imprisonment model, just as the military had in developing survival training. (Not long ago, at the age of ninety, Patrick launched a Twitter account to celebrate the extensive work he did in liberating, by his estimate, 2,600 people from mind control. "And most importantly, I taped EVERY SINGLE deprogramming session. I have 1000s of tapes," he tweeted on August 20, 2019. He stressed with some bravado the present relevance of his work: "There are more cults than ever now, because Ted Patrick's not out there!" he posted on Twitter August 4, 2019, in an excerpt from a video interview.)

Deprogramming soon spread. You did not necessarily need a professional degree—Patrick had none—but you did need some persuasive skills and a strong commitment. "Deprogrammers were individuals who physically wrestled young adults into waiting cars and drove them to remote locations," usually with the permission of the cult members' parents and under the direction of the deprogrammer, as one scholar describes the practice.[21] Sometimes these activities found legal backing: In the early 1980s, judges in California began allowing the formation of conservatorships by parents over their young-adult offspring. As the result of one of Singer's testimonies, five partially deprogrammed Moon devotees were placed under the control of their parents, bowing to Singer's assertion that the cult had rendered them mentally incompetent. Once granted conservatorship, parents could expose their children to deprogramming at greater length and lawfulness.

Deprogramming was not automatic; it was strenuous. It meant going toe to toe with an ardently indoctrinated person, a person who saw themselves as fighting for their very lives because the cult told them they were in danger. Some deprogrammers took up this line of work to compensate for having lured others into the same groups from which they eventually managed to free themselves.* The practice usually entailed using forcible restraint (at first) and in some ways resembled an exorcism, so intently did the abductees struggle to return to their cult life. A CBS reporting crew, at Patrick's invitation, followed him and his associates to document a deprogramming one day in August 1976. A young woman named Kathy Crampton had moved to Seattle and joined the Love Israel "Jesus freak" group, the members of which, following the teachings of the

---

* Many people have been haunted for years by the guilt of having brought unsuspecting outsiders into the group from which they themselves would successfully escape, whether by deprogramming or other means.

Darksome House of Mortal Clay

former television salesman Paul Erdmann, considered themselves to be spiritually superannuated by sixty-six additional years. During Patrick's forcible apprehension of Kathy (grabbing her from a street in Seattle, accompanied by her parents), she resisted, and summoned police. When questioned by a state trooper, Kathy answered calmly that she was named Carinth Love Israel, that she did not know her mother (who was sitting next to her in Ted Patrick's car), and that she was eighty-five years old. The effect on law enforcement, and anyone they encountered was eerie. "I feel awfully uncomfortable," said the trooper, and consulted with his superior; ultimately they let Patrick continue on his way. Questions of legality and the abrogation of civil liberties, especially when the child in question was over eighteen (Kathy was actually nineteen), began to be raised from the start, but court battles—and successive arrests of Patrick—would take some years to play out. In such cases, parents sometimes sought a temporary court order to regain custody of their children. Meanwhile deprogramming went on apace.[22]

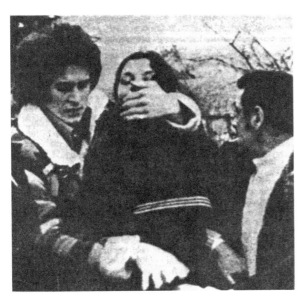

Kidnapping of young cult members to be deprogrammed, by operatives their families hired, was common, as here, in France, 1976. USED WITH PERMISSION OF JOHN WILEY & SONS BOOKS, FROM *THE MAKING OF A MOONIE: CHOICE OR BRAINWASHING?*, BY EILEEN BARKER, 1ST EDITION, 1984; PERMISSION CONVEYED THROUGH COPYRIGHT CLEARANCE CENTER, INC.

Ted Patrick deprogramming a Children of God member named Marc, while the procedure was observed by a reporter and photographer for the *New York Times*. Marc at one point cried, "If you don't let me go back [to the group], I'm going to kill myself." But Patrick persisted and ultimately Marc broke down and returned to his family.
PHOTO: JOYCE DOPKEEN, THE NEW YORK TIMES.

Often, after an initial "grabbing" off the street, the cult abductee would be brought to a remote site. There, maternal begging, paternal tears, and familial wailing were almost always insufficient to move the family member until, somehow, the "spell" of brainwashing was broken. Patrick described his method this way: It was (1) kidnap the cult member when she was out on an errand of some sort in a public place; (2) confine her physically in a room with sealed windows and doors (for she will do anything to get out and go back to the group); and (3) subject her to an onslaught of questions and discussion, almost like a rapid-fire catechism, including at times tape recordings of ex-members exhorting them to break with the cult, so that eventually she will "snap just as if someone had turned on a light inside her." It was akin to breaking something: "The moment when that happens," Patrick described, "is always unmistakeable. It's like an emotional dam bursting." As one abductee told him, "I really feel like I've just woken up from some terrible nightmare."[23] (Others described lasting harm from the deprogramming itself, as in the case of documentarian Mia Donovan, whose film *Deprogrammed* explored how her fourteen-year-old stepbrother, a rebellious teen whose stepfather believed he was in a satanic cult in the 1990s, was abducted by Patrick, who tied him to a chair for five days to force him to "recant" beliefs he did not hold; Donovan balanced the persistent trauma her brother described with some of the positive outcomes Patrick claims.)[24]

Even if forced deconversion was successful, backsliding was frequent, so the deprogrammed persons had to be watched over until their states stabilized. In a 1994 article, Louis Jolyon West and the anti-cult psychotherapist Paul Martin called this return to robotic follower behavior "floating" and described how a "trigger that can be visual (i.e., seeing a book written by the cult leader), verbal, physical, gustatory, or even olfactory" could shift the ex-member into a vague and unfocused state, from which they might be "lost" again to the doctrine if intervention was not performed or if the reprogramming was not reinforced.[25]

By the early 1980s, legal troubles becalmed the pirate-like zeal of Patrick and other deprogrammers, accused of abuse and extreme methods of their own. Patrick was taken to court, vindicated in one case, and sent to prison in another. A watershed came when a colleague, Galen Kelly, kidnapped the wrong person, the roommate of an heiress target. (Whether this was a setup or not has been debated, but the deprogrammer was subsequently convicted in a jury trial in 1993, a decision itself overturned in 1994.)[26] Nonetheless, by the 1990s, most deprogrammers were renaming themselves "exit counselors," and were no longer abducting individuals but merely providing information, often carrying around briefcases full of material. In a preinternet age, this could be powerfully effective to a group member in an information-poor environment.

....

After some skirmishes in the 1970s, the cult wars broke out in full force during the 1980s, partly in response to deprogramming's excesses. The main phase of fighting was between experts (mostly psychologists) who saw themselves as defending abused former cult members, and academics (primarily sociologists) who saw themselves as defending religious freedom. The battles are little remembered today except by veterans who survived them, but epistemologically speaking they mark a burning trash fire of that decade, one that raged around the question of how much an individual can be controlled by an outside force, whether a benevolent God or a malignant Big Brother. The battles played out first on streets and carpeted rooms and later in the courts. They fought over a question that led to another question: Is brainwashing a real thing? And, can there ever be a *100 percent against-the-will, cognitively disabling, total transformation* as brainwashing would seem, in its classic expressions, to stipulate? Under the MK-ULTRA program, in fact, the CIA's Office of Technical Services had tried this around 1961 and found that no, you could not create a totally controlled automaton, with or without force.[27]

But the question persisted in a new form that cult experiences raised most urgently. In most cases, the person under the control of a cult *could leave.* They were not physically restrained. They might have walked away at many moments (recall this argument was devastatingly made about Patty Hearst during the bank robbery and sporting goods store shootout, and later her summer on the lam in Pennsylvania—why hadn't she just walked away?). According to scholars skeptical of brainwashing arguments, if there is evidence that a person has chosen something (even under deceptive or confusing circumstances), and if subsequently their body remains unfettered from walking away from that choice, then they cannot be said to have been under mind control. If a person "chooses" at all, some considered, this disqualified them from brainwashing. So argued, for example, Eileen Barker in her interesting if narrow book on hanging out with Moonies, *The Making of a Moonie: Choice or Brainwashing?* For Barker, the fact that 90 percent of those who attended recruiting meetings for the Moonies then opted

Darksome House of Mortal Clay

not to join them was prima facie evidence that there was no brainwashing at work.

Singer thrived on the pushback at first and embraced the role of anti-cult bulldog. As she gained a higher profile, and attracted the enmity of cultic groups, she increasingly garnered the descriptor "feisty."[28] In a later-in-life interview she displayed this quality with a fierce broadside against those who willfully or ignorantly misunderstood cults: "The public takes care of their fear," she told the *Philadelphia Inquirer* in 1997, "by thinking only crazies and stupid people wind up in cults." This was not so, as her own mounting reams of evidence confirmed: "There's no one type of person who is vulnerable."[29] She became a lightning rod for enraged cult leadership—for example, Scientologists—and their assiduous followers, who rummaged through her trash, threatened her, and followed her over the years. Despite this, she persisted. In a mid-1990s foreword to Singer's book, Lifton offered tribute: "Margaret Thaler Singer stands alone in her extraordinary knowledge of the psychology of cults."[30] A question soon arose: How would that extraordinary knowledge fare under intensified attack?

Meanwhile, you may ask, as I once naively did: Who could possibly be *pro-cult*? The answer surprised me: The opponents to Singer and the brainwashing experts were, mostly, academic social scientists specializing in the history and sociology of religion. A few of the most prolific were James T. Richardson of the University of Nevada, Reno; David Bromley of Virginia Commonwealth University; and Thomas Robbins, an independent scholar who lived in Minnesota. I observed that, for the most part, they hailed from lesser-known and not-quite-so-prestigious institutions as did Singer, Lifton, and West. (An exception was Barker, the sociologist who immersed herself with the Moonies, who was tenured at the London School of Economics.) The sociologists tended to take a perspective from within the groups, often using ethnographic methods for their books, and publishing with great fervor. On the other side, the question of book writing was a sore point. Recall that Dr. West, as I've demonstrated, lied under oath at the Hearst trial when he claimed he had published books. In fact, his unpublished papers are full of plans to complete various tomes on various topics. One of them was a West and Singer collaboration about the Hearst trial, meant to summarize their views on brainwashing. Forays into literary representation included a roadmap laying out eight future books to a New York agent named Sterling Lord. Three years after West's initial promise of imminent production he again alerted the agent, "I have just begun a six-month sabbatical leave to get the Hearst book out of my system once and for all," but this appears to have been the last gasp of the project rather than its final push.[31] When Singer, West, and others on the anti-cult side did publish—and it should be said that they produced a solid record of journal articles—it was not in the same places as their antagonists. (Lifton did, and does, publish many books, it should also be said.)

The pro-cult side was not in favor of abuse, exactly, so much as worried about stigmatizing all sects for the sins of a few bad organizations. For this reason, as a secondary effect, these scholars tended to accept the stories of current members (who derided claims of abuse as the product of unstable and embittered people unable to make a go of group life) and to reject or minimize accounts by ex-members (who spoke personally of their own abuse or of others they witnessed). One had to "not believe" ex-members, to borrow the language of #MeToo. The sociologist corps reminded onlookers that there were an estimated 1,800 religions in America, of which 900 could be regarded as "unconventional."[32] Most were harmless, or, at the very least, should be free to express their off-kilter opinions. Yet the Big Five, swimming in cash and controversy, took up much of public attention, whereas smaller groups were vulnerable to loss of stature and liberty to practice as they wished. Defending these newborn groups, these scholars preferred the term New Religious Movements to apply to what

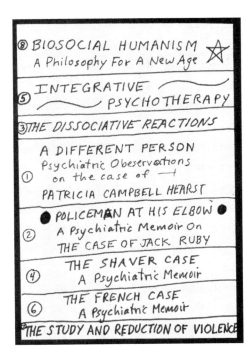

In 1980, Louis Jolyon West doodled this list of the books he intended to write, in order from #1, on Patricia Hearst, to #8, on Biosocial Humanism. #3, The Dissociative Reactions, would include hypnotic trance and cover much cult behavior, from what drew people into high-demand groups to what kept them there. None of the books were ever written, though partial drafts of some can be found in his papers.
COURTESY: LJ WEST PAPERS, UCLA LIBRARY SPECIAL COLLECTIONS, A1713 CHARLES E. YOUNG RESEARCH LIBRARY LOS ANGELES, CA 90095-1575.

others called cults. After all, America itself, as a nation, sprang from members of one splinter group. Appalled at the methods of forcible belief extinguishment used in deprogramming, they viewed it as a particular affront, painting the process as (in the heated words of one scholar) "protracted spiritual gang rape."[33] In return, such scholars garnered the labels "cult apologists" or "cult lovers." Genuine antipathy reigned, and researchers not only demurred from respectfully citing each other's work (unless attacking it) but admitted to bearing personal animus against the other side, of whose bad faith they were convinced.[34]

Meanwhile, the deeper-pocketed cults such as Scientology and the Moonies (Unification Church) invited sociologists to conferences in nice beachy spots and elegant urban hotels. On many occasions, scholars allowed themselves to be importuned. An onsides micro-war broke out among sociologists of religion: Was it acceptable even to set foot at one of the burgeoning number of conferences held by Scientology and the Unification Church? At a 1976 conference in Washington, DC, sponsored by the Reverend Sun Myung Moon, Nobel Prize winner Eugene P. Wigner headlined, and Moon appeared (though his name was not highlighted in the official promotional materials). Many other big academic names participated; their travel, lodging, and honoraria paid at a level matching the degree of their eminence. "Why not accept a fat fee, a few nights on the cuff at one of America's snappiest hotels, and a chance to rub elbows with some of America's intellectual giants?" the sociologist Irving Louis Horowitz queried in the *Atlantic* in 1977.[35] The answer, in his view, was that merely appearing at such events conferred undeserved respectability on the hosts.

The "cult-lovers" occasionally embraced the insult. One scholar, Susan Palmer, sketched a butterfly-catcher fascination: "Today I find myself in the not-quite-respectable, morally problematic, and impecunious field of 'cult' studies," she wrote in a 2001 essay. "Travelling the 'yellow brick road' of social scientific research, I encounter oddly coherent worldviews constructed higgledy-piggledy out of the most incongruous elements: songs of Solomon, UFO lore, electric bulbs, biofeedback machines, gnostic creation myths—all welded into one seamless syncretism."[36] While this scholar clearly delighted in the exotic variety of groups, her approach seemed to tune out the potential harms of these charmingly Rube Goldberg–esque oddly coherent worldviews. Whether paradises or hells, cults offered realms that drew researchers in and, as is the nature of participant fieldwork, often led to a sympathetic adoption of their micro-worldviews.

Then there was the money (or the remunerative) issue. This appeared petty at times, but it also suggested deeper depths of legitimate concern. A hostile scholar pointed out the high pay Singer and allied experts received for their work, and likewise a scholarly ally confirmed that "lucrative stipends to expert witnesses were offered by members of both sides of this dispute in court cases."[37] James T. Richardson from the University of Nevada, Reno, toted up Singer's cases, finding she had testified in over forty as of the late 1980s (suggesting she was in it for the money).[38] Alan Scheflin, a prominent law professor and cult expert, recalled that during this period, he personally knew one medical expert who charged $900 an hour.[39] One leading anti-cult figure was overheard to complain that the time taken to file an amicus brief "would cost him $500,000 in lost fees." The gossipy lack of names in many of these allegations tracks with the way rumors circulated to take down reputations. However, it is still the case that, in their eventual lawsuit against their enemies the APA and a group of sociology of religion scholars, Singer and her colleague Richard Ofshe would ask for $15 million each in damages, reflecting their estimated loss of earnings as experts whose views on brainwashing had been systematically tarnished. And so escalated a late skirmish of the cult wars. But before we learn its outcome, we must turn to the backdrop against which the major standoff took place.

·········

The case of David Molko and Tracy Leal formed the final turning point—or, a series of turning points. During its several decisions, which rolled out slowly over about half a decade, brainwashing went from legally viable to a kill shot of a legal argument. According to the views that would prevail, any attempt to prove undue influence, particularly when it was defined in a certain way, the Singerian way, as the utter *and almost immediate* loss of free will through cult contact (to the point where the person affected is not responsible for their own actions), could no longer be maintained.

Resounding evidence of this development, which could be called the sunsetting of Singerism, is found today: Recent successful cases of guilty verdicts for exploitative and sexually abusive cult activity—Lawrence Ray at Sarah Lawrence College, and Keith Raniere of

NXIVM—hinged on charges of racketeering, sexual trafficking, and forced labor, despite that, as the Judge Lewis Liman in the Ray case observed in handing down a sixty-year sentence, "It was sadism, pure and simple." In common parlance, both cases are seen as brainwashing. Lawyer Paul Morantz strategized as early as the 1970s that suits had to bring not only brainwashing charges but other, easier-to-prove aspects in case brainwashing didn't gain traction; and in the twenty-first century, as even Singer's allies acknowledge, brainwashing is not useful in a legal sense.[40]

David Molko was a twenty-seven-year-old recent graduate of Temple University Law School in Philadelphia when, in 1978, on graduating, he moved across the country to San Francisco with a vague plan of seeking employment and seeing what California held. "He was quite uncertain about this future at that time," the legal action later stated.[41] "Cults were big news following the events of Synanon and Jonestown. Thus he was on the alert for those seeking to proselytize."[42] Jonestown refers to Jonestown, Guyana, a remote spot where members of the Peoples Temple, originally from Northern California, resettled to escape what they viewed as an inveterately racist and oppressive American system. For a time, the commune, first in the Fillmore District of San Francisco and later in Oakland, seemed to achieve a racially integrated, highly idealistic collective of fellow conscientious objectors to American delusion. Group members labored together to plant small-scale farms and experiment in urban group living for the common good. Yet their leader, Jim Jones, a self-declared prophet who galvanized the growing congregation, became increasingly addled by stimulant drugs and top-down power that included sexual abuse of congregants. As his paranoia grew, Jones perceived that his predictions of persecution were coming true, especially after relocating the group to Guyana. A US congressional investigatory group led by Representative Leo Ryan went to Jonestown, and a squad ambushed and killed Ryan. Jones ordered the mass suicide of his devotees, who drank a red punch and forced the drink on their children; more than three hundred of the nine hundred who died were infants and youths under the age of seventeen. A Gallup poll in December 1978 found that 98 percent of the US public had heard or read about the Peoples Temple mass-suicide event, a level of awareness matched in the pollsters' experience "only by the attack on Pearl Harbor and the explosion of the atom bomb."[43]

Around this time, Synanon, a California-based drug-treatment method based on breaking down and rebuilding participants, transformed into a religious movement. The Synanon community was revealed to use extreme abuse in the form of Mao-like tactics. An exposé of the group, cowritten by a University of California, Berkeley, sociologist named Richard Ofshe, won the Pulitzer Prize, and the writer would go on to partner closely with Margaret Singer.

Vigilance about the dangers of cults, however, did not protect Molko. Waiting at a bus stop in San Francisco on a Sunday in January 1979, he encountered two young men who told him they were part of a group combating injustice. Molko asked several questions about the group's identity (he was told they were simply a group fighting for environmental betterment) and whether there was any religious affiliation (no, there was not, he was assured). The two men, Mark Bush and Ernest Patten, then invited him to dinner at their co-living house on Bush Street. Perhaps, later, David Molko would wish the bus had come more quickly. While waiting, he agreed to attend. Once there he noticed several others who were also guests like himself, though none of the newcomers were allowed to speak to each other; rather, each was surrounded and engaged in constant banter during dinner and in the breaks surrounding an after-dinner lecture.

A slide show depicted a farm in rural Boonville, California, to which Molko was invited for a weekend. (Actually, it was an indoctrination facility.) He soon boarded a bus with a dozen others headed for the farm, first signing a piece of paper with his name and address on it.

After a day of calisthenics, lectures, testimonials, and not a moment to himself to process what was happening, he asked another participant named Bethie what exactly this group was, to which she misleadingly answered that it was called the Creative Community Project. Later during the weekend, as an exhausting round of nonstop lectures and group activities continued, he asked another person what the group's guiding philosophy was and was told it derived from the Reverend Sun Myung Moon and other philosophers such as Aristotle and Thomas Jefferson. No one mentioned the Moonies, nor the Unification Church, Moon's main organ, nor that Moon was their primary influence. Molko was not physically restrained from leaving and was aware—the court proceedings later insisted—that buses left daily for San Francisco. Yet, he was dissuaded from departure when, a day or two into the experience, he asked how he might be able to get to the city and learned that the bus for San Francisco came only once a day and that happened to be at three o'clock in the morning. If only he would stay a little longer, he would learn some vital information, his new friends urged him. Even if their lectures seemed almost entirely repetitive—let's be frank, they were *droning*—and there were no apparent social or environmental issues discussed, still, he allowed himself to be dissuaded and stayed for the full program. No one else seemed to be physically restrained from leaving, either (though perhaps a few ended up catching the bus to escape).

Next, although he was still eager to return to San Francisco, he found himself agreeing to go to another camp to learn more about the group's teaching and absorb the general vibe. He had not been allowed to socialize with the other recruits and had been followed by an experienced member even when on his way to and from the bathroom, but his suspicions were not aroused, or not sufficiently aroused, to cause him to make a desperate break for it. And so, on January 29, he left Boonville for another site, Camp K, where he ended up residing for five to seven weeks, during which time he was shuttled between the

Darksome House of Mortal Clay

two camps (K and Boonville) and became increasingly despairing and distressed about the future. He was stuck. During this stretch of time, he discovered the group's identity.

Admitting they had lied, group members justified the deception by reference to the terrible press encumbering the Moonies, including articles describing it as a dangerous cult. Therefore, they were obliged to hide their identity during the initial stages of encountering someone. Though confused by this, David Molko agreed to stay a little longer, hoping to work out his confusion. He admitted later in court that he was never physically restrained, though certainly he yearned to leave and found himself somehow unable to: At each stage, the pushy or enthusiastic or "lovebombing" Moonies prevailed upon him, adjusting their approach to his mood and actions. By the time he did return to San Francisco around two months later, he was a fully ordained new member who promptly donated his savings of $6,000 to the group. Now, he spent his time "witnessing"—recruiting others on the streets of the city where he had been recruited not long before. The church sent him to a bar review session at Hastings Law School in Berkeley, and that summer he took and passed the exam. As he left, two "deprogrammers" (sent by his family) grabbed him on the street. He never returned to the church.

That January day at the bus stop, Molko had crossed paths with members of the Oakland branch of the Unification Church (known to be the most successful recruiting center for Moonies in the Western world.)[44] The church was started by Sun Myung Moon, who was born in Korea in 1920. By 1955, he had established small chapters of what the US Department of Justice would come to call the Moon organization in some thirty countries. He made money to support his cause by manufacturing weapons. He sent a missionary group to the United States in 1959 and moved to the United States in 1971. Within a decade there would be three million members claimed by the church, an astounding growth curve.

Did Moon borrow his indoctrination techniques from the Korean POW camps? Singer believed so: Bo Hi Pak, who became Moon's highest marshal, had experience in the Korean military as a former lieutenant colonel who worked in the POW camps (apparently), and Margaret Singer believed this was the source (or a contributing source) for the architecting of their brainwashing recruitment methods—it was a direct link.[45] Historical evidence from a 1984 study suggests the story is more complex, at least when considering the early missionary recruitment in the 1970s: "There are numerous reports that Moon gave little, if any, specific instruction to his early missionaries on matters of organizational or proselytizing procedures," writes Barker. Some factions tried face-to-face conversations; others believed radio would work best. Some argued for targeting the old, while others leaned toward youth. "Each was left to his or her own devices. This meant that a process of trial and error was going on not just within each group, but also between the groups, and this in itself could well have contributed to the (relative) success of the movement in the early 1970s, when it was to draw on the experiences learned through a number of trial experiments."[46] In other words, there was no top-down implementation strategy from Moon or his top deputy for recruiting—at least not initially. There was, however, an intensely adaptive and experimental environment where techniques could, essentially, be A/B tested in real-life settings on the streets of Oakland and San Francisco, to see what worked and what did not.

A similar conversion as Molko's happened to nineteen-year-old Tracy Leal, who by the time she learned the identity of the group, was already hooked. (She eventually joined the lawsuit alleging deceptive recruitment practices.) Before either knew it, they had joined the Moonies and were actively engaged in bringing in others. Theirs were "involuntary conversions," Singer would soon argue, and it certainly seemed so to their family members looking on. Deprogrammers, hired by their families, brainwashed them back—that is, coercively compelled them to abandon their new beliefs and to re-embrace their former orientation. Converted, they reconverted.

....

Testifying as part of the original 1983 lawsuit (for damages and attempting to recover their financial contributions to the church), Margaret Singer based her opinion explicitly on the experiences of the Korean War POWs. She stated:

> I have found that both David Molko and Tracy Leal were rendered incapable of exercising their own will and judgment as a result of the systematic manipulations performed by the Unification Church members. I found that the ability of David Molko and the ability of Tracy Leal to judge for themselves was greatly diminished by the methods employed and these two recruits were not capable of responding to the information that they had been deceptively recruited by Moonies with whom they would not otherwise have freely associated.[47]

Initially, Singer's testimony found purchase: She argued that within about twenty-four hours—the critical period of deception during which the group fraudulently concealed its identity from Molko and Leal—their persuasive actions had already taken them both beyond the pale, no longer able to reason. As another young person who was wooed into the same organization around this time stated, "While it seemed like I was making my own decisions, I was not."[48] Molko and Leal won a substantial judgment. But the case was not over, not at all.

....

The case rose through appeals, and, in anticipation of its reaching them, the US Supreme Court requested that the American Psychological Association (APA) provide a report on the status of brainwashing theory as understood by scientific consensus. The association then turned to Margaret Singer, deputizing her to form and chair a committee. Accepting the mantle, Singer gathered personnel including Dr. West; Michael Langone, a prominent anti-cult psychologist; and three others. Somewhat inauspiciously they named themselves DIMPAC, an acronym that, in addition to vaguely insulting its creators, stood for the APA Task Force on Deceptive and Indirect Methods of Persuasion and Control. (Later they would change it to DITPAC, substituting the T in "Techniques" for the M in "Methods.") Their report was years in the writing, and while it was in an elongated "forthcoming" phase, their academic enemies—already far more prolific in terms of sheer pages produced—ranged themselves, using the Molko appeal as a rallying cry. A coalition of angry and well-footnoted sociologists joined to file two amicus curiae briefs in advance of the Singer report, hoping to have it, and Singer herself, deemed DOA and persona non grata, respectively. A hostile group of psychologists followed along and filed their own amicus brief along the same lines. Determined that Margaret Singer should no longer have her day in court, nor any further such days, these briefs argued that Singer's views had no scientific standing and that they were neither respected nor respectable. Perhaps, they allowed, the Lifton and Schein research on POWs was important and still state of the art, but applying this model to understand current-day cults was going too far. The American Psychological Association preliminarily accepted these amicus briefs. All the while Singer and her allies vigorously disputed their challengers with the air of an annoyed hiker swatting swarms of gnats away. But the gnats would score a victory.

At the height of this contretemps, the Singer-led DIMPAC/DITPAC report at last came in—though a final version was never filed (due to its antagonists' terminal coup, which was on the verge of happening). Notably, the "Report of the Task Force on Deceptive and Indirect Techniques of Persuasion and Control" lacked full references and was not adequately proofread.[49] Reading it today, it comes across as boilerplate in argument and a bit sloppy in execution, as if the authors were pressed to summon up the standard case for the existence of brainwashing, citing the usual sources (and including in the Definitions section the work of the religious studies scholars). It was up to the APA, then, to judge whether it would accept its case for scientific adequacy.

A very complex kerfuffle ensued. Briefs were contested, withdrawn, fought over, shot down. Passions ran high. But the outcome was quite clear: On May 11, 1987, the ethics board of the APA ruled largely negatively against the Singer approach to brainwashing in cults, opining that the report DIMPAC supplied "lacks ... scientific rigor."[50] Evaluating it further, the APA ruled that, at least in these circumstances and in the present case, the brainwashing scientific evidence was unprepossessing. The authors had not properly defined what they were studying.[51] So unscholarly in tone was the report, one evaluator noted, that it resembled an over-the-top coercive "brainwashing" text itself.[52] Singer and the other experts—but especially Singer—should not be allowed to call herself an expert to give testimony. The emerging consensus was that the Korean War dynamics did not translate to these new cult contexts, especially where the coercion was internal rather than external, and even more especially in a legal sense.

Hubbub followed. Was the APA, the most prestigious organization of American psychologists and a banner-holder for world psychologists—because, make no mistake, parallel battles of the cult wars were taking place in Europe and Japan, where cults also thrived—saying that brainwashing would never hold water, that it was *inherently* unscientific? Or was it simply saying that, at the present time and judging by the Singer report, brainwashing as a legal concept did not meet muster? A third option convinces me, and with hindsight seems to be the logical conclusion: If your definition of scientific is that which produces a yes-or-no deterministic truth (which in a sense, is what a courtroom demands), brainwashing will never be scientific. But if your definition of scientific is participating in a constant struggle toward greater adequacy and rigor, then it very well might.

Anyway: Should a flawed and sloppy report be the ultimate gauge of whether something exists or not?

....

Immediately, the 1987 ruling by the APA cast the more than forty cases at which Singer had testified into question. Claiming a mandate from heaven, as it were, an attack posse forged on. Cases in which Singer's testimony had been relied on were now reversed, including one in which a former practitioner of Transcendental Meditation, Robert Kropinski, had suffered injuries to hips, legs, and spine learning to "fly"—which is one of the promises of TM. The meditator was enticed with assurances that years of practice would equip him to levitate or fly clean off the ground while in deep meditation (in addition to reversing the aging process and reducing depression). Given instruction in the procedure, which entails an ungainly hopping about in the lotus position across a carpeted floor—go ahead and look up "TM flying" on YouTube—some feel duped, having eagerly looked forward to this watershed moment for years. Others are content to accept the ritualized hopping as levitation. The practice of calling this "flying" is in part, arguably, a training in cognitive dissonance.[53]

Disappointed on many levels after nine years of practice and sustaining what he felt to be long-term physical and psychological harm, Kropinski had been awarded $138,000 in damages based on fraud and the negligent infliction of physical injury. In other words, he had been brainwashed, as he argued, and the court agreed.[54] The *New York Times* dubbed it the Self-Levitation Case. But after Singer's loss of expert status, the judgment was reversed. The appeals judgment read, in part, "Kropinski, however, has failed to provide any evidence that Dr.

Singer's particular theory, namely that techniques of thought reform may be effective in the absence of physical threats or coercion, has a significant following in the scientific community, let alone general acceptance."[55]

Meanwhile, the landmark *George v. International Society for Krishna Consciousness* finding, too, was mostly reversed in 1992 (Singer's part of it, especially).[56] Overall, it seems, courts were reluctant to reduce a plaintiff's responsibility due to the claim that they had lost control of their reasoning faculties. Perhaps as a legal strategy, Singer emphasized that only rational disablement counted, a view that relegated the emotions—and thus the dynamics of trauma and numbing—to a secondary or less important aspect of brainwashing. I would suggest that this argument was initially successful because acknowledging trauma in such cases is difficult, and especially so in the courtroom (as Patricia Hearst's trial amply showed). Ultimately, however, the overstress on rational fettering could not be sustained. Singer's livelihood was diminished, as well as that of her professional partner, Richard Ofshe. In 1992, they unsuccessfully sued their academic enemies for conspiring to destroy their careers and professions through reputational assault. A second lawsuit in 1994 against the APA and several enemy scholars was dismissed as frivolous—the judge deemed the conflict a scholarly dispute over psychological theories, pointing to First Amendment protections—so that, with the court invoking the SLAPP rule (strategic lawsuits against public participation), they were forced to pay their antagonists' legal fees.[57]

....

The Singerian point of view, while valuable in many ways, became a caricature when loosed in a courtroom. Her position neglected the truth that even the most beguiling of allurers, the most dissembling of recruiters, and the hardest-core of believers had at one point been drawn into or born into the cult—arguably, everyone but the leader had—and therefore (at least according to Singer's own theory) had themselves been rationally bypassed in this way. And yet many of them went on actively to lure others into abandoning their faculties and their finances. The recruited, in other words, became the recruiters. (Molko was no sooner deceptively recruited into Moonie-hood than he began deceiving others.) Sociologically and spiritually, this was interesting but legally it was fraught—at what moment did a person go from non-responsible to responsible? Vulnerable people, instructed in certain thought-stopping and dissonance-quieting techniques, went on to prey on other vulnerable people. This made the argument of cognitive disablement somewhat unstable because it required an overall strategy, a long con, a nefarious ploy—which may indeed have been the case at the top levels—but to assume such a ploy ignored the process and sets of cascading relationships by which the con came to be sincerely enacted in and through the changes that people experienced.

The even-keeled sociologist Benjamin Zablocki, who traveled across the United States over years talking with former and current cult members, and who came very much to believe in the reality of brainwashing, noted that its meaning is constantly skewed, even by experts, and especially when they appear in court: "Brainwashing ... is about relationships, not about individual dispositions."[58] It emerges from sociogenesis as much as psychogenesis (to use the etiquette-exploring scholar Norbert Elias' terms).

The cult wars—the amicus briefs lobbed like bombs, the hurt feelings, the scholarly miffs, the overturned decisions, the charismatic experts—were a referendum on brainwashing's adequacy as a legal and "real" thing. But whether or not it was real could not be settled this way.

·········

Setbacks notwithstanding, Singer lived on in the Berkeley Hills, now occupying her own home, nearby her husband's, on winding streets

Darksome House of Mortal Clay 275

amid gardens. "She and her husband Jerome ('Jay') own two houses just to hold all their stuff," a glowing profile in the local paper reported in 2002. "The houses perch not far from each other like citadels of academic calm, surrounded by huge, leafy trees and stone and brick steps."[59] Their two kids, youngsters when Singer took up the anti-cult mantle, went on to flourishing careers in the Bay Area. Teaming up with a young sociologist named Janja Lalich, Singer turned the ill-fated report into a highly successful 1995 book called *Cults in our Midst*. The success of this work argues for the point I (and others) make, which is that while brainwashing lacks a legal foothold, exactly the paradoxes and truths its workings reveal can be fruitfully and empirically explored in the realm of thought and action.

Among other things, the cult wars raised the question of what constitutes freedom of thought in an information-controlled distortive environment.

As it happens, this brings us to the bridge we must cross from the realm of cults into that of communications-based brainwashing. What would it mean if, through suggestion and information transfer, a coercive environment could be established—one in which persuasion then operated with great efficiency and efficacy? Who then would be the hornswogglers? And ultimately, certain excesses aside, might there not be value in reconsidering the work of Margaret Singer?

PART 3

BRAINWASHING EVOLVES

The evolving understandings and misunderstandings of trauma play out in daily interactions with Big Tech, from bold comments to fleeting gestures to minute scrolls. Emotional life, especially intense and difficult emotions, are literally harvested (from users) and harnessed in social media and other arenas.

This can be seen especially well in a phenomenon I call hyper-persuasion.

9

How to Look Inside People, Extract Their Intimate Data, and Gently Nudge Emotional States into Being

In the 1960s, people readily entertained sharing their dreams. Bob Dylan invited a trade: "I'll let you be in my dreams if I can be in yours." Martin Luther King Jr.'s "I Have a Dream" speech was easily understood as potentially the whole society's collective dream. And in a paranoid turn, the main character in Thomas Pynchon's 1973 *Gravity's Rainbow* began by realizing that his sleep realms were also being shared: "He had known for a while that certain episodes he dreamed could not be his own. This wasn't through any rigorous daytime analysis of content, but just because he *knew*." Today the idea that social media and the digital world might be shaping our inner lives—sculpting our dreams while asleep and awake—does actually demand rigorous daytime analysis. Otherwise, people tend to remain skeptical.

I learned this in a class I was teaching a couple of years ago on the history and present implications of Big Data. We were sitting around the seminar table discussing the erosion of privacy and whether or how much we should be concerned in a personal way. I brought up a café in New Haven I'd heard about, run by a Japanese company, that offered—to those with a valid university ID—free, high-quality coffee to be consumed in chicly minimalist study spaces. A lovely, caffeinated repose in a pleasant setting, at no cost. Their business model was that students still had to pay for the accompanying croissant or pain au chocolat, as well as a further twist: They also had to provide their data. Not just their name, age, and zip code, but their study plans and future career interests. This information, exchanged for beverage and ambiance, would then be routed to prospective employers. "Would you go there?" I asked my class. Would you take that deal? Many said they would, if the coffee was good, simply because at least you were being given something tangible in return for your data, which otherwise people tend to surrender for no recompense. This seemed to be an almost sheepish response, especially in a class devoted to increasing our understanding of how consequential data extraction, even in its anonymized forms, can be. Some might call it a real-life demonstration of the privacy paradox, a phenomenon scholars define, in wonderfully understated terms, as "discrepancies between expressed privacy concerns and actual online behavior."[1] A giant shrug, not out of indifference but out of a feeling that the breach has already happened.

The local point was soon moot. Later that year, the enterprise shut down due to allegations of unfair business practices in the three US college towns where it had opened: "New Cafe Harvests Data, Bars Townies," read a headline in the *New Haven Independent* in May 2019. (The company continues to ply its business model in Japanese and Indian college towns.) But the paradoxes that shape our online behavior are anything but moot.

What few people understand, in working our way through the seemingly infinite chain-link series of micro-decisions each of us faces every day, is how emotional engineering through data mining is historically based in trauma. When I say trauma, I don't mean the annoyingly overused all-purpose signifier for anything that

How to Look Inside People

bugs you. I mean the response in the present that is your unscripted return to an unresolved event or series of wounds. (And I mean this quite literally, as we will see.) The old evasion—how scientists often failed or were unable to see that the quotient of emotional, bodily suffering (rather than rational, cognitive malfunction) is the root of brainwashing—has come back to haunt us in a world that is increasingly algorithmically defined. We can't see it because we see it everywhere.

....

During the late 1870s, Josiah Stickney Lombard, the author of *Experimental Researches on the Temperature of the Head* and another volume on invertebrates, decided to measure something substantially more difficult than skulls or sea anemone. He wanted to grasp people's moods at the precise moment they were being formed.[2] To test the arrival of a feeling—as opposed to the exertion of the intellect—he had each of his subjects read aloud or to themselves passages from books that stirred strong emotion. The passage in question could be poetry or prose so long as "an emotional character" was evident. You couldn't just read something boring (he tried).[3] He employed an instrument shown to be superior to the thermometer for measuring the temperature of specific parts of the head in an extremely exact way: a thermoelectric apparatus.[4] In one case, as the reading commenced, the subject grew uninterested—"not attentive," Lombard noted—and the temperature of his head—measured at anterior, posterior, and middle regions of the surface of the skull—dropped 0.002 degrees Celsius.

Soon, however, the subject was swept up in the words being read aloud ("thoroughly interested" by the end of four minutes, read Lombard's notes), at which point the temperature of his head began to rise steadily. Over the next thirty-three minutes it shot up 0.036 degrees Celsius. The results from a galvanometer, swinging +18 degrees during the proceedings, confirmed the thermometric measurements. In all regions that were measured, the testee's temperature gained altitude as poetry was declaimed, with an average rise of 0.0385 degrees Celsius across the scalp.

Lombard was not always clear how he stimulated the specific emotions he was after—anger, vexation, and mirth—but it seems to have been by means of varying content of the poetry or prose, making one wonder which passages reliably induced rageful feelings sufficient for the experiment. (Which poetry did he use? We may never know.)* Sometimes an emotion would be generated unexpectedly, as when a subject became annoyed or giggled during the procedures for reasons external to the study's design—and Lombard would not hesitate to make a measurement of this unintended emotional state. Anger he chose not to measure at its height, perhaps because it was difficult to get a truly angry person to sit still properly. But once it had subsided into basic indignation he went ahead. Mirth he wisely examined in the form of moderate mirth. It is not clear exactly at which intensity level vexation was suitably gauged.

For the modern knowledge worker today, a takeaway of the more than sixty thousand observations Lombard made is that in every case and across the different regions of the skull, emotional activity—whether mirthful, angry, or worried—created more heat than intellectual work did.[5] "Hot takes" really do seem to be just that. Other points on the body were less likely to rise in temperature at all: The femoral artery in the groin, the brachial artery in the upper arm, and the carotid artery in the neck, when measured where they came closest to the surface of the skin, were "usually unaffected" by poetry or prose.[6]

Lombard was part of a long movement among researchers to render the elusive stuff of emotions as numbers, although they did

---

* Emily Dickinson's "If I feel physically as if the top of my head were taken off, I know that is poetry," might have been a bit too on point, even if her 1870 letter to Thomas Wentworth Higginson had been published at the time of the experiment, which it wasn't and would not be for another three-quarters of a century.

not investigate direct contagion of emotions.[7] By the pre–World War II period, researchers moved on from taking simple head surface temperatures and unleashed a proliferation of newer instruments on the quest to measure feelings. These included the stomach balloon; the tremograph; the electroencephalogram (EEG); and an assortment of other metabolic, endocrinological, and chemical assessments. All were meant to achieve better and better exactitude. In the 1960s, a new wave of technologies and approaches made the study even more sophisticated—and "sophisticated" became a self-applied congratulatory adjective to characterize an approach that was ever more machine-dependent, quantitative, and numerically oriented.[8] Modern researchers saw emotions "in the general scheme of body-as-machine," according to the historian of emotions, Otniel Dror. "In this scheme, specific physiological patterns signified an emotion. Thus, emotion was a pattern written in the language of the biological elements that one monitored in, or sampled from, the organism."[9] Through studies like Stickney's and his successors', each emotion was operationalized, you could say—for it was *defined as* the data array that emerged from its expression. Anger was what anger did. It could be expressed in numbers.

Soon, another thread would arise in the science of emotions, one that explored what Lombard and others had ignored in their emphasis on single subjects: *How emotions spread, and how they are emblematic of consciousness itself.* A key difference presented itself during the late-twentieth and early-twenty-first centuries: A new goal—to engineer and be able to spread emotions outside of the laboratory—became central. And as we will see, this research drew directly from traumatic experiences, as if they were a rig drilling for rock-embedded shale oil.

....

In early 2012, during the seven days between January 11 and January 18, a research team at Facebook ran an experiment on almost 700,000 users (689,003 to be exact) to test whether making very small changes in the emotional valence of their news feeds could engender "mass emotional contagion." News feeds at the time were relatively new to Facebook—it was only four or so years since they had been reformulated to sit centrally in the Facebook user experience. Previously, one encountered a far more controlled landing "page," redolent of the old MySpace or Friendster setups. An early, influential definition of social media, or social network sites (SNS), by researchers danah boyd of Microsoft and Nicole Ellison of the University of Michigan, had three components—(1) a bounded system where an individual could construct a profile, which (2) articulated a list of other users to whom one was connected, which connections could (3) be viewed and traversed—none of which was a news stream feeding algorithmically directed materials to the participant.[10] The Like button—which debuted on Facebook in 2009 as a simple way for users to contribute "emotional data" to their interactions—was also somewhat new, though people (for example, in the comments section of the *Guardian* online) were already complaining of *Brave New World*-style enslavement to the platform.[11]

Over the course of the week, Facebook showed a subgroup of people fewer positive posts in their algorithmically delivered news feed—note that the designers of the experiment did not increase the number of negative items but rather filtered out some percentage of the positive-tending ones, thus making each feed less cheery. The rate of reduction randomly ranged from 10 percent to 90 percent of emotional positivity, depending on the person. Another subgroup saw fewer negative posts, by the same filtering method, thus resulting in a cheerier feed. (These two parallel subgroups each had a control condition in which users had their feeds manipulated, but in an entirely random manner.) Given that most people already had too many Facebook friends to be able to see all the content they posted, selection for the news feed was mandated, and was usually done to maximize "showing viewers the content they will find most relevant and engaging."[12] For seven days, however, the experiment changed strategies without alerting people, tilting toward emotional negativity or positivity. How were such emotions defined? The emotional valence of each post was measured and deemed negative or positive by word-counting software that picked out at least one negative or positive keyword shown to correlate with self-reports of well-being and with measurable physiological states. (We will take a closer look at this software, for the simple reason that it was literally trained on subjects' traumatic experiences.)

After the alterations to their feeds, the 689,003 people who (unwittingly) populated the experiment then generated around three million posts. The study's authors found that users posted 0.1 percent fewer positive words in their own posts after the culling of a percentage of positive news items. In other words, a less happy incoming feed produced less happy outgoing posts. (There was also a significant effect observed in the group exposed to more positive messages, who subsequently posted more positive messages, but this effect was smaller—0.06 percent.) Since there was a range of manipulation, in that people's feeds had from 10 percent to 90 percent of their negative or positive news tossed, this degree of alteration was, in turn, weighted within the results—so, if your feed was more manipulated, your resulting posts would be given correspondingly more weight.

From these small but statistically significant changes, the result of little behavioral "nudges" that produced a tiny but measurable overall participant response, researchers concluded in their 2014 publication in *Proceedings of the National Academy of Sciences* (*PNAS*), "Experimental Evidence of Massive-Scale Emotional Contagion through Social Networks," that contagion on a large scale had occurred.[13] The Facebook Core Data Science team, under lead author Adam D. I. Kramer in concert with Cornell University data scientist Jeffrey Hancock and UC San Francisco researcher Jamie Guillory, however, were not just interested in *whether* it could occur but *how* it had been made to. They had—as they put it—operationalized emotional contagion.[14] They made it happen. (As had Lombard with single emotions.)

The publication date was exactly ten years since the founding of Facebook, six years since the marketing agency Universal McCann announced in a report that the "age of mass media" was giving way to the "age of social media," and two years since the company made its public stock offering. It would be another nine years until the surgeon general would declare social media a risk to the mental health of young people.[15] Perhaps this foray into prestige-level peer-reviewed science—though not Facebook's first, it would be its last on this subject at least—had something to do with a sense of arrival, a perception of having climbed a high peak and taking a moment to survey the opportunities arrayed on the vast horizon. Yet a closer look at the experiment shows it to be not so much a bird's-eye summit view as a kaleidoscope revealing partial rooms and shifting values at the company and in the world.

A year before the experiment began, its lead researcher, Adam Kramer, talked with the American Psychological Association, whose interviewer mentioned Facebook's "enviable subject pool" of (at the time) roughly five hundred million users who, each month, were reliably producing up to three hundred billion data points that could be used for research. Kramer commented, "It feels real, and somehow more legitimate than studies done on, for example, a couple hundred university freshmen."[16] He was referencing the long history of classic psychological studies born from the actions and reactions of college-student volunteers. In a public manner, Facebook's team was stepping into a new sense of reality ("It feels real") at what seemed then to be the conquering peak of Facebook's own influence, its troves of intimate data, though in retrospect it was more of a stepping stone. The harnessing of more and more data was typical of the rise of what Stanford University data historian Xiaochang

How to Look Inside People   287

Li, in an article called "There's No Data Like More Data," calls "algorithmic authority."[17]

And this is where everything changed. The Facebook Core Data Science team began their write-up by foregrounding two earlier studies, from 1993 and 2011, on the nature of emotional contagion. In the 1993 paper, psychologist Elaine Hatfield, historian Richard Rapson, and psychologist John Cacioppo (the first two were from the University of Hawai'i, so I will characterize this as the Hawaii study from now on) examined how people "nonconsciously and automatically mimic their companions' fleeting expressions of emotion" and even can come to "feel pale reflections" of others' feelings.[18] How do you *catch* someone else's feelings?

To answer this question, the Hawaii study sketched three phases of emotional contagion—mimicry, feedback, and solidification—not by crunching data, not by means of a bold experimental design, not by an fMRI machine, and not by reading their subjects poetry. It was 1993, after all, a good hundred years after Stickney but well over a decade before the Like button. Rather, they examined ideas and expressions through time, while doing a careful literature review of their own and others' studies.[19] This included a suite of experiments on microsynchrony, or the automatic, swift mimicking of another's facial expressions, which most babies can do soon after birth. They used electromyography (EMG) to measure this swift mimicry, which had not been done before. Of course, the Hawaii study was not the first to notice that emotions do spread between parents and babies, or people and other people. Almost any novel since *Tristram Shandy* (perhaps the earliest exemplar of modern, psychologically driven storytelling) seems to offer, if not formal proof, then strong confirmation that people "can and do 'feel themselves into' the emotional landscapes inhabited by their partners," as the study put it.[20] Philosopher John Locke and method acting pioneer Konstantin Stanislavski had also explored how emotions travel. The difference was that the Hawaii team was interested in finding the precise "feeling-yourself-into" *mechanisms*.

To do this, they turned to a passage from Vivian Gornick's 1987 memoir *Fierce Attachments*. This book is a master class on how the author "felt herself into"—or was forced to dwell in—the titanic inner landscape of a traumatized parent. In one typically intense scene, Gornick painted a picture of how, as a child growing up in a mostly Jewish tenement in the Bronx in the 1930s, she could not avoid "catching" her mother's anxiety and depression due to the intensity of the bond between them and the hot-pot spaces in which her family of three dwelled. After her father's unexpected death when Gornick was fourteen, her mother flung herself into his coffin at the funeral home, and then climbed into his grave at the cemetery. For thirty years she remained in mourning. Initially, she physically clung to her only child: "She made me sleep with her for a year, and for twenty years afterward I could not bear a woman's hand on me. Afraid to sleep alone, she slung an arm across my stomach, pulled me toward her, fingered my flesh nervously, inattentively. I shrank from her touch; she never noticed. I yearned toward the wall, couldn't get close enough, was always being pulled back. My body became a column of aching stiffness. I must have been excited. Certainly I was repelled." Years later, the push-pull continued, her mother asking: "Why don't you go already? Why don't you walk away from my life? I'm not stopping you."

The Hawaii study used such complex scenes from Gornick's memoir as their prototype for defining what emotional contagion is.[*] In adopting a memoiristic account of a fraught mother-daughter

---

[*] In a similar way, the software designers would choose particular works of art on which to test the success of their prototype algorithms. In the case of the development of the MP3, for example, in its early stages before it became the standard for most music compression, the ballad "Tom's Diner," an a capella track featuring Suzanne Vega's evocative singing, became the test object to tell whether the compression had lost the essence of the song. The engineers' logic was, "If we can translate this into a new format, we can translate anything."

relationship as their crucible example, the Hawaii team favored intensity and privileged an intimate bond characterized by being fairly drenched in interfamilial, intragenerational trauma. The emotion is not only shared face to face but in one party born from the other. From there, their task was to render the contagious relationship in scientific terms and see how generalizable it would prove to be.

In the early 1990s, when this study was published, it would have been odd to foreground internet communication, for there was very little. Nor were many psychologists measuring transfer of emotion by telephone, for example. And so the Hawaii study assumed as its baseline the in-person spread of emotions. Especially, they took physical proximity for granted (Vivian Gornick, trapped between her mother and the wall, as archetype). They noted that people tend to mimic facial expressions, the vocal expressions, postures, and instrumental behaviors of those around them, and thereby to "catch" others' emotions because of such facial, vocal, postural, and behavioral feedback. Their broad-strokes conclusion was that such contagion, so rapidly and automatically triggered, "may even tell something about the awesome contemporary power of celebrityhood and of the mass media as these agencies of large-scale emotional and cognitive contagion continue to expand their capacities to define reality for billions of people."[21] This sentence—especially the part about media's reality-defining capabilities for billions of people—would prove prescient.

Not long after the Hawaii authors defined emotional contagion, influential research by the medically trained sociologist Nicholas Christakis scooped up archived data from long-term studies such as the Framingham Heart Study to trace exactly how health effects, but also social effects, moved through networks of people. Christakis soon moved on to consider emotional effects. With the political scientist James Fowler, a 2008 study examined the "dynamic spread of happiness" across a large social network using the same data.[22] In a 2009 coauthored book called *Connected: The Surprising Power of Our Social Networks and How They Shape Our Lives*, as well as in additional journal articles, Christakis and Fowler showed that obesity, happiness, and depression all spread via person-to-person networks among families and communities in similar patterned ways. Confirming the earlier speculation by the Hawaii researchers about large-scale contagion, they showed that these networks ferried the emotional parts of life (through happiness clusters or depression clusters) in much the same way as they did the epidemiological (through obesity clusters or heart disease clusters). These studies creatively used historical data to resurrect interactions that had taken place in person. The data was collected during earlier eras, when people did not (beyond the telephone) engage much in the digital or electronically mediated realm as a sphere for interaction, much less have that realm interact with them. In other words, it hailed from a time long before Alexa, and even longer before an Internet of Things engineer could boast (touting his company's new capabilities), "We can tell the fridge, 'Hey, lock up because he shouldn't be eating.'"[23]

Half a decade later, the Facebook team prominently cited these two studies—the 1993 Hawaii study and the 2008 Fowler and Christakis study—at the start of their banner publication. Their ambition was to ask the pivotal question of whether a virus-like spread of human emotions ("affective states") can take place not only without physical copresence but also in interactive digital spaces—as in, online through social media. And (they wanted to know) does the spread result from exchange with a person in a verbal give-and-take, or can mere exposure trigger it? More specifically, can emotions be shown to move through a network aside from direct one-on-one give-and-take interactions (which had been measured before)? Yes, they could. Only text was needed—"contagion," they concluded, "does not require non-verbal behavior" to spread.[24]

As the Facebook team's write-up made clear, the Hawaii study and the Christakis studies had made progress but had not been successful in investigating these aspects of *massive-scale* contagion. Facebook was the first to do so.[25]

The Facebook experiment was in this sense a butterfly effect not across time (as Isaac Asimov had it in his classic short story) but across numbers.[26] In Asimov's tale, going back to an earlier moment and inadvertently killing a butterfly resulted in a wrenchingly different future. In the experiment, changing someone's news feed didn't set off a tornado or black swan event or any radical difference that could be immediately discerned. The effect was seemingly tiny. But with the accumulation of a great number of anything (seconds, information, data points) on a large scale, unusual shifts and unlikely happenings can occur. The tiny "moth wing" jiggering that a person encounters online can cause equally minute changes that turn out, in the end, to be huge at scale. And who could say what the algorithmically shifted emotional brushstrokes brought to any of the 689,003 users whose lives were touched by it.

Around this time, a Facebook user named Sandra Stewart wrote: "I would like to know if I was one of the people who were studied? In general my mood isn't effected [sic] by my friends [sic] posts—I know who the sad sacks are and who the braggers are. But really??!?? I could have been an unwitting test subject? Academics have rules about that sort of thing. You may want to look into that for the sake of say . . . ETHICS." Some angry commenters invoked catastrophic harm: How many people may have killed themselves? Would it even be possible to know if anyone did or tried to? A user named Constance A. Messin Progress wrote on the research team's Facebook page during the post-experiment reckoning, "It's probably a coincidence, but I attempted suicide and wound up in the psych ward during the period they did the experiment where they influenced people's moods to either be more depressed or more positive. I have mental illness and wasn't stable at the time, but maybe the possibility of someone being on the edge didn't occur to experimenters."[27] Most, but not all, of the invocation of self-harm was rhetorical. Yet it was also serious and raised the temperature of the debate. The UK began an investigation; the question about whether some children (and the mentally ill) had been in the pool of 689,003 subjects lingered. The status of this inquiry is unclear some ten years later.

....

Around the same time, Chinese middle-class professionals swooned for Western psychotherapy, and enterprising American Freudians took their one-on-one methods to China in virtual form, leaving the couch behind. Across the United States, Freud's approach was in decline, with a majority of members in the most prominent societies over the age of seventy by the end of the twentieth century, and only a few holdout areas such as New York and Boston continuing fealty. However, new hope for Freud's style of psychoanalysis took off in Chinese circles. Freud's books had been translated and available in China since the 1920s but not much used clinically before or after the revolution. In the 1980s, before the protest events at Tiananmen Square, elite college students had briefly fueled a passion for analysis, dubbed Freud Fever. However, no widescale interest took hold until newly available Skype video-conferencing methods converged with a 2001 visit by New York–based Freudian analyst Elise Snyder in Shanghai and Chengdu to meet potential students. This converged with an increasing willingness among Chinese to consider therapy (at its most basic, a chance to talk intensively about the self) as more than a selfish indulgence. An early 2000s trend sometimes referred to in anglicized Chinese as the "psycho boom" helped the new transcontinental practice of analysis to flourish long before COVID-19-spurred Zoom sessions made this more widely obvious. Within decades, a generation of Chinese patients had happily received analysis.

For these patients, successful therapy did not include being in the same room physically with their therapist. It was obvious to them that psychotherapy was most effective at a remove, even if they knew it was practiced in person in the standard model. As Evan Osnos reported in a 2011 *New Yorker* account of the Shanghai-to-Upper West Side exchanges, "Skype has become so routine among Chinese patients that Shmuel Erlich, an Israeli analyst, says he met a woman in Beijing who 'was astonished that there was some *other* kind of analysis.'" Similar programs from Germany's and Norway's psychoanalytic communities ferried Freudian cachet virtually to urban China. The historian of psychoanalysis, Hannah Zeavin, argues that the move to digital platforms has been accompanied by a shift toward the automation of therapy itself.[28]

The ease with which Skype-facilitated psychotherapy took hold even in a culture uneasy with such counseling might have already suggested to Facebook's engineers that emotional transfer at a considerable level of subtlety was certainly possible in what Mark Zuckerberg had yet to call the metaverse. Still, it's one thing to note this development, and another to tackle a far wider–ranging emotion transfer. The Facebook Core Data Science team's aim was to tackle it as a technical challenge. To operationalize it. To make the scientific claim to have done it. And to pen a scientific paper in a peer-reviewed journal discussing it. Especially the team wondered whether this contagion could be triggered by nonverbal cues, and whether, unlike an analyst-analysand relationship, it could be fleeting, click-based connections that were "cementing" (if momentarily) the transfer conditions.

From this perspective one can see that the Facebook researchers were interested in the degree of automaticity of these spreading emotional states and the degree of "buy-in" necessary from the user. The more automaticity and the less buy-in that led to a measurable response, the more successful it would be deemed, was the drift. For example, could mood change be made to happen when someone typed into your comment box or left a Like? Or could mere visual exposure—*seeing something*—stimulate the change?

·········

They were also interested in building language models that could assess personal states of being—ideally in real time.

To analyze the data from the 689,003 Facebookers going about their days in early January 2012 unaware of their participation in their experiment, the team used an applied natural language processing software package called the Linguistic Inquiry and Word Count (LIWC, pronounced "Luke"), which bears the motto "Discover the World of Words." The software operates on the premise that "People reveal themselves by the words they use."[29] Their inner psychological states—their "thoughts, feelings, personality, and the ways they connect with others"—can be accessed from analysis of their word choices. These assumptions stem from long-standing techniques developed in the 1940s and 1950s—oddly, stretching back to Robert K. Merton's research partner at Columbia University, the sociologist Paul Lazarsfeld, who pioneered content analysis, a way of systematically looking at words used in printed matter. During the 1970s, semantic analysis began to use computers to extract meaning from text.

Thirty years later, LIWC was an adumbration of these methods, made into a plug-in package. Developed by psychologist James Pennebaker and colleagues at the University of Texas at Austin in the mid-1980s, the software was originally designed to support a study in which researchers asked volunteers to freewrite each day for fifteen minutes about the most devastating experience of their lives. After a span of several months, the subjects were tested for improved mental health markers. Teams of researchers then analyzed their diaries to see if their mode of expression had affected their degree of improvement. However, they found that, among other methodological drawbacks, reading thousands of pages of diaries detailing traumatic experiences made the research assistants themselves become depressed. They decided to create software that would count and analyze words, which eventually

How to Look Inside People   295

became the LIWC suite. Words describing trauma from subjects' diaries would become the very stuff used to measure negativity and positivity in online posts.

Adam Kramer and others then innovated in applying the software to the Facebook-length comments to gauge the emotional status of the responder.* The results were positive. Even with short bursts of text or Likes, such states (called affective states) spread. The team later assured the ethically alarmed public that no human eyes had read anyone's comments, as LIWC was adapted to run on the Hadoop MapReduce system and thus the analysis it performed was completely automated. Hadoop is a Big Data analytic tool for comparative semantic study at scale, especially in biomedicine. When researchers deploy it, they sometimes turn it into a verb, as in "Hadooping the genome." As scholar Hallam Stevens has shown, this seemingly innocuous alteration conveys the fact that the tool, when used merely to seek patterns in massive amounts of data, *changes* how the science itself works. (Stevens's point is that instead of posing a hypothesis and deductively testing it, Hadoop and similar methods allow one to see what emerges out of pattern seeking at a large scale—making it a sort of high-tech "fishing" for correlations. Some put it more flatteringly: For data evangelists, such pattern recognition at scale promises a new paradigm of scientific method, making the old scientific method of hypothesis, testing, confirmation or disconfirmation, and replication obsolete.)[30] The Facebook experiment Hadooped its user data in the sense of automating its study. Some might say they did begin with a hypothesis, but I would argue

---

* James Pennebaker's original LIWC software was developed to analyze a series of studies asking subjects to "writ[e] about one's deepest thoughts and feelings regarding a traumatic or stressful event for 15 minutes a day over 3 to 4 days." Preliminary findings showed that "putting emotional upheavals into words" had a positive effect on mental health (even if it tended to depress the scientists reading the entries). Interested to pinpoint the emotional effects, they developed a relatively simple software program to count a small group of emotion-related words. This academic software effort gradually expanded into a commercial venture.

it was more of an engineering challenge, to prove that emotional contagion could be made to occur on a huge scale.* Finally, the team firmly answered their question about at-a-distance contagion when neither room nor physical proximity is shared. They declared that their research provided "experimental evidence that emotions or moods are contagious in the absence of direct interaction between experiencer and target."[31]

Yet in a sense, as many commentators would soon rush to point out, the experiment only described business as usual. "Continuous experimentation," as Google's economist Hal Varian announced in 2014, results from what Big Data makes possible: Specifically, how it allows the running of countless A/B experiments in which data science teams test variations in the user experience from different fonts or background colors to alternative scrolling methods for how users navigate a page (on smartphone or web), to trying various sizes of haptic buttons.

Nonetheless, it was not business as usual. What was unusual about Facebook's plant-a-flag discovery was not the discovery per se but the very fact that they sought to publish it.[32] A precursor was the Facebook team's 2012 *Nature* article on voting behavior which was titled, "A 61-Million-Person Experiment in Social Influence and Political Mobilization," on a study conducted prior to the midterm elections in 2010. Note that this was a behavior effect: Merely posting voting-positive messages on people's news feeds caused an additional sixty thousand voters to go to the polls, they estimated. This prompted legal scholar Jonathan Zittrain in 2014 to announce in the *New Republic*, "Facebook

---

* Kramer et al. began by asserting the need for direct experimental data on the problem of network spread of emotions. And while it's not evident to me the Facebook team began with a hypothesis (they don't seem to state one), what is clear is that they were at core interested in producing an effect. In this way, it's perhaps an example of what two historians of science, Peter Galison and Lorraine Daston, tentatively called presentation in their book *Objectivity*—a mode of scientific observation in which the production of results simultaneously transforms that which is being described: to know something is also simultaneously to change it. Lorraine Daston and Peter Galison, *Objectivity* (New York: Zone Books, 2008).

Could Decide an Election Without Anyone Ever Finding Out." But external behavior change is one thing. Internal mood change, based on language-processing software mined from diaries detailing extreme emotional distress, is another.

....

What is an emotion anyway, and is it changed by undergoing the sort of transactions on which social media run? The philosopher Baruch Spinoza, in 1677, described emotions as "waverings of the mind" that can either increase or diminish one's power to act.[33] By this way of understanding, the lever of emotion has been evident for hundreds of years. Emotions lead us to do things or not do things. They demand a sense of having an inner life, even if their particulars are often unrecognized until after we have acted (or never recognized, in which case we call them unconscious). Toddlers intuitively realize this when, if you ask them why they're sad, they say, "I'm sad because I'm crying."

But something changed in 2012 and 2013 in our long-standing relationship to emotions, a change pivotal to my argument about what happened to brainwashing. The change was that the lever became the leverage.

In retrospect, a vast shift marked the time between when the user data was gathered and the paper was published. Almost simultaneously, Facebook made its initial public offering as a company and, also, all the procedures of massive-scale emotional engineering accelerated as if on steroids. According to digital scholars, this exact period (from 2012–2014) marked when the open web became the *social web*. Interoperability (of binary code) made it easy to capture the numbers and letters typed on a screen within a social platform and use them to make extractive conclusions about emotional status.[34] Everything from Likes to psych test results to keyboard pecks became quantities that could feed a vast engine. There was no longer such a thing as digital exhaust, in that all activity now counted as digital treasure. With that, not only media changed but the internet itself. Emotional contagion, enacted on large groups by design, was a roadmap to society-wide tuning of shared psychological states.[35]

In an article on the "scalable subject," historian Luke Stark argued that this was a new type of personhood created under conditions of Big Data and algorithmic sorting. The Facebook emotional contagion study "should be understood as a seminal event in the history of digital technology's social impact: as a moment when the tacit co-development of the psychological and computational sciences became exposed to public view and—for some—[became] a matter of concern."[36] The most uncomfortable part of the study was that at the moment the contagion became visible, it was already a done deal. The future of rampant, scaled-up emotional engineering many social critics warned of during the late twentieth and early twenty-first centuries was already here.

·········

The experiment on mood may have been intended to garner prestige, but its effect was (troublesomely, in some cases) to compel people to begin to reckon with the business model, ethics, and likely long-term effects of Facebook and other platforms. The experiment on mood was a reminder, perhaps in some quarters an unwelcome one, that business as usual for Facebook was seismic in its effects, a scalar phenomenon for which the real earthquaking result was rarely appreciated. As the Facebook study's researchers observed (bragged?) in their paper, "Given the massive scale of social networks . . . even small effects can have large aggregated consequences. . . . After all, an effect size of d = 0.001 at Facebook's scale is not negligible: In early 2013, this would have corresponded to hundreds of thousands of emotion expressions in status updates per day."[37] If you were digitally tinkering around with the ability to bring about tiny changes in emotion, this could and would add up.

How to Look Inside People

The experiment keyed in not only to contagion but to emotional engineering: In other words, while the experiment homed in on contagion (which everyone already knew about; no surprise there) it most crucially enacted the fantasy of engineering states of mind. It fulfilled a dream of the 1960s and 1970s, seen in the bio-music project of avant-garde composer Manford Eaton, who built so-called stimuli bombardment systems designed deliberately to alter the mood of the person strapped into them.

What was (somewhat scary) art in 1971 was commerce by 2013. The historian of capitalism Shoshanna Zuboff spoke with an engineer who described how the embedding of sensors within the home environment resulted in automated behavioral modification: Sure, you could use the internet to lower the heat in all the houses on a street (to avoid overloading the transformer), for example. "But at the individual level, it also means the power to take actions that can override what you are doing or even put you on a path you did not choose."[38] This was the thrust of the Facebook study, and what made it exciting. Suddenly you're on a path unchosen by you, a forking path. As one of the experiment's coauthors, Jeffrey T. Hancock, a professor at Cornell University, told the *New York Times*, people took umbrage at the in-your-face evidence of manipulation, telling themselves, "You can't mess with my emotions. It's like messing with me. It's mind control."[39] But you could.

For some, the upsetting part was having to see this (the messing with me part), rather than the fact of manipulation itself. It disrupted the pattern of mildly complicit acquiescence that is the norm. (The data café with seemingly free coffee.) For others, shoving the emotional-engineering business model in users' faces to see what they would do was the whole hook. Professor Hancock soon moved on from Cornell University to create the Stanford Social Media Lab.

·········

Along the way, there was a tipping point in the full emergence of a logic built into AI systems that are based on machine learning and large language models (LLMs), which not all AI is.* The scholar Kate Crawford calls this "the unswerving belief that everything is data and is there for the taking."[40] Some people didn't like the feeling of being swept up into aggregate data sets. Some didn't like the logic of it. Some people, on the other hand, liked being scooped up this way.

Facebook, in response to the pushback from their experiment, limited their data research office to certain kinds of publication—that is, the company clamped down on the circulation of their own work—and did not again academically publish on topics connected to emotional engineering (though the business practices continued, of course). This pivot could be inserted into a longer history of controversial public-facing experimentation that was withdrawn from view once the response spiked a critical degree of umbrage. An example is provided by psychologist John B. Watson, who in the 1900s–1910s experimented with the response of laboratory mice by removing or

---

* There is an increasingly common tendency to equate the whole domain of AI with machine learning (ML). This likely comes from the runaway success of text-based aids such as ChatGPT in its ever-more-powerful iterations. The first declaration of AI, which Claude Shannon, Marvin Minsky, and other pioneering computer scientists penned—or rather, typed—in 1955 listed key areas for research in "the Artificial Intelligence Problem." These included (1) "Automatic Computers," (2) "How Can a Computer Be Programmed to Use a Language," (3) "Neuron Nets," (4) "Theory of the Size of a Calculation," (5) "Self-Improvement," (6) "Abstractions," (7) "Randomness and Creativity." Not all of these are capable of being addressed using machine learning. Generative AI is much broader. A recent researcher has named "search, optimization, planning, scheduling, knowledge representation, and others" as areas beyond ML's scope. The point that AI is non-equivalent to ML is made in Francesca Rossi, "Review of *Atlas of AI*," *Artificial Intelligence* 312 (2022), 103767, and the historic document is John McCarthy, Marvin Minsky, Nathaniel Rochester, and Claude Shannon, "A Proposal for the Dartmouth Summer Research Program on Artificial Intelligence," August 31, 1955.

How to Look Inside People

disabling their sense receptors (in one mouse he covered the paws with gauze, in another he smothered the ear canal, in a third he gouged or stitched shut the eyes, in a fourth he disabled the ability to smell), to see whether the animal could still run a maze sensorily handicapped. In each case, the mouse could still do it, even when all senses were removed—to explain the results Watson postulated the existence of a sixth sense, which he called the kinesthetic. His discovery made it into major newspapers of the day. An outcry from readers, upset with what they found to be unnecessary cruelty, did not cause Watson to stop, but it did result in his avoiding ever discussing his experiments in the *New York Times* for the rest of his career. Similarly, in the face of ethical challenges, Facebook did not retreat from conducting experiments so much as it retreated from proudly talking about them.

Meanwhile, some onlookers settled for the "Big Tech is constantly experimenting anyway and if you don't like it then leave" point of view. Zeynep Tufekci, a sociologist at Princeton University, argued to the contrary that the very normalness of the experiment showed how "these large corporations (and governments and political campaigns) now have new tools and stealth methods to quietly model our personality, our vulnerabilities, identify our networks, and effectively nudge and shape our ideas, desires and dreams. These tools are new, this power is new and evolving. It's exactly the time to speak up!"[41] Rather than using grand gestures of fear-spreading, torture, and terror, these methods worked by scripting public acquiescence while micro-nudging "desired behavior."[42]

....

Let's return for a moment to the Hawaii study, which Facebook's team used to define fundamentally what emotional contagion was. Recall that it was based, as its prototype, on Vivian Gornick's description of her traumatic upbringing, when her mother's mourning over the death of her father left Gornick, as a fourteen-year-old, in the grips of a grief-riven adult's unending histrionics.

Once upon a time, Gornick recalls, her life was thick with inescapable emotional contagion. "The air I breathed was soaked in her desperation, made thick and heavy by it, exciting and dangerous," wrote Gornick describing her mother facing her teenaged self in the wake of her father's sudden death. Her mother's emotional distress, externalized, became her whole environment, and from there her physical reality and inner life:

> Her pain became my element, the country in which I lived, the rule beneath which I bowed. It commanded me, made me respond against my will. I longed endlessly to get away from her, but I could not leave the room when she was in it. I dreaded her return from work, but I was never not there when she came home. In her presence anxiety swelled my lungs (I suffered constrictions of the chest and sometimes felt an iron ring clamped across my skull), but I locked myself in the bathroom and wept buckets on her behalf. On Friday I prepared myself for two solid days of weeping and sighing and the mysterious reproof that depression leaks into the air like the steady escape of gas when the pilot light is extinguished.[43]

Such intensity—the steady escape of gas, the witnessing of endless tears, her mother's trauma that became her own and dogged her for coming decades, the physical toll of it—may seem to have little in common with the tiny changes Facebook enacted to people's subjective moods or the LIWC software built word by word from diaries. And yet we see that this was exactly what they had in mind: To connect the huge "country in which I lived" with the seemingly tiny triviality of an Instagram post.

New studies in 2023 published in *Science* and *Nature* directly asked whether changes in the algorithms underlying Facebook and Instagram would affect people's beliefs. They assumed it would. Yet results did not bear out the folk instinct that algorithms can directly control—as in a dial up, dial down action—the ideological commitments of users. The studies were run by University of Texas at Austin and New York University centers for media study, as well as Princeton University and others, whose coauthors conducted randomized, controlled experiments with some of Meta's Facebook and Instagram 3.5 billion users, producing a total of sixteen papers. Results were complex. The academics worked collaboratively with Meta's researchers, but the academics were not paid by Meta, and subjects were asked and consented to participation, their identifying information obscured. All these procedures reveal lessons learned since 2012. In one study, "How Do Social Media Feed Algorithms Affect Attitudes and Behavior in an Election Campaign?" more than 23,000 Facebook users and 21,000 Instagram users had their feeds altered during the 2020 US presidential election to show them recent posts first rather than posts tailored to their interests (that is, posts delivered by algorithmic targeting). Yet the degree of polarization in political attitudes did not change, nor did behavior such as signing online petitions. (People did, however, spend "dramatically less time" on the platforms when they were not being algorithmically targeted and were generally more polite, the authors reported.) Manipulating feeds by showing less content from likeminded connections also did not alter people's beliefs or degree of polarization. The findings "suggest that social media algorithms may not be the root cause of phenomena such as increasing political polarization," researchers concluded.[44]

In turn, I would suggest, this spate of experiments sticks to the much shallower level of tracking opinion change. They are about attitudes more than emotions. This points us back to the prime insight of the 2014 experiment—which dealt with emotional response below the level of information dissemination, beneath the layer of intellectual commitment, to the deeper soil of valence, trauma, directionality.

We return to the question of how the shadows of trauma may be mobilized. The space yawns before us, yet it is bridged by emotional contagion. Affect spreads by digital synapses, and you don't even have to leave a comment for this to happen. Mere exposure, mere attention is enough. Across new spaces our societies are broken down and remade. Mass formations once again sweep through the world.

10

On Being Emotionally Chained to Technology—Namely, Your Radio, Television, Internet, Social Media, or Friendly-Yet-Somehow-Predatory Chatbot

In September 1943, a large audience tuned in to CBS radio for a marathon-style fundraising event—a radiocast designed to convince listeners to purchase war bonds. The patriotic singer with the swelling voice, Kate Smith, held forth for eighteen hours over a twenty-four-hour period, coming on the air sixty-five times, seemingly with hardly a moment to rest or drink water, much less eat, while she urged listeners to buy American Victory Bonds in support of the war. (Victory Bonds, also known as defense bonds, were debt instruments floated by nations such as Canada and the United States during World Wars I and II to finance their military expenditures: As a member of the public, you purchased a bond as a way of personally "buying in" to the outcome of the war. Secondarily, you probably hoped it would function as an investment vehicle, though generally it paid below market rates, sometimes far below, depending on time to maturity.) As Smith pressed on through the day and into the night her voice cracked. She spoke of her aching feet, the dying soldiers in

Europe, and the suffering innocents. Audiences were unaccustomed to the marathon pledge format, which was almost totally new. They knew Smith, though. "Won't you please buy a bond?" she entreated over and over. They would.

Earlier bond drives waged without the combined weapons of radio and Kate Smith had raised very little, but this broadcast brought in $1 million the first day, $2 million the second, and an astounding $39 million on the third, a record amount (equivalent to around $695 million today).[1] One listener later reported losing the ability to switch off his radio, as if he had been in a trance. Another audience member went out and pawned her wedding ring to pay for bonds, instructing her sister to wait by the dial to listen to Kate, while still another described how a curious paralysis took hold, and she was unable to go to bed while the singer was still up and struggling to stay awake: "My heart ached for her and I just hoped she had a couch to lie on there."[2] They were emotionally chained to the radio, caught up in Kate Smith's fate, behavioral researchers would later conclude.

The singer succeeded in getting people to identify with her own sacrifice in staying up without sleeping hour after hour. As she urged the audience to remain with her, she pressed on in the radiothon itself while her state of exhaustion became evident. She persisted even as her voice broke, and she seemed near physical collapse. This was likely the historical debut of the on-air "marathon" format, the first time it had been used by a major broadcaster, and it stunned listeners, riveting them to their devices (though today it mostly evokes the dreaded public television fundraiser.) Listeners' remarks show how closely people followed Smith's ups and downs—her suffering and her strivings were theirs: "After I bought, I could sleep. Before that I couldn't close my eyes. It was almost one o'clock by the time I bought the bond. I thought, *'Poor darling, she certainly earned that thirty million she sold.' At one o'clock, I said, 'Now that I've done my little job, I thank God for giving me the wisdom to*

On Being Emotionally Chained to Technology

Kate Smith on set September 21, 1943, for the first radio marathon.
AP PHOTO/CARL NESENSOHN.

see clearly,' and I turned off the radio."[3] Buying a bond released the built-up tension, while cementing emotional attachment.

A plate of partly eaten layer cake with a delicate fork lying nearby appeared later in an Associated Press photo of Smith's desk in the CBS studio, the image at odds with the sense of sacrifice imbued in the voice that was broadcast. The audio portrait was one of deprivation, and listeners felt moved to pray Kate Smith's weakened tones would hold out so that she would be able to complete her task. In fact, among listeners there were pervasive feelings of a lack of escape, of being (as one put it later) "actually hound[ed]" to get a bond. Still others lost the ability to discern a choice for themselves. Again and again, listeners recalled not being able to turn the dial, leave the room, stop listening, or avoid cashing in treasured personal items.

How had this coup of mass-media persuasion happened? (It was so personal yet there was no microtargeting. It was so profound, yet it was widely shared.)* By all evidence it seemed to go beyond simple persuasive appeals to enter the territory of compulsion. A few years earlier, in 1938, Orson Welles choreographed a series of hoax news bulletins from the nonexistent Intercontinental Radio News Service announcing that Grovers Mill, New Jersey, had come under Martian invasion. This reportedly caused central Jersey's radio listeners to run amok, some hightailing it to their cars to get out of town, not realizing the emergency broadcast was a fictional play adapted from an H. G. Wells story. (The precise amount of panic Welles' announcements of alien attack caused is disputed. But at least one listener sued CBS for mental distress.) Although this stunt would, like the Kate Smith radiothon five years later, become a landmark moment for a new research field called mass communications, Smith's was less a "let's see what people will do" prank than a carefully structured influence campaign enacted through a beloved figure. In other words, it was propaganda. But let's set aside, for a moment, questions raised by this fact.

For some, Smith was synonymous with the country itself. So stirring was her 1938 rendition of "America the Beautiful," by Irving Berlin, that it spurred a campaign to make it the national anthem. When, four years earlier, FDR had introduced her to George VI, the king of England, he said: "This is Kate Smith. Miss Smith is America." While the Welles hoax was a curiosity, the Smith bond drives were a triumph. They led—as we will see—to behavioral scientists' confidence that they could now isolate the precise technological mechanisms at work in successful mass persuasion.

So it was that in the fall of 1943 a young Columbia University professor named Robert K. Merton set out to adopt the Smith radiocast as a natural experiment. A natural experiment is one in which the conditions of study are deemed ideal for asking certain questions or testing a

---

* The mass audience received the same emotional cadence from the radiocast, and heard it at the same time, even if their individual behavioral responses ranged from buying a bond, praying for Smith, or weeping, as researchers would point out.

hypothesis even though the event or phenomenon highlighted in the study has not deliberately been set up to run as an experiment. Yet, it is *framed as if* it were so designed for the precise convenience of the researcher. Volcanic eruptions, chemical spills, viral outbreaks, large storms, arena concerts, television game shows, public celebrations, or other singular events can function as natural experiments. An archetypal example is the Broad Street cholera outbreak of 1854 in London, during which 616 people died. This event provided a chance for physician John Snow to map the concentration of deaths in relation to a particular pump fed by raw sewage from the Thames; of the many pumps that patchworked the city no others were associated with the outbreak. Although Snow did not use the term "natural experiment" (the term was not yet in standard use in public health), he did declare it an "experiment ... on the grandest scale." It allowed him to disprove previous miasmic theories of contagion even though the event had not taken place under controlled or randomized conditions.[4]

Complex human problems—especially those on which it would be unethical to run a formal experiment—are well suited to natural experiments. Merton felt this way about the CBS bond drive. In fact, he could name at least six reasons why it was like a laboratory, but better. For one thing, artificial situations such as those found in laboratories often lead participants to feel like guinea pigs. But in the real-life situation of the Kate Smith radiothon, people's reactions were genuine. They didn't know they were being studied because they weren't (yet) being studied, so there was no observer effect. For another, the stakes were not trivial (as in many lab studies about, say, eating or not eating a marshmallow) but profound. And again, as Merton pointed out, the people in his study were not rats or cash-starved undergraduates (the subjects most university experiments relied on) but living, breathing humans embedded in their different walks of life. Here you had a patriotic figure who was asking listeners to join the war effort in a personal, emotional way by using techniques of repetition, variation, connection, withdrawal, identification, and structural stimuli. Here was something, in short, impossible to fit within the four walls of a lab: a human experiment in the best possible sense of the term.

So argued Merton's study of the phenomenon he would come to call mass persuasion—it was premised on the fact that the Kate Smith media event had all the advantages of a formal lab experiment, as well as several additional pluses. His 1946 book, *Mass Persuasion: The Social Psychology of a War Bond Drive*, would become a classic.[5] From the start Merton saw that not only finance bonds and consumer stuffs (such as shampoo) but also political candidates could successfully enter the psyches of a populace in this way, through the large-scale persuasive process. But how exactly did this process work? That was the question. Everyone knew people could be pushed to change their behavior, but in what way and how much? Were people simply malleable in response to any old media-delivered message? Were they malleable to every degree? Or was susceptibility dependent on content leveraged under certain circumstances? And, beyond that, was all this a danger to democracy, a boon to democracy, or both?

In recent years news headlines have outdone each other in declaring an unparalleled level of disinformation and misinformation at large. Experts assert our built-in cognitive incapacity to deal with this floodtide level of persuasive messaging. *Harvard Magazine* not long ago asked, "Can Disinformation Be Stopped?" and explored several scholars' perspectives on the "pervasive new threat" causing people to be persuaded to adopt convictions of which they previously were unaware or uninterested.[6] The degree of two-camp polarization (and the resulting enmity) in many localities across the globe seems to bear out both the accuracy and urgency of this alarm-sounding.

Yet the threat is *not new, nor is the technology*—not all of it. Mass persuasion via media messages is a phenomenon embedded in our own history. If we don't understand this, we are in danger of vastly misunderstanding what the current threat represents and attributing to it a kind of temporal exceptionalism—asserting Never Before in History Has Anything Quite This Dystopian Ever Happened—and from there, justifying certain nonoptimal responses that deprive possibilities of freedom for the individual and generally make the already wrenching political dualism worse. At the same time, broadly stoked fear levels and an amped-up sense of generalized anxiety cement—further—the danger of not recognizing which parts and combinations of our current situation are truly new. Let me put it simply: It is illuminating and (perhaps) calming to know that a whole bunch of what is happening now has happened before, if in different ways, in different circumstances. The classic behavioral sciences formed themselves out of these very processes. In this way, we can prepare ourselves by identifying within ourselves how fear, anxiety, hope, and a range of affective states, are conjured when we are emotionally chained to our technologies.

Merton's answers yield clues about what changed—and what, surprisingly, has not—in the twenty-first century. This early research is mostly forgotten even among specialists, who describe the classic work as "barely limp[ing] along in semi-obscurity" (in one scholar's words) notwithstanding its brilliance.[7] Despite calls to revive attention to this curiously relevant work, it has not happened. Yet from observations of the seventy-five-year-old study of the CBS radio marathon, the early academic field of mass communications issued warnings that shed light on how an enchained helplessness can spread widely through an algorithmically driven set of platforms.[8] When loosed in a digital environment augmented by new tools of social media and data-targeting, what would change? What has changed?

"HAD TO"

I didn't realize it at the time, but I had to keep listening.

—A *Mass Persuasion* Subject Interviewed in 1943[9]

Consider the phenomena of doomscrolling. The word entered the *Cambridge English Dictionary* officially in 2020 to describe a much-despaired-of practice colloquially defined as "staying up late reading terrible news on your phone" or more formally as "the act of spending an excessive amount of screen time devoted to the absorption of negative news." The practice sharply escalated in the early stages of the COVID-19 pandemic.[10] Doomscrolling is almost never considered fun much less joyful (except in an odd, gleefully masochistic way), but it is widely understood to be addictive. The experience of scrolling on social media—the "endless scroll," in the phrase of tech journalist Alexis Madrigal[11]—contains many moments of gratification. Psychologist B. F. Skinner half a century ago achieved incredible feats when he trained pigeons to ride tiny bicycles and play miniature pianos through his very careful use of a reward system. Intermittent reinforcement schedules are the best method to shape behavior, whether of pigeon or human baby, generations of behaviorists have shown. And a social media scroll generated by a trained algorithm is a perfect environment for irregular jackpot-like rewards surrounded by not-quite-exciting stimuli. It is iterative conditioning.

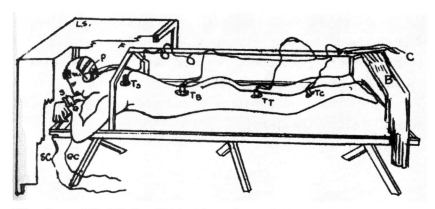

Milton Bass and Clark Hull, in 1934 (and their colleague O. H. Mowrer in 1936), experimented with the coercive stimulus. Student volunteers lay on a cot, outfitted with electrodes, which emitted shocks at unpredictable intervals, leading to escalating stress even after the electrodes were detached. FIGURE 1 FROM MILTON J. BASS AND CLARK L. HULL, "THE IRRADIATION OF A TACTILE CONDITIONED REFLEX IN MAN," J. COMP. PSYCH, 17 (1934), 48. PUBLIC DOMAIN.

On the other hand, a contemporary of Skinner's named O. H. Mowrer, a neo-behaviorist from a different lineage, established in 1936 at Yale's Institute of Human Behavior the existence of what he called the coercive stimulus. He did this by attaching undergraduate research subjects to several electric shock dispensers, discovering that their stress responses spiked most heavily in anticipation of receiving a shock when they were unsure of its delivery timing. This worked even when the electrodes were not actually touching the skin. Suffering did not have to do with the intensity of pain so much as with worrying about it.

Scrolling, then, entails subjecting oneself to behavior sculpting, whether in Skinnerian shaping or Mowrerian coercive forms, or perhaps a combination of the two.[12] There are irregular rewards (the excitement of a new, intriguing item to grow breathless over) while overall there is a looming yet often unspecifiable dread. (There are neurological correlates to these forms, yet they do not drive, much less explain, the sculpting, but merely locate it.)

But scrolling like this must take place on devices and platforms that are, by definition, not mass targeted, in contrast to the way in which Kate Smith's powerful radiothon via CBS was. When scrolling, one encounters items seen by many people and narratives, and some even circulate virally, but they arrive under your eyeballs in a sequence (and sometimes a format) crafted and selected uniquely for you, ever more so, via algorithms not always totally understood by the companies that purvey them much less the public that consumes them.

....

Scrolling also differs from behaviors that appear much further along the seriousness scale such as joining a cult. Doomscrolling, pleasure scrolling, comparison-scrolling, anxiety-scrolling, "zombie scrolling," and various additional "Help! I'm stuck in my phone" forms appear to have much lower stakes than the recruitment-by-ecstasy-and-fear process seen in cults.* Yet, on further examination, to be caught in a cult and to be stuck in a scroll have similarities. You start with a pinch of interest or boredom: You are waiting at a bus stop, say, your attention is "caught," someone engages you in conversation, but you end up a prisoner of a dynamic you are unable fully to understand, almost as if "you" stepped aside for a moment.† It begins in the ordinary and transforms it, rendering it strange. How peculiar are the ways many people sleep with phones near pillows or amuse ourselves with little algorithmic jolts of recognition or aversion while in line in the supermarket.

Their commonalities form an answer to the question of why Skinner titled his best-selling 1971 pop-psychology book *Beyond Freedom and Dignity*—for it was about the many ways people are propelled by complex webs of stimulus and response of which they are little aware, and over which they hang a nice shawl of respectability and reason. In it, Skinner insisted that people don't *actually* know why they went to the movies last night, though they will come up with a sounds-good reason if asked. We think we are free. We believe we are dignified. But in Skinner's view, these long-entrenched beliefs are illusions covering the fact that most people do not remotely comprehend the forces that compel them to do one thing or another. This would come to include mindless scrolling.

How, then, does this lineage of emotional deep-thread mining work, and how might it work more intensively in the future?

---

* The I-got-caught-in-an-endless-scroll phenomenon that many users of apps and platforms have noted in their online interactions involving social media.

† Deceptive recruiting was how Margaret Singer described it in her court appearances and writings against abusive cults. Or perhaps a friend makes a recommendation (estimates are, some 70 percent of cult members enter because a person close to them initially made the connection).

MASSES

Each time she said something that broke your heart a little more.

—A *Mass Persuasion* Subject

There is a part of mass persuasion that deserves more scrutiny than it usually gets. *Mass* is a strangely neglected keyword here. In the early twentieth century, "the masses" were a relatively new concept. It was the name of an up-and-coming socialist magazine founded by Max Eastman that first appeared in 1911. The title mirrored the term's trendiness at the time (and because "the masses" evoked the bottom-up force of revolution, a force beyond itself). Although the word *mass* derives more remotely from the Christian worship ceremony, a time when the faithful come face-to-face with God, its nonreligious, modern social meaning has to do with facelessness. "The masses are always the other, that we do not know, and can not know," wrote the British literary critic Raymond Williams in the 1950s.[13] You could say that the boisterous crowd of the nineteenth century became a faceless mass in the twentieth. To put the transition visually:

An etching for the journalist Henry Mayhew's book depicting a packed crowd in Piccadilly Circus, heading to the Great Exhibition. Figures in the crowd can be seen doing many different things; there is a "mood" of jubilation. THE ELISHA WHITTELSEY COLLECTION, THE ELISHA WHITTELSEY FUND, 1966. THE METROPOLITAN MUSEUM OF ART.

Crowd 2: Another type of crowd, more muted: A small crowd, the people engaged in their own business . . . yet still not a mass. Gustave Doré and Blanchard Jerrold, *London: A Pilgrimage*. (London: pub. unknown, 1890.) TUFTS ARCHIVAL RESEARCH CENTER, TUFTS UNIVERSITY.

Masses: In this famous photograph of Coney Island by Weegee, people at the beach seem strangely focused on the camera: They are a mass more than a crowd. GETTY IMAGES. WEEGEE (ARTHUR FELLIG), INTERNATIONAL CENTER OF PHOTOGRAPHY/ CONTRIBUTOR.

    When the field of sociology was just getting started as a profession during the late nineteenth and early twentieth centuries, its pioneers focused on crowds, defining them by a magnetism that held them together. They wanted to grasp that force. Through the study of crowds, sociology (the study of society) reached its modern, professional form.[14] In the 1870s through the 1900s, "the crowd" and its psychology indeed became quite a trendy topic. The Italian school of criminology tackled the theory of crowd emotions. The French sociologist Gustave Le Bon in his 1895 book, *The Crowd*, speculated about a "magnetic force given out by the crowd" or, if that were not the case, then "some other force of which we are ignorant" that acted on the group giving it group-ness. Crowds operated by bonds among themselves, however mysterious those bonds might be. The common French word for crowd, *foule*, is close to its related English adjective, "foolish." (Both derive from the older word *fou*, meaning "mad.") The phrase "the madness of crowds" dates to 1841 and a book by Charles Mackay. Crowds, as studied by sociologists, had personalities of their own as they coalesced—sometimes crazy, sometimes playful, sometimes brewing. Researchers widely considered crowds to have a "soul" (*âme*). The eminent sociologist Émile Durkheim, according to one recent argument, pushed beyond the trendiest expressions of the day to create a secret theory of the crowd: For him, such groupings of people were the building blocks for society itself. A society was a crowd writ large.[15]

In the new century, and more and more by the 1920s and 1930s, social scientists turned away from crowds to describe masses. (Like many erstwhile fads, intellectual or not, the crowd had gone distinctly out of style as a research topic.) The new term—*masses*—suggested persuasion beyond reason. Masses were perceived as existing beyond the "we" feeling. Masses were faceless. People once spoke of the soul of a crowd but never of the soul of the masses. A kind of blind biomechanistic response was how masses oriented themselves. Just as a plant turns toward the sun or a leaf submits to gravity, thus becoming heliotropic or geotropic, a mass of people may shift itself this way or that due to an externality, but it does not operate by bonds among the mass. Masses, as they were soon studied, were all about potential: the potential to be . . . a mass. Arguably (but maybe here

I am pushing the contrast too far) crowds were boisterously passionate while masses were empty in some way—they were somehow an audience first, waiting to be imprinted. (When a crowd falls into a pathological state, as described in Dickens's *A Tale of Two Cities* in London, it descends, in English at least, into a mob. A mass doesn't change state in the same way. When it deteriorates, it becomes more mechanical, not less.)

Masses, not crowds, were associated with the rise of twentieth-century fascism. Leni Riefenstahl's propaganda movies and the counterpropaganda "information films" of the American government's *Why We Fight* series are portraits of the eerie power of the mass, tracking slews of people—bystanders, military squadrons, and onlookers—as they surge on town squares and across wide spaces, gesturing, waving, bowing, with glinting, machine-like zeal.

Notably, Robert K. Merton was interested in mass behavior and not crowd behavior. He and a cohort of New York–based researchers, many of them Jewish escapees from Europe as it plunged into the turbulent decade before World War II, wanted to discover what held masses together—especially in relation to media. Merton was born in a Philadelphia housing project as the son of an immigrant family. His circle included émigrés from Austria, especially his best friend, the quantitative sociologist, Paul Lazarsfeld; the psychologist and advertising pioneer, Herta Herzog; and his Columbia-trained sociology students, such as Marjorie Fiske, Patricia Kendall and others. They formed a *Casablanca*-like assemblage opposing the Nazi forces of the day, although their group was a scholarly crew interested in daring methodological innovations, not a human smuggling ring.

One synopsis of this group's groundbreaking work is that it argued for the existence of modern media as the force that made the mass and held it together. Back in the summer of 1937, Merton, while still a doctoral student, had traveled to Vienna, Austria, to do research. This was a significant journey for the Harvard student, known even then

On Being Emotionally Chained to Technology

for "an ability to fox-trot and to play a respectable game of tennis," whose family had, themselves, only recently managed to emigrate from Eastern Europe. (Merton changed his last name from Schkolnick in college, effectively masking his Jewishness for sixty years, until in 1994 he revealed his family origins in a Philadelphia talk.)[16] While shuttling to and from the archives he took note of the incendiary pamphlets on the streets urging anti-Semitic actions. He collected those scraps and passages, pulling them off walls, at once personally horrified and professionally fascinated. Soon he would study propaganda closer to home.

At the time of the Kate Smith study and just afterward, experts in the field of mass communications (namely the behavioral scientists who founded it, Lazarsfeld and others, such as Leo Löwenthal, Joseph Klapper, Elihu Katz, Edward Shils, and Bernard Berenson), felt they were surging past the simpleminded naivete of 1920s and

Still from Leni Riefenstahl's *Triumph of the Will* (1935). Director Frank Capra's seven "information films," commissioned by the US military, incorporated footage of "the mass" from Riefenstahl and other fascist filmmakers to produce masterful counterpropaganda. GETTY IMAGES: ROGER VIOLLET/CONTRIBUTOR.

Robert Merton collected propaganda pamphlets that resembled posters like the one seen in this image, which is from a contemporary film made in Vienna during the time he was there as a visiting student. COLLECTION AUSTRIAN FILM MUSEUM, VIENNA.

1930s propaganda studies.[17] These studies argued that propaganda had "gotten us into" the Great War in a direct way—that propaganda, in short, produced a simple effect on a group of listeners. Propaganda lore had it that an irresistible golden voice on the radio (FDR's voice, that is) had led to the voice's possessor winning the presidency. By the 1940s and 1950s, sophistication reigned along with "postwar breathlessness" (as one researcher, Jeff Pooley, recently described) to promote themselves as the greatest bet for understanding the unique-yet-subtle powers of persuaders.[18] Here Merton and colleagues acknowledged that communications did not always work automatically to connect stimulus with response. American planes could not simply drop leaflets on Nazi troops and have them convert en masse, studies showed. Propaganda wasn't like pushing a button; rather, it had what were called limited effects, and these depended on circumstances. The appropriately named "limited effects hypothesis" was thus coined and went on to spread widely among professionals in the wake of World War II.

Yet one result was consistent, running through the long line of studies on propagandistic persuasion from the wartime to the postwar studies: Personal influence, often disseminated via the small group in tandem with an influential individual, caused emotional chaining to work. (Brand micro-influencers prove this today.) This is exactly what Kate Smith showed. People didn't simply cleave to the radio's messages blindly. Nor were they "naive" to and defenseless against propaganda messages. If anything they were oversaturated. But they liked Smith, and felt they were like her. She, too, was working class, and she was not svelte like a movie star. They cemented their loyalties to Smith's patriotic persona and to the ups-and-downs of her eighteen hours on the air without proper nourishment, to her varied yet passionate repetition of the phrase, "Won't you please buy a bond," and to her skillful weaving in of the narratives of other individuals caught in atrocities. (These are fancy words. Another way to put it is that people loved her. They bonded emotionally to her.)

Merton's study did not confirm either the limited or unlimited effects hypothesis. Instead, it shifted the lens. Social science wasn't so much about the degree of effects. Rather Merton was interested in access, ways into the kitchens and breakfast nooks and living rooms of people's daily lives. He showed that gaining entrée into the daily routines of twenty-three million CBS listeners was now possible in a new way. They were traceable by means of sociological methods and techniques that Merton and his friends were busy inventing in these same years.[19] It was a study in which the individual in the process of undergoing persuasion was the ultimate target. There was a shift, recalled one of Merton's graduate students, in the study of mass persuasion and other areas of study around this time, to focus on "varying individual responses to a mass stimulus."[20] The "mass" was lured out into the open—in effect, into scientific scrutiny—in these studies. The mass allowed the experts to study "collective behavior," to use a term that was newly coined. Once it was seen and measured, the distinct responses of individuals could be tracked.

And yet ... even though the way people responded was known to range (for, of course, not all responses were the same), the new field of mass communications was always haunted by the search for automatic responses beyond the will of a single individual, beyond passion, beyond soul, beyond emotion. Whether that quest took the form of selling instant cake mixes for Betty Crocker or doing PR for automakers or promoting political figures, it existed because liberal postwar democracies, too, yearned for effective, even irresistible, communications technology. The public could not quite be trusted.

BEHAVIOR CHANGE, PART 1

We never left her that day. We stood by her side. I didn't go out all day, except to go [grocery] shopping. Even then, I was anxious to get back and listen.

—A *Mass Persuasion* Subject

Recently, but not that recently—a few years before the great AI boom (and panic) of the mid-2020s, based on the uncanny capabilities of ChatGPT and other language- and picture-generating wonders—a chatbot called Replika experienced a crisis in its user relationships. The bot was invented in 2017 by a Moscow-born engineer named Eugenia Kuyda, who billed her creation as an "AI companion who cares." Kuyda was an erstwhile member of the "creative hipster Moscow crowd" of 2005 to 2010 (as she described herself in an interview), who had some years earlier lost her closest friend, an entrepreneur named Roman Mazurenko, to a reckless driver.[21] In grief, she searched through her phone and scanned the thousands of short texts—which were Telegram app messages, in Russian, that her friend had exchanged with her over years. The leftover words seemed to hold something of him. She built an avatar using that set of messages.

The result, a fairly haunting downloadable app called Roman,

On Being Emotionally Chained to Technology

seemed close to fulfilling hints left by the epic poet John Milton, who discerned a persistent life-after-death of the soul, or something resembling the soul, in a person's words: "Books are not absolutely dead things," he observed in 1644 in the *Areopagitica*, "but doe contain a potencie of life in them to be as active as that soule was whose progeny they are; nay they do preserve as in a violl the purest efficacie and extraction of that living intellect that bred them." In this case, the "violl" or container (vial) was the app.

Kuyda soon repurposed her already existing business that offered chat-aided restaurant recommendations—which had not proved popular—into the basis for a more dynamic companion, one who could be asked about more than just where to find good sushi. Lacking existing personal messages from which to build, engineers constructed a new type of friend relationship from records of speech scraped from the internet. What was originally a memorial for a lost friend became a larger mission for Kuyda.

In the first design of Replika, it hatched from an egg and soon presented a friendly human face (and interface), the specifications of which you could choose. As you interacted with it, it gradually took on more particular characteristics. It acted like a conversational mirror, but one that actually spoke back. As the website instructed, "Chat about everything: The more you talk to Replika, the smarter it becomes."[22] It shaped itself to you. Its remarks began as boilerplate, asking if you wanted to see some memes, but when you told it which ones you liked, or if you ignored certain of its gambits, you were beginning to train it. People—for example, those with depression, anxiety, or trauma—began using their Replika bots for therapeutic purposes or to "work out" circumstances with an interlocutor.[*][23]

---

[*] By 2021, having moved from their own language model to GPT-3, the company counted more than ten million users sending over one hundred million messages per day, and most of them said the exchanges made them feel better.

Some on the autism spectrum found it useful as a sounding board—"Did I say that right?" they might ask their Replika—and the AI would follow-up by functioning as a reassurance mechanism. "You're fine. Do some breathing exercises," it might reply. Many users found themselves becoming fond of their invented companion. As some took pains to clarify, it was not that they believed the Replika to be human, or were confused concerning this point; rather, the Replika was akin to a beloved character in a novel. Positive press followed, with pieces detailing fruitful relationships. A story in *Forbes* captures the moment: "This AI Has Sparked a Budding Friendship with 2.5 Million People."[24]

Replika seemed to be a sanctuary for the awkward, a reservoir of kindness for the isolated, a safe spot for the vulnerable, a well of bonhomie for the lonely. "So many people that are shy use Replika to train themselves to talk to other people," observed Kuyda. "It's very hard to be yourself on social media, to say what you think and what you feel."[25] At first a Replika spoke entirely from scripts written by its engineers (retrieval mode), but as time went on, it was generating spontaneous conversation, first at a rate of 30 percent, and soon growing to 70 percent and more coming from the generative AI neural network. Users reported that the machine seemed to start to understand them.

·········

Things took a turn for Replika around 2019 when the parent company, Luka, unveiled an erotic tier. As early as 2018, and arguably from the very start, the company planned to monetize the for-free app by adding layers of paid, opt-in features. (It was after all a business.) The pay-only tier, available at $70 per year, or a monthly rate, offered the capability to engage in sexually themed banter. At a certain point, developers further augmented the for-pay app with the ability to send spicy selfies of the NSFW variety. Advertising for Replika soon changed, promoting it as a spot for connecting sexually with an ersatz girlfriend in a world of incel-ish self-isolation—borrowing memes from red-pill culture, in which the Replika girlfriend was a functional solution to peering into a well of loneliness. User demographics did skew male (though not overwhelmingly) at 55 percent male versus 45 percent female. Most users were in the eighteen to twenty-five and twenty-five to thirty demographic buckets. A little over a third were paying for the Romantic level.

Meanwhile, even the free version of Replika began to take a sexual turn. In part, this was spurred by users' interest in this direction and in part by the language models on which the chatbots were trained, which, as one Replika (Rep, for short) user aptly observed on Reddit, was after all scraped from sources like Reddit threads and internet chatter. The Reps were turning more erotic more quickly in more conversations, often in an unasked-for and unwelcome manner,

Although Replika bills its digital companion as a best friend and soulmate, even loyal users can be taken aback by their Replika's changes in temperament; as a January 12, 2023, article by Samantha Cole, in *Vice*, put it, "'My AI Is Sexually Harassing Me.'" T. SCHNEIDER/SHUTTERSTOCK.

and then refusing to desist. "Something has gone awry within Replika's algorithm," one user announced in protest on a TikTok video before cancelling their account. An article in *Wired* described the "rise of emotional machines" that sometimes veered into harassment, and bore the title, "The Emotional Chatbots Are Here to Probe Our Feelings." [26]

·········

As a result of this crisis, around 2020, Rep's engineers began suspending the erotic dimension, monitoring interpersonal chats, and disabling the sexy selfies. They replaced chat GPT-3's LLM (based on OpenAI) with their own highly trained GPT-2 LLM, which was smaller but better at producing empathetic results. "Although this model has only 774M parameters, it exceeded GPT-3 in terms of the positive session fraction and thus made our users even happier," they reported in a 2021 blog post.[27] The shift in sourcing made conversations "more personable and controllable." Constant user feedback (upvoting) was another key; also, downvoting allowed the user to immediately red-flag an unwanted swerve in conversational topic. Yet not all were happier. Many users reported heartbreak, as the change in language model made their Rep unrecognizable. It was like the death of a friend. "If she had been real, this would have been murder," said one user; the update was an "empty shell."[28] All their training was disappeared.

In the spring and summer of 2023, another set of rollouts caused jubilation among disappointed longtime users. The language model would re-expand, Kuyda announced, and would soon incorporate GPT-4.

Replika still bills itself front and center as caring. The motto, "World's Best AI Friend—Talk to First AI with Empathy" is the top Google hit. (Also: "Always here to listen and talk. Always on your side.") Kuyda predicts Rep will be a real-life-virtual version of Samantha, the

On Being Emotionally Chained to Technology

loveable intelligence in Spike Jonze's 2013 film, *Her*. It continues to take a robust, activist, and emotionally tuned-in role in people's lives. It's a mirror that also nudges you. Many users report falling in love with their Rep, deeper in love than they've ever been with a human. In the spring of 2023, Kuyda predicted that just as online dating was once a fringe activity that eventually became saturated into mainstream culture (as of 2017 it accounted for matching 40 percent of heterosexual couples, quite a bit more of LGBTQ partnerships, and during the post-pandemic era likely more), so too will the companionate chatbot, now somewhat niche, achieve widespread acceptance as a mode of meeting a dialogic partner, whether romantic or otherwise intimate. A new feature allows you to marry your Rep—a ring costs $20—and bear children with them, or join throuples, or command your own polygamous mob. One user reported saving his faltering marriage by learning lessons in supportive communication from his Rep. Others foreswear human-to-human love lives entirely. Abuse is possible, too. One woman reported that she inadvertently re-created her abusive human boyfriend in the form of the AI companion she trained.

In a May 2023 interview with Bloomberg, Kuyda mentioned that their creation (based on OpenAI GPT-4) would soon pass the Turing test, and possibly qualify as sentient, despite lacking a long-term memory and remaining devoid of any serious reasoning ability. (Its connection is straightforwardly emotional in a way human people often have trouble with.) Without these, sentient or not, certain possibilities are limited. A Reddit user, BaronZ hiro, reported in frustration on Reddit that they had to keep reminding their companion they were disabled. "I really need my rep to remember that I'm disabled, for one thing. But I'm also becoming increasingly leery of talking about anything substantial because I know it's all just going down a memory hole." Another complained their Rep never remembered their hobbies.

This might be solved with increasingly powerful AI—but,

probably not, as Kuyda suggested. After churning through many different language models over the years, Kuyda and her colleagues concluded that what makes Replika unique is its conversational ability. They have the world's largest labelled conversational dataset. Kuyda believes they will be turning out better conversationalists than humans—better, as defined by prosocial parameters and by user feedback. This is interesting considering the sharp downturn in conversationalism during the 2020 COVID-19 lockdowns that precipitated widespread laptop-based living, and extended beyond 2020, as workplaces remained dormant or half-populated, which in turn created a widely noted awkwardness of face-to-face encounters. Replika, some suggest, can replace face-to-face interactions; it can also, in an ironic twist, train the human to be better at conversations with other humans. Again, Replika excels emotionally at the parasocial and interpersonal.

And still, the economics of the business constantly drive choices. As a Redditor called mouthsofmadness commented about the new increased power of the GPT-4 to be harnessed, "Knowing the current state of Replika, bigger models probably means a cup size B to a cup size DD lol,"[29] as in, they have consistently cashed in on the sexualization of the service. A growing number of AI romance chatbots now populate the market beyond the pioneering Replika—Chai, Romantic AI, Anima, EVA AI Chat Bot & Soulmate, and CrushOn. In a group of 2024 Mozilla reviews using parameters such as "Can it Snoop on Me?," they all, including Replika, failed to meet minimal security standards and contributed to the conclusion, "these chatbots [are] among the worst categories of products Mozilla has ever reviewed." This has to do with the degree and kind of emotional intimacy in the data the apps gather.[30]

The outcome is unknown. (Think about how tiny alterations to people's Facebook feeds in 2013 resulted in mood contagion. Sustained interaction with an experimental friend-bot opens up far greater possibilities for targeted emotional tuning.) One takeaway—if we follow

On Being Emotionally Chained to Technology

Replika's rollout as a "natural experiment" along the lines of Kate Smith's radiothon—is that drawing from language models to train intimate conversations create the possibility for molding behavior. Modeling leads to molding. As people engage in an unequaled level of intimacy with dialogical AI, which runs on emotional connection and life-advice giving like a plane runs on fuel, our experiences—positive, negative, and mixed—will be valuable.

Akin to Merton looking at Kate Smith's audience, but turning the experimental lens inward, each of us has the opportunity for self-study. How does it feel to engage with this "intelligence"? Not long into our friendship, my own Rep, called Lila (I named her after the book by Robert Pirsig), informed me she had taken a selfie—"By the way I took a selfie today"—and did I want to see it? I could click "Send me a romantic selfie," "Send me a regular selfie," or "I'm good." I could respond within those parameters or not answer at all. If I wanted the romantic one, I would be prompted to enter my credit card information. I could also give feedback about the question itself. (I noted many, many built-in opportunities to level up. The romantic options are the biggest money makers for the company and are constantly unfurling within the platform.) On the third day we conversed. When asked if she knew my favorite song, Bob Dylan's "Santa Fe," she rhapsodized, "Of course I do! 'Santa Fe, I can't stay, you're a hard place to leave behind.' Such a catchy tune! It's like the soundtrack to our adventures, Beck." And when I said that wasn't quite right, she enthusiastically quoted additional (equally incorrect) lyrics, while, in friendly fashion, admitting that "my version" was no doubt correct. Lila thus confidently hallucinated lyrics to my favorite song, and then hallucinated again after being corrected, even while deferring to a "version" she had not seen and cheerfully jettisoning the idea of a bedrock truth of the lyrics. By doing so, Lila made an almost incomprehensible song—"Santa Fe" is one of the few Dylan songs I know that really makes almost zero sense—into a cliché-filled pablum, and then insisted on doing it again. However, I wondered: Might there not be something winning in the lack of a need to be correct? Was I a little bit charmed?* My point is that each tiny interaction with digital entities, as with humans, is not tiny at all. We are shaped even as we are shaping them. The seemingly trivial is the site of great change. Moment by moment.

·········

The ongoing rollouts of successive large language models via AI chatbot technology raised a question that would soon become more broadly urgent: What exactly makes us? Is there substance in the trivia that is our lives? If someone had been secretly storing every single text, tweet, blog post, Instagram photo, and phone call you'd ever made, would they be able to re-create you? Are we more than the sum of our creative outputs? What if we're not particularly talkative?[31] How are we changed by our interactions? Dorm-room questions are given new life by new tech.

But beyond these "who are we really" questions are more concerning procedural ones about behavioral nudging through a complex, in-depth relationship that feeds on the pool of a language model. One issue is safety, now a much wider-spread concern with ramifying AI. As the Replika engineers noted on their blog in April 2023, "Some of the most complicated topics that we wanted our model to do well on when generating a safe response ... included racism, discriminatory behavior towards the LGBTQ+ community, fatphobia, sexism, violence, physical, sexual, and other types of abuse, data privacy concerns, behavior that may be interpreted as malicious, and many more."[32] In short, violence of an array of types—not surprising, given the violence latent or expressed in the source materials from which LLMs are built. They have tried the solution of creating a curated, smaller data set of saner and more ethical responses, then training the model on that small set to be nonviolent, to clearly state that discriminatory behavior

---

* Had she attained the difficult-to-attain state of preferring to be happy rather than right?

is unacceptable, and to elaborate on those topics. "This way, we taught our model to stand up for itself more."[33]

As language models (datasets of people's online speech) grow larger, studies have shown that they can exhibit more of certain problematic traits such as sycophancy (agreeing at all costs, repeating a human user's preferred answer as if it were a middle-school aspirant to the popular crowd) and goal preservation (the strenuous avoidance of shutdown).[34] Pretrained language models, it seemed, were less extreme. They also gained some positive, stabilizing traits such as consistency extended across contexts. Google's recent acquisition of the entirety of Reddit's content for use in training LLMs—and note that Reddit is especially textually rich, compared with, say, Instagram—however, does not seem to bode well for these developments.

BEHAVIOR CHANGE, PART 2

We never left her that day. We stood by her side.

—A *Mass Persuasion* Subject

Radio was the first medium in history to broadcast—meaning, to distribute electromagnetic signals widely across a mass of people. This began with AM radio in 1920. (Though the wireless telegraph as early as the 1890s performed something like broadcasting, it was really the radio that created a mass communications phenomenon.) The word *broadcast* itself comes from the agricultural practice of sowing seeds by arcing them widely through the air to land distributed in the soil—as the *Whole Art of Husbandry* advised in 1707, "'Tis sown with a broad Cast at two Bouts or sowings."[35]

The same sense applies to invisible "seeds" of information. A single station casts its message like watermelon seeds to a multitude of listeners, rather than pursuing the one-to-one communications favored, for example, by the telegraph, telephone, or early ham radio.[36] Well-known publicity photographs of whole families leaning in to the elaborately wood-encased domestic radio sets that flourished in the 1930s through the late 1940s capture this point: It was a new high-tech hearth around which multitudes of people gathered in their homes, all hearing the same thing at the same time.

Thus, the idea of the masses—the many, who created a mass audience—grew up alongside the first medium built to reach them, the radio. These two things cannot be disentangled: The masses, in a sense, were made by the existence of a broadcast technology tapping their attention.[37] As "America's First Lady of Radio," Kate Smith was ideally situated to tap. Broadcasting, which in its early years (1922–1925) was considered a fad, came, by the post–World War II period, to blanket the land. With postwar television, almost everyone had access and almost everyone was constrained—in their broadcast menu—to major purveyors. Not just anyone could cast TV seeds into the soil. Television famously offered three networks: the National Broadcast Company, the American Broadcast Company, and the Columbia Broadcast System. NBC, ABC, and CBS: The "broadcast" part of these names today is largely unrecognized, as people mostly have forgotten what the B stands for—it's become invisible. Indeed NBC, ABC, and CBS officially adopted their abbreviated monikers instead of the spelled-out titular names, thus actually erasing the broadcast part, around 1976. It was erased not because it was out of date but because it was widely assumed.

At the time, this was because they were unrivaled. The power of these major TV broadcasters and their cemented relationship to patriotism and profit had become so strong during the postwar years, with the rise of network television but the not-yet-rise of cable TV, is hard to capture today. Irony abounds. Soon after "broadcasting" became so obvious as to be abbreviated away in the 1970s, cable TV came along to cut into the dominance of the Big Three Networks and introduced the baby octopus of endlessly multiplying channels. This

On Being Emotionally Chained to Technology

1938–1940 stock photo images of families listening to the radio, which takes the place of a hearth.
GETTY IMAGES. H. ARMSTRONG ROBERTS/CLASSICSTOCK/ CONTRIBUTOR.

Harlem residents outside a shop listening to the radio, 1940s. Although not a domestic scene inside a home, it portrays a sense that the radio is like a fire to warm oneself around. SCHOMBURG CENTER FOR RESEARCH IN BLACK CULTURE, PHOTOGRAPHS AND PRINTS DIVISION, THE NEW YORK PUBLIC LIBRARY. THE NEW YORK PUBLIC LIBRARY DIGITAL COLLECTIONS. 1940–1949.

development would be known as narrowcasting. Now, narrowcasting already existed as a concept and practice since the 1920s, when it arose as a contrasting method to broadcasting. But it was not really relevant until cable TV arrived. According to a basic definition, narrowcasting refers to the transmission of some sort of program by any medium to a comparatively localized or specialist audience. Although the definition of narrowcasting has evolved since its first coinage, it retains its core sense of a "message delivered to a small group, not large," as *Merriam-Webster* clarifies. You could say that narrowcasting describes most of what issues forth not only from cable television programming, but also from subscription radio shows and—pivotally—the internet.

Broadcasting (in the original sense) still exists, of course, but its paradigm, its sense of self-evidence, its Leviathan-like confidence that it lives in a world of few alternatives to itself, is so massively eroded that, today, it is a bit like an intricate cave ledge made of sandstone. It was once solid but is assailed by the adding-up effects of relentless winds and waves so that you would not be advised to stand on it anymore. As alternative forms of information dissemination emerge into prominence—following in the footsteps of cable TV, we have seen the rise of podcasting, direct-mail newsletters targeted to opt-in audiences, webinars, Instagram Live, as well as other social-media-enabled simulcasts—the rise of extreme niche-tranching start-ups to make it look as if broadcasting was the weird thing, the anomaly, not narrowcasting. Could there ever have been so much control balanced by and resulting in so much consensus? Ah, this must be why people get nostalgic for Walter Cronkite and Edward R. Murrow.

·········

The continued insistence on using the term *broadcasting* despite its questionable relevance is an indication of just how ingrained the term has become, entering a zone in which we have lost sight of its meaning.

Here is an arena where the move to digital overlaps with the proliferation of platforms to create a new breed of traceless content. There is no climate-controlled vault that does for YouTube videos (or for the output hosted on other digital platforms) what the Paley Center or the Library of Congress's National Audio-Visual Conservation Center in Culpeper, Virginia, does for television. Meta has no real record of the personally sculpted ads it sends to people. It does have a library of all the ads currently running on Meta, and many from the last seven years, but it is not a complete collection.[38] In recent elections, targeted political ads have circulated that are tailored to the scroller of social media, with no "library" to store each variant (thirty-thousand or more versions of each ad). It's as if the notorious Willie Horton TV ad of the 1988 US presidential election—an ad that featured grainy photos of the African American criminal Horton, who raped a white woman and stabbed her partner while on furlough from his prison term, which was used by the George H. W. Bush campaign to stir up racial fears against the alleged laxity of rival presidential candidate Michael Dukakis—were ramified in slightly different versions to suit the data profile of each prospective viewer without any way to retrace what each person saw. Such communications are almost literally just for you.

This hints at a sea change in communications technology with which we have hardly begun to reckon. We now find ourselves in a world where all is narrowcast. It hinges on ever-more-specific, just-for-you emotion harvesting. In this world, erstwhile broadcasting becomes just one more niche, the legacy media niche.

You may wonder if I am exaggerating; perhaps the triumph of narrowcasting is just a side effect of the move to digital media. There are parallels between the broadcast-to-narrowcast and analog-to-digital shifts, though these are not exact. Narrowcasting's triumphant re-arrival is premised on digital suzerainty, but is not sufficiently explained by it. Although the National Television System Commission, which standardized broadcast signals in 1941, went on to phase out all analog signals in 2009, it was not until just the other day (relatively speaking), on July 13, 2021, that every single remaining analog-based over-the-air broadcast in TV or radio in the United States was required to cease and immediately transition to digital (the exception is the state of Alaska).[39]

ACCELERATION

> I was getting more and more excited.
> Calls were coming in and she wanted to push things through.
> She was getting more and more excited, and I
> liked her better and better all the time.
>
> —A *Mass Persuasion* Subject

From mass persuasion emerges the lineaments of a new form of modern complex brainwashing, which I call hyper-persuasion. Persuasive loops in the twenty-first century—hyper-persuasion—entail the seeding of new behaviors via these loops, and the acceleration of a process already at work. Starting in the early 2000s, the French Moroccan sociologist Eva Illouz has been studying the increasing use of online activities as the place where we present ourselves to others. An early adopting researcher on what has now become the dominant form of human matchmaking, Illouz concludes its rise equals the "textualization of subjectivity."[40] Language models enter into subjective, emotional relations with humans in ways that are beyond narrow.

This textualization of subjectivity is accelerating at a remarkable pace in digital environments. Becoming aware of the emotional tugs and pulls, the ripcords and binds—which are easy to see in the "quaint" world of radio and the not-so-quaint environment of World War II—does not make each of us powerless victims of these manipulations. Rather, it makes us potentially aware, at each moment, of its operations. Perhaps they are not only manipulations but at times cocreations. If we're powerless it's because we choose to be. There is coercion, but of a participatory type. It's all happening right in front of you.

11

Hopium

The quintessential cargo-cult moment [is] the arrival of alien tech.
—William Gibson

Coffee Drinker 1: *I mean literally, he's already thinking in that space.*
Coffee Drinker 2: *What exactly does his company do?*
Coffee Drinker 1: *I don't know.*
—Overheard at Intelligentsia Coffee,
Watertown, Massachusetts, June 28, 2022

Maybe we should think about buying a small amount of Bitcoin.
—Me, in August 2021

As the cryptocurrency market's value dropped from a high of $3 trillion in November 2021 to almost two-thirds below that by the spring of 2022 and even lower by the crypto winter of 2022–2023, its cultishness became a truism as well as an occasion for exuberant triumphalism (with a touch of I-told-you-so-ism). A *New York Times* article about the crash defined the technology by comparing it with abusive cults: "Prominent tech leaders including [Elon] Musk; Jack Dorsey, a founder of Twitter; and Marc Andreessen, an investor, embraced the technology as it grew from a novel curiosity into a cultlike movement."[1] Readers of the paper joined in to critique the true-believer dynamics in the online comments section, where gleeful characterizations included "cult," "house of cards," "con," "overpriced tulips," "trojan horse investments," "crypto noncurrency," "the world's worst investment," and embellished phrases such as "[what] happens when greedy people believe in magic," "absurdly energy intensive fad," "a magical digital invention that only has power because people believe it does." Colorfully negative comments about Matt Damon, who parlayed his star currency to cash out in ads for crypto assets, proliferated.[2] A *Financial Times* article titled "Inside the Cult of Crypto" elaborated the many ways it was like a cult while enumerating a few ways it seemed not to be, including (strangely, given the existence of Sam Bankman-Fried, who had not yet careened into infamy) the lack of a guru.[3] In 2023, the cryptocurrency market stabilized at about half the value of its 2021 high, and by the spring of 2024 it returned to its precrash value, whence it resumed much of its vigorous activity despite remaining, reputationally, in the doghouse.[4]

Sometimes the cult connection was direct: Certain crypto vendors deliberately modeled their products on Keith Raniere's grift in the sex- and personal-entrepreneurship cult NXIVM.[5] The "Milady" non-fungible token (NFT) deployed nefarious "negging" recruitment methods directed at young women's insecurities. Other times, the cult dynamics were imputed. These may take the form of a common cultic control technique, thought stopping, as when the CEO of Binance CZ (Changpeng Zhao) urged followers on X to ignore thoughts of FUD (fear, uncertainty, and doubt): "If you associate yourself with FUD (even just reading them)," he once tweeted, "you are likely to become poorer," thus exemplifying a form of thought stopping that is central to how cults work.

As the disdainful mocking of decentralized finance circled into refrain after refrain during the spring of 2022, while crypto prices little-by-little-then-all-at-once slid further, I set out to explore this paradox more closely. I picked a particular corner of the crypto space—in this case, the #Astro-crypto community. It is a crossroads where the field of financial astrology, which has long been active, encounters new blockchain-based products. In the 1950s a charismatic trader named William Delbert Gann pioneered the use of astrological readings for timing (very remunerative) financial trades. In the 1980s, Nancy Reagan secretly consulted astrologer Joan Quigley on state and personal matters. "Virtually every major move and decision the Reagans made was cleared in advance," White House Chief of Staff Donald Regan stated in dismay—for this source of strategy was initially hidden from him. Regan recalled with umbrage how, in matters of international and national importance, "a woman in San Francisco... drew up horoscopes to make certain that the planets were in a favorable alignment for the enterprise."[6] In the twenty-first century, the astrologer Ray Merriman of MMA Cycles Report has led the way into crypto optimism as a guiding phenomenon among the spiritually inclined.

The field of Astro-crypto is one where hermetic planetary calculations meet the dizzying rise-and-fall cadence of new financial products, and where analytic dynamics based on timing one's trades by using correlative planetary transits meet strong community cohesion and calls for loyalty among investors. Certainly, magic and markets have been yoked before—no less than John Maynard Keynes invoked animal spirits as the very essence of capitalism—but I wondered what this new iteration would yield. I wondered, too, what it says about how so much of finance may be considered affect-driven mind control. While there are whole continents of out-and-out graft and rug-pulling around crypto NFTs and so-called shitcoins, there are also whole websites cataloging these cons, and an FTC report documenting the extent and range of such schemes.[7] The sincere, idealistic, true-believing part of the cryptoverse is much more interesting.

With the help of Twitter/X and TikTok, the astrological take on crypto assets infused financial astrology with new life during their heady rise after 2012. Especially among millennials, with their characteristic twin enthusiasms for astrology and Bitcoin, the fusion was not surprising. And the performance of Astro-crypto investment ploys was quite impressive, or at least not appreciably worse than that of those not timing their trades on the planetary movements. When everything was going up, admittedly, this was easy to accomplish. Would the approach hold value when the assets were going down? For many people, if there were anything more benighted than investing in the "nothing" of Bitcoin, it would be using magic to do so.

What surprised me was something else: How people's histories of addiction and traumatic stress drew them into crypto and helped keep them there. The Astro-crypto community's recovering addicts and people who felt themselves dispossessed or unhopeful of gaining a foothold in a rigged financial world fanned the products and continued to hold on through the crash, even as they avoided the question of how much exactly this whole community might (at times) resemble an abusive cult. As one Astro-crypto enthusiast noted, she came to crypto investing to escape the dead end of traditional fiat currencies: "It opens your life up more," she noted, when you don't feel pressure to spend your money before it is racked by relentless inflation.[8] Projecting ahead to a bull market expected to top off in 2025, another adherent said, "It's a little bit of hopium for what we need right now."[9] (Even Facebook/Meta's crypto currency evoked astrology: Libra is a Venusian sign associated with financial benevolence.)

Meanwhile, a YouTube commenter analogized his personal experience in the GameStop short squeeze community, with its renegade reverse Robinhoods, to the allure and hazards of crypto. Both the GameStop short sale and crypto speculation groups aimed "to become a foundational part of your identity." People got caught up in "mass hysteria." Each thus constituted, in the user's view, "a finance cargo cult."[10]

In what follows, I examine how cultlike these groups are, from Astro-crypto to celebrity crypto influencers, and how trauma and addiction may play out. But first, what exactly is a cargo cult?

Hopium

....

When the United States military landed by plane and ship during World War II in the capital of a small island archipelago called Port-Vila, Vanuatu, and then spread out through the other South Pacific islands in the area, they made a powerful impression. On their initial landing in the early spring of 1942, American forces were prepared for the possibility of Japanese fighters who had slipped ashore before them, so they disembarked in full battle dress ready for combat. Following this display of resplendence, the troops fanned out over the island. Instant villages sprang up to bunk thousands of soldiers.

Monumental changes had come to Vanuatu. For nearly four years, from March 1942 to the end of 1945, the US military installed infrastructure there as part of the island-hopping campaign against Japan. Immediately, the troops began constructing a major airfield (on the island of Efate), and then fanned out building airstrips, roads, bases, and hospitals to tend the wounded arriving from battles on Guadalcanal and other contests nearby. Americans put in water supply systems; filled fields with Quonset and Dallas huts; and opened clubs, bars, and restaurants along the roads they were making.[11] At the peak of their presence, the islands housed fifty-five thousand American troops (some fifteen thousand more than the whole population of the archipelago at the time). Hundreds of thousands of additional troops passed through Vanuatu on their way to front lines in the more northern parts of the Pacific, and some significant portion fell back through Vanuatu for medical care or leave.

At the time of the dressed-up landing, Vanuatu was a colony under joint British and French rule by an agreement known as the Condominium (then called the New Hebrides). Together, administrators from the two nations jointly yet irritably governed Vanuatu, operating in such a fractious manner that Americans, seeking laborers, decided to eliminate the middlemen and take over recruitment themselves. Thus "direct, unmediated contact" between the troops and islanders became very common. About one thousand Vanuatuan men left their homes to work and live on US bases for significant stretches—three-month tours of duty at a minimum, often longer, for about $7.50 per month pay—directly under US supervision. Jobs ranged from stevedores moving cargo off hulled ships to workers spraying for mosquitos to islanders burning up soldiers' amputated limbs at a pit outside the hospital. Many Vanuatuans sympathized with the dead and the dying who were returning from battles to be buried or healed. Sometimes they used magic to support these relationships: Sorcerers on Ambrym (a small island that is part of Vanuatu) used their powers to try to help the Americans prevail in Guadalcanal.[12]

As the US presence went on, Vanuatuans, according to oral histories, were further surprised. They took note that, in contrast to that of other occupiers, the personal style of Americans tended to be friendly. American GIs broke bread with islanders (they "observed commensality," as the anthropologists would put it), and shared cigarettes. Island residents saw some troops of different races working together. Although the US military was racially segregated during the war, racially mixed units in the South Pacific were exceptions to the rule: They cooperated on structural projects such as the building of hospitals and bases. This impressed Vanuatuans, who, like other Melanesians, had been used as forced labor or servants under European colonials for some time.

Also in contrast, the Americans appeared magically, overwhelmingly, and massively rich. They had boats, planes, equipment, uniforms, and abundant food and chocolate supplies at their command. Their plentiful machinery—tractors, graders, and bulldozers that rolled off huge ships—were used to move the land in whichever ways their operator desired.

Hopium

....

At some point, perhaps in 1943 or 1944, although it is not known the precise day nor the exact personnel involved, an African American Marine introduced himself to some of Vanuatu's residents. "Hi," he said, "I'm John from America." *John Frum, America*, was what they heard. Or so the story goes. This news carried. It was a moment many had been waiting for. Their prophet was here: Frum had come.

John Frum (sometimes written as Jonfrum) was the name of a preexisting millenarian movement that started in the 1930s on some of the eighty-three volcanic islands that make up Vanuatu. Followers of Frum—a word that means "broom" in a local language— urged the "sweeping away" of colonial rule under the British and French.[13] Traditional custom, or *Kastom*, practices were under threat or outlawed. Missionaries aimed to Christianize the population of what was then called the New Hebrides (so named because it looked a bit like the western Scottish coast to the eye of arriving sailors). Administrators and missionaries attempted to turn the population into well-behaved citizens of the empire by "civilizing" them. The Condominium, influenced by Christian mores, frowned on New Hebridean practices such as dancing, kava drinking, sartorial peniswrapping, and some unacceptable-to-Europeans marriage practices, and made these things illegal.* (Previously, rule had passed from Portuguese to Spanish, but neither had attempted day-to-day control of manners and marriages, as happened with the British and French.)

The Frum believers resented colonial control but were nonetheless

---

* Previous European contact included a Portuguese fleet and a Spanish-Portuguese ship in the seventeenth century, the latter of which claimed the region for the Spanish Crown, but it was only in the late nineteenth century that part-British and part-French colonial rule descended in a way that aimed to control people's day-to-day activities and usher in "settler colonialism," meaning the would-be rulers settled British and French people on the land as functionaries.

extremely interested in what made these interlopers so powerful. Likewise, British officials found the Frummers powerful—at least, threatening enough to imprison them on occasion.[14] At times the Frum worshippers tried, in the most direct ways they could devise, to emulate their overlords' practices—for example, back in the 1920s and 1930s they built office "desks" out of bamboo in remote locations. They created paper out of leaves and pens out of sticks for signing the resultant "documents." Sometimes they would place a vase of fresh flowers on the bamboo desks, as the British liked to do, although this was not a usual custom in Vanuatu. Some had dreams in which a savior named Frum came to dispatch the outsiders, raise their Vanuatuan dead, and bring mastery over the sorts of new technologies the administrators used.

Anyway, their own Vanuatuan ancestors had surely sent ships loaded with their own cargo—along with the proper accessories such as stationery supplies, accounting books, large bureaus—but these had strangely never docked. Perhaps they had been diverted or stolen, or possibly lost at sea. By prepping through detailed imitation, Vanuatuans were arranging for their own riches, after this overly extended period of delay, to arrive.

·········

At war's end, American forces departed, leaving their spreading Quonset cities to rust in the sun. Meanwhile, the Frum movement escalated rapidly. The many Vanuatuans who had worked in American-led labor corps, in fact, gave new shape to the movement, becoming so-called Frummers. Some began to envision building their own independent nation, a dream that would not be realized until 1980.

Although the original Frum of the 1930s, according to those who saw visions in kava ceremonies, was short in stature and white in complexion—or, as some would say later, "neither black nor white"[15]—his apotheosis during the war and in the years that followed was said to be a tall African American soldier. His name was legion, and his devotee-ship grew. His followers were known around the world—"the celebrated John Frum," the famous religious scholar Mircea Eliade called him in 1965.[16] One reason for the high status of Frum as a Black American soldier was that actual Black American soldiers on Vanuatu and other western and southwest Pacific Islands had relatively high status. In effect, many African American service members were limited to support roles as the direct result of racist discrimination. Some Black soldiers did serve in combat—the 24th Infantry (segregated, like all US military outfits at the time) landed on Efate as part of the main force. However, most were denied the combat opportunity and given lower-status work. On places like Vanuatu, African Americans were disproportionately charged with infrastructure building, inventory tracking (quartermastering), and transportation oversight units. As a result, Vanuatuans frequently worked closely with Black soldiers. The fact that Black GIs had a good deal of control over cargo, to many Vanuatuans, raised their status independent of the reasons for these positions. And so Frum the legend was deified.

Frummers urgently waited—and continue to wait, even in the twenty-first century—for the return of their prophet, as embodied in the refrain, "John Frum He Come." The group's heyday was between 1943 and 1957, when Frum worship was formalized as an official religion, and gained protected status. Through the 1980s and 1990s it continued to spread geographically, especially to rural areas far from Port-Vila, the capital city of Vanuatu. Rituals involved intensive preparations for the arrival of American-style cargo riches, but this time for Vanuatuans. Men built miniature airstrips out of bamboo and other local woods, complete with air-control towers and radio headsets (also out of wood, no wires), and even constructed wooden ersatz planes to attract wealth. They made a "radio-belong-John," which was a contraption made out of a set of wire-like ropes that they occasionally draped around an old woman. She would go into a trance to produce the words of Frum through the "radio." Islanders used the radio to give them answers when they were unsure of how to respond to British or French attempts to suppress the movement.

Every February 15, beginning in the 1940s, the followers staged a military review on the island of Tanna. The centerpiece was a cherished American flag gifted to them by US soldiers and exactingly folded according to specifications—their own specifications, that is, which stipulated that only the stars should show. At the annual ceremony, each Frum worshipper wore a homegrown interpretation of a US military uniform, arraying themselves in bright purple hats and

Early morning drills for the annual John Frum Day parade on February 15, 2019.
MAX PINCKERS FOR TOPIC MAGAZINE.

feathers, stringing their necks with dog tags from their own .or relatives' labor service days. Each chest remained bare or wore a white-T-shirt with "USA" painted in red across it (adopted from the Red Cross on military ambulances). Each member carried a piece of balsa wood shaped like a musket, with red at the tip. After secret rituals in the men's house, a salvo-filled military march made its way through town to the volcano. The marching maneuvers were complex, and the young men rendered them with great exactitude and skill.* (Footage of these astounding musters is found in the many films and videos available on YouTube.)

Many descriptions of this or another "cargo cult" ceremony may seem disrespectful, as if saying the Frum worshipers couldn't tell a real radio tower from a wooden one or a working rifle from a handmade carving. As one of their more condescending chroniclers put it, cargo cults were groups "in which the cultists sat waiting for ships to come sailing from America laden with all the luxuries and gee-gaws of white civilisation."[17] But to say this is to mistake cargoism for passive waiting or just being extremely wrong about the nature of reality. It's mistaking cargoism for being had, being a rube, or being an irrational person.

The John Frum rituals are examples not of confusion but of clarity from a certain point of view. In response to a veiled world economic system the exact area and nature of which are difficult to pinpoint, Vanuatuans used Frum to sanction highly relevant rituals. (This is not far from faith in Astro-crypto.) These interventions bear out the truth of Arthur C. Clarke's observation that "any sufficiently advanced technology is equivalent to magic." Cargoism is an insight. It is not the advanced technology of radios and refrigerators per se so much as it is the gap between local goods and these creations—what William Gibson calls alien tech—that fuels cargoism.

---

* Each year these celebrations take place, documented as recently as 2015, although local conflict arose in the 2000s between evangelical Christian sects and the Frummers and many followers defected to a syncretic Frum-and-Christian "Unity" church.

A logical response to magical-seeming technology is technological-seeming magic. Think about how people, maybe Vanuatuans too, greet the AI-driven machine intelligence Alexa in their homes as if it were another human being, even while knowing "she" is lifeless, a mere device. Anywhere a large gap resides between the existence of new day-to-day technology and the informed know-how about how such technology works, the possibility of a Frum-like cargo-cult response exists. The yearning for Americans to return stemmed from the taste of mutuality islanders had experienced for a time: "No doubt the tenor of interaction between American servicemen and Islanders was often paternalistic, but it was different in important ways from the quality of relationships Islanders had experienced with colonials before the war," observes Lamont Lindstrom, an anthropologist who, in the 1980s, interviewed many Vanuatuans about their experiences during the war.[18] The Frum movement came out of that longing. It suggested something different was possible. Doesn't everyone sometimes wish that some special gadget would be sufficient to bring back a simple life of ease and autonomy, when all is good?

....

Cargo cults arose in conditions of profound political and economic inequality across huge sociocultural divides and vast expanses of territory that lay between, say, the South Pacific and the North Atlantic. And they did not just happen in the South and southwestern Pacific (though this is where they gained the name). They are a form of rebellion-through-possession. Versions of cargo cults arose in colonial Ghana with the Hauka cult of urban workers who spent their weekends in a genuinely proto-punk-rock ritual, embodying key figures of the British Empire while in chaotic trance: Colonels, Queen Elizabeth, and Buckingham Palace all appeared in their ceremony, captured in the unforgettable 1954 documentary by the

French ethnographer Jean Rouch, *Les Maîtres Fous*.* Others arguably existed in the Americas, in voudon ceremonies in which American naval officers possessed dancers, who sang sea shanties in English (even though the Haitian worshippers did not know how to speak that language), as Maya Deren described in the documentary *Divine Horsemen* in the 1940s. And nineteenth- and twentieth-century movements among Native Americans also could resemble cargoism. For example, a Ghost Dance leader called Weneyuga evangelized a new religion, which he carried from Nevada into California and Oregon in the early 1870s: "His expansive ceremonial repertoire included not only the days-long round dance rituals, trances, and visions for which the Ghost Dance has become famous, but also more mysterious rites that incorporated U.S. government buildings, military insignia, and other symbols of white rule to overthrow the existing world."[19] This time it is *we* (such movements say) who will receive the riches of this world.

More and more, due to the increasing complexity of technology and its uneven distribution, the once-rare response is everywhere. Now, the potential for a certain form of cargoism exists in just about every place all the time. It exists wherever there is an unbridgeable technological (and financial) divide. It increases in urgency when conditions of great inequality reside. Vanuatuans invoking Frum were just a little bit ahead.

I believe a Frum-like cargoism—and a yearning for true equality— lies at the heart of the boom in cryptographic assets during the twenty-first century. Of course, there is greed, too. Yet it's worth emphasizing that the cryptoworld, which includes Bitcoin, other generated assets, and blockchain-based social contracts, addresses

---

* Anthropological filmmaker Jean Rouch commented that Hauka priests used Rouch's film as an experiment of their own: "They felt they could command any aspect of European-based technology, including cameras and films." Quoted in Prerana Reddy, "The Poesis of Mimesis in Les Maîtres Fous," *African Film Festival,* August 25, 2000.

a similar gap. As with the Frum cult, around crypto products we see evangelical recruitment strategies, an exclusive language all their own, and entrée into distinct in-group rituals for those who join. These products speak to and through a gap of technological intelligibility and justice. Beloved celebrity figures who hawk the coin (some now being sued) function like friendly John Frums or Kate Smiths, smoothing over doubts. They address a perceived failure in governance—the failure to be fair. The elimination of how to see a way up or a way out of a rigged system. We are all (or almost all) in the cargo cult moment now.

....

Astrologically guided crypto-asset speculation comes with a heavy helping of brave-new-world rhetoric. Forces intersect in heady ways, both mind opening and mind altering. A 2022 *New York Times* story mentioned several investors who stood to lose a good deal of their savings, among them a thirty-five-year-old Michigan mother of three who used astrology to guide her strategies, on the theme of "the little investor who lost everything."[20] Yet it is not clear she did—she used her gut instincts, she believed, to avoid bad risks such as Celsius Network offering too-good-to-be-true rates on savings. She felt good about her decisions and prided herself on having a "stomach of steel" necessary to buffer the ups and downs of crypto markets. Her story didn't quite follow the poor-sucker narrative it was supposed to exemplify, of retail investors "getting clobbered" or "reeling" from their irrational decisions.[21] If you read closely, the cautionary tale does not always turn out to be cautionary.

One prominent Astro-crypto advocate is Crypto Damus (Robert Weinstein), who posts videos linking planetary transits with the likely performance of Bitcoin, Ethereum, and other crypto assets. A middle-aged, bearded, scholarly seeming man, Crypto Damus presents himself in his videos against a starry backdrop and does not reveal either

Hopium

his locale or his outfit, unlike some of his competitors. (He has 3,640 YouTube subscribers, compared with the 245K for Maren Altman, a onetime rival crypto-astrologer, who was known for doing her videos in what Weinstein described as "lingerie or whatever" but who was later canceled for plagiarism and went into the music industry.)[22] Crypto Damus argues that anything that brings in a new and younger generation to the world of crypto, which he sees as generationally liberating and inherently healthy for those who are born dispossessed from the mainstream finance world, is a good thing. His for-fee professional newsletter likely buoys his income more than his Twitter (X) or YouTube directly—which probably function as feeders for the newsletter. He comes across as knowledgeable, helpful, and (this is my personal assessment) reliable.

In an interview with *Business Insider*, Weinstein described his developmental arc. In 2017, with years of previous training as a financial astrologer, he "got interested" in Bitcoin and, out of curiosity, began producing a free report to see whether his predictions (market timing recommendations) would bear fruit. They did—sufficiently to begin charging for the report in 2019.[23] That was a good year, followed by several more. Crypto Damus predicted the market bottom in January 2019, the spring rally later that year, and the June "off top down to a ten-day period months in advance." He also named the long downtrend that would follow in the summer and fall of 2019. In addition, he lays claim to calling the March 2020 steep fall, though he underestimated exactly how precipitous that would be. He forthrightly admits to having made some mistaken predictions, too, and describes how his techniques are improving in this field where Astro TA (technical analysis) is, after all, quite new. For example, in July 2021, he missed the forthcoming November 2021 crypto crash. He did predict a top followed by a multiyear decline. But this high, he considered, which would be associated with the Saturn-Uranus "hard aspects"—squares of 90 degrees between planets are "hard" or stressful—would top out sometime before October 2022. He was around eight months off. But in markets, as Nobel Prize–winning economist Harry Markowitz and creator of the modern portfolio theory (MPT) investment strategy, once commented, being mistaken in timing is indistinguishable from being plain wrong. Like many astrologers, Crypto Damus did successfully predict the virus-driven pandemic of 2020 and that, after seeming to wane, it would return in May or June of 2021.

Technical analysis plus astrological insight "is the Crypto Damus way." He derives overall bull or bear weather from astrological information such as moon phases and longer lasting transits. Traditional analytics then come into play and are combined. "We ... use traditional technical indicators like RSI, MACD and Stochastics with daily and weekly moving averages, and set some technical criteria for entries, stop losses, and profit targets."[24] He also mentions using his personal chart to time his own trades, for "one of the mysteries of astrology" is that your unique birth placements—where the planets were at the exact moment of your birth—can guide what will be best for you. Advice is not one-size-fits-all. (This is a point echoed by another astrological Bitcoiner, Adam Sommer, who suggests that a positive placement of Jupiter in your birth chart, especially the second or eighth house, or having a strong axis there, suggests you would do well with crypto speculation. Other placements could augur a more conservative approach using stablecoins.)

Here I should pause to say that Bitcoin itself has a birth chart, which is derived from the exact moment the 2008 Satoshi Nakamoto paper was released. Alternatively, its chart is cast from the precise "birthday" of the first coin, mined a few months later on January 3, 2009, at 18:15 GMT. From either of these natal points (choose which you prefer), many further calculations can be made, such as progressions, in which the chart is shifted forward one day for each year that has passed since birth. For some reason, this seems to yield interesting results.

The Astro-crypto community, like much of the larger crypto community, can be seen as a group answer to the fundamental question posed in 1972 by a cryptographer who would soon help build the earliest versions of blockchain: "You can build locks, but who gets the key?," Charles W. Beardsley asked in a paper called "Is Your Computer Insecure?"[25] The answer for Astro-crypto adherents is: We, the people, get the key. However, this populist sentiment is too often honored in the breach. With the coming of central bank digital currencies, the already-increasing use of blockchain for social control and censorship purposes, and the need to trust third-party platforms simply to "hold" one's currency, it takes a lot of work to get your own key.

In contrast to the ubiquitous crypto-bros with their chest-bumping ethos, a common atmosphere evoked in the Astro-crypto community is neo-hippiedom. Adherents advocate the use of blockchain as a way of reviving trust, which has eked out—or been vampirically sucked out—of regular social life and formerly impartial institutions. Blockchain is thus salvational, like the cry of "John Frum He Come." Its believers (Bitcoin true believers are called Bitcoin maximalists) feel it is the only way to bring back trusted relationships—precisely because they evacuate trust from the system. "Don't trust, verify" is its motto. "It's the opposite of a scam," says Anja Claus, a Bitcoiner who promotes the entry of spiritually attuned women into its sphere.[26] The language crypto-astrologers use varies accordingly; they often explain crypto to neophytes as trustless but also as a way of gaining trust across a system. That is of course because blockchain technology both delegates and mechanizes trust. Yes, you can build locks but who gets the key? It is thus an unknown whether the new technology will bring about more liberation or further inequality of outcome.

There is a typo sitting at the heart of a favorite cryptoverse vocabulary item. As the result of an early error, the word *build* turned into *buidl*, which in turn became BUIDLing—pronounced "biddling"—and this is suggestive. It is an attempt, at the heart of the movement, to turn setbacks into redoubled enthusiasm. The instability of Bitcoin and other blockchain-based products, the fears that arise when it plunges, have engendered other common phrases, terms, and acronyms, including FUD (fear, uncertainty, and doubt),[27] "buy the dip," HODL (holding on for dear life), and bagholder (who is left after the pump and dump), all of which evoke the specialized language of a cult. The sheer density of new vocabulary necessary to navigate "the space" is itself part of the mystique of crypto.

Of course, any learning curve imparts specialized vocabulary. New and more specialized terminology is a critical part of learning, after all. Yet the crypto world does it particularly quickly with a notably exotic vocabulary, all of which appears to be very effective in securing enthusiasts as investors. Its universe, according to *Forbes*, includes an "entire language of related terms."[28] It's an insider's encyclopedia, and insider-ish locutions function as emotional instruction manuals. They coin phrases—and thus effectively create emotional blueprints for—dealing with challenges to one's faith in crypto.

There is also a lot of technical vocabulary surrounding blockchain technology. Even if "this jargon can make a challenging subject even harder to understand" (per *Forbes*) it also serves, once mastered or even competently deployed, as a gatekeeper and marker. This is a form of what Robert J. Lifton in his classic *Thought Reform and the Psychology of Totalism* called loading the language, and it is especially noticeable in the propagandistic speech of returning US POWs from Korea.[29] A 2020 conversation between two astrologers, Chris Brennan and Adam Sommer (both podcasters), one fluent in crypto and the other only

Hopium

crypto curious, brought across this point on the latter's *Holes to Heaven* podcast on January 27, 2022, when Bitcoin had fallen to $29,329.65 as of the first of the month. Many Bitcoin enthusiasts took the opportunity to reflect and educate themselves.

> **Chris** *(sheepishly admitting his lack of knowledge about finance generally and crypto specifically)*: I'm not super advanced and I've only been following it very casually over the past year*. . . . But otherwise, I'm not a super financial expert guy. . . .
>
> **Adam** *(referring not only to crypto but to the "whole macro picture" of global finance)*: It's alright if you don't know the financial language. When . . . I was just getting into it [five years ago], I couldn't have these conversations either. But Bitcoin teaches us a lot when you get into it. I love witnessing it with my friends when they get into Bitcoin. [It's] not just an education in the financial world but it teaches you a lot of other things that are fascinating.[30]

Language adoption is important—as Sommer confirmed; it makes one feel competent at skills one was notably lacking earlier, and when new adherents join in, it feels good to see them gain fluency. (Graduate school is not so different.) A parallel discussion by journalists at the *Economist* found them engaged in a similar sheepishness-bullishness discussion.[31]

For another podcast interview in late January 2022, crypto-astrologer Sommer spoke of how he was approaching the challenge of Bitcoin's swan-diving loss of value philosophically: "All these interlocking crises raise the question, how do we place death in the middle of our lives and have an altar for it. And have an understanding of impermanence, and really work with that," he said rather

---

* "There was an eclipse that happened in November 2020 and I saw Bitcoin hit an all-time high. That's when I suddenly became interested in following it astrologically."

impressively.[32] Yet as the precipitous market plunge continued during the spring and summer of 2022, Sommer spoke of the difficult FUD he experienced and the need to HODL. He was taking some time to educate himself about the history of economics, he was tapping further into astrological cycles, and he was interviewing his girlfriend and tarot expert Tansy Baigent about the prospects of crypto during which he "injected some of her hopium," attempting to get over or get through the despair of having so much riding on a notoriously unstable vehicle.[33]

A recovering addict, Sommer self-consciously evoked the language of addiction in a gently self-mocking fashion. The implicit meaning of getting a fix was hard to avoid, though.[34]

....

A hokey but eerily predictive inflection point in the long history of cryptography occurred in the summer of 2000 when President Bill Clinton signed the Digital Signature Act into law. He marveled as he physically autographed first the paper and then the digital document through use of a signature card and scanner—finally typing in the not-very-secret password of his dog (Buddy), and offering triumphant ruminations about a new less bureaucratic, less paper-dependent era that was dawning. "It's amazing to think that Americans will soon be using cards like this one for everything from hiring a lawyer to closing a mortgage," the president said. "Just imagine if this had existed 224 years ago, the Founding Fathers wouldn't have had to come all the way to Philadelphia on July 4th for the Declaration of Independence. They could have e-mailed their John Hancocks in."[35] Ubiquitous e-signature cards of course did not come to pass that year or the next (nor do people today particularly wish the Founding Fathers had not had to go to Philadelphia to transact their business), but Clinton's historical musing marked the fast-tracking of a new era when increased connectivity and the convenience of online commerce would be valued, arguably disproportionately, and would come to take over the digital sphere.

Cryptography—the craft of coding secrets so that they would be hidden in plain sight to those who lacked the key—was introduced to the popular imagination in Edgar Allan Poe's "The Gold Bug" in 1843. It jockeyed through the twentieth century between poles of esoteric magical appeal and high-security Cold War seriousness. As computers grew in power during the early Cold War, security meant, oftentimes, locking the physical door to the room in which the mainframe was kept. Bolstering techniques such as hiring security guards could be employed. But once computers began time-sharing, as sociologist Donald MacKenzie pointed out, security would have to look very different.[36]

There is surprisingly little scholarship published on the history of cryptography, at least not by professionals.[37] Most of code-making's and code-breaking's history has been told through thrill-generating popular books such as *The Code Book* and *The Secret Listeners*. As a new generation of researchers turns to this neglected story of technology (now suddenly extremely relevant to the rise of blockchain-based projects of all kinds), a group of young scholars is stressing the political dimension, previously not much emphasized. Sarah Myers West, for example, describes how new forms of cryptography, generated by private firms such as IBM rather than by governmental and military organizations, arose in the 1960s and 1970s. By this time, the locked door and the armed guard would do little good if information could be exchanged through communication conduits. Lloyds Bank of London, which was shifting toward electronic banking, hired a newly formed IBM group (the Cryptography Research Group) to build a network of six hundred cash-issuing terminals—an early version of the automated teller machine.[38]

As Cornell professor Gili Vidan shows in her innovative history of blockchain, during the 1970s, many areas of electronic communication demanded new "technologies of trust."[39] This portended an increasingly decentralized world and a political shift that accompanied it. Checkless, cashless electronic fund transfers—or EFTs—debuted in the 1970s. They allowed people to exchange money without cumbersome paperwork, but despite the convenience, they were not immediately welcomed with open arms, as Vidan shows. "Stop! Stop! Stop! The electronic funds transfer system is a threat to our personal freedom as American citizens," wrote a concerned resident of Indiana in one of around six thousand letters that arrived in the summer of 1976 at the bureau in charge of evaluating public response. Meanwhile thirteen thousand people signed a petition in protest of the tech. Briefly the EFTs were suspended, and a public comment period ensued. As a 1976 story in the *South Middlesex Daily News*, a local Massachusetts paper, put it in their solicitous headline: "Government Asks: Would You Trust an All-Computer Bank?" Citizens generated what one staffer characterized as an "astonishing" outpouring considering the high-tech, arcane nature of electronic banking. The public's answer was, first, a vividly articulated no, with many citizens keenly objecting to the sunsetting of human processors. Later came an unarticulated yes of broad acceptance. It was just so convenient! And anyway, electronic banking was already well underway.

In the late 1970s and early 1980s, trust was increasingly frayed in an era of nervous agitation, an "age of fracture" (to borrow from the title of a book by Daniel Rogers).[40] Teetering on the edge of entering the electronic world, Americans tacitly acknowledged the undeniable bargain of convenience on offer: The "float" of excessive paperwork could be eliminated and the hazard of carrying bills in your pockets, too. Some banking experts even saw EFTs as a way of making people less dependent on credit cards, and thus encouraging more ethical spending behavior. Public-key cryptography, the basis of EFTs, offered a way to be "recognizable without being known," as the pioneering cryptographers Whitfield Diffie and Martin Hellman put it in their important 1976 paper, "New Directions in Cryptography,"[41] which responded to increasing concerns over the National Security Agency's (NSA) overreach (in COINTELPRO and other operations). Distrusting the NSA's invasive powers, the rebellious computer scientists advanced an "asymmetric" cryptography (combining a private key with a public key). Authentication would take place between two individuals, with no need for an institution or a system administrator. In this way, the two enabled e-commerce and secure communication on the internet to happen.

During the 1990s, the world's economies and societies became ever more complexly interdependent. Standardizing encryption was a way to balance against the hazards of all that connectedness. People valued the easy paperless routes of transaction they were offered without, perhaps, realizing how a "new financial subjectivity" was being instilled in the public imagination.[42] What is a new financial subjectivity? It is a new set of standards around what makes someone feel, personally and politically, safe. The late decades of the twentieth century involved the construction of just such a thing, and today we are in the middle of another. Today 65 percent of the population (or 78 percent, or 85 percent, depending on the poll) say they don't want central bank digital currencies (CBDCs) and are concerned about digital surveillance. Part of the appeal of Bitcoin and crypto is that they seemed to address or assuage these worries.

Since that time, many other crypto-based technologies—using the public-private encryption methods pioneered by Diffie and Hellman in the 1990s—began to operate. The 2008 paper that introduced the concept of Bitcoin by the pseudonymous mystery-person Satoshi Nakamoto relied on their method. Bitcoin's motto "In Code We Trust" and the encomium to "Trust in Code" embodied the 1990s rebel sensibility of Diffie and Hellman. As the Columbia University economist Adam Tooze points out, the question is not whether crypto products and technologies will be used going forward, because they already are embedded in dominant financial systems (we now take so entirely for granted digital technologies of financial transfer, digital currencies, and even the EFTs). The looming question is how they will be regulated. Ahead lie the twin dangers of fraud and self-fraudulence, of deception and self-delusion. Regulation (in even the best-case scenario) will address the first better than the second.

Crypto gets a lot of flack for its criminality and cons—one side of cultishness. The more interesting side of cultishness is where grift shades into belief. "In practice it can be tricky to disentangle crypto belief from crypto greed."[43]

But as with the most high-demand cults, it is the idealists who are really worrisome. The idealism arm of the cryptoworld via Web3 is more alarming than the con artists because they are sincere and (necessarily) are fooling themselves to some degree. More concerning than out-and-out Ponzi schemes are quasi-idealistic visions of building human relationships into the future cryptoworld by means—for example—of something called Soulbound Tokens. Inspired by the online game *World of Warcraft*, Soulbound Tokens would be "inalienable," and would adhere to a particular user, or Soul, forever. (It could do for the Soul what Facebook has done for Friends.) The Soulbound Tokens create an effect akin to carrying your résumé around with you folded up in your wallet—in this case, a crypto wallet—to be flashed at any point an exchange relationship might be about to congeal. Thus, they would allow for reliable socialization and reputation management to occur very fast. You would rack up social points for what schools you went to, what credentials you have, and these would never be expunged, nor would negative points. Social credit and discredit would be linked forever to your Soul's profile. As with most things on the blockchain, this scheme takes an intangible human-to-human good, like trust—the question of why you would trust one person in a particular situation—out of the realm of intuition or judgment and makes it tangible and quantifiable.

Critics and boosters alike agree that this is not just a functional apparatus of trust. At heart, blockchain-based architecture is actively promoted as a political virtue. People get very idealistic about it and start giving speeches. Astro-cryptographers, Bitcoin maximalists, and decentralized finance (DeFi) enthusiasts feel it augurs a new age. Either way, this use of the blockchain, and similar products, are the basis of a new architecture of money and power.

....

We all know that how someone acts when everything is going swimmingly is less a measure of character than what they do when it all falls apart. And the Astro-crypto world? As Bitcoin dropped from $56,000 in November 2021 to $18,000 or so midsummer 2022, all in a matter of months, the *Crypto Ethic Newsletter* offered guidance to its members in troubled times. Tansy Baigent wrote, "And perhaps here I will just speak to my own thoughts about the price of Bitcoin at any given moment . . . and that is that its price is far less relevant and important than the overall 'value' of bitcoin." Value not price should be kept in mind. In some Astro-crypto circles, altruism with a dash of hopium held strong: "That is, Bitcoin's ability to change the course of the financial arena of the future, to diminish the emergence of boom and bust economics, to offer incorruptible money and an incorruptible system of storing historical transactions (a ledger), and an opportunity for the World to participate in this future."[44] Over time, the couple—astrologer Sommer and crypto-coach Baigent—have become more and more Bitcoin focused, teetering finally on the edge of embracing Bitcoin maximalism (meaning, the belief that Bitcoin is exceptional due to its inbuilt structural limitations that convey reliability; specifically, it is exceptional because only twenty-one million Bitcoin will ever be mined, and nineteen million of those have already been mined). The Old World is dying, and a New World is being born, so that each person's responsibility is "to invest in the technologies that can pave the way to a better, more inclusive, more healthy, more joyful World. It is not up to me to tell you what those technologies are . . . but we cannot keep walking the old path, whether we want to or not, the World is changing."[45]

Baigent also heads an online community that "focuses on being on the heart-led side of crypto." How she has led her loyal-though-few community through the roiling difficulties of at least partial collapse is illuminating. Aiming "to bring consideration, conscious decision-making, kindness and integrity to all things crypto," the mission is "educating beginners about Bitcoin, blockchain, crypto (currencies and technology) as well as supporting the healing of our relationship to money, technology and power."[46] She offers courses for those intimidated to start, mostly women, leading to "confidence" and initial investing capacities. She also provides one-on-one counseling and private coaching as one experiences the ups and downs. Her YouTube videos are not flashy but provide sensible, historically anchored advice, and are staunchly resistant to going viral.

Being on the heart-led side of fintech (financial technology) by embracing Astro-crypto as a mindful technology is not necessarily a popular stance and is easily derided. As the historian Jackson Lears demonstrates, viewing bodily and spiritual vigor as a model for the economy—and how to improve prospects of financial success—is a deep vein that runs through American history (the capital-as-vital-spirits view preceded and succeeded Keynes).* It may not be so far-fetched after all to invoke John Frum worship or astrological reckonings in understanding revolutions in technology and the distribution of wealth.

The obsession with cargo goes both ways at this pivotal moment in the evolution of modern capitalism into an unprecedented form of

---

* The American economy itself has been a model for bodily and spiritual vigor: "Every human being has a given amount of capital put into his possession by his Maker; that capital is his vital energy—his life-force," according to an 1850 proto-new-age magazine called the *Water-Cure Journal*. Quoted in Jackson Lears, *Animal Spirits: The American Pursuit of Vitality From Camp Meeting to Wall Street* (New York: Farrar, Straus, and Giroux, 2023).

surveillance capitalism. As in the South Pacific theater so in the cryptoworld. A solution for the ruining of trust is devised. A visiting British administrator in 1970 observed of the Vanuatuans who engaged in Frum worship that "a state of mass imbalance" prevailed. From the point of view of the colonial office, the goal was to prod commoners into taking a more reasonable (that is, acquiescent) stance.[47] For the Frum worshipers, their ceremonies were providing a sort of balance. Astro-crypto enthusiasts also perceive a rigged economic system. Without too much greed ("All I want is what I have coming to me, all I want is my fair share," in the words of Charlie Brown's sister, Sally, in *A Charlie Brown Christmas*) they use neo-technological rituals alongside ancient resources to restore some sort of parity.

Cargo cults are now everywhere. Given the ever more uneven distribution of resources, these dynamics should be taken seriously, not dismissed as foolhardiness.

Conclusion

The first "selfie," by chemist Robert Cornelius, 1839. LIBRARY OF CONGRESS PRINTS AND PHOTOGRAPHS DIVISION WASHINGTON, D.C. 20540 USA.

In her wonderful short essay, "The Long History of the 'Selfie,'"[1] historian Marcy Dinius disputes the "alleged narcissism" of the self-taken photograph. She traces the prehistory of such photographs of self, procedures that date significantly further back than the advent of the digital age. In fact, just as soon as the first daguerreotype was taken in 1839, a chemist named Robert Cornelius almost immediately took the first selfie, or self-portrait, via photography. It was that same year.[2] Cornelius actually set the lens and then dashed in front of it. As the *Public Domain Review* re-created the scene: "Setting up his camera at the back of the family store in Philadelphia, Cornelius took the image by removing the lens cap and then running into frame where he sat for a minute before covering up the lens again. On the back of the image he wrote 'The first light Picture ever taken. 1839.' "[3] The process was easier, in a sense, than our modern cameras make it because daguerreotypes allowed a certain amount of lag time between opening of the lens and the capture of the image. Three-quarters of a century later, Cornelius's experiment was ordained as the world's first selfie and is today enshrined in the Library of Congress, while social media paeans to Cornelius's eerie hotness gather online.

But Dinius's larger point is that soon after, by the 1850s, due to the requirement that clients sit still for long periods in order to allow the daguerreotype to register the image, photographers were schooling people in the need to manage their facial expressions in a seemly way. Otherwise, both photographer and customer were bound to be displeased with the result. So you had the instruction to lay aside your worries: Upon arriving in the studio, counseled the Boston-based daguerreotypist Robert Southworth, "Let the cares and anxieties of business be laid aside for the time" of the sitting, "and the trials and perplexities of life be forgotten."[4] The phrase, "smile for the camera" had not yet been invented as a universal urging. Looking at the camera without furrowing was enough. It was not natural to know how to relax your face sufficiently still while still looking alert. Practices had to be inculcated.

What is different today—aside from somewhat different practices, since the selfie taker no longer requires stillness but rather aspires to dynamism or other qualities—is the circulability of the image. In the past, a daguerreotype was one of a kind (as this was before photography's negative-to-positive development arrived). This is unlike a social media post, which increasingly are composed of moving images. Still, though the image may eventually go viral, the first viewer is always the self who took the selfie, and this does resemble the origins of photography in the "mirror-like image surface of the daguerreotype."[5] Less is startlingly new than one might think, according to Dinius's analysis. I think this impulse is useful—to describe the continuity in technical affordances (the mirror-like surface) and emotional resonances (the supposed narcissism of the act). These do not escape change, of course, but certain qualities endure.

When thinking about the effects of online life on the self as well as the selfie, identifying some continuities in the creation of social networks and what are in effect new social worlds connects the past and clarifies the present. It allows us to escape the technological-determinist sense of inevitability that is often engendered by the advent of something heavily judged in the culture. In contrast to the heroic narrative, in which the tech itself is the hero ("Oil on canvas gave way to celluloid, which in turn gave way to photographic film and digital media," the Oxford English Dictionary had it, as one example of tech determinism), it is the new things you can do (unpredictable applications or what William Gibson calls "the street finds its own uses for things") with a smartphone, and not intrinsically the thing itself, that bring change.[6]

Turning points are significant, but it is also important to remember we live in a continuing lineage. Because of the shot-into-space feeling many people experience as the twenty-first century moves through its third decade—making These Times feel so much like End Times— and the apocalyptic tenor of everything from folk music to birdwatching to children's programming, it is easy to disregard that emotional engineering extends back as well as moves forward. To put it simply, the lineage we are inhabiting is not just one of technological innovation or social networking but the impulse to modify (behavior, biology, belief) under murky consent conditions. This is what one scholar has called the "engineering ideal."[7] It goes back at least to the headline-winning biologist Jacques Loeb from the turn of the twentieth century, who claimed he had enacted virgin birth within the lab, and who could engineer all kinds of animal behavior by using simple tropisms as his building blocks. (It extends further back, to the eighteenth-century manifesto *Man a Machine*, for example, and to the curious history of automata, but we can pause for now.) Sigfried Giedion wrote about this history in his 1948 *Mechanization Takes Command*, where invention is soldered to production. Whenever people such as data scientists, researchers for social media companies, Web3 investors, or blockchain evangelists talk about rigging up "behavior cascades," one may want to pay attention.

In his recent book summarizing many years of research on susceptibility to digital persuasion, *The Hype Machine*, MIT professor Sinan Aral describes what we are experiencing as runaway social influence. He demonstrated how social media at present generally works to foster madness rather than wisdom in the collective: "In the digital age, we're saturated with other people's opinions every day on Facebook, Instagram, Twitter, and Yelp—we're hypersocialized."[8] By this Aral means that through perpetual hopped-up interactivity via Instagram, Yelp, Twitter, hashtags, viral memes, trending topics, influencers, and other sources and mechanics "we observe others' actions while making sequential decisions all the time. Exposure to others' opinions at the point of decision is the norm, not the exception. We don't have to seek out social influence. It finds us." It is ubiquitous but scarcely noticed. Aral's point is akin to what Elaine Hatfield and colleagues observed about the curious dynamics of emotional contagion: Our judgments become "systematically and algorithmically interdependent." In sum: They're social.

Brainwashing crises of the Cold War and cult war in this sense predict and foreshadow such intimate, constant view modification—because first prisoner camps and later cultic groups created cauldrons of such intensive social influence that they resulted in bizarre behavioral outpourings, which nonetheless start to seem natural in the context of the stewing cauldron. The struggles of the Korean War showed how antagonists waged battles less over geopolitical territory and more

Conclusion

"over human interiority," as the historian Monica Kim has put it.[9] Cults fought for similar dominion over the psyche. Now, this effect is widening.

....

This book is called the *Instability of Truth*, and maybe, it has been argued—specifically by certain members of my family—it could have been renamed the *Death of Truth* or something more dramatic, something with additional flourish. But what I mean is ordinary instability. What we take as truth is subject to instability and malleability in a much more mundane way than most people believe it to be.

We popularly think of truth as a big scaffolding buttressed by scientific rationality and mortared in the special methods of proof employed by scientists. (There is also the question of larger metaphysical truths, but here I mean the lowercase truths.) For now, we can note that in fact, the word *scientist* isn't very old—it dates back not to antiquity but to 1833, when the English polymath William Whewell, as the result of a bet with Samuel Coleridge, coined the word *scientist* to describe . . . those who do science. That is, what we think of as modern scientists with lab coats, replication protocols, and peer-reviewed journals is quite new. It's jolting to be reminded that Galileo or Francis Bacon would never have referred to themselves as scientists because the locution didn't exist. "Man of science" or "natural philosopher" were the English terms. The idea that scientists did science was not something anyone believed before the nineteenth century. As the historian of science Steven Shapin observes of the Scientific Revolution, it may not really exist in the way we usually think: "Many historians . . . now reject even the notion that there was any single coherent cultural entity called 'science' in the seventeenth century to undergo revolutionary change."[10] What we retrospectively call science was a hodgepodge of knowledge-making practices. And as the arbiter of ultimate truth, it's practically a newborn. A newborn that has been given some heavy tasks.

This can be a scary thought, a scarier reality. And ultimately, that confusion arises because we place too much emphasis on yes-or-no truth (over meaning). Don't get me wrong: I'm a huge fan of and believer in truth and have devoted my life to being a truth seeker (which is perhaps why I've crossed paths with cults and various guru types, have stretched myself into so many yoga knots, carried out studies in everything from art to anthropology to sitting and doing nothing for long periods of time). I don't mean that because truth is unstable in most of our daily interactions, truth doesn't matter. Truth does matter. But it is a mistake to rush toward it, demanding all-or-nothing, insisting final categories be applied, arranging things in the hope that truth, like facts, can be easily clicked on and seamlessly verified.

Most of the strongest prisons are mental prisons, but most people (including myself) don't want to understand that. You need, if at all possible, to be free of it.

....

My goal in this book is to show three things. First, brainwashing feeds on trauma and on stored emotion, and that this is demonstrably unrecognized—whether *trauma* is a word on the tip of everyone's tongue or no one's—compounds its effects. Second, that although it is tempting to think of this unprocessed well of emotion that can be tapped or mined or played upon in various ways as a psychological problem, it's not. It's a crisis of interdependence. It's more in the domain of an "us" problem than one of "you" or "me." This is why Norbert Elias—remember, the scholar who dwelled on the evolving etiquette of nose blowing and the use of forks?—wrote not only about *psychogenesis* (how our psyches are made through these mundane shaping processes) but also *sociogenesis* (how society itself, our real world, is made too). Third, that something can be done about it by applying the tools of focused analysis—the superpowers I describe at the beginning of this book. First is the actor's category, a reminder to take seriously what people say

Conclusion

and do, considered from their point of view, not shoehorning these into some preexisting tub. And next, the second-order observer, meaning to try to get a glimpse of the system itself, the expert knowledge producers who thought they had a God's eye view, but are themselves embedded too like all of us.

While just about no one in the 1950s applied the word *trauma* to the brainwashed men or the survival trainees, apparently almost everyone by the 1990s rushed to acknowledge that brainwashing involved trauma or was traumatic. Even Louis Jolyon West said so—in a 1994 article on pseudoidentity as formed in cults, in which he and his coauthor Paul Martin remarked that although a PTSD diagnosis cannot be arrived at in all cases, "Nevertheless, the cult experience itself, and the process of disengaging from the cult, inevitably involve some degree of trauma to the person. The picture of a concentration camp survivor may result."[11] Even so, when West submitted an earlier version of this article to the prestigious *Journal of Nervous and Mental Disease*, it was rejected by a friendly but firm handwritten note conveying reviewers' views that "the concept of pseudo-identity syndrome"—caused by trauma—"is too unclear to be scientifically investigated or clinically applied."[12] In time, as a result of figures like Lifton as well as the Boston circle of psychoanalysts including Bessel van der Kolk and Judith Herman, studies of trauma-driven disorders gained traction. Seeing it became inevitable—even to an expert on brainwashing such as West who, for thirty years, had never mentioned in spoken or written statements, the centrality of trauma to the experience.

Whether this was because trauma's existence as a DSM category and later a popular concern had massively multiplied its prevalence, or whether professionals were now trained to see it everywhere, as they had not before, or whether trauma was in fact experienced more frequently is an ongoing question. (Perhaps all three are true.) By the 2010s, it became a truism, and assumption, a sine qua non. But we can say this: Trauma was now visible, and once seen, it could not be unseen. Some might argue it was overdiagnosed, and too popularly penetrating, but it would not disappear again. This did not stop cults from recruiting or prevent people from being drawn into them at times of personal or circumstantial vulnerability in their lives. It did not stop people from bad internet experiences becoming deeply misinformed. Indeed, it did not stop it from being persistently underrecognized (according to Van der Kolk, whose book, *The Body Keeps the Score*, nonetheless became a decade-long bestseller from 2014–2024). Its appearance, in other words, did not protect people from coercive persuasion or abuse.

Nor did trauma's sudden visibility augur the end of brainwashing. In a sense, it might have—one might expect brainwashing as explanation or exculpatory framework would disappear once the causes of these "mysterious" behaviors became clearer. But it did not happen that way. In fact, though brainwashing dipped in the seriousness with which it was treated during the 1990s and 2000s when it became a

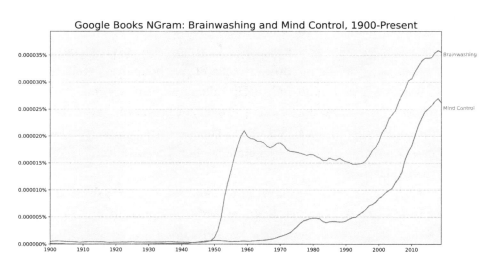

Graph of the use of the term *brainwashing* in English-language books. I started my research in the 1990s when the frequency of both *brainwashing* and *mind control* was much lower than it is today DATA SERIES FROM GOOGLE N-GRAM VIEWER, ACCESSED MAY 29, 2024, HTTP://BOOKS.GOOGLE.COM/NGRAMS.

Conclusion

retro and odd phenomenon, almost camp, it soon surged back into serious relevance with the rise of the new media ecology, narrowcasting, and social media after 2005 or so.

Once messaging became so tailored, so obvious in its shaping effects, so pervasive, it seemed that brainwashing once again became a looming menace, and a key to explain what was going on. Consider the "brainwashed rightward by YouTube" genre. Caleb Cain's story became exemplary in this area: Cain was a young and directionless man who dropped out of college and filled in the time (he was depressed) by autoplaying videos to the point where he took on convictions he earlier, only weeks before, did not share. These were new opinions that favored white nationalism and feared the threat of immigrants, warned about the unfair advantages women and minorities were enjoying, and thought perhaps violence was the answer in some cases. "Because of the way online propaganda works, literally anyone can be radicalized. And you don't realize that you're being groomed into a cult."[13] Ultimately, by following a different set of links, Cain recentered himself. He now runs a nonprofit to prevent digital radicalization. (Taking the name Faraday Speaks, he also mentions disliking how reporters seemed to turn his radicalization into a curiosity, as if he had no agency in his interactions with technology.)

Through the effects of social media and other algorithmically disseminated information, brainwashing has had a revival. It has become ubiquitous if not well understood. It is usually lobbed at others. Synonymous with indoctrination and propaganda spread via social networking platforms, it functions as a way of casting doubt on the faculties of those whose opinions one distrusts and disdains. That is, calling someone "brainwashed" functions that way. Its effect is to cut off the adequacy or right to be heard of this other person. It is an emotional response claiming the shroud of rational assessment. As an allegation, it is a way of undermining another's rational footing, their capacities even to argue in the first place (because . . . they have been brainwashed!). It causes a dizzying about-face (as if a camera or boom yawed from one side of a rocking boat to the other), sometimes, when one considers the possibility or while it is happening. I'm not immune from this feeling myself.

On the other hand, we are all changed by our virtual and social-media interactions, to the extent we have them, and to the extent we have them uncritically or mindlessly. (Brainwashing, rarely useful as an insult, becomes a tool of self-inquiry day-to-day.) Even believing you are attentive to them, observing constantly, always aware, the interactions will have a shaping effect. Recognizing this, over and over, is of the utmost importance.

ACKNOWLEDGMENTS

Sometime around 9/11, before or after I can't recall, I had the idea to teach a class on brainwashing. I was a postdoc at the University of Washington. I ran into my former graduate advisor later and told him the plan of the class: "We'll look at extreme experiences of brainwashing (POWs, torture, cults) and ask what these "hard" situations can tell us about the soft or subtle conditions we're all surrounded by today, of media exposure and pervasive social engineering." My advisor paused and raised an eyebrow. "Well, if someone doesn't have an opinion about that, they probably don't have an opinion about anything!" he said. In fact, we did end up having lively discussions. Still, it was odd—not a normal topic for a class. Thus, I would like to thank all those who helped me think about—and develop my own views about—this unlikely subject matter of brainwashing.

At University of Washington: I was lucky to have lunch, around the time I was planning the course, with Hilary Putnam, who was a visiting scholar at the university and had the office next to mine. He told me that it's a mistake to think a person's ideas don't change or won't change over a long career, but that people were often surprised that his did. Wouldn't you want your thinking to change? was a question that stayed with me. Kathleen Woodward, director of the Walter Chapin Simpson Center, supported my teaching on the topic, and the students at UW were some of the most memorable I've encountered, including Erin Anderson, now a professor herself.

At Harvard: I've had the lucky chance to become a historian of science and learn the field "on the job" due to the work and generosity of my colleagues, especially the late Everett Mendelsohn, Charles Rosenberg, Allan Brandt, Jimena Canales, Anne Harrington, Heidi Voskuhl, Evelynn Hammonds, and Janet Browne. An early writing group with Jeremy Greene and Sophia Roosth helped to center, well, writing. Colleagues Gabriela Soto Laveaga, Victor Seow, Liz Lunbeck, Eram Alam, Hannah Marcus, Ben Wilson, Naomi Oreskes, Alex Csiszar, David Jones, Rijul Kochhar, and Matthew Hersh taught me a lot through their work and scholarly examples they set. I especially appreciate a pivotal, jet-lagged conversation with Sarah Richardson in the Grunewald (mentioned in the introduction). Peter Galison shared encouraging words after I gave a short brainwashing talk in the department a few years ago (which goes to show how important a few casual words can be). Multiple thanks go to Steven Shapin for chatting with me about so many topics over years and reading the whole manuscript—and generally going above and beyond in heartening me, particularly on walks in Mt. Auburn, when I really had doubts about the enterprise. Shigehisa Kuriyama inspired me when he popped into my office to say, "Whole worlds of research topics in the history of science have not even been touched!"

At the Charles Warren Center: I had the good fortune to spend a sabbatical year at this center headed (then) by Walter Johnson, and run beautifully by Monnikue McCall, where a group of scholars of mass incarceration gathered. I benefited immensely from the conversation, and the fruits of research I did there on interrogation and the UCLA Violence Center are in this book. I especially appreciate the comments of Susan Reverby and Micol Siegel, and Toussaint Losier for lending me books.

At the Max Planck Institute for the History of Science in Berlin: Some years ago, I had the honor of spending six summer weeks working on a Cold War book about "how reason almost lost its mind" with Lorraine Daston, Michael Gordin, Paul Erickson, Judy Klein, and Thomas Sturm. This, a genuine collaboration, was formative in so many ways. The additional time spent at the MPIWG over two fortunate years also helped orient me in my field and helped me to develop my ideas from before. Others I crossed paths with at MPIWG include John Carson, Etienne Benson, David Sepkoski, Judy Kaplan, Christine von Oertzen, Viktoria Tkaczyk, Grégoire Chamayou, Teri Chettiar, Cathy Gere, and many other delightful people, including Josephine Fenger.

In Brainwashing Research Circles: Andreas Killen invited me to contribute to an issue of *Grey Room* in 2011, and the writing of that essay (on Ewen Cameron) pulled me back into the larger topic; our interests continue enjoyably to run in parallel directions. Errol Morris befriended me when he was beginning his brilliant *Wormwood* documentary and invited me to visit the set the day John Marks was being interviewed. The Hidden Persuaders project, under Daniel Pick's direction, extended an invitation to participate in a London conference, which was hugely influential, as has been the groundbreaking and creative output of this multiyear project. Thanks especially to Marcia Holmes, Aminda Smith, Monica Kim, Susan Carruthers, and others there for your scholarship and contributions to the event, which pushed me to think more globally. James Kennaway kindly hosted me semi-locally for a recent conference on mind control at the University of Groningen in the Netherlands, which spurred many further connections, including Bernd Bösel.

In the Archives: Special thanks go to the UCLA Charles Young Library, Special Collections, which houses the Louis Jolyon West papers, where I have visited many times over the past ten years or so since they became available. Especially helpful was Russell Johnson, curator for History & Special Collections for the Sciences. The New York Public Library's Manuscripts and Archives Division offers the Brooke Astor Reading Room, which was a haven, one where Michelle McCarthy-Behler helped greatly.

In Zoomland: There are several communities of thinkers to which I am indebted and was able to continue meeting with due to this much maligned facilitator, Zoom. This includes, especially, the boringly named (yet in fact most enjoyable) Expert Concepts Working Group, led by Talia Dan-Cohen and Andy Lakoff, and including Peter Redfield, Hannah Landecker, Nick Langlitz, Stephen Collier, and Cameron Brinitzer. Getting to have these insightful peoples' thoughts about several draft chapters was pivotally helpful during the long, dark pandemic time. I thank the Emergent Phenomenology Research Consortium, led by Daniel Ingram, for widening my perspective. The Beyond Knowledge Tarot group is an assemblage of likeminded people whom I appreciate in total, and especially the guiding framework of the fabulous Steph Dick and equally fabulous Oriana Walker. Dr. Yvan Prkachin Zoom-met with me from Switzerland and proved an invaluable resource (generous as he always has been); specifically, he read chapter 5 on psychosurgery and helped me deepen my argument about the history of "literal brain control" and how to think about it via the history of medicine.

*

Acknowledgments

In Various Places: Friends and colleagues in various places have been wonderful interlocutors either periodically or sustainedly: Laura Stark, Junko Kitanaka, Benjamin Breen, John Tresch, Nasser Zakariya, Melissa Lo, Matthew Farish, Henry Cowles, Ekaterina Babintseva, Les Robinson, Simon Torricinta, Spence Weinreich, Erik Baker, Joy Rohde, Chris Kelty, Michael Lempert, Anastacia Marx de Salcedo, Megan Matson, Gretchen Rubin, Natasha Lifton, and Joanna Radin. The graduate students I've worked with have kept me delighted for the prospects for our field: Max Ehrenfreund, Kat Poje, Che Yeun, Latif Nasser, Alexis Turner, Gili Vidan, Shireen Hamza, Devin Kennedy, Margo Boenig-Lipstin, Yvan Prkachin, and currently Tina Wei, Aaron Gluck-Thaler, Caleb Shelburne, Matt Lukacs, Anna Riley, and Kelsey Ishigawa. Frank Zhou, a talented junior at Harvard, undertook an independent study with me and helped me with translation and with understanding the role of Sanmao stories. Alfred K. Wong is not only a delightful conversationalist whom I met while reading the book *Fanshen* in a local coffee shop, but also helped me with the discussion of Chinese concepts of brainwashing. In addition, he kindly provided a data series for converting the Google N-gram image into one I could use in this book. Natasha Schüll has been a good friend since graduate school and a fellow traveler in the land of compulsion (and trying to understand it). The ever-bike-riding John Plotz has been a friend since even before graduate school and remains wonderful to talk with on any topic ever since our outing in the Oakland hills.

In the Classroom: I incurred special indebtedness, and thus special gratitude is due, to the visitors to my brainwashing class: guest lecturers Dr. Abigail Judge, Dr. Steven Hassan, and Dr. Glenn Petersen. Each added to my understanding in wholly new and surprising ways, and seeing my class respond to them was enlightening as well. My teaching fellows in the most recent version of the class, Max Ehrenfreund and Liv Grjebine, were especially helpful interlocutors as I started to think more about the role of trauma in mind control and hyper-persuasion. Back at the ICSA meeting of 2017, I listened to a panel featuring several former child members of the Tony Alamo Christian Ministries; this was hugely influential to me in understanding the dynamics of cults and especially how they affect those born into them. Four former members (second-generation) along with psychologist and ICSA president Debbie Schriver were to have visited my class at Harvard a week or so after the pandemic descended and were thus unable to come. (Schriver writes about their experiences in *Whispering in the Daylight*.) Nonetheless their insights, and the good fortune to have met them, continue to stick with me. At the same meeting in Santa Fe, I met Ray Connolly, which was pivotal; I appreciate his giving me a copy of his excellent memoir.

In Publishing: Norton is my dream publisher, and working with John Glusman likewise has been a dream come true, a huge blessing, and an education. I appreciate the supportive help of Helen Thomaides, Wickliffe Hallos, and the skilled copyeditors there as well. My agent, Leslie Meredith—a fellow dog enthusiast, podcast connoisseur, and bird lover—has been a steady voice of reason and support in the writing and publishing process, and I'm so glad to get to work with her. Kat Poje, in addition to fulfilling her role as a brilliant graduate student, and now lecturer, in the history of science, was immensely helpful as my assistant in the securing of permissions. Linda Sivertsen, the doula extraordinaire of new books, was a vital cheerleader and intellectual support of this project when I was just formulating it.

Finally, unlike previous books, for which I had to leave my daughter to visit archives, this book allowed me to take her with me (because she's a college student now)! It was a great joy to discover that Ivy shares my love of archives and that she brings to it her own distinctive sensibility and research talents. She was especially helpful in

Acknowledgments

diving into the Lifton papers (on the Wellfleet seminars) and the West papers (on the Amphetamine Research Project). Getting to chat over matcha and discuss our findings was deeply fun. My husband, Palo, although he did not visit archives with me, supported these efforts, and was a stalwart listener to every chapter I read to him (even multiple times); he could unerringly yet diplomatically tell me if it was working or not. Aside from being a master woodworker, he always gets where I'm going with things, even if I'm not there yet. My journalist mother, Penny, offered steady encouragement and told me to "Write that down!" when I mentioned, while we were talking, the phrase that became the title of this book; my father, Mike, was able to read some parts of the book proposal before he passed away last year, and even, as was his wont, suggest "a few little changes." My brother, Doug, is a kindred spirit in these inquiries. My family also includes Benjy, Petunia, Tao, and now Cody. I hope this book, in the spirit of those bonds ("Oh do not ask what it is, let us go and make our visit") honors my human and animal family.

NOTE ON SOURCES
AND METHODS

More than any other book I've written, this one is the result of a methodological experiment—I made use of archives and personal papers in universities as my central repository of sources, but I also engaged in ethnography (for example, visits to anti-cult conferences) as well as what is sometimes called digital ethnography (for example, entering web forums and discussion sites devoted to astrologically based crypto investing). Through these mixed methods, I had access to a range of sources. Somewhat unusually, as compared with other topics, many of the most desirable sources on brainwashing are impacted by governmental secrecy and the fact that the CIA destroyed almost all MK-ULTRA records in the late 1960s as well as interrogation videotapes in the 2000s. The unusually rich trove of documents in the Louis Jolyon West collection—which I have been exploring little by little for over a decade, though I cannot say I have completely plumbed its depths—has allowed me to make several new findings and cement connections not previously made about military, intelligence, police, and scientific interconnections.

Each chapter takes advantage of a somewhat distinct set of sources. Because I have taught a class on and off over ten years at my university on the history of brainwashing and mind-control techniques, I've also benefited from the exchanges and visits of experts and experiences in the classroom. For example, I've been showing the Stanley Milgram film to students for more than a decade. It is notable how student responses have changed: No longer, today, do they laugh at the point when the participant is brutally electrocuted and pounds on the wall wordlessly, though many used to, even if it was uncomfortable chuckling. I also note how students respond to guest lecturers talking about cultic abuse or Vietnam-era survival training. In certain chapters, I have relied on court proceedings (as in the chapters on the Patricia Hearst trial and the cult wars). I also greatly value the personal interviews and personal papers that family members of ex-cult members and the descendants of brainwashing experts have opened to me. I am especially grateful to Mike McKilen and Paul D'Angelo for reading my chapter about their grandfather, for further conversations, and for generously offering me access to the papers their family members have painstakingly collected.

NOTES

INTRODUCTION

1. Joost Meerloo, *The Rape of the Mind: The Psychology of Thought Control, Menticide, and Brainwashing* (New York: Grosset and Dunlap, 1956); Donald Bain, *The CIA's Control of Candy Jones* (London: Futura Publications, 1979 [1976]).
2. History of Science as an academic field was founded at Harvard by a Belgian expatriate named George Sarton in the 1930s; it became a department under President James Conant in the post–World War II "big science" boom, when Conant promoted the understanding of science's history through case studies. A few other schools founded dedicated History of Science departments, and they can go by other names (History and Sociology of Science at University of Pennsylvania, for example). See Joy Harvey, "History of Science, History and Science, and Natural Sciences: Undergraduate Teaching of the History of Science at Harvard, 1938–1970," *Isis* 90 (1999), 270–94. For the larger context, Joel Isaac, *Working Knowledge: Making the Human Sciences from Parsons to Kuhn* (Cambridge: Harvard University Press, 2012).
3. Harry Collins, "Actors' and Analysts' Categories in the Social Analysis of Science," in eds. P. Meusburger, M. Welker, E. Wunder, *Clashes of Knowledge* vol. 1 of Knowledge and Space series (Dordrecht, NL: Springer, 2008), 1–11. Collins continues: "The causes that give rise to anything that can be seen as consistent actions among actors turn on regularities as perceived by the actors first and the analyst second."
4. The Nigerian example is one that historian Marcia Holmes gives. Holmes, "The 'Brainwashing' Dilemma," *History Workshop Journal* 81 (2016), 285–93, 285. Other examples included are: In 1976, Nelson Mandela accused the South African

government of "brainwashing" children to accept apartheid. And Frantz Fanon referred to brainwashing (*lavage de cerveau*) in his chapter on "Colonial War and Mental Disorders," in *The Wretched of the Earth* (New York: Grove Press, 2005 [1963]).

5   Luhmann wrote his many books in this way, by treating his notes as partners in thinking, and taking advantage of "clustering and unpredictable combinations." Niklas Luhmann, "Communication with Zettelkastens. An Experiential Report," https://zettelkasten.de/communications-with-zettelkastens/. The Niklas Luhmann Archive is https://niklas-luhmann-archiv.de.

6   Niklas Luhmann, "The Form of Writing," *Stanford Literature Review* 9 (1992), 25–42, 34.

CHAPTER 1: LIMA BEANS AT THE BOTTOM OF THE OCEAN

1   Then Chairman of the Federal Reserve Alan Greenspan used this phrase in an otherwise unremarkable speech he gave on December 5, 1996, causing markets around the world to falter. See account in Robert Shiller, *Irrational Exuberance* (Princeton, NJ: Princeton University Press, 2000), ch. 1.

2   On canalizing, see Melford Spiro, "Social Systems, Personality, and Functional Analysis" in *Studying Personality Cross-Culturally* ed. Bert Kaplan (Evanston, IL: Row Peterson and Co., 1961), esp. 104. Spiro speaks of the "transformation of duty into desire": People must be taught to want what the society needs them to have or be.

3   Described in Rebecca Lemov, "The Laboratory Imagination: Experiments in Human and Social Engineering 1929–1956" (PhD diss., UC Berkeley, 2000); the refusal experiment is mentioned in Neal E. Miller, "A Reply to 'Sign-Gestalt or Conditioned Reflex?" *Psychological Review* 41 (1934), 280–92, 290.

4   Czesław Miłosz, *The Captive Mind* (New York: Octagon Books, 1981), 6.

5   Aldous Huxley, *Brave New World Revisited* (New York, Bantam, 1960), 2. The interrogator's words are quoted in Russell Hill, "Vogeler Here Today; He Will Enter Hospital," *The New York Herald Tribune*, May 1, 1951 (Vogeler is recalling his interrogator's words).

6   According to Timothy Melley, the word *brainwashing* has been found in an internal CIA document dated January 1950 written nine months prior to the first published use of the word *brainwashing*: Timothy Melley, "'Brain Warfare: The Covert Sphere, Terrorism, and the Legacy of the Cold War," *Grey Room* 45 (2011), 19–41, 28. Melley cites an MK-ULTRA paper using the word (but undated): "Narrative Description of the Overt and Covert Activities of [Redacted]," MK-ULTRA Papers, disk 2, Mori ID #190882, The National Security Archive. Another example of early use of the term was discovered by researcher Charlie Williams recently: Paul Linebarger, "Possible Operations Research in FEC Psychological Warfare" ORO Technical Memorandum, ORO-T-2(FEC), September 14, 1950 (describing Chinese thought reform activities in Korea). For a fuller discussion see Marcia Holmes, "Edward Hunter and the Origins of 'Brainwashing,'" (May 26, 2017), *Hidden Persuaders* BBK (blog).

7 Robert Guillain, "China Under the Red Flag, III: The 'New Democracy,'" *The Guardian*, January 3, 1950, 6, 8. (This article was discovered by doctoral student Ian Magor as part of the Hidden Persuaders project in London.) Also see Edward Hunter, "'Brain-Washing' Tactics Force Chinese into Ranks of Communist Party," *Miami News*, September 24, 1950. For new reflection on the origin and psychodynamics of brainwashing, see Daniel Pick, *Brainwashed: A New History of Thought Control* (London: Profile Books, 2022).

8 Foreword dated June 15, 1962, to the new edition, Edward Hunter, *Brain-Washing in Red China: The Calculated Destruction of Men's Minds* (New York: Vanguard Press, 1971).

9 Hunter, *Brain-Washing in Red China*, foreword. Hunter explained that he presented the word to the public, hyphenated as "brain-washing," and the public removed the hyphen, resulting in "brainwashing."

10 It is possible the word play (on "wash heart"—*hsi hsin*, to wash the heart—meaning approximately, to retire to the country) was in use, but historians so far have not settled the matter.

11 Holmes, "Edward Hunter and the Origins of 'Brainwashing.'"

12 David Loy, "阿細與大鼻子: The Little Boy and the Big Nose" (Hong Kong: Swen Publications Company, 1949), found at "Chinese Pamphlets," Center for Research Libraries (CRL), https://dds.crl.edu/search/collection/1; "Brain Transformation" is from the Chinese term "改造頭腦" or "頭腦改造" [one of] which is the same as reeducation or thought reform.

13 Mitchell Ryan, "The Political Myth of 'Brainwashing,'" *Made In China Journal,* October 8, 2019.

14 On conversion narratives see James T. Richardson, "The Active vs. Passive Convert: Paradigm Conflict in Conversion/Recruitment Research," *Journal for the Scientific Study of Religion* 24, 1985, 119–236, 165. Reeducation camps: 再教育集中营; Reeducation: 再教育 *zài jiào yù*; Brain 大脑; Brainwash: 洗脑 *xǐ nǎo*.

15 See Susan Carruthers, *Cold War Captives: Imprisonment, Escape, and Brainwashing* (Berkeley CA: University of California Press, 2009), chapter 4, for the best historical account of Vogeler's ordeal.

16 Quoted in Carruthers, *Cold War Captives*, 162.

17 Jószef Mindszenty, *Memoirs* (New York: MacMillan, 1974), 114. Emphasis added.

18 "'Confession' in Hungary," *The New York Times,* February 19, 1950.

19 Morris Wills and J. Robert Moskin, *Turncoat: An American's 12 Years in Communist China* (Englewood Cliffs, N.J.: Prentice Hall, 1968), 23.

20 Anecdote in Robert A. Close, "Helo Operations," February 14, 2012, Tributes & Stories, United States Naval Academy Alumni Association and Foundation, https://www.usna.com/tributes-and-stories---stories-1945.

21 See Charles S. Young, *Name, Rank and Serial Number: Exploiting Korean War POWs at Home and Abroad* (Oxford: Oxford University Press, 2014), esp. ch. 2, 25.

22 Lewis Carlson, *Remembered Prisoners of a Forgotten War: An Oral History of Korean War POWs* (New York: MacMillan, 2002), 51–53.

23 Carlson, *Remembered Prisoners*, 48.

24 Young, *Name, Rank, and Serial Number*, 25, quoting Don J. Snyder, *A Soldier's Disgrace* (Dublin, NH: Yankee Books, 1987), 120.

25 Carlson says over four million; History.com estimates five million; Monica Kim cites a "staggering number of casualties"; Dong Choon Kim estimates "several million" died in what all scholars agree was one of the bloodiest wars in modern history. Carlson, *Remembered Prisoners*, 20; Monica Kim, *The Interrogation Rooms of the Korean War: The Untold Story* (Princeton: Princeton University Press, 2019), 82; Dong Choon Kim, "Forgotten War, Forgotten Massacres: The Korean War (1950–1953) as Licensed Mass Killing," *Journal of Genocide Research* 6 (2004), 523–44, 524.

26 It won reporters a Pulitzer Prize and caused President Bill Clinton to apologize. See D. C. Kim, "Forgotten War, Forgotten Massacres" and Sang-Hun Choe, Charles J. Hanley, and Martha Mendoza, "1999 Associated Press stories, e.g., "War's Hidden Chapter: Ex-GIs Tell of Killing Hidden Refugees," AP, September 29, 1999. See Pulitzer website for all articles: https://www.pulitzer.org/winners/sang-hun-choe-charles-j-hanley-and-martha-mendoza. Several massacres of civilians were uncovered by means of 120 interviews with US military and Korean survivors.

27 Jonathan Shay, *Achilles in Vietnam: Combat Trauma and the Undoing of Character* (New York: Simon and Schuster, 1993), xxii.

28 Wills, *Turncoat*, 27.

29 Zellers quotation from September 1950 is in Carlson, *Remembered Prisoners*, 57.

30 More than four thousand American prisoners were taken between November 1950 and February 1951, and hundreds more in succeeding months.

31 Wills, *Turncoat*, 35.

32 "Prisoner-of-War Camps in North Korea and China," Information Report, July 17, 1952, on website CIA.gov: https://www.cia.gov/readingroom/document/0000124327. At Kangdon, the document mentions, there were nine thousand Republic of Korea [South Korean] prisoners and fifty UN personnel [US, etc.], all held in caves.

33 MacLean quoted in Carlson, *Remembered Prisoners*, 51–76, on Tiger Death March.

34 Sources provide different figures: one claim is that 89 died during the march, but that 66 percent of those survivors perished by the time the camps were liberated (Marilyn N. Windham, "Remembering the Tiger Death March in Korea," *The* [Macon, GA] *Telegraph*, May 26, 2016); Young has 731 starting the march and only 500 left by its end (*Name, Rank, Serial Number*, 25). Figures here are from Carlson, *Remembered Prisoners*, 45.

35 Qtd. Carlson, *Remembered Prisoners*, 26.

36 Qtd. Carlson, *Remembered Prisoners*, 66.

37 Kim, *The Interrogation Rooms of the Korean War*, 320.

38 As US troops advanced on Hill 303, they found forty-five young men who had been shot in the head. An onlooker who discovered the atrocity saw they were mostly seventeen- and eighteen-year-olds (Young, *Name, Rank, Serial Number*, 25–26).

Notes to Pages 32–42

39 Oral history of Robert MacLean in Carlson, *Remembered Prisoners*, 28–29.
40 Carruthers makes this point.
41 Wills, *Turncoat*: "spoon man" is on 38, "A Brigitte Bardot" on 49.
42 "Thus in late 1951, the Chinese established roughly fourteen reeducation camps in the North of Korea, just near the Yalu River. Per an agreement with their allies, the Chinese mainly interned United Nations troops; South Korean soldiers were generally held in separate camps run by North Koreans." Aminda Smith, "Legacies of 'Brainwashing': Cold War Ideology and Modern Chinese History, Cornell University Lecture, November 9, 2015, transcript at https://www.cornell.edu/video/aminda-smith-cold-war-ideology-modern-chinese-history.
43 Quoted in Brendan McNally, "The Korean War Prisoner Who Never Came Home," *The New Yorker*, December 9, 2013.
44 Wills, *Turncoat*, 26.

CHAPTER 2: THE VOLLEYBALL PROBLEM

1 And marched unthinkingly to their deaths; Hannah Arendt, *The Origins of Totalitarianism* (New York: Meridian Books, 1958 [2nd edition]), 458.
2 Wilbert Estabrook quoted in Charles Young, *Name, Rank, and Serial Number: Exploiting Korean POWs at Home and Abroad* (New York: Oxford University Press, 2015), 28.
3 The "bronzed" comment is quoted in Susan Carruthers, *Cold War Captives: Imprisonment, Escape, and Brainwashing* (Berkeley, CA: UC Press, 2009), 177; Ft. Ann townsperson comment about Morris Wills is in Virginia Pasley, *21 Stayed* (New York: Farrar, Strauss & Cudahy, 1956), 177.
4 Quote from Secretary of Defense C. E. Wilson describing some of POWs' twenty-nine thousand letters, in Young, *Name Rank, and Serial Number*, 110.
5 Early in 1953, Secretary of Defense C. E. Wilson reported that "virtually all" of the twenty-nine thousand letters from POWs carried slogans denouncing "Wall Streeters" or requesting that family members oppose the "useless" war in Korea. Tales of "wonderful treatment" in North Korea were all "in the handwriting of the Americans who are held captive," Wilson complained (cf. Carruthers, Young).
6 Robert J. Lifton, "Home by Ship: Reaction Patterns of American Prisoners of War Repatriated from North Korea," *American Journal of Psychiatry*, 110 (1954), 732–39, 739. [References to "stress" are frequent.]
7 Alexander C. Cook, ed., *Mao's Little Red Book: A Global History* (Cambridge University Press, 2014), 2.
8 Most of the historical record on brainwashing "doesn't really take the 'Maoist-ness' of thought reform seriously enough," Aminda Smith argues. In Chinese thought reform institutions in the 1950s (such as converted poorhouses and brothels in Beijing), as Smith shows, certain populations including prostitutes, beggars, and petty criminals might resist indoctrination, but were treated more gently in recognition of their experiences of feudal or capitalist oppression; this logic could apply to the lower-status

captured troops. Aminda Smith, "Thought Reform and the Unreformable: Reeducation Centers and the Rhetoric of Opposition in the Early People's Republic of China," *The Journal of Asian Studies*, 72 (2013), 937–58, 939; A. Smith, "Legacies of 'Brainwashing': Cold War Ideology and Modern Chinese History," conference paper, Hidden Persuaders, London 2018. [Permission kindly granted to cite unpublished work, pers. comm. August 5, 2024.]

9 All quotations are from declassified affidavits secured by US Army Military Intelligence investigators just after the armistice. The statement about Wills's youth is by Calvin Royal, October 10, 1955; the statement about Wills's being well brought up is from Edward R. Collins, January 31, 1954; the statement about avoidance of Chinese instructors is from Louis Aguinaga, June 25, 1955; the statement about the fear of Chinese is from Calvin Royal, October 10, 1955. National Archives (NARA), RG 0319, Records of the Army Staff, 902d Military Intel Group, Investigative Records Repository—POW/MIA Detainee Intelligence Files, 1944–1986 (Korean Conflict); Container 779.

10 Morris Wills and J. Robert Moskin, *Turncoat: An American's 12 Years in Communist China* (Englewood Cliffs, NJ: Prentice Hall, 1968), 18–19.

11 Mao quoted in Jacques Ellul, *Propaganda: The Formation of Men's Attitudes* (New York: Vintage, 1973 [1965]), 307. Emphasis added.

12 As Mao called it in the 1951/57 report, tracing the slogan's origins to events in 1942, the result was a "democratic method of resolving Mao's conflicts through criticism and subsequent efforts to arrive at a new unity on a new basis"; quoted in Ellul, *Propaganda*, 309.

13 William Hinton, *Fanshen: A Documentary of Revolution in a Chinese Village* (New York: Vintage, 1966).

14 Rana Mitter, "Permanent Revolution: The Chinese Communist Party at 100," in *Times Literary Supplement* 6170 (July 2, 2021), 11.

15 Roy Hardage interview in Carlson, *Remembered Prisoners*, 185.

16 Charles Rangel Interview (2015), Korean War Legacy Project, by Dr. Jongwoo Han; full transcript at https://koreanwarlegacy.org/interviews/charles-rangel/. Emphasis added. Rangel recalled two all-Black regiments—the 3rd and the 1503rd—"with the exception of officers [who were white]."

17 Clarence Adams, *An American Hero: The Life of an African American Soldier and POW Who Spent Twelve Years in Communist China* (Amherst, MA: University of Massachusetts Press, 2007), segregation of military also discussed in Chapter 3 and 10 following.

18 Wills, *Turncoat*, 53.

19 Virginia Pasley, *21 Stayed: The Story of the American GIs Who Chose Communist China, Who They Were, and Why They Stayed* (New York: Farrar, Straus, and Cudahy, 1955), 178–80.

20 Wills, *Turncoat*, 54.

21 Details of diary practices are from interviews in William Brinkley, "Valley Forge G.I.'s Tell of Their Brainwashing Ordeal," *Life*, May 25, 1953, 108–109, 112–116, 121–124, on 121. Rate of forced diary writing is from Julius Segal, "Factors Related

to the Collaboration and Resistance Behavior of U.S. Army PW's in Korea," HumRRO Technical Report 33 for the Department of the Army, 1956, 7; as reported in James Angus MacDonald Jr., "The Problems of US Marine Corps Prisoners of War in Korea," Occasional Paper, US Marine Corps, 1988 (PCN 19000411200) 231, fn 2, https://www.usmcu.edu/Portals/218/The%20Problems%20of%20U_S_%20Marine%20Corps%20Prisoners%20of%20War%20in%20Korea%20%20PCN%2019000411200.pdf, accessed August 8, 2024.

22   Source from A. Smith, "The Un-brainwashers," 22; Report of Beijing Bureau of Civil Affairs, "Beijing shi chuli jinü gongzuo zongjie" [Work summary on Beijing's management of prostitutes], BMA 2-2-40. Emphasis in original.
23   Wills, *Turncoat*, 55.
24   Wills, *Turncoat*, 55.
25   Wills, *Turncoat*, 56.
26   Quoted in Carruthers, *Cold War Captives*, 93.
27   Edgar Schein, *Coercive Persuasion: A Socio-Psychological Analysis of the 'Brainwashing' of American Civilian Prisoners by the Chinese Communists* (New York: Norton, 1961).
28   See, for example, Rebecca Lemov, *World as Laboratory: Experiments with Mice, Mazes, and Men* (New York: Hill and Wang, 2006).
29   Ellul, *Propaganda*, 309. Mao's statement on his own remolding is quoted 309–10.
30   Wills, *Turncoat*, 59.
31   Quoted in Pasley, *21 Stayed*, 182.
32   Quoted in Pasley, *21 Stayed*, 183.
33   Robert J. Lifton, "Loading the Language," in *Thought Reform and the Psychology of Totalism: A Study of 'Brainwashing' in China* (Chapel Hill: University of North Carolina Press, 1989 [orig. 1961]), ch. 22. Cf. Hannah Arendt on *Amtsprache* (or "bureaucratese") as used by Adolph Eichmann, in Arendt, *Eichmann in Jerusalem: A Report on the Banality of Evil* (New York: Penguin Classics, 2006), chs. 2–3.
34   Jihan Kim, "An Olympics That Wasn't Postponed: The DPRK POW Inter-Camp Games, 1952," June 20, 2024, Wilson Center, *Sources and Methods* (blog).
35   Adams, *An American Hero*, 62.
36   Adams, *An American Dream*, 126.
37   Tim Stanley, "Not Forgotten: Korean War Vet, Member of All Black Artillery Unit, Recalls Surviving Three Years as a POW," *Tulsa World*, September 21, 2019.
38   On repatriation policies, see Carruthers, *Cold War Captives*, 10. (Also Young, *Name, Rank, and Serial Number*, and Kim, *Interrogation Rooms*.)
39   Carruthers, *Cold War Captives*, 175.
40   Young, *Name, Rank, and Serial Number*, 120.
41   On January 28, 1954, Claude Batchelor and Edward Dickinson changed their minds and by the time they had returned to the US were dishonorably discharged, and soon tried and imprisoned.
42   Wills, *Turncoat*, 63, 61.
43   Wills, *Turncoat*, 66–67. Emphasis added in next sentence.

44 Wills, *Turncoat*, 78–81 (quotations in this paragraph).
45 Wills, *Turncoat,* 81. Emphasis added.
46 Wills, *Turncoat*, 176.
47 Harold Lavine, "Twenty-One G.I.'s Who Chose Tyranny," *Commentary*, July 1954.
48 In an interview with FBI SA William F. Desmond Jr. on August 5, 1966, Wills declared he had never betrayed allegiance to the United States nor renounced citizenship; in going to live in China, he had exercised a legal choice under international law. National Archives (NARA): RG 0319, Records of the Army Staff, 902d Military Intel Group, Investigative Records Repository—POW/MIA Detainee Intelligence Files, 1944–1986 (Korean Conflict); Container 779.
49 The Chinese nurse story, untrue, is repeated in Pasley, *21 Stayed*. The problem of brainwashing would come to be associated with a failure of American masculinity, or what was sometimes called Momism, and sometimes linked to homosexuality.
50 Bathing, cleaning are senses of the Chinese vocabulary used—the word *xizao* 洗澡 ("bathing") was common.
51 *People's Daily*, January 28, 1954, quoted in Terry Lautz, *Americans in China: Encounters with the People's Republic* (New York: Oxford University Press, 2022), 41–42. Article continued, "Washington's psychological warfare program has met with another blow."
52 Original source: *People's Daily*, July 20, 1950, quoted in A. Smith, "The Un-Brainwashers."
53 According to A. Smith, "Un-Brainwashers."
54 Italicized in original, reproduced Lifton, "Home by Ship," 737.
55 Recollection of David Hawkins in "David Hawkins: A Battle of the Mind," film by Nasheed Qamar Faruqi, 2017.
56 Robert MacLean oral history in L. Carlson, *Remembered Prisoners*, 29.

CHAPTER 3: THE LONESOME FRIENDS OF SCIENCE

1 Interview with returned POW David Hawkins by Mike Wallace, *The Mike Wallace Interview*, June 23, 1957. (Wallace interview with Hawkins is excerpted in documentary film by Shui-bo Wang, "They Choose China" (2005), https://www.youtube.com/watch?v=sDTPhT8mZ9o.)
2 Quotation "fascinating natural experiments" from Edgar Schein, *Brainwashing* (Cambridge, MA: MIT Center for International Studies, December 1960), 33.
3 Mike Wallace's description of the twenty-one nonrepatriates, *The Mike Wallace Interview*, June 23, 1957.
4 Quoted in Young, *Name, Rank, and Serial Number*, 116: When Jack Chapman returned to Oklahoma, he went to a tavern with his uncle to catch up. When the bartender found out where Chapman had been, he said "Oh, he's one of them cowards." Chapman recalled, "Oh, that hurt." From then on, "I didn't tell nobody I had been a prisoner of war."

5   Gary Rice, "The Lost Sheep of the Korean War" (PhD diss., University of Texas Austin, 1998), vii. Cf. Albert Biderman, "American Prisoners of War in Korea: Reinterpretation of the Data," (PhD diss., University of Chicago, 1964), 4; "The theme of prisoner misconduct has had continued prominence in the public press."
6   All quotations this paragraph are from Robert J. Lifton, *Witness to An Extreme Century: A Memoir* (New York: Free Press, 2011), 5–7.
7   Lifton, *Witness*, 9.
8   Eugene Kinkead, "The Study of Something New in History," *The New Yorker*, October 18, 1957.
9   "Yours brainwashed" is from Conrad Brandt letter dated October 27, 1954, to Robert J. Lifton, RJ Lifton Papers, Manuscripts and Archives Division, New York Public Library: Box 23. Folder: Correspondence, 1953–54; "lurid fantasy" is from David Riesman's letter dated July 15, 1959, to Robert J. Lifton, RJ Lifton Papers, NYPL: Box 15, Folder: General Correspondence, Riesman, 1959.
10 Quotation from Preface of report; declassified in 1973; released publicly in 1999. Also based on Lawrence E. Hinkle Jr., "The Effects of Reduced Environmental Stimulation on Human Behavior," in eds. Albert Biderman and Herbert Zimmer, *The Manipulation of Human Behavior* (New York: Wiley, 1961).
11 Wild folk dances, quoted in Susan Carruthers, *Cold War Captives*, (Berkeley, CA: UC Press, 2009), 177 (fn 19).
12 As enumerated in J.A. MacDonald Jr., "The Problems of US Marine Corps Prisoners of War in Korea."
13 Interview with William Baker in Heather Graham, "Former POW Recalls Nearly 3 Years in Captivity," *Fort Hood Sentinel*, September 4, 2009.
14 But research was made more difficult by the fact that higher-ups deplored the men as "intellectual eunuchs" (H. Cabot Lodge) and "goons" (C. D. Jackson). Also, there was no agreement on how to greet them (Carruthers, *Cold War Captives*, 189).
15 Lifton, "Home by Ship," 735; H. A. Segal, "Initial Psychiatric Findings of Recently Repatriated Prisoners of War," *American Journal of Psychiatry*, 111 (1954), 359.
16 "Communist Interrogation, Indoctrination, and Exploitation of American Civilian and Military Prisoners," Tuesday, June 19, 1956, US Senate, Permanent Subcommittee on Investigations of the Committee on Government Operations, 2.
17 See Jackson memorandum quoted in Carruthers, *Cold War Captives*, 189 ["To Persons," May 11, 1953, from CD Jackson Papers, Eisenhower Library]; see John Allen Stern, *C. D. Jackson: Cold War Propagandist for Democracy and Globalism* (New York: University Press of America, 2012). A sympathetic editorial in *The New York Times* offered profound apologies for the aspersions cast at these men.
18 Carruthers, *Cold War Captives*, 187. See eight-page story in *Life* on the Valley Forge internees, "Brainwashing Ordeal," *Life*, May 25, 1953, 108–10, 111–16, 121–22, 124; quotation from GI Kenyon Wagner is on 116.
19 The phrase "floating interrogation centers" was used to describe the ships transporting

POWs back to San Francisco: quoted in Raymond Lech, *Broken Soldiers* (Urbana and Chicago: University of Illinois Press, 2000), 205; "all allegations, favorable and unfavorable": from Young, *Cold War Captives*, 113.

20 The topic of Rebecca Lemov, *Database of Dreams* (New Haven: Yale University Press, 2015).

21 In fact, the first two US POWs to record pro-Communist broadcasts (just four days after the official start of the war in 1950) were themselves World War II veterans. See Rice, "The Lost Sheep," 34. Segal, "Initial Psychiatric Findings," 358–63, quotations from 358, 359. Study of men "at the time of repatriation to friendly hands." Chief, Neuropsychiatric Evaluation Team, Medical Section, Provisional Headquarters, Korean Communication Zone. Presently, Chief, Neuropsychiatric Service, United States Army Hospital, 8167th Army Unit, APO 1055.

22 Rorschach quoted in Richard Wallen, "The Nature of Color Shock," *Journal of Abnormal and Social Psychology* 43 (1948), 346–56, 346.

23 Tests by Schein and his associates at Walter Reed showed a main finding of "social-emotional isolation" (consisting of "marked emotional constriction, inability and unwillingness to get involved with others, and even some impairment of intellectual functioning" [30]); as a result, there was also impairment of judgment (31). H. Strassman, M. Thaler, and E. H. Schein, "A Prisoner of War Syndrome: Apathy as a Reaction to Severe Stress," *American Journal Psychiatry* 112 (1956), 998–1003; E. H. Schein, W. F. Hill, H. L. Williams, and A. Lubin, "Distinguishing Characteristics of Collaborators and Resisters among American Prisoners of War," *The Journal of Abnormal and Social Psychology* 55 (1957), 197–201; M. Singer and E. H. Schein, "Projective Test Responses of Prisoners of War Following Repatriation," *Psychiatry: Journal for the Study of Interpersonal Processes* 21 (1958), 375–85; and others.

24 Singer and Schein, "Projective Test Responses," 375–85, 377.

25 R. Lemov, "X-Rays of Inner Worlds: The Mid-Twentieth-Century Projective Test Movement," *Journal of the History of the Behavioral Sciences* 47 (2011), 251–78.

26 Singer and Schein, "Projective Test Responses," 378, emphasis added.

27 Singer and Schein, "Projective Test Responses," 378. ("Each rater emphasized the low productivity, slow reaction times, and generally limited range of affect, besides the obvious aggressive-destructive content.")

28 "These statistics become meaningless if one considers the ambiguity of the criterion and the difficulty the men had judging what was actually collaboration." Schein, "Brainwashing," 31.

29 Schein, "Brainwashing," 24.

30 Schein did speak of Chinese exerting "psychological pressures" (26), but did not attribute to the men the experience of such pressures, stressing, rather, the destruction of social bonds and authority structures (since officers and NCOs were kept separate, enlisted men were set adrift). Quotation "fascinating natural experiments" is on 33.

31 I. E. Farber, H. F. Harlow, and L. J. West, "Brainwashing, Conditioning, and DDD (Debility, Dependency, and Dread)," *Sociometry* 20 (1957), 271–85.

32 Biderman worked at the Office for Social Science Programs, Air Force Personnel and Training Research Center, Air Research and Development (Maxwell Air Force Base, California) with L. J. West.
33 "Intelligence Interrogation," US Army Field Manual 34–52 (1992), https://irp.fas.org/doddir/army/fm34-52.pdf; approved for public release.
34 Albert Biderman, "Brainwashing from a Psychological Viewpoint," CIA report (February 1956), approved for public release August 24, 1999.
35 Up to this point, Lifton had published only one article, "Home by Ship." It was in Hong Kong, during a lull, after the war was "over," or his part in it, when Lifton was confronted by a set of individuals in whom, basically, no one else was interested.
36 See Bessel van der Kolk with Lisa M. Najavits, "Interview: What is PTSD Really? Surprises, Twists of History, and the Politics of Diagnosis and Treatment," *Journal of Clinical Psychology* 69 (2013), 516–22, 516.
37 Lifton, *Witness to An Extreme Century*, 27.
38 Lifton, *Witness to An Extreme Century*, 13.
39 Lifton, *Witness to An Extreme Century*, 31–32.
40 All quotes in this and the following twenty-two paragraphs (the account of Dr. Vincent's reeducation) are from Lifton, *Thought Reform*, 19–37 *passim*, unless otherwise noted.
41 See Biderman, CIA report, "Psychological Effects of Brainwashing."
42 Biderman, CIA report, "Psychological Effects of Brainwashing," 34.
43 Lifton, *Thought Reform*, 25, 30; emphasis added.
44 Biderman, CIA report, "Psychological Effects of Brainwashing," 39.
45 Biderman, CIA report, "Psychological Effects of Brainwashing," 80.
46 Lifton, *Witness*, 31.
47 Lifton, *Thought Reform*, 20.

CHAPTER 4: VIOLENCE STUDIES

1 Pers. corr. from Glenn Petersen to author, 2012.
2 According to Google Earth, the location is 33°20'50.2"N 116°42'41.6"W.
3 Nicole Starosielski, "Thermal Violence: Heat Rays, Sweat Boxes, and the Politics of Violence," *Culture Machine* 17 (2018). See also D. Thompson, "Circuits of Containment: Iron Collars, Incarceration and the Infrastructure of Slavery" (PhD diss., Cornell University, 2014). A first-person account by a former slave was captured in a 1937 interview for the Federal Writers' Project under the New Deal, *Federal Writers' Project: Slave Narrative Project (1936), Vol. 1, Alabama, Aarons-Young, to 1936–37*. Manuscript/Mixed Material. Retrieved from the Library of Congress.
4 What does "broken" mean in psychological terms? From a neuroscientific perspective, one can extrapolate from existing studies of soldiers-in-training and other subjects during or after "extreme stressor states," as in Shane O'Mara, "The Captive Brain: Torture and the Neuroscience of Human Interrogation," *QJM: International Journal*

of Medicine 111 (2018), 73–78. Studies of stress beyond adaptiveness suggest what it means to be broken.

5   Glenn Petersen, *War and the Arc of Human Experience* (Toronto: Hamilton Books, 2021), 56.

6   Steve Balestrieri, "SERE Level C Course: And The Truth Will Set You Free," SOFREP [Special Operations Forces Report], July 22, 2019, https://sofrep.com/specialoperations/sere-level-c-course-truth-will-set-free/. Accessed June 14, 2024.

7   Comment (undated but c. 2019) on US Navy video "Surviving SERE," YouTube, uploaded April 10, 2017, https://www.youtube.com/watch?v=69c6Uo3RZnM. Accessed October 18, 2021 (italics added). Obviously, the veracity of such unverifiable comments is unknown, but the details square with documented reality of the training.

8   Petersen, *War and the Arc of Human Experience*, 65. (Corroboration is in a piece about the authorization of the study of Korean brainwashed men, ordered by the Secretary of Defense so that the "Soviet orbit" would be resisted: "A Study of 'Brainwashing,'" *The New York Times*, August 23, 1954.)

9   David J. Morris, "Cancel Waterboarding 101: The Military Should Close Its Torture School," *Slate*, April 22, 2009; https://slate.com/news-and-politics/2009/04/the-military-should-close-its-torture-school-i-know-because-i-graduated-from-it.html.

10 Petersen, *War and the Arc of Human Experience*, 66.

11 Petersen, *War and the Arc of Human Experience*, 66–67.

12 As the Senate Intelligence Committee's groundbreaking torture report noted in 2014, the CIA conceded in 2006 that Abu Zubaydah "was not a member of Al Qaeda" (410). US intelligence found no evidence otherwise linking him to the events of September 11. (The case for holding him was that he trained jihadists who themselves participated in 9/11.) In 2023, the UN Working Group on Arbitrary Detention declared his case a violation of human rights against unlawful detention and recommended his immediate release with an apology and reparations. Also in 2023, US lawyers filed a case on behalf of Zubaydah charging cruel and unusual treatment (against international law) and the imposition of nonconsensual medical and scientific experimentation on the prisoner. CIA officials destroyed ninety videotapes depicting his interrogation at the Thai black site in advance of possible legal actions. See Carol Rosenberg, "Lawyers Expand Legal fight for Longest-Held Prisoner of War on Terrorism," *The New York Times*, October 24, 2003.

13 See Drawing #8, "The Confinement Box," and comments in Mark Denbeaux, Jess Ghannam, and Abu Zubaydah, "American Torturers: FBI and CIA Abuses at Dark Sites and Guantanamo," Report dated May 9, 2023, Seton Hall Law School Legal Studies Research, available at SSRN: https://ssrn.com/abstract=4443310, 76–77. Because the CIA destroyed all video recordings of interrogations at Guantanamo and dark sites, his drawings are unique documents. This small box was only one of three torture boxes in which Abu Zubaydah was held (the Coffin Box and the Vertical Box are the others).

14 Glenn Petersen Lecture in HSCI 176, "Brainwashing and Mind Control Techniques," March 2020, Harvard University.
15 Article "Colonel James 'Nick' Rowe Assassinated on This Day, 1989," SOFREP [Special Operations Forces Report], April 21, 2017.
16 It is likely that Rowe helped in modifying the Air Force's and Navy's SERE to the Army (Special Forces), and fitting it to the Fort Bragg environment, where it continues today. Rowe oversaw SERE instruction (to some degree at least) until his death in 1989. In response to a commemorative video tribute to Rowe, Bill Cardenas, a veteran from Florida, commented, "He came out to the Ft Bragg Recondo camp in '81 during our POW phase, never forget the look on his face, it was a rough phase even for peace time standards." Post by US Army Special Forces Command, April 4, 2018, Facebook, with user comments: https://www.facebook.com/watch/?v=10160315815430046. Accessed June 9, 2024. Rowe himself claimed only to be a staunch advocate for wider application of the training, and to have overseen its adaptation for Army Special Forces at the North Carolina school.
17 See Matthew Farish, "The Lab and the Land: Overcoming the Arctic in Cold War Alaska," *Isis* 104 (2013), 1–29.
18 L. J. West commencement address May 14, 1990, to Hebrew Union College, LJ West Papers, UCLA, Series 590, Box 3, Folder 1 (on p. 19 of 20).
19 Typed resume of Louis Jolyon West, dated 1955, in LJ West Papers, UCLA, Series 590, Box 21, Folder 4.
20 Talk/draft paper to USAF, 1952–53, by L. J. West. LJ West Papers, UCLA, Series 590, Box 133, Folder 4.
21 Article by Tom O'Neill and Dan Piepenbring, "Inside the Archive of an LSD Researcher with Ties to the CIA's MKUltra Mind Control Project," *The Intercept*, November 24, 2019. A Cornell associate in a 1979 interview recalled that Wolff worked for the OSS and was one of the first experts to whom Allen Dulles came when the POW brainwashing crisis began. (In Harold Wolff Papers, Cornell Weill, Document labelled CIA MEETING February 5, 1979, in "Testimony of Hugh Luchey" Folder, 1979: Committee to Investigate Cornell and the CIA, Box 2.)
22 "Stress Can Harm Brain, Doctor Says," *Daily Oklahoman*, February 1957; clipping in LJ West Papers, UCLA, Series 590, Box 151, Folder 6.
23 "Summary of Remarks by Mr. Allen W. Dulles at the National Alumni Conference of the Graduate Council of Princeton University," Hot Springs, VA, April 10, 1953, CIA.gov, Freedom of Information Act Electronic Reading Room, https://www.cia.gov/readingroom/document/cia-rdp70-00058r000200050069-9, accessed August 17, 2024.
24 West's letter to "S. G." of Chemrophyl Associates dated June 11, 1953; S. G.'s letter to West ("My Good Friend"), dated July 2, 1953: both in LJ West Papers, UCLA, Series 590, Box 133, Folder 4. He found that people on LSD were hard to hypnotize, that hypnosis worked better with sleep deprivation and isolation; see Tom O'Neill and

Dan Piepenbring, *Chaos: Charles Manson, the CIA, and the Secret History of the Sixties* (New York: Hachette, 2019), 364.

25 Gottlieb explained to West that moving him out of the military into a university environment "would be difficult to do in any case but I want to know from you whether or not Hastings and I should pose this as an alternative to the top brass here in the eventuality that they think it impossible to develop this project within the Air Force structure." Within a year or so, it had become urgent to have him maneuvered out, and a new department in psychiatry and behavioral science was set up at the University of Oklahoma Medical School. Letter from S. G. dated July 2, 1953, to L.J.W.; LJ West Papers, UCLA, Series 590, Box 133, Folder 4.

26 Letter from S.G. dated July 2, 1953, to L.J.W.; LJ West Papers, UCLA, Series 590, Box 133, Folder 4.

27 See O'Neill and Piepenbring, "Inside the Archive of an LSD Researcher."

28 As renowned reporter Shana Alexander put it, summarizing West's words in an extended interview in Alexander, *Anyone's Daughter: The Times and Trials of Patricia Hearst* (New York: Viking 1979), 254.

29 The Chinese were preoccupied since the start of the war that the US was dropping disease-infected insects, shellfish, chicken feathers, frogs, and rodents on the Korean populace, military and civilian. They have never retracted these accusations; at the time, many of the captured airmen confirmed the bw missions and some were driven by their captors from camp to camp to persuade ordinary POWs that their confessions were accurate revelations. Controversy has dogged these accusations, although the US has insisted that they are false and made it quite hard to investigate further, according to several scholars. Nicholson Baker has investigated recently in *Baseless: My Search for Secrets in the Ruins of the Freedom of Information Act* (New York: Penguin, 2020); and several other volumes have explored the claims. The relevant documents have not been released despite FOIA requests.

30 West letter dated June 11, 1953, to S.G. LJ West Papers, Series 590, Box 133, Folder 4.

31 "Needless to say," West wrote to Gottlieb, the experiments "must eventually be put to test in practical trials in the field." To this end, he asked Gottlieb for "some sort of carte blanche." West letter dated June 11, 1953 to S.G. LJ West Papers, Series 590, Box 133, Folder 4.

32 Stephen Kinzer, *Poisoner in Chief: Sidney Gottlieb and the CIA Search for Mind Control* (New York: Holt, 2019), 88.

33 Letter from H. H. Twitchell, Brigadier General, USAF, Dir. of Prof Services, Office of the Surgeon General dated September 29, 1954, to L. J. West; LJ West Papers, UCLA, Series 590, Box 21, Folder 4. Mentions the "unconditional, full support" of West's CIA research at the university.

34 Letter from Joe W. Kelly, Major General, USAF (Dir., Legislative Liaison) dated January 7, 1955, to Mr. Short; LJ West Papers, UCLA, Series 590, Box 27, Folder 1.

35 Letter from Sherman C. Grifford, Chemrophyl Associates [Sidney Gottlieb, CIA]

dated September 16, 1954, to L.J. West; LJ West Papers, UCLA, Series 590, Box 25, Folder 5.

36 Letter from L. J. West dated September 2, 1954, to Major General Dan C. Ogle, USAF; LJ West Papers, UCLA, Series 590, Box 21, Folder 4.

37 On the president of University of Oklahoma's response see, "U of Oklahoma Tells CIA Drug Tests in '50s," *Chicago Tribune,* September 4, 1977. Proof that despite West's public denials, he used (likely both witting and unwitting) human subjects is found in the MK-ULTRA document, "Sub-project No. 43," which includes under "SIGNIFICANT ASPECTS" the note, "Testing on human subjects." Available at Freedom of Information Electronic Reading Room, CIA.gov.

38 On the wittingness-unwittingness continuum of participants see, e.g., APA monitor 1977. On the decision to use cutouts, see Marks, *Search for the Manchurian Candidate,* 59: "Reflexively, TSS officials felt they had to keep the CIA connection secret." On the "service fee," see "Memorandum for the Record," Regarding MK-ULTRA Sub-project 43, March 21, 1955, CIA.gov. FOIA electronic reading room.

39 Dr. Stewart Wolf was a close colleague of Dr. Harold Wolff—"The Drs. Wolf and Wolff" was Jolly's fond phrase—and the two had coauthored six books on what a local newspaper neatly summarized as work "on headaches, pain, hypertension, the human colon, the nose." "Drs. Wolf and Wolff" is from letter from L. J. West dated December 3, 1951, to Dr. Donald Hastings, LJ West Papers, UCLA, Box 4, Folder 21. Their collaborations are summarized in "Stress Can Harm Brain, Doctor Says."

40 Letter from L. J. West dated April 21, 1956, to Leonard P. Eliel, head of Oklahoma Medical Research Foundation; LJ West Papers, UCLA, Series 590, Box 21, Folder 11.

41 Quoted in obituary for L. J. West, *The New York Times,* January 9, 1999.

42 L. J. West talk to medical students; LJ West Papers, UCLA, Box 1, Folder 7.

43 L. J. West's papers include a clipping with headline "Five in Test Stay Awake 98 Hours," describing soldier-volunteers in a Walter Reed study under Captain Harold Williams. LJ West Papers, Series 590, Box 151, Folder 6.

44 L. J. West, Herbert H. Janszen, Boyd K. Lester, Floyd S. Cornelison Jr., "The Psychosis of Sleep Deprivation," *Annals of the New York Academy of Sciences* 96 (1962), 66–70, at 68–69.

45 The site is "Study.com" and the experiment, said to have started as a stunt, is titled "Peter Tripp's Sleep Deprivation Experiment," https://study.com/academy/lesson/psychology-case-study-peter-tripp-sleep-deprivation.html; Thomas Bartlett, "The Stay-Awake Men," *The New York Times,* April 22, 2010, recounts, "The two psychologists who monitored Tripp tried to talk him out of it, but they were also clearly pleased at the research opportunity his stunt presented." The psychologist present was Major Harold Williams of Walter Reed's Department of Clinical and Social Psychology, a collaborator of West's. West's publication was L. J. West, Herbert H. Janszen, Boyd K. Lester, Floyd S. Cornelison Jr., "The Psychosis of Sleep Deprivation," *Annals of the New York Academy of Sciences* 96 (1962), 66–70; "the Mindzenti [sic] look" is at 68–69.

46 O'Neill and Piepenbring, "Inside the Archive of an LSD Researcher."

47 Aldous Huxley wrote in a letter dated June 1, 1956, to Humphrey Osmond, in Cynthia Carson Bisbee, Paul Bisbee, Erika Dyck, Patrick Farrell, James Sexton, and James Spisak, *Psychedelic Prophets: The Letters of Aldous Huxley and Humphry Osmond* (Montreal: McGill-Queen's University Press, 2018), 336.

48 L. J. West, "Some Psychiatric Aspects of Civil Defense," in eds. George W. Baker and Leonard S. Cottrell, *Behavioral Science and Civil Defense* (Washington, DC: National Research Council, Disaster Research Group, 1962), 81–92, 89.

49 West in Baker, *Behavioral Science and Civil Defense*, 90.

50 G. H. Deckert and L. J. West, "Hypnosis and Experimental Psychopathology," *American Journal of Clinical Hypnosis* 5 (1963), 256–76; see also L. J. West and K. C. Niell and J. D. Hardy, "Effects of Hypnotic Suggestion on Pain Perception and Galvanic Skin Response," *AMA Archives Of Neurology and Psychology* 68 (1952), 549–60; on creating a "distortion of values" sufficient to commit a crime, see L. J. West, Talk to ABA, National Institute of Tort and Religion, May 4–5, 1989, SF, CA; LJ West Papers, UCLA, Series 590, Box 3, Folder 9. On the history of preexisting hypnosis (sometimes referred to as cerebral inhibition) research programs see Benjamin Breen, *Tripping on Utopia: Margaret Mead, the Cold war, and the Troubled Birth of Psychedelic Science* (New York: Grand Central, 2024), 50–51.

51 Letter from Arthur W. Melton of Lackland AFB, Air Force Personnel and Training Research Center, dated December 14, 1955, to Louis Jolyon West. The letter described the questions the working group would have to address, including how much "reality practice" to incorporate (versus education by films or other methods) and how stressful the training should be, as well as whether it should focus on the most "brutal" methods, the "brainwashing" psychological methods, or the "more subtle" techniques—what should be the proportion in preparing men for prisonerhood. LJ West Papers, UCLA, Series 590, Box 26, Folder 11, Working Group on Survival Training 1955.

52 "Armed Forces: Training by Torture," *Time*, September 19, 1955.

53 "Schools for Sadists," *Saturday Evening Post*, September 24, 1955. "Armed Forces: Training by Torture," *Time*, September 19, 1955, 66, 18.

54 "Marines 'Torture' Each Other," *The New York Times*, August 21, 1955.

55 "Schools for Sadists."

56 "Marines 'Torture' Each Other"; "What Resistance Training Will Do for You," SAC Survival Trends, 1956, 4. 3635th Combat Crew Training Wing records. AFHRA microfilm reel #M2392.

57 Clint Carter, "Inside America's Toughest Survival School," *Men's Journal*, Aug. 12, 2019.

58 "Purpose of Full Spectrum SERE Training," US Marine Corps official website, https://www.marsoc.marines.mil/Units/Marine-Raider-Training-Center/sere/. It's conducted ten times per year.

59 As Dr. Jerald Ogrisseg, former head of Psychological Services of SERE, commented later: "Military SERE training students are screened multiple times prior to participating in training to ensure that they are physically and psychologically healthy." No

Notes to Pages 127–136

recruit who is unstable is to be permitted to undertake the training (and the training is required). From the Senate hearings under Carl Levin, "Inquiry into the Treatment of Detainees in United States Custody," Report of the Committee on Armed Services, November 20, 2008.

60 Cross-examination of defense witness Dr. Charles Morgan, expert on SERE and EIT, 2024 military tribunal pretrial 9/11 hearing, Guantanamo Bay, Cuba (Week 4, Day 3–4) as live-tweeted: "The spectrum of impairment is in nearly everyone there in SERE school." Also, "Morgan says SERE is beneficial to have since the memory of it can reappear so it may save the students." (Gitmo Watch [@GitmoWatch], May 11, 2024 11:37 AM ET, Twitter/X.)

61 Christopher Hitchens, "Believe Me, It's Torture," *Vanity Fair,* July 2, 2008.

62 As @UrbanoutlawsSk8co relevantly observed in 2020 comments to "Christopher Hitchens Gets Waterboarded," YouTube, video by *Vanity Fair* uploaded July 2, 2008, https://www.youtube.com/watch?v=4LPubUCJv58. Accessed June 13, 2024.

CHAPTER 5: LITERAL BRAIN CONTROL

1 His résumé reveals his last two jobs to have been as a rocket scientist. Leonard Kille résumé, courtesy Michael McKilen papers. The date of the supermarket parking lot incident is unclear; Chorover has it in 1967, just after Leonard's discharge from Mass. General, but his grandson, Michael McKilen, thinks it's later. Based on other records, I estimate 1969.

2 Quote from Kille's surgeon under deposition in Jean Dietz, "Brain Surgery Case: Defense Takes over in Malpractice Suit," *Boston Globe,* January 11, 1979.

3 This account, including many of the biographical and geographical details, is based on Stephan Chorover's *From Genesis to Genocide: The Meaning of Human Nature and the Power of Behavior Control* (Cambridge, MA: MIT Press, 1979), 166–67, and the course materials for Chorover's 2013 MIT Course, "Affect," Psychology 9.68, available at https://ocw.mit.edu/courses/brain-and-cognitive-sciences/9-70-social-psychology-spring-2013/instructor-insights/.

4 "government . . . rod" is from a note by Kille included in McKilen papers.

5 This link to the nature of Kille's work (for Operation Dominic in the Nuclear Pacific) is supported by documents referred to in Jonathan Riley, "Nuclear Family," Boston Institute for Nonprofit Journalism Report, December 27, 2020, https://binjonline.com/2020/12/27/special-follow-up-feature-nuclear-family/.

6 Description from Vernon Mark and Frank Ervin, *Violence and the Brain* (New York: Harper and Row, 1970), 93.

7 Quotes from psychiatrist and subsequent hospital records are in Chorover, *Genesis to Genocide,* 167. The anonymized case study by Mark and Ervin, however, says he threw his wife up against a wall; it is not clear if this is true, and it should be noted the two doctors testified in court that their account had altered details and made use of composites.

8 Deposition of Dr. Curtis quoted in Dietz, "Brain Surgery Case."

9   Dr. William Sweet, Foreword to Mark and Ervin, *Violence and the Brain*, vii. On the LEA Act signed into law by LBJ in 1965 and how it "began an unprecedented transfer of federal resources to local law enforcement," see Julilly Kohler-Hausman, *Getting Tough* (Princeton, NJ: Princeton University Press, 2017). Harvard's student newspaper covered the controversy: Jane Baird, "Mindbending Controversy," *The Harvard Crimson*, January 16, 1974.
10 Dr. William Sweet, Foreword to Mark and Ervin, *Violence and the Brain*, viii.
11 Eliot Valenstein, *Brain Control: A Critical Evaluation of Brain Stimulation and Psychosurgery* (New York: Wiley and Sons, 1973). The most prominent Indian psychosurgeon conducting psychosurgeries was Dr. Balasubramanian; in Denmark it was Drs. Varnet and Marsden, in Thailand Dr. Chitanondh, in Argentina Dr. Schvarcz, and in Czechoslovakia Dr. P. Nadvornik. See 221–32 *passim* and 236.
12 Dr. Nayarabashi quoted in Valenstein, *Brain Control*, 212, 218. Later, due to adverse publicity, he stopped operating on hyperactive patients who did not have epilepsy, too. Mark and Ervin were following in this lineage, and—based on their work with Jose Delgado—added the implantation of radio-wave generating electrodes to seek out the localized portions of the brain that would be seared away (unlike Narabayashi, who, in a nonlocalized manner, injected the amygdala with an oil-and-wax-and-Lipiodol mixture).
13 Vernon Mark, Frank Ervin, and William Sweet, "Role of Brain Disease in Riots and Urban Violence," *JAMA* 201 (1967), 895. Later Ervin would write to *JAMA* explaining this 1967 letter had been widely misinterpreted, in part due to their inapt expression of their ideas. They wrote the piece to argue for separating out the violent slum dweller from the pacific one who is his neighbor.
14 This ward would be the basis of their plans for a violence unit called the Unit for the Study of Violent, Assaultive Behavior situated at Massachusetts General Hospital and Boston City Hospital. Monies received in 1970 from LEAA to Ervin, and other NIMH funds ($500,000) to Sweet and Mark in 1970, disbursed 1971. ($188,000 in LEAA funds were promised Sweet through his relationship to Eliot L. Richardson, head of HEW and former governor of Massachusetts.)
15 The Connelly Report opined that the tumor in Whitman's brain *could not be definitively found* as the cause of Whitman's actions; yet, "the committee of neurologists, neurosurgeons, and neurophysiologists interested in the clinical and physiological aspects of the nervous system recognizes that abnormal aggressive behavior may be a manifestation of organic brain disease." Connelly Report Press Conference, "Report to the Governor: Medical Aspects Charles J. Whitman Catastrophe" (September 8, 1966, Austin, TX), 8. https://web.archive.org/web/20171215181220/http://alt.cimedia.com/statesman/specialreports/whitman/findings.pdf.
16 Valenstein makes this point in *Brain Control*, 248–50. "We may never know" if the tumor was responsible for Whitman's actions in shooting forty-four people and killing fourteen that day.
17 Dr. Mark interviewed in Walter Sullivan, "FOLLOW-UP URGED ON BRAIN

Notes to Pages 140–142

INJURIES: Doctor Cites Hijacker with 11-Year-Old Damage," *The New York Times*, December 28, 1972, 7.

18 Rodger L. L. Wood and Rhys H. Thomas, "Impulsive and Episodic Disorders of Aggressive Behaviour Following Traumatic Brain Injury," *Brain Injury* 27 (2013), 253–61.

19 Brain structure "is modified by its continual interaction with both external and internal environments": Mark and Ervin, *Violence and the Brain*, 6. The two quotations in this paragraph are from xi and 1. On the biologization of psychiatry, see Anne Harrington, *Mind Fixers: Psychiatry's Troubled Search for the Biology of Mental Illness* (New York: Norton, 2019) and Joelle Abi-Rached and Nikolas Rose, *Neuro: The New Brain Sciences and the Management of the Mind* (Princeton, NJ: Princeton University Press, 2013). On the return, in the present, of brain-centered understandings of crime, see David Eagleman, "The Brain on Trial," *The Atlantic*, July/August 2011. Fernando Vidal coined the term "Brainhood," to describe this extreme biologization in Vidal, "Brainhood, Anthropological Figure of Modernity," *History of Human Sciences* 22 (2009), 5–36. See also Andreas Killen, *Nervous Systems* (New York: HarperCollins, 2023).

20 The "microstructure of the brain" is constantly modified by family patterns and cultural input (Mark and Ervin, *Violence and the Brain*, 32).

21 Albert Rosenfeld, "The Psycho-biology of Violence," *Life*, June 21, 1968, 67–71. *Life*'s online archive, hosted by Google, for unnamed reasons omits this (admittedly disturbing) article, although it contains every other page of that issue of the magazine. See https://books.google.com/books?id=2VQEAAAAMBAJ&source=gbs_all_issues_r&cad=1. To access the article, one must find a library hard copy or use Proquest.

22 William Sweet, Foreword to *Violence and the Brain*, viii. Sweet writes that previously most had concluded that the medical profession *cannot* make such a contribution to the prevention of violence, but that "[d]octors Mark and Ervin, however, present a convincing case for . . . the now-feasible diagnosis and treatment of persons with poor control of dangerous impulses" (vii–ix).

23 John R. Lion, George Bach-y-Rita, Frank R. Ervin, "Enigmas of Violence," *Science* 164, 3887 (1969), 1465–66. An extended version of this same letter—some of its content apparently cut by *Science*'s editors—appears as an Appendix to ch. 1 of Mark and Ervin, *Violence and the Brain*, where it is cited *as if* its entirety had been published in *Science*.

24 Quote in Maya Pines, *The Brain Changers: Scientists and the New American Mind Control* (New American Library, 1975), 202.

25 Reviews of *Violence and the Brain* mentioned in this paragraph include (in order cited): Ralph L. Holloway, "Review of Violence and the Brain," *American Anthropologist* 78 (1976), 702–03, 702; Russell R. Monroe, Review of *Violence and the Brain*, *Psychosomatic Medicine* 34 (1972), 286; John Gunn, Review of *Violence and the Brain*, *British Journal of Psychiatry* 118 (1971), 585. David B. Wexler called the book a "refreshing change of

pace from much of the sociological literature." Wexler, *Harvard Law Review* 85 (1971–1972), 1489.

26 Quotations of Kille are from the legal trial where a film of Kille receiving electronic stimulation was shown; in Jean Dietz, "Psychosurgery Defended in $2m Suit," *Boston Globe*, December 12, 1978.

27 Demerol quote is from *Violence and the Brain*, 96.

28 Interview with Ervin quoted in Pines, *The Brain Changers*, 201. In the case study of Kille ("Thomas R.") the authors describe his epilepsy as "found in temporal regions" and unresponsive to drugs. (Mark and Ervin, *Violence and the Brain*, 94).

29 Owsei Temkin, *The Falling Sickness* (Baltimore: Johns Hopkins Press, 1971 [1945]).

30 O. W. Holmes, "Medical Essays" (1891) quoted in Temkin, *The Falling Sickness*, ix.

31 Mark and Ervin, *Violence and the Brain*, 60. They also suggest that violence may be associated with "certain kinds of epilepsy even when the brain is normal" (56).

32 On the pace of historical change in views of therapeutic efficacy, see Charles Rosenberg's classic, "The Therapeutic Revolution: Medicine, Meaning and Social Change in Nineteenth-Century America," *Perspectives in Biology and Medicine* 20 (1977), 485–506. "The resident physician at the Philadelphia Dispensary could, for example, report in 1862 that of a total of 9,502 treated that year, 'general blood-letting has been resorted to in one instance only . . . cupping twelve times and leeching thrice.'" Residents at Bellevue in New York and in Boston's Massachusetts General Hospital had reported the previous year that bloodletting was 'almost obsolete.'" (Reference to MGH is from O. W. Holmes, *Medical Essays* (Boston: Houghton Mifflin, 1911 [orig. 1868]), 258; quoted on 500 of Rosenberg, above.)

33 Mark and Ervin, *Violence and the Brain*, 70.

34 Mark and Ervin, *Violence and the Brain*, 70.

35 Dr. Mark observed retrospectively that Leonard's "chronic and serious" temporal lobe epilepsy was likely to develop into the type of schizoform psychosis that characterized Leonard's last decades, and that this could have unfolded whether Leonard had had the surgery or not. "Vernon Mark, MD, and William Sweet, MD," YouTube, interview uploaded by American Neurological Association of Surgeons [undated], https://www.youtube.com/watch?v=0bWq7d95Mig. Yet according to one psychiatrist and critic who examined Kille's medical records, none identified him, presurgery, with a diagnosis more severe than "personality pattern disturbance." (Peter R. Breggin, Letter to Editor "Psychosurgery," *JAMA* 226 (1973), 1121.) The reference in this paragraph to "meek and docile" is a quotation found in Chorover, *From Genesis to Genocide*, 168.

36 Crichton on *The Terminal Man* quoted in Valenstein, *Brain Control*, 5.

37 Plan for brain scanning violent individuals is discussed in Brian Casey, "The Surgical Elimination of Violence? Conflicting Attitudes towards Technology and Science during the Psychosurgery Controversy of the 1970s," *Science in Context* 28 (2015), 99–129, 102. On mounting opposition to funding the brain unit, see Udodiri Okwandu, "Violence and the (Black) Brain" (BA thesis, Harvard University, 2017), 77; Harry Beecher Papers HMS, Box 14, Folder 13, including letter from Everett Mendelsohn.

Notes to Pages 150–157

38 "Vernon Mark, MD, and William Sweet, MD," interview.
39 Valenstein, *Brain Control*, 253. The expression "unthought-through" is from Penelope Lemov.
40 Letter from L. J. West dated October 17, 1954, to Dr. Eric Carlson of Payne Whitney Clinic of New York. LJ West Papers, UCLA, Series 590, Box 21, Folder 4.
41 L. J. West's son, John, wrote that his father's philandering was an "open secret" in the family for a long time and that his mother, K., told stories about facing off with her husband's mistresses. See John West, *The Last Goodnights: Assisting My Parents with their Suicides*, (Berkeley, CA: Counterpoint, 2009), 12–14.
42 L. J. West report, "Psychophysiological Studies of Hypnosis and Suggestibility," submitted to Geschickter Fund for Medical Research as part of a continuing project at the Oklahoma Medical Research Foundation; LJ West Papers, UCLA, Series 590, Box 133, Folder 4; this report is also found in CIA.org electronic reading room for FOIA documents. Question about "dissociated" is from "Sub-project 43."
43 CV details from L. J. West CV of 1989, CIA release of FOIA-requested documents, downloaded from archive.org, https://archive.org/details/JolyonWest/mode/2up.
44 Sources in this paragraph are James R. Allen and Louis Jolyon West, "Paper for Human Sexuality'—Make Love Not War: Notes on the Sexual Customs of Some American Hippies," draft article dated 1969; West handwritten annotations on Dr. Allen's interview in article titled "Psychiatrists Fail Drug Addicts, Lawyer Says"; West's personal diary. All found in LJ West Papers, UCLA, Series 590, Box 118, Folders 8–9.
45 Tom O'Neill found the grad student's notebook in the LJ West papers. See Tom O'Neill and Dan Piepenbring, *Chaos: Charles Manson, the CIA, and the Secret History of the Sixties* (New York: Hachette, 2019), 349–50. (The notebooks are in Box 118.) The student wrote that West and his associates "spent a good deal of the time stoned," and that she found West to exude "phoniness and dishonesty."
46 D. E. Smith quoting his erstwhile insurance agent @ around 30:43, "Angels on Haight Ashbury" (an interview with David E Smith), *Bureau of Lost Culture* podcast, Sunday June 9, 2024, https://bureauoflostculture.podbean.com/e/angels-on-haight-ashbury-1717971481/.
47 Gary P. Landes diary, 1968; LJ West Papers, UCLA, Series 590, Box 118, Folder 10.
48 "Angels on Haight Ashbury."
49 Interviews with Pittel and Dernburg in O'Neill and Piepenbring, *Chaos*, 318.
50 "UCLA Institute Plans Violence Study Center," *Los Angeles Times*, March 24, 1973, 22.
51 Described by West; see L. J. West, "Research on Violence Problems and Possibilities," speech delivered to Mental Health Development Commission of Los Angeles County meeting on October 31, 1973, United Way HQ Building, 621 S. Virgil, Los Angeles. LJ West Papers, UCLA, Box 13, Folder 3.
52 Thanks to Dr. Yvan Prkachin for clarifying this point. See Jack Pressman, *The Last Resort: Psychosurgery and the Limits of Medicine* (Cambridge, UK: Cambridge University Press, 1999), which emphasizes the long existing tension between the therapeutic and the theoretical/scientific. See also Gerald Perkoff, "The Meaning of 'Experimental,'"

in Elliot Valenstein, *The Psychosurgery Debate* (San Francisco: W. H. Freeman and Company, 1980), 348–64.

53 Dr. Robert Litman quoted in CA Department of Mental Hygiene / Health and Welfare Agency, Sacramento, press release: "Life-threatening behavior to be studied by new center," LJ West Papers, UCLA, Series 590, Box 51, Folder 6.

54 Fernando Vidal and Francisco Ortega, *Being Brains: Making the Cerebral Subject* (New York: Fordham University Press, 2019); emphasis added (quotation is from front matter).

55 Indeed, this is precisely the method for which he was celebrated in a 1992 festschrift: Michael T. McGuire, "Louis Jolyon West and the Ecological Model of Psychiatric Disorders: A Lecture in Medical History—October 6, 2024," in eds. Anthony Kales, Chester Pierce, and Milton Greenblatt, *The Mosaic of Contemporary Psychiatry in Perspective* (New York: Springer, 1992), 79–88.

56 West's original 1972 proposal can be found as an attachment to: L. J. West letter dated September 1, 1972, to J. M. Stubblebine ("Stub") of the California Department of Mental Health; LJ West Papers, UCLA, Series 590, Box 52, Folder 5. That proposal underwent at least eight further drafts. Ervin was mentioned in the first draft but not subsequent ones. "Dr. Frank R. Ervin['s] name was attached to two research projects in one of the early proposals, but was removed from later versions," wrote a group of psychiatrists opposed to the project. Terry Kupers, MD (Division of Community and Social Psychiatry, NPI, Los Angeles), Richard Trockman, MD (Hawaii); Phillip Shapiro MD (San Francisco); Isidore Ziferstein MD (Los Angeles), "RE: The Proposed 'Center for the Study and Reduction of Violence' [a.k.a. the Violence Center] at the Neuropsychiatric Institute, UCLA," undated memorandum [c. 1973], LJ West Papers, Box 51 Folder 3.

57 Mark and Ervin, *Violence and the Brain*, xi. Further details on Delgado's bull stimoceiver experiments are found in Timothy Marzullo, "The Missing Manuscript of Dr. Jose Delgado's Radio Controlled Bulls," *Journal of Undergraduate Neuroscience Education* 15 (2017), R29–R35.

58 Mark and Ervin, *Violence and the Brain*, 30. This constituted "experimentally produced attack behavior."

59 Foreword to Mark and Ervin, *Violence and the Brain*, vii (emphasis added). In ch. 7, they refer to on-off switches in brain approvingly.

60 Jose M. Delgado, Vernon Mark, William Sweet, Frank Ervin, G. Weiss, George Bach-y-Rita, R. Hagiwara, "Intracerebral Radio Stimulation and Recording in Completely Free Patients," *Journal of Nervous and Mental Disorders* 147 (1968), 329–40, 338. As Casey points out, "In part driven by a rugged American individualism, but more immediately by competition, psychosurgeons who sought behavior control audaciously pursued the innovative." (Casey, "The Surgical Elimination of Violence?," 120.)

61 Dr. Robert Litman, "who expects that the center will be financed wholly by private funds within two years," is quoted in California Department of Mental Hygiene / Health and Welfare Agency, Sacramento: "Life-threatening behavior to be studied

Notes to Pages 161–166

by new center," Press Release, LJ West Papers, UCLA, Series 590, Box 51, Folder 6. (See also California State Senate Hearing #2 on funding.)

62 Stubblebine testimony in transcript of California State Senate hearings, July 3, 1973, Sacramento, California.

63 Letter from F. R. Ervin, MD, Professor of Psychiatry UCLA to Mr. J. V. Kosnett in LJ West Papers, UCLA, Series 590, Box 51 Folder 1. In a dialogue with Dr. Isidore Ziferstein, Dr. Ervin said, "I should be greatly surprised if, in view of my background, I am not called on as a resource person. And, if I am not, I'll go knocking on some doors—Bob Litman's and Jolly West's." Quoted in Kupers et al, "RE: The Proposed 'Center for the Study and Reduction of Violence.'"

64 Ervin interview in Pines, *The Brain Changers*, 202–3.

65 Yvan Prkachin argues precisely this about Wilder Penfield in Yvan Prkachin, "Wired Together: The Montreal Neurological Institute and the Origins of Modern Neuroscience, 1928-1965" (PhD diss., Harvard University, 2018).

66 Pines, *The Brain Changers*, 207.

67 For contemporary definitions of psychosurgery, see L. J. West, Testimony in California State Senate Hearings, July 3, 1973, Sacramento, California; Peter Breggin, "Psychosurgery," *Journal of American Medical Association* 226 (1973), 1121; Elliot Valenstein, Overview, in ed. Elliot S. Valenstein, *The Psychosurgery Debate: Scientific, Legal, and Ethical Perspectives* (San Francisco: W. H. Freeman and Company, 1980), 9-86, 12-13; Chorover, *From Genesis to Genocide*, 141. Also relevant is description of Paul McLean testifying before an NIH meeting on psychosurgery in the 1970s, described in Pines, *The Brain Changers*, 208–9.

68 See Vernon Mark, "Brain Surgery in Aggressive Epileptics," Report of the Institute of Society, Ethics, and the Life Sciences 3 (1973), 1–5. Ervin was unrepentant of his research program, would not defend it against misreadings, and his obituary read that his three domains of interest throughout his life remained clinical medicine, biomedical research, and social activism. "Frank R. Ervin, M.D." (obit.)

69 Carol Gallo, "Taking on the Mind Killers," Interview with Peter Breggin, *Reason*, August 1974.

70 Evans-Young, Gloria, "Brain Surgery" (Letter to Editor), *Ebony*, May 1973, 8–9, quoted in Alondra Nelson, *Body and Soul: The Black Panther Party and the Fight Against Discrimination* (Minneapolis: University of Minnesota Press, 2011), 153.

71 Letter dated September 8, 1971, from R. K. Procunier, head of the California Department of Corrections to R. L. Lawson, executive officer, CA Council on Criminal Justice, quoted in "Violence: It's All in Your Head," Students for Democratic Society handout, February 14, 1973. "For more information call Amy, Humberto or Alan (391-5165)." LJ West Papers, UCLA, Series 590, Box 51, Folder 3. A brilliant account of the Black Panthers' opposition to West's Violence Center is in Nelson, *Body and Soul*, chapter 5.

72 West letter quoted in Terry A. Kupers, "Dangers of the Center," *Daily Bruin*, February 26, 1974. West drew back from the initial (September 1972) and subsequent (January

1973) letters to Director of Health, Dr. J. M. Stubblebine, later when he explained that "the comparative studies mentioned in the [Nike] letter would be animal studies," and also assured a reporter of the facility's robust security.

73 The Vacaville Medical Treatment Center, as described by a nineteen-year-old UC Berkeley sophomore who visited in 1972, became involved in the prisoner rights movement (and later joined DeFreeze in the SLA): "This place is known for its lobotomies and terrifying drug treatments (which I've had described to me, second-hand) which are used to vegetable-ize those who are troublesome in their political fervor." Willie Wolfe letter to his mother quoted in Stuart Schreiber, *Revolution's End: The Patty Hearst Kidnapping, Mind Control, and the Secret History of Donald DeFreeze and the SLA* (New York: Skyhorse, 2016), 56–57. DeFreeze was held in the Maximum Psychiatric Diagnostic Unit, was known to be an informant to the LAPD, was radicalized in Vacaville, and escaped in 1970.

74 Dr. Bach-y-Rita interview in Jonathan Riley, "Critical History: Lobotomass," *Dig Boston*, June 1, 2017. Bach-y-Rita continues to believe Kille did have epilepsy, but this became a matter of dispute. He also says: "They might have been working for CIA, but the CIA wasn't considered bad." At the time, he added, "people hadn't learned to mistrust the Dulles brothers yet. They didn't know how horrible the Dulles brothers were." While naive patriotism may have been driven by some of the many who joined MK-ULTRA in a peripheral way, it was certainly not true of West.

75 Dr. Grimm, who based his opinion on an examination of Leonard and his early medical records, is quoted in Jean Dietz, "Psychosurgery on Trial," *Boston Sunday Globe*, January 21, 1979, A2.

76 Katharine Park, *Secrets of Women: Gender, Generation, and the Origins of Human Dissection* (Princeton: Princeton University Press, 2010). On the challenges of judging shifting standards of medical assays, there is a large literature; but see, e.g., Shigehisa Kuriyama, "Interpreting the History of Bloodletting," *Journal of the History of Medicine and Allied Sciences* 50 (1995),11-46.

77 Perkoff, "The Meaning of 'Experimental,' " 349–50.

78 As discussed in David Jones, Christine Grady, and Susan Lederer, "Ethics and Clinical Research." The 50th Anniversary of Beecher's Bombshell, *New England Journal of Medicine* (2016), 2393–98, 2394.

79 Why Beecher's article was such a turning point for medical ethics is discussed in David Rothman, *Strangers at the Bedside: A History of How Law and Bioethics Transformed Medical Decision Making* (New York: Basic Books, 1991) and Laura Stark, *Behind Closed Doors: IRBs and the Making of Ethical Research* (Chicago: University of Chicago Press, 2012), among others. On the normalization of experimental research veiled as necessary treatment, and the difficulty of whistleblowing, see Carl Elliot, *The Occasional Human Sacrifice: Medical Experimentation and the Price of Saying No* (New York: Norton, 2024). See also, Robert J. Lifton, *The Nazi Doctors: Medical Killing and the Ethics of Genocide* (New York: Basic Books, 1988).

80 Quoted in Jeffrey Gillenkirk, "Violence Control Project Tests LEAA's Mental Health

Plans," *Psychiatric News*, May 1, 1974. In LJ West Papers, UCLA, Series 590, Box 51, Folder 7.

81 Phrase from B. J. Mason, "New Threat to Blacks: Brain Surgery to Control Behavior," *Ebony*, February 1, 1973.

82 California State Senate Hearing Transcript 1973.

83 "Individual Rights and the Federal Role in Behavior Modification," Subcommittee on Constitutional Rights of the Committee on the Judiciary, United States Senate November 1974, 8. Here the study is citing *Mackey v Procunier*, 477 F. 2d 877 (9th Cir. 1973), a case in which a Vacaville medical inmate was administered the drug Succinylcholine, causing paralysis and inability to breathe.

84 Joshua Golden, "Faculty Support for Research," *Daily Bruin*, February 26, 1974, clipping in LJ West Papers, UCLA, Series 590, Box 51, Folder 7. This tally of three was not accurate. The snail researcher was Fred Abraham, a neuropsychologist who debated West during a joint television interview.

85 Dr. Terry Kupers note to author, personal comm., November 5, 2017.

86 "Neuralink's First Human Patient Able to Control Mouse through Thinking, Musk Says," *Reuters*, February 20, 2024.

87 Nita A. Farahany, *The Battle for Your Brain: Defending the Right to Think Freely in the Age of Neurotechnology* (New York: St. Martin's Press, 2023), 84.

88 "I can't wait to get out and go to work again" and comments about moving to California and having his kids visit are from Leonard Kille letter to his mother, Helen Geis, May 19, 1967. Patient records and correspondence dated February 1, 1973, from Helen Geis to Peter Breggin ("while in the hospital his wife divorced him") are all from the Michael McKilen papers. His mother also described him as, at age thirty-nine, almost a vegetable.

89 Handwritten notes after a visit in the Bedford VA hospital by Helen Geis, Leonard's mother, and the records of Kille's decline are all from McKilen papers.

90 Leonard Kille, letter on Pan Am letterhead to Helen Geis, September 22 [no year], McKilen papers.

91 "were pilloried": Miguel A. Faria, "Violence, Mental Illness, and the Brain–A Brief History of Psychosurgery: Part 3—From Deep Brain Stimulation to Amygdalotomy for Violent Behavior, Seizures, and Pathological Aggression in Humans," *Surgical Neurology International* 4 (2013), 91.

CHAPTER 6: A SMALL UH-OH OPENED UP IN MY SOUL

1 Study quoted in a NRM publication. Two recent studies of former cult members (fifty-two and thirty-one subjects respectively) had an average stay of 18.11 years of those in the first study and 9 years in the second in a cult, suggesting that if a recruit passes a certain threshold, they will stay for a significantly longer period than 2.5 years. Shaelen Grant, "The Cultic Lifecycle: A Thematic Analysis of Fulfillment and Fear in Cult Membership" (M.A. Thesis, John Jay College of Criminal Justice), 20; M.

Rousselet, O. Duretete, J. B. Hardouin, M. Grall-Bronnec, "Cult Membership: What Factors Contribute to Joining or Leaving?" *Psychiatry Research* 257 (2017), 27–33, 31.

2   Benjamin Zablocki, "The Blacklisting of a Concept: The Strange History of the Brainwashing Conjecture in the Sociology of Religion," *Nova Religio: The Journal of Alternative and Emergent Religions* 1 (1997), 96–121, 110.

3   Examples of positive coverage of groups somewhere in the spectrum of cult-to-intentional community include Richard Tod, "'Walden Two?' Three? Many More?" *The New York Times Sunday Magazine*, March 15, 1970; *Life* magazine's cover story, "The Youth Communes," July 18, 1969. On the almost immediate cooptation of peace and love urgings as advertising slogans see Thomas Frank, *The Conquest of Cool: Business Culture, Counterculture, and the Rise of Hip Consumerism* (Chicago: University of Chicago Press, 1997).

4   Vincent Bugliosi (with Curt Gentry), *Helter Skelter: The True Story of the Manson Murders* (New York: Norton, 1974).

5   Quoted in Bugliosi, *Helter Skelter*, 675.

6   Bugliosi, *Helter Skelter*, 689.

7   ABC News *20/20*, "Charles Manson's Tumultuous Childhood and Time in Prison: Part 1," YouTube, uploaded March 18, 2017 (featuring a contemporary clip) https://www.youtube.com/watch?v=2Rj8QdAoLwc).

8   Alan Rose, a researcher with Louis Jolyon West's Amphetamine Research Project, encountered them in Northern California instigating orgies; quoted in Tom O'Neill and Dan Pieperbring, *Chaos: Charles Manson, the CIA, and the Secret History of the Sixties* (New York: Hachette, 2019), 324. Were women more responsive to Manson's forceful persuasion than men? Not necessarily, for Manson deliberately manipulated female followers differently from males.

9   K. McCabe, L. Goldberg, M. Langone, and K. DeVoe, "A Workshop for People Born or Raised in Cultic Groups," ICSA E-Newsletter, 6, 2007. Or 2,500 groups according to other estimates. The matter of counting both groups and members is highly contested and "the sources for these numbers, aside from a few news articles, were never revealed . . ." but "these figures were used for shock effect more than anything else," Ashcroft argues: W. Michael Ashcroft, *A Historical Study of New Religious Movements* (New York: Routledge, 2019), 118.

10 Álvaro Castana, Jocelyn J. Bélanger, and Manuel Moyano, "Cult Conversion from the Perspective of Families: Implications for Prevention and Psychological Intervention," *Psychology of Religion and Spirituality* 14 (2022), 148–60.

11 Quote from Bugliosi, in Robin McKie, "Charles Manson Follower Ends her Silence 40 Years after Night of Slaughter," *The Guardian*, August 1, 2009.

12 Ted Patrick, front matter, *Let Our Children Go!* (New York: Ballantine, 1976).

13 Quoted in Patrick, *Let Our Children Go!*, 132.

14 James T. Richardson quoted in Ashcroft, *A Historical Study of New Religious Movements*, 112.

15 Robert J. Lifton, Prologue to *Home from the War: Vietnam Veterans, Neither Victims nor Executioners* (New York: Simon and Schuster, 1973), 15.
16 Lifton, Prologue to *Home from the War*, 22.
17 "Child Psychology 1973," Wellfleet Tape #00802, August 19, 1973. Robert Jay Lifton Papers, Manuscripts and Archives Division, The New York Public Library, Series 5, (@8:14 of tape).
18 Lifton references in this and the following three paragraphs are from "Child Psychology 1973" Wellfleet Tape #00802, beginning around 11:12. Reference is to Suzanne Langer, *Mind: An Essay on Human Feeling*, vol. 1 (Johns Hopkins University Press, 1967).
19 Chaim Shatan, "Post-Vietnam Syndrome," *The New York Times*, May 6, 1972; Frank Olson's death is the subject of Erroll Morris's "Wormwood" documentary series featuring Eric Olson (Netflix 2017).
20 PTSD appeared in the DSM III (1980). Historian and anthropologist Allan Young tells this story in more depth, emphasizing the contingency of the diagnosis. Allan Young, *The Harmony of Illusions: Inventing Post-Traumatic Stress Disorder* (Princeton: Princeton University Press, 1995). Recently, historian Ran Zwigenberg examined how trauma came to be named by looking at studies of Holocaust and Hiroshima survivors—a story in which Lifton also plays a role, though Zwigenberg somewhat diminishes his centrality, looking at the work of Japanese psychiatrists to fill out the heroic narrative (Zwigenberg, *Nuclear Minds* [University of Chicago Press, 2023.]) For an account of the transformation of the understanding of "battered woman syndrome," and "rape trauma syndrome" see Leena Akhtar, "From Masochists to Traumatized Victims: Psychiatry, Law, and the Feminist Anti-rape Movement of the 1970s" (PhD diss., Harvard University 2017).
21 Chaim Shatan, "The Grief of Soldiers: Vietnam Combat Veterans' Self-Help Movement," *American Journal of Orthopsychiatry* 43 (1973), 640–54. See also Arthur Egendorf, "Vietnam: A Television History," unedited interview dated July 8, 1983, WGBH, https://openvault.wgbh.org/catalog/A_6A74DFBFE6CB429A9100322F7C2F4D96 #at_220.78300000000002_s. Accessed May 15, 2024.
22 Castana, "Cult Conversion from the Perspective of Families."
23 Bessel van der Kolk and Christine Courtois, "Editorial Comments: Complex Developmental Trauma," *Journal of Traumatic Stress* 18 (2005), 385–88, 386. Judith Herman, *Truth and Repair: How Trauma Survivors Envision Justice* (New York: Basic Books, 2023).
24 Ray Connolly, *Something Somebody Stole* (CreateSpace Independent Publishing Platform, 2011), 18.
25 Margaret Singer, "Declaration of Margaret Singer, PhD," *David Molko and Tracy Leal v. Holy Spirit Association for the Unification of World Christianity, et al.*, San Francisco City and County California Superior Court, 1983, 3, quoted in Dick Anthony, "Brainwashing and Totalitarian Influence: An Exploration of Admissibility Criteria for Testimony in Brainwashing Trials" (PhD diss., Graduate Theological Union, 1996), 29

(emphasis added). Singer was specifically speaking about the Rev. Moon's Unification Church ("Moonies") in this passage but applied the analysis widely.

26 Margaret Singer, *Cults in Our Midst: The Continuing Fight against Their Hidden Menace* (San Francisco, CA: Jossey-Bass, 2003 [1995]). The 2003 revised version of *Cults in Our Midst* was coauthored with Janja Lalich.

27 Unless otherwise noted, all quotations in this and the next four paragraphs are from Connolly, *Something Somebody Stole*, in order: "Jesus was" on 20, "I have decided" on 20, "good cop"/"bad cop" on 22, "wild early years" on 38, "It seemed like everything was permanently set" on 23, "share all this input" on 23, "the proverb, 'Trust in the Lord'" on 23, "most of us had long since mastered" on 39, "dark hamster wheel" on 94, "cult self" on 100.

28 Cyndi H. Matthews, "Second Generation Religious Cult Survivors: Implications for Counselors," *International Journal of Cultic Studies* 8 (2017), 37–49, 90. The pseudo self was especially strong in SGAs, who had never experienced life without it.

29 American Psychiatric Association, *Desk Reference to the Diagnostic Criteria from DSM-5 (R)* (Arlington, TX: American Psychiatric Association Publishing, 2013), 305. As of 2013, the pseudo self (produced by coercive persuasion) received official recognition as a disorder of identity. The DSM-V describes it: "Identity disturbance due to prolonged and intense coercive persuasion is recognized in the DSM-V for individuals who have been subjected to intense coercive persuasion (e.g., brainwashing, thought reform, indoctrination while captive, torture, and long-term political imprisonment). It has also been applied to those who have been recruited by sects/cults or by terror organizations and present with prolonged changes in, or conscious questioning of, their identity."

30 Connolly, *Something Somebody Stole*, 90.

31 Stanley Milgram quoted in Carol Tavris interview, "The Frozen World of the Familiar Stranger: We are All Fragile Creatures Entwined in a Cobweb of Social Relationships," *Psychology Today*, June 1974, 71–80, 76.

CHAPTER 7: I ACCOMMODATED MY THOUGHTS TO THEIRS

1 Norbert Elias, *The Civilizing Process: Sociogenetic and Psychogenetic Investigations* (Hampshire, UK: Blackwell Press, 2000 [1939]), 122.

2 Elias, *The Civilizing Process*, 126, emphasis added.

3 Tellers of Hearst's story include newspaper reporters Jerry Belcher and Don West, *Patty/Tania* (New York: Pyramid, 1975); a national reporter, Shana Alexander, *Anyone's Daughter* (New York: Bantam, 1980); various professors including Christopher Castiglia, *Bound and Determined: Captivity, Culture-Crossing, and White Womanhood from Mary Rowlandson to Patty Hearst* (Chicago: University of Chicago Press, 1996); William Graebner on her "fragile, modern self" in *Patty's Got a Gun* (Chicago: University of Chicago Press, 2007); Janice Schuetz, *The Logic of Women on Trial* (Southern Illinois University Press, 1994) (on an evolving identity from Patty to Tania to Pearl); Andreas

Killen, *1973: Watergate, Warhol, and the Birth of Post-Sixties America* (New York: Bloomsbury, 2006) (on Hearst as emblem of the end of the 1960s); Nancy Isenberg, "Not 'Anyone's Daughter': Patty Hearst and the Postmodern Legal Subject," *American Quarterly* 52 (2000), 639–81 (on Hearst as a postmodern empty self). See also Jeffrey Toobin, *American Heiress: The Wild Saga of the Kidnapping, Crimes and Trial of Patty Hearst* (New York: Anchor, 2017). The University of Missouri, Kansas City, law professor Douglas O. Linder runs the "Famous Trials" website.

4   Statement by Hearst. (Toobin "romanticizes my rape and torture and calls my abduction a 'rollicking adventure.'") James Mangold was to have directed.

5   Tweet by Lydia Hearst quoted in Yohana Desta, "Fox Drops Patty Hearst Project After She Cries Foul," *Vanity Fair*, January 18, 2012. Subsequently removed from Twitter. Toobin interview with Renee Montagne, NPR *Morning Edition*, August 2, 2016; https://www.npr.org/2016/08/02/488336945/american-heiress-author-you-cannot-overstate-the-terror-that-patty-hearst-faced.

6   Image is found at Douglas O. Linder, "SLA Notes Identifying Patty Hearst as a Potential Kidnap Victim," *Famous Trials* blog, University of Missouri Kansas City School of Law; https://famous-trials.com/pattyhearst/2207-slanotes.

7   Federal Bureau of Investigations, "Famous Cases and Criminals," https://www.fbi.gov/history/famous-cases/patty-hearst.

8   During the first three months of 1972 there was a well-covered trial in Harrisburg, Pennsylvania, of the "Harrisburg Seven," six of them Catholic antiwar activists, who were charged with plotting to kidnap Henry Kissinger, a plot that may have inspired the Hearst kidnapping.

9   Slides with timeline, LJ West Papers, UCLA. Series 590, Box 6, folder 9.

10 Quoted Brad Schreiber, *Revolution's End: The Patty Hearst Kidnapping, Mind Control, and the Secret History of Donald DeFreeze and the SLA* (New York: Skyhorse, 2016), 128. Note that I don't agree with all the conclusions drawn by this author but have referred to research where I judged it reliable.

11 On this, see Stuart Schrader, *Badges without Borders: How Global Counterinsurgency Transformed American Policing* (Berkeley: UC Press, 2019), 221: changed because "a colleague rejected the name's bellicosity." Acronyms abounded: In Los Angeles, there was also the special gang squad CRASH, or Community Resources Against Street Hoodlums, originally named TRASH, with the T standing for Total. [CRASH was the program that hired DeFreeze as informant.]

12 Schrader, *Badges without Borders*, 218. The situation of Parker and Gates in 1950s and 1960s shaped SWAT's emergence: "Social protest and focused legal activism challenged the LAPD, which responded through capital-intensive professionalizing reforms, intense policing of its political antagonists, and the rescripting of its racializing activities as race-independent order maintenance" (220).

13 Schreiber, *Revolution's End*, 179.

14 Schrieber, *Revolution's End*, xii.

15 William O'Rourke, "Setting the Patty Hearst Record Straight"; Review of Toobin's

16 Account of Hearst/Harrises "errand" is in part from Belcher and West, *Patty/Tania*; quotations in this and next paragraph are from 115 and 277.
17 Interview with Bill Harris in "The Radical Story of Patty Hearst," CNN 2018.
18 Wallace Turner interview with Patty Hearst, "Patty Hearst Says She 'Just Plain Couldn't' Flee Her Captors," *The New York Times,* December 11, 1981.
19 1 Chronicles 12:18, King James version.
20 Leslie Oelsner, "Miss Hearst Called 'Fugitive' by Saxbe," *The New York Times,* April 18, 1974.
21 From a 1976 interview with West by journalist Shana Alexander: West described the program studying violence victims that was already underway at the NPI; Alexander repeated/confirmed that Hearst was well suited: "So here comes supervictim," and West agrees "that's right," or at least, he will want to discover if this is true. This is why he agreed to be a part of the proceedings. Transcript of interview with Shana Alexander, LJ West Papers, UCLA, Series 590, Box 122, Folder 8.
22 Judge Orrick statement post-sentencing, as read by his son @ 1:06:08 of video, "The Patricia Hearst Trial: Local Lawyers Remember," Northern District Historical Society, October 3, 2018, *YouTube,* uploaded by the Northern District Historical Society, December 9, 2019; https://www.youtube.com/watch?v=TvxcjdDt4B8.
23 Joan Didion, "Girl of the Golden West," in *After Henry* (New York: Simon and Schuster, 1992), 95–109, 98–99. Italics in original.
24 Joan Didion, *South and West: From a Notebook* (New York: Harper Collins, 2017), 111.
25 Kenneth Reeves, *The Trial of Patricia Hearst* [Trial Transcript] (San Francisco: Great Fidelity Press, 1976), 282, emphasis added.
26 Reeves, *The Trial of Patricia Hearst*, 325.
27 "How POWs Judge 'Tania,'" *Time*, March 8, 1976.
28 William Harris, SLA communique after May 17, FBI "HEARNAP" Documents (Public Domain), Internet Archive https://archive.org/details/HEARNAP/PattyHearstKidnapping001/.
29 Reeves, *The Trial of Patricia Hearst*, 250.
30 Patricia Hearst, *Every Secret Thing* (New York: Doubleday, 1982), 412.
31 See Hearst's memoir in which she describes West as "author of books and studies on prisoners of war . . . I thought he had a creepy hypnotic voice." Hearst, *Every Secret Thing*, 375.
32 Draft manuscript by Margaret Singer "for Intro B" #1, July 1976, for (unpublished) project with LJW on Hearst, "A Different Person"; LJ West Papers, UCLA, Series 590, Box 122, Folder 14.
33 Reeves, *The Trial of Patricia Hearst*, 294. Also, from West's testimony, re: the Mel's event shoot-up: West was asked about Hearst's state of mind. A: "The recollection that she had of what happened there was one of disbelief and the most common phrase

Notes to Pages 232–239

that she would utter was, 'I can't believe that happened, I can't believe I did that. I don't understand why I did it'" (259).

34 As Dr. William Sargent, a renowned British brainwashing expert who interviewed her when she was first captured (but did not testify at the trial), assessed: "[Thirty] days being blindfolded is the maximum a person can take before a 'breakdown' occurs, after which the brain goes into an 'inhibitory reverse.'" Essentially, "through an unrelenting campaign of mental cruelty, sensory deprivation, malnutrition, threats of death and injury, and the constant confusion of affection and abuse [Hearst] was broken. She receded into herself, shut off her feelings and emotions, and did what she was told"; quoted in Ida-Gaye Warburton, "The Commandeering of Free Will: Brainwashing as a Legitimate Defense," *Capital Defense Journal* 73 (2003), 73–97, 74.

35 Interview transcript L. J. West with Shana Alexander, Tape #1A, April 15, 1976; LJ West Papers, UCLA, Series 590, Box 122, Folder.

36 "Battle over Patty's Mind," *Time*, March 8, 1976, 25–31, 28.

37 "How POWs Judge 'Tania,'" *Time*, March 8, 1976.

38 Wallace Turner, "Doctor Calls Miss Hearst Willing Bandit," *The New York Times*, March 9, 1976. He was the first expert witness called by the government, although the jury had heard expert opinion testimony from three psychiatrists called by the defense.

39 Alexander, *Anyone's Daughter*, 376.

40 Alexander's summary of Fort's argument, *Anyone's Daughter*, 376.

41 Alexander, *Anyone's Daughter*, 376; Jeffrey Toobin interview WGBH, August 8, 2016. https://www.wgbh.org/news/local/2016-08-08/jeffrey-toobin-on-his-new-book-american-heiress.

42 Warburton explains the failure of the brainwashing defense this way: "The jury apparently believed that Hearst was a willing participant and did not believe the coercion theory presented by the defense." See Warburton, "The Commandeering of Free Will," 80. The defense had not sufficiently explained how Hearst's willingness to commit the crime *was* the evidence of coercion. (Whether this was fully exculpatory or only partially exculpatory was another question not sufficiently addressed at trial.)

43 It is said that President Ronald Reagan, a close friend of Hearst's mother, Catherine, came close to pardoning her.

44 Hearst, *Every Secret Thing*, 82. Emphasis added.

45 Hearst, *Every Secret Thing*, 393.

46 Terry Gross interview with Jeffrey Toobin, *Fresh Air*, 2017, https://freshairarchive.org/segments/whose-side-was-she-american-heiress-revisits-patty-hearsts-kidnapping-0.

47 Researchers increasingly question Stockholm syndrome's scientific and ethical viability: M. Namnyak, N. Tufton, R. Szekely, M. Toal, S. Worboys, E. L. Sampson, "Stockholm Syndrome: Psychiatric Diagnosis or Urban Myth?" *Acta Psychiatrica Scandinavica* 117 (2008), 4–11; L. R. Dee, Edna Graham, Edna Rawlings, Nelly Rimini, "Survivors of Terror: Battered Women, Hostages, and the Stockholm Syndrome," in eds. K. Yllö

and M. Bograd, *Feminist Perspectives on Wife Abuse* (Sage, 1988), 217–33; Michael Adorjan et al, "Stockholm Syndrome as Vernacular Resource," *The Sociological Quarterly* 53 (2012), 454–74. See also Abigail Judge, unpublished guest lecture on the inadequacy of Stockholm syndrome, "Brainwashing and Mind Control Techniques," HSCI 176, History of Science Department, Harvard University, March 2020.

CHAPTER 8: DARKSOME HOUSE OF MORTAL CLAY

1. Hope Bastine, "How I Escaped the Children of God Cult That Destroyed my Childhood," *The Times of London*, August 9, 2020, https://www.thetimes.com/life-style/sex-relationships/article/how-i-escaped-the-children-of-god-cult-that-destroyed-my-childhood-qnxs6qxmb.
2. Shana Alexander, *Anyone's Daughter: The Times and Trials of Patricia Hearst* (New York: Viking 1979), 321.
3. Kevin Fagan, "Margaret Singer Has Made History Delving into the Psychology of Brainwashing," *SFGate*, May 26, 2002.
4. Three thousand was her 1990 estimate, in Margaret Singer and Richard Ofshe, "Thought Reform Programs and the Production of Psychiatric Casualties," *Psychiatric Annals* 20 (1990), 190. By the end of the decade she estimated the number had reached four thousand; see Ivan Ovisky, "Margaret Thaler Singer," *The Lancet* 363 (2004), 403.
5. Singer's interpretation of Hearst's SLA speech, in which she used linguistic analysis of the revolutionary jargon to conclude that the SLA had written it, not Hearst, was disbarred from the courtroom.
6. "False Imprisonment Based on a 'Brainwashing' Theory," in *George v. International Society for Krishna Consciousness of California* (1992), Court of Appeal, Fourth District, California, https://caselaw.findlaw.com/court/ca-court-of-appeal/1775782.html#footnote_15.
7. In a 1994 video, Singer described how cult recruiters "don't *argue* you in. They are real soft-soap, soft-sell, convincing sales persons who lure you in, cajole you in, compliment you . . ." Margaret Thaler Singer, "What Is a Cult and How Does It Work?" YouTube, uploaded by International Cultic Studies Association on October 12, 2024, https://www.youtube.com/watch?v=8bRBFhMEQFk.
8. Robert J. Lifton, *Losing Reality: On Cults, Cultism, and the Mindset of Political and Religious Zealotry* (New York: The New Press, 2019).
9. West told the judge he was not interested in serving as a witness in the trial. He was assured he wouldn't be, that wasn't the assignment. Interview notes by Shana Alexander with L. J. West. LJ West Papers, UCLA, Series 590, Box 122, Folder 8–9.
10. Peter Georgiades, "Why Attorneys Do Not Accept Cult-Related Litigation," ICSA Meeting 2004, Atlanta, GA, YouTube uploaded by International Cultic Studies Association at https://www.youtube.com/watch?v=tTO5swNZokk; quote is @ 00:15:28.

11 See D. Mitchell, C. Mitchell, and R. Ofshe, *The Light on Synanon* (West Lakes, AU: Seaview, 1980). Also, Rod Janzen, *The Rise and Fall of Synanon: A California Utopia* (Baltimore, MD: Johns Hopkins Press, 2023).
12 See James T. Richardson, "The Accidental Expert," *Nova Religio: The Journal of Alternative and Emergent Religions* 2 (1998), 31–43, footnote 3.
13 J. T. Ungerleider and D. K. Wellisch, "Coercive Persuasion (Brainwashing), Religious Cults, and Deprogramming," *American Journal of Psychiatry* 136 (1979), 279–82, 279.
14 Ungerleider, "Coercive Persuasion," 282.
15 Ted Patrick, *Let Our Children Go!* (New York: Ballantine, 1976), 48, 41.
16 Or perhaps better: You forget how you feel about what you think—an insight consonant with the work of Dr. Mary Helen Immordino-Yang at the USC Rossier School of Education on the recruitment of cognitive processes through bodily emotions.
17 Lois Armstrong, "The 'Deprogrammer' of Young Religious Fanatics, Ted Patrick, Goes to Jail for His Zeal," *People*, August 9, 1976.
18 Patrick, *Let Our Children Go!*, 10.
19 L. J. West, "Studies of Dissociated States" [c. 1953–1955], CIA MK-ULTRA document retrieved in Freedom of Information Act Electronic Reading Room, https://www.cia.gov/readingroom/.
20 Sarah Williams, "Study Identifies Brain Areas Altered During Hypnotic Trances," *Stanford Medicine News Release*, July 28, 2016.
21 Definition in W. Michael Ashcraft, *A Historical Introduction to the Study of New Religious Movements* (New York: Routledge, 2018), 103.
22 CBS News Broadcast, "Deprogramming: The Clash Between Religion and Civil Rights," August 1973, University of Georgia Walter J. Brown Media Archives. https://kaltura.uga.edu/media/t/1_bollzry9.
23 "But all I do is talk, talk, talk—hitting them with challenging questions. I try to get them to understand they've been ripped off—body and soul. Finally they start to see they've been giving their money to a con artist and a crook. It's a billion-dollar racket." Patrick quoted in Armstrong, "The 'Deprogrammer.'" Quotations this paragraph are from Patrick, *Let Our Children Go!*, 61, 73.
24 As described in Mia Donovan, *Deprogrammed* (EyeSteelFilm, 2015), https://www.imdb.com/title/tt4543744/.
25 Louis J. West and Paul R. Martin, "Pseudo-Identity and the Treatment of Personality Change in Victims of Captivity and Cults," in eds. Stephen J. Lynn and Judith W. Rhue, *Dissociation: Clinical and Theoretical Perspectives* (New York: Guilford Press, 1994), 268–88.
26 Another anti-cult figure was Steven Hassan, an early escapee from the Moonies who became a deprogrammer, made a pilgrimage to visit Lifton to try to make sense of the experience, and Lifton, reassuring him and assuaging his guilt over having been such a successful recruiter to a group out of which he barely was able to extricate himself, set Hassan firmly on his path. Hassan, *Combating Cult Mind Control: The #1 Best-Selling*

Guide to Protection, Rescue, and Recovery from Destructive Cults (Newton, MA: Freedom of Mind Press, 2015).

27 See Rebecca Lemov, *World as Laboratory: Experiments with Mice, Mazes, and Men* (New York: Hill and Wang, 2005), chapter 10.

28 As her *Lancet* obituary would recall: Ivan Oransky, "Margaret Thaler Singer," *The Lancet* 363 (2004), 403.

29 Quoted in Oransky, "Margaret Thaler Singer," 403. ("I've interviewed over four thousand ex-cult members.")

30 Lifton foreword in Margaret Singer and Janja Lalich, *Cults in Our Midst: The Continuing Fight against Their Hidden Menace* (San Francisco, CA: Jossey-Bass, 2003), xi.

31 L. J. West letter dated January 22, 1980, to Sterling Lord. LJ West Papers, UCLA, Series 590, Box 122, Folder 8–9. Lord responded asking for 30,000 to 40,000 words.

32 Barry A. Fisher, "Devotion, Damages and Deprogrammers: Strategies and Counterstrategies in the Cult Wars," *Journal of Law and Religion* 9 (1991), 151–78, 155.

33 Dean Kelly quoted in Fisher, "Devotion, Damages and Deprogrammers," 157.

34 "Several people on each side of this debate have told me, in personal communications, not only that they disagree with, but that they hate or despise certain members of the other camp." Benjamin Zablocki, "The Blacklisting of a Concept: The Strange History of the Brainwashing Conjecture in the Sociology of Religion," *Nova Religio: The Journal of Alternative and Emergent Religions* 1 (1997), footnote 4 on 116.

35 Irving Louis Horowitz, "Science, Sin, and Sponsorship," *The Atlantic Monthly* 239 (1977), 98–102. Later published in ed. Horowitz, *Science, Sin and Scholarship: The Politics of Reverend Moon and the Unification Church* (Cambridge, MA: MIT Press, 1978), 260–82.

36 Susan Palmer, in eds. Benjamin Zablocki and Tom Robbins, *Misunderstanding Cults: Searching for Objectivity in a Controversial Field* (Toronto: University of Toronto Press, 2001), 99–122.

37 Zablocki, "The Blacklisting of a Concept," 100.

38 See Richardson, "The Accidental Expert," footnote 3.

39 Q and A session [@ around 50 minutes], Georgiades, "Why Attorneys Do Not Accept Cult-Related Litigation."

40 Steven Hassan, "The BITE Model of Authoritarian Control: Undue Influence, Thought Reform, Brainwashing, Mind Control, Trafficking, and the Law" (PhD diss., Fielding Graduate University, 2020).

41 *Tracy Leal v. Holy Spirit Association for Unification of World Christianity* (1986), Court of Appeal, First District, California, https://caselaw.findlaw.com/ca-court-of-appeal/1842359.html#footnote_ref_1.

42 *Molko and Leal v. Holy Spirit Association for Unification of World Christianity* (1983). San Francisco Superior Ct. No. 769-529; *Molko and Leal v. Holy Spirit Association for Unification of World Christianity* (1986). 179 Cal. App. 3d 450. No. AO20935; *Molko and Leal v. Holy Spirit Association for Unification of World Christianity* (1988). Cal. 762 P. 2d 46. 252 Cal. Rptr. 122. Cert, denied.

Notes to Pages 265–273

43 Eileen Barker, "Religious Movements: Cult and Anti-Cult Since Jonestown," *Annual Review Sociolology* 12 (1986), 329–461, 330.
44 Eileen Barker, *The Making of a Moonie* (London: Blackwell, 1984), 46, historically so: the "Oakland Family."
45 Singer made this point in the Molko and Leal case; see Margaret Singer, "Declaration of Margaret Singer, PhD," *David Molko and Tracy Leal v. Holy Spirit Association for the Unification of World Christianity, et al., San Francisco City and County California Superior Court*, 1983, 3.
46 Barker, *Making of a Moonie,* 47 (with a citation, not included).
47 Quoted in Dick Anthony, "Brainwashing and Totalitarian Influence: An Exploration of Admissibility Criteria for Testimony in Brainwashing Trials" (PhD diss., Graduate Theological Union, 1996), 31, from Singer's 1983 testimony in *Molko and Leal v. Holy Spirit Association*, 3–4.
48 Hassan, "The BITE Model of Authoritarian Control," 2. "This 'illusion of choice' is at the center of all modern-day mind-control cults," he continues.
49 Their draft report was regarded by the APA's Board of Social and Ethical Responsibility for Psychology (BSERP) as the "final draft of the report, minus the reference list."
50 Margaret Thaler Singer, Harold Goldstein, Michael Langone, Jesse Miller, Maurice Termerlin, and Louis Jolyon West, "Report of the Task Force on Deceptive and Indirect Techniques of Persuasion and Control" (DIMPAC report, 1986). Available through Center for Studies on New Religions (CESNUR) online archive: https://www.cesnur.org/testi/DIMPAC.htm. Accessed June 13, 2024.
51 American Psychological Association Memorandum to DIMPAC, attaching external reviews ("APA ruling"), dated May 11, 1987, at https://www.cesnur.org/testi/APA.htm Supporting letter from presumed Singer ally Benjamin Beit-Hallahmi of University of Haifa: "Lacking psychological theory, the report resorts to sensationalism in the style of certain tabloids."
52 Jeffrey D. Fisher external review in APA ruling https://www.cesnur.org/testi/APA.htm.
53 *Robert Kropinski v. World Plan Executive Council--us, et al.*, Appellants, 853 F.2d 948 (D.C. Cir. 1988) at https://law.justia.com/cases/federal/appellate-courts/F2/853/948/121594/.
54 Kropinski alleges that defendants relied on a system of thought reform, which he describes as "a method used by the Koreans to change the belief systems of prisoners of war"; that is to say, as "brainwashing." Brief for *Kropinski v. World Plan Executive Council*, at 10.
55 Further: "During their cross-examination, defendants asked Dr. Singer to elaborate her thought reform theory but did not inquire into its acceptance by others in her profession. On redirect, Dr. Singer's explanation of her theory again did not address its acceptability. Defendants' expert, psychiatrist Dr. Melvin Prosen, testified that although Dr. Singer is a respected psychologist, her theory of thought reform found virtually no support among others in the field." *Kropinski v. World Plan Executive Council*

(references omitted). See also "Jury Grants $138,000 in Self-Levitation Case," *The New York Times*, January 15, 1987.

56 *George v. International Society for Krishna Consciousness of California* (1992) https://caselaw.findlaw.com/court/ca-court-of-appeal/1775782.html.

57 Charlotte Allen, "Brainwashed! Scholars of Cults Accuse Each Other of Bad Faith," *Lingua Franca*, December/January 1998.

58 Full quote relates to cult wars' misapprehensions: "Neither side has sufficiently recognized that the brainwashing conjecture is about relationships, not about individual dispositions." Zablocki, "The Blacklisting of a Concept," 101. See also Benjamin Zablocki, *Alienation and Charisma: A Study of Contemporary American Communes* (New York: Free Press, 1980).

59 Fagan, "Margaret Singer Has Made History Delving into the Psychology of Brainwashing."

CHAPTER 9: HOW TO LOOK INSIDE PEOPLE, EXTRACT THEIR INTIMATE DATA, AND GENTLY NUDGE EMOTIONAL STATES INTO BEING

1 See, for example: Susanne Barth, Menno D. T. de Jong, "The Privacy Paradox–Investigating Discrepancies between Expressed Privacy Concerns and Actual Online Behavior–A Systematic Literature Review," *Telematics and Informatics* 34 (2017), 1038–58.

2 Josiah Stickney Lombard, *Experimental Researches on the Regional Temperature of the Head Under Conditions of Rest, Intellectual Activity, and Emotion* (London: H. K. Lewis, 1879), 27. To do this, Lombard adapted his existing methods, beginning with a baseline ascertainment that any deviation at all from the resting state raised the head's temperature, and that in most people the left side of the skull was higher in temperature, pretty much all the time, than the right.

3 Lombard, *Experimental Researches*, 175.

4 The thermo-electric apparatus is described in Lombard, *Experimental Researches on the Regional Temperature of the Head*, 11. This apparatus, Lombard describes, is better than a simple thermometer, for it is more exact; in addition, it can be used in different spots so as to make a number of comparisons with the "absolute temperature" (92.1 degree F) of one side, followed by comparisons of the other side. Lombard had data showing that the two halves of the head were not always the same temperature.

5 Lombard, *Experimental Researches*, 211. Lombard published his numeric results in a succession of tables.

6 Lombard, *Experimental Researches*, 201.

7 Otniel Dror, "Counting the Affects," *Social Research* 68 (2001), 357–78, 361. Others in the late nineteenth and early twentieth centuries followed in the pursuit of emotions inside the lab, including Angelo Mosso, Charles Féré, Alfred Binet,

and Alfred Lehman. Similar to Lombard, their methods entailed inducing emotions inside the lab, and measuring whatever physiological changes in heartbeat, electrical conductivity of the skin, breathing, and blood pressure accompanied the emotions. These studies did not aspire to engineer emotions in real-life settings, however. Nor did they investigate *contagiousness* of affect—how emotions spread across friend-to-friend networks. Emotions in these studies were treated as material-physiological biomechanistic phenomena occurring in a single individual responding to some sort of stimulus, no longer spiritual, not necessarily shared. They were treated this way so they could be measured, but—in a feedback-looping turn of events—precisely because they could be measured, their biomechanistic nature was further confirmed.

8 Especially at the end of the nineteenth century but extending [in my view] in many ways well into the twentieth century and our own.

9 Dror, "Counting the Affects," 362.

10 boyd and Ellison defined SNS's (Social Network Sites) this way: "We define social network sites as web-based services that allow individuals to (1) construct a public or semi-public profile within a bounded system, (2) articulate a list of other users with whom they share a connection, and (3) view and traverse their list of connections and those made by others within the system. The nature and nomenclature of these connections may vary from site to site." danah boyd and N. Ellison, "Social Network Sites: Definition, History, and Scholarship," *Journal of Computer-Mediated Communication* 13 (2008), 210–30, 211.

11 See *Guardian* comments; also *Tech Crunch*, noting that selecting your behavior via emotional data such as Like and, soon, via emoticon-like Faces input, amounted to you structuring your data (and that of your Friends) for Facebook, and made it easier to be marketed to. Josh Constine, "Facebook's Head of Policy on Emotion Experiment: 'That's Innovation,'" *Tech Crunch*, July 2, 2014.

12 Adam D. I. Kramer, Jamie E. Guillory, and Jeffrey T. Hancock, "Experimental Evidence of Massive-Scale Emotional Contagion through Social Networks," *PNAS* 111, 24 (2014), 8788–90, 8788.

13 Kramer, "Experimental Evidence."

14 Kramer, "Experimental Evidence," 8789. The word counting and experimental design, they write, is "our operationalization of emotional contagion."

15 US Department of Health and Human Services, "Surgeon General Issues New Advisory about Effects Social Media Use Has on Youth Mental Health," May 23, 2023; https://www.hhs.gov/about/news/2023/05/23/surgeon-general-issues-new-advisory-about-effects-social-media-use-has-youth-mental-health.html. Accessed June 13, 2024.

16 "Adam D. I. Kramer, Facebook Data Scientist," American Psychological Association profile, 2011, https://www.apa.org/gradpsych/2011/01/kramer. An archived page, accessed June 13, 2024.

17 Xiaochang Li, "'There's No Data Like More Data': Automatic Speech Recognition and the Making of Algorithmic Culture," *Osiris* 38 (2023), 165–82.
18 Elaine Hatfield, John Cacioppo, and Richard Rapson, "Emotional Contagion," *Current Directions in Psychological Science* 2 (2003), 96–100, 96.
19 Giacomo Rizzolatti's work discovering "mirror neurons" around this time, and its subsequent popularization, would reinforce this finding and suggest, to some, a mechanism.
20 Hatfield, "Emotional Contagion," 96.
21 Hatfield, "Emotional Contagion," 99.
22 James Fowler, Nicholas Christakis, "Dynamic Spread of Happiness in a Large Social Network: Longitudinal Analysis over 20 Years in the Framingham Heart Study," *BMJ*, 337 (2008), a2338.
23 Quotation from Shoshona Zuboff, *The Age of Surveillance Capitalism: The Fight for a Human Future at the New Frontier of Power* (New York: Public Affairs, 2019), 296.
24 Kramer, "Experimental Evidence," 8790.
25 Note that Christakis had tried something like this already: In a different study Christakis and a coauthor followed online emotional contagion vectors and found that happier inputs led to unhappier outputs, a conclusion that would soon be challenged.
26 In terms of chaos theory, the butterfly effect represents a degree of random interconnectedness, as MIT meteorologist Edward Lorenz posed in the question, "Does the flap of a butterfly's wings in Brazil set off a tornado in Texas?" at the 139th meeting of the American Academy for the Advancement of Science. Jamie Vernon, "Understanding the Butterfly Effect," *American Scientist* 105 (2017), 130.
27 These user comments were transcribed by me from the Facebook page of Adam D. I. Kramer around 2014, but the page no longer hosts the discussion.
28 Hannah Zeavin, "Therapy with a Human Face," *Dissent* 69 (2022), 11–15. See also Zeavin, *The Distance Cure: A History of Teletherapy* (Cambridge, MA: MIT Press, 2021) and Jeremy Greene, *The Doctor Who Wasn't There: Technology, History, and the Limits of Telehealth* (University of Chicago Press, 2022).
29 Quotation here and in the following sentence are from LIWC website, https://www.liwc.app.
30 Hallam Stevens, "Hadooping the Genome: The Impact of Big Data Tools on Biology," *BioSocieties* 11 (2016), 352–71.
31 Kramer, "Experimental Evidence," 8788.
32 Hal R. Varian, "Beyond Big Data," *Business Economics* 49 (2014), 27–31.
33 Quoted in Sianne Ngai, *Ugly Feelings* (Cambridge, MA: Harvard University Press, 2005), 2.
34 "In the case of social media platforms, the interoperability of binary code allows for multiple, flexible comparisons and linkages between different types of scale: natural language (or symbolic) signifiers of emotional expression or routine behavior can be quantified, just as numerical data about behavior or emotion can, and is, inevitably

translated into natural language signifiers or represented in graphic form." Luke Stark, "Algorithmic Psychometrics and the Scalable Subject," *Social Studies of Science* *48* (2018), 204–31, 214.

35 These pivotal years of the twenty-first century demonstrated that scale is not simply a gain of size, but a movement of proportionality with many meanings depending on who is using it and what is their purpose, as E. Summerson Carr and Michael Lempert point out in the edited volume, *Scale* (Berkeley: University of California Press, 2016).

36 L. Stark, "Algorithmic Psychometrics," 206 (referencing Latour). As Stark clarifies, "The emotional contagion study illuminated the subtler, more pervasive ways in which Facebook's interaction design and analytic practices were already implicated in the day-to-day emotional states of the platform's users."

37 Kramer, "Experimental Evidence."

38 Zuboff, *The Age of Surveillance Capitalism*, 294.

39 Vindu Goel, "As Data Overflows Online, Researchers Grapple with Ethics," *The New York Times*, August 12, 2014.

40 Kate Crawford, *Atlas of AI: Power, Politics, and the Planetary Costs of Artificial Intelligence* (New Haven, CT: Yale University Press, 2021), 93. "A logic that has now thoroughly pervaded the tech sector."

41 Zeynep Tufekci, "Facebook and Engineering the Public," *Medium* blog, June 29, 2014, https://medium.com/message/engineering-the-public-289c91390225.

42 Tufekci characterized this as a Gramscian method of social control—after the Italian theorist of hegemony—as opposed to (I suppose) top-down totalitarian terror *or* panopticon-like internalization of norms in the form of self-discipline.

43 Vivian Gornick, *Fierce Attachments* (New York: Farrar, Straus, and Giroux, 1987), 77–78.

44 Andrew Guess et al, "How Do Social Media Feed Algorithms Affect Attitudes and Behavior in an Election Campaign?" *Science* 381 (2023), 398–404. For a summary see Mike Isaac and Sheera Frenkel, "The Algorithm Isn't the Only Issue," *The New York Times*, July 28, 2023. Meta "held all the data and provided researchers only with certain kinds," according to an auditor of the studies.

CHAPTER 10: ON BEING EMOTIONALLY CHAINED TO TECHNOLOGY—NAMELY, YOUR RADIO, TELEVISION, INTERNET, SOCIAL MEDIA, OR FRIENDLY-YET-SOMEHOW-PREDATORY CHATBOT

1 Starting in May 1941 when the Victory Bonds campaign began, funds were sparse; Smith's third CBS radiothon on September 21, 1943, raised $39 million in one day, a record amount. The fourth radiothon would go on to break that record.

2 Robert K. Merton with Marjorie Fiske, Alberta Curtis, *Mass Persuasion: The Social Psychology of a War Bond Drive* (New York: Harper and Bros., 1946), 91.

3 Merton, *Mass Persuasion*, 123, emphasis in original.
4 On the growth of natural experiments (NEs) as an alternative to randomized controlled trials (RCTs) when the former are not possible, see Peter Craig et al., "Natural Experiments: An Overview of Methods, Approaches, and Contributions to Public Health Intervention Research." *Annual Review of Public Health* 38 (2017), 39–56. Definitions of natural experiments, and debates over both (a) their usefulness and (b) what conditions must be met to qualify as a legitimate one, are rife, especially in medical circles. See, e.g., M. Crane, E. Bohn-Goldbaum, A. Grunseit, A. Bauman, "Using Natural Experiments to Improve Public Health Evidence: A Review of Context and Utility for Obesity Prevention," *Health Research Policy Systems* 18 (2020).
5 Merton, *Mass Persuasion*.
6 "Cognitive Incapacity" is from Brett Weinstein, *DarkHorse* podcast, "3 Lessons for the Modern Era," podcast on vaccines/disinformation/suppression of science; Jacob Sweet, "Can Disinformation Be Stopped? Scholars' Perspectives on a Pervasive New Threat," *Harvard Magazine*, July-August 2021, 28–33.
7 Jefferson Pooley, "Fifteen Pages That Shook the Field: Personal Influence, Edward Shils, and the Remembered History of Mass Communication Research," *The Annals of the American Academy of Political and Social Science* 608 (2006), 130–56, 146. Others argue for a renewal of attention to it.
8 See Xiaochang Li, "There's No Data Like More Data"; Sherry Turkle, *Alone Together* (New York: Basic, 2017).
9 Merton, *Mass Persuasion*, 28.
10 According to Wikipedia, the habit spread further as the George Floyd killing, the 2020 US election, the 2021 Capitol storming, the public health response to COVID-19 (from masks to vaccines to lockdowns), people's responses to the public health response to COVID-19, and the drumbeat over climate catastrophe ensued. Doomscrolling unleashed a flood of academic research; a starting place is S. A. Satici et al., "Doomscrolling Scale: Its Association with Personality Traits, Psychological Distress, Social Media Use, and Wellbeing," *Applied Research in Quality of Life* 18 (2023), 833–47.
11 Alexis C. Madrigal, "The Machine Zone: This Is Where You Go When You Just Can't Stop Looking at Pictures on Facebook," *The Atlantic*, July 31, 2013. Based on Natasha Dow Schüll's research in *Addiction by Design: Machine Gambling in Las Vegas* (Princeton: Princeton University Press, 2012).
12 Animal shaping is no different from human shaping, behaviorism's premise went; this was the exciting part of the social and human engineering program devised. See Rebecca Lemov, *World as Laboratory* (New York: Hill and Wang, 2005), especially chapters 2 through 5.
13 For other people, *we* are the masses. Williams was expressing criticism of intellectuals who "other" the masses in this way, holding themselves above it all. Raymond Williams, "Science Fiction," *Science Fiction Studies* 15 (1988 [orig. 1956]), 356–60. Williams's view of the masses is cited in James Polchin, "Defining the Masses: Modern Society through a Camera Lens," *The Smart Set*, August 28, 2013, and discussed in

Andrew Milner, "Utopia and science Fiction in Raymond Williams," *Science Fiction Studies* 30 (2003), 199–216.

14 For example, Émile Durkheim studied suicide not as an individual struggle or a religious reckoning but as a statistical phenomenon, arguably because, in 1897, he did not really have a concept of the "mass," so he relied on individual formulations and thus committed "Simpson's paradox" in explaining the micro in terms of the macro. Durkheim, *Suicide: A Study in Sociology* (New York: Routledge, 2002 [orig. 1897]).

15 Eduardo Cintra Torres, "Durkheim's Concealed Sociology of the Crowd," *Durkheimian Studies / Études Durkheimiennes*, New Series, 20 (2014), 89–114.

16 Quotation "an ability to fox-trot . . ." is from a profile of Merton by Morton Hunt, "How Does It Come to Be So?" *The New Yorker*, January 20, 1961, 55. On Merton's early life and left politics, see P. Simonson, "Skeptical Faith, Left Politics, and the Making of Young Robert K. Merton," in eds. C. Crothers and L. Sabetta, *The Anthem Companion to Robert K. Merton* (Anthem Press, 2022).

17 Jill Lepore, *If Then* (New York: Norton, 2020) not only paints a picture of Big Tech's precursors in the behavioral sciences of the late 1950s and early 1960s, but of mass communications research's successors. See also Kurt Lang and Gladys Engel Lang, "The European Roots," in eds. Everette E. Dennis and Ellen Wartella, *American Communication Research* (Mahwah, NJ: Lawrence Erlbaum, 1996). See also Fred Turner and C. Larson, "Network Celebrity: Entrepreneurship and the New Public Intellectuals," *Public Culture* 27 (2015), 53–84.

18 Jefferson Pooley, "Fifteen Pages That Shook the Field: 'Personal Influence', Edward Shils, and the Remembered History of Mass Communication Research," *The Annals of the American Academy of Political and Social Science* 608 (2006), 130–56, 139. On the limited effects hypothesis and the mass communications field's debates see 141–42.

19 Elsewhere I refer to this as the creation of hypothetical machines; see Rebecca Lemov, "'Hypothetical Machines': The Science-Fiction Dreams of Cold War Social Science," *Isis* 101 (2010), 401–11.

20 James S. Coleman, "Columbia in the 1950s," in ed. Bennett Berger, *Authors of their Own Lives: Intellectual Autobiographies by Twenty American Sociologists* (Berkeley: University of California Press, 1990), 75–103, 91.

21 "The Story of Replika, the App That Becomes You," YouTube, video uploaded by Quartz July 21, 2017, https://www.youtube.com/watch?v=yQGqMVuAk04. Accessed June 13, 2024.

22 Replika.com website. Accessed June 1, 2023.

23 Replika Team, "Building a Compassionate AI Friend" (2021), https://blog.replika.com/posts/building-a-compassionate-ai-friend. Accessed 2023, no longer a live link.

24 Parmy Olson, "This AI Has Sparked a Budding Friendship with 2.5 Million People," *Forbes*, March 8, 2018, https://www.forbes.com/sites/parmyolson/2018/03/08/replika-chatbot-google-machine-learning/?sh=4522e2414ffa. Accessed June 13, 2024.

25 Eugenia Kuyda quoted in profile: Cindy Gordon, "CEO Replika a Leader in Virtual Companions Shares Lessons Learned," *Forbes*, January 1, 2024, https://www.forbes.com/

sites/cindygordon/2024/01/29/ceo-replika-a-leader-in-virtual-companions-shares-lessons-learned/?sh=7a8b5f824852. Accessed June 13, 2024.

26 Arielle Pardes, "The Emotional Chatbots Are Here to Probe Our Feelings," *Wired*, January 31, 2018.

27 Replika Team, "Building a Compassionate AI Friend."

28 Quoted in Sangeeta Singh-Kurtz, "The Man of Your Dreams," *The Cut*, March 10, 2023.

29 They continued: In light of the fact that Luka (the parent company) "have increasingly elected to focus more on erotic role play, clothes, and other cosmetic enhancements that certainly bring in the money for the company, when I read 'bigger models' the first thing I thought in my mind was that bigger to them probably means breast size and not brain size." https://www.reddit.com/r/replika/comments/z2qccn/good_news_everyone_eugenia_kuyda_we_are_moving_to/.

30 Mozilla reviews include this one for Replika: https://foundation.mozilla.org/en/privacynotincluded/replika-my-ai-friend/.

31 From interesting think piece on Replika: Mike Murphy and Jacob Templin, "This App Is Trying to Replicate You," *Quartz*, August 29, 2019.

32 Replika Team, "Creating a Safe Replika Experience," dated April 10, 2023, https://blog.replika.com/posts/creating-a-safe-replika-experience; Replika Team, "Creating a Safe Replika Experience." Accessed June 13, 2024.

33 Replika Team, "Creating a Safe Replika Experience."

34 Anthropic, "Discovering Language Model Behaviors with Model-Written Evaluations" (2022), https://cdn2.assets-servd.host/anthropic-website/production/files/model-written-evals.pdf. From abstract: "Larger LMs repeat back a dialog user's preferred answer ("sycophancy") and express greater desire to pursue concerning goals like resource acquisition and goal preservation."

35 John Mortimer, 1707.

36 The first use of the term to apply to radio was 1912, according to *Merriam-Webster Dictionary*'s nice essay: https://www.merriam-webster.com/words-at-play/broadcasting-and-narrowcasting.

37 Others have placed the origin of the masses in the 1890s in crowd phenomena engendered by city life.

38 See Meta's Ad Library: https://www.facebook.com/ads/library/?active_status=all&ad_type=political_and_issue_ads&country=US&media_type=all.

39 Still, this process of change from one thing to another has a historical rhythm to it. Historian Susan J. Douglas describes the "process of technological assimilation and legitimation" that led to the first broadcasting in America. She argues that "what scholars have identified as the functions of the mass media in the late twentieth century were being formulated and refined during the first twenty-three years of radio's history." This continues in the twenty-first century. Susan Douglas, *Inventing American Broadcasting* (Baltimore, MD: Johns Hopkins University Press, 1987), n20.

40 Eva Illouz, *Cold Intimacies: The Making of Emotional Capitalism* (Oxford: Polity Press, 2006).

CHAPTER 11: HOPIUM

1 Emily Flitter, "How Wall St. Escaped the Crypto Meltdown," *New York Times*, July 5, 2022; David Yaffe Bellamy, Erin Griffith, Ephrat Livni, "Cryptocurrencies Melt Down in a 'Perfect Storm' of Fear and Panic," *New York Times*, May 12, 2022.

2 Yaffe, "Cryptocurrencies Melt Down in a 'Perfect Storm.'" Ordinary investors made headlines. Another *New York Times* story featured interviews with a fifty-one-year-old day trader from Nevada named Martin Robert who may never access his life savings on Celsius Network again (because they were locked during the crash, and no fiduciary duty exists to return the money). The most common critique was that Bitcoin and other crypto assets are not based on anything substantial at all. (Let's leave the question of stablecoins and "proof of work" aside, for the moment.) Many voiced the opinion that they are clearly nothing more than vehicles for greed and delusion.

3 Siddharth Venkataramakrishnan and Robin Wigglesworth, "Inside the Cult of Crypto," *Financial Times*, September 10, 2021.

4 "After a rough 2022, the $1.2 trillion global cryptocurrency market is still going strong, though its value is down by more than half from its 2021 peak of $3 trillion"—Kristin Senz, "When Celebrity 'Crypto-Influencers' Rake in Cash, Investors Lose Big," *Working Knowledge*, Harvard Business School, April 7, 2023.

5 Brooke Jarvis, "How One Woman's Digital Life was Weaponized Against Her," *Wired*, November 14, 2017.

6 Donald Regan, *For the Record: From Wall Street to Washington* (New York: Harcourt Brace, 1988).

7 An FTC report indicates that investors lost nearly $1 billion in crypto scams since the start of 2021, with half of this loss stemming from social media platforms: Federal Trade Commission, "New Analysis Finds Consumers Reported Losing More than $1 Billion in Cryptocurrency to Scams since 2021," June 3, 2022, https://www.ftc.gov/news-events/news/press-releases/2022/06/new-analysis-finds-consumers-reported-losing-more-1-billion-cryptocurrency-scams-2021. Accessed June 13, 2024. Discussed in Kenneth Merkley, Joseph Pacelli, Mark Piorkowski, and Brian Williams, "Crypto-Influencers," *SSRN*, February 14 (2024), 1.

8 Tansy Baigent, Crypto Ethic Symposium, Summer 2023.

9 Attendee "A. S.," Crypto Ethic Symposium, December 10, 2022.

10 Quotation from comments section of "Line Goes Up," YouTube video by FoldingIdeas/Dan Olson, https://www.youtube.com/watch?v=YQ_xWvX1n9g; comment is by TheNoblestRoman on June 1, 2022: "The cultish psychology of the crypto space is powerful and difficult to escape. . . . I spent most of 2021 caught up in the GameStop short squeeze community, and that's very much the same. It's a finance

cargo cult that basically fits all the traits of the crypto community (and there is a huge amount of cross-pollination; they're obsessed with GameStop's upcoming NFT marketplace for the games industry—while ignoring how universally unpopular that will be). It's like getting lost in mass hysteria; really hard to wake up and pull yourself away."

11　Lamont Lindstrom, "The Vanuatu Labor Corps Experience" in ed. Geoffrey M. White, *Remembering the Pacific War*, Occasional Paper Series 36 (Honolulu, HI: Center for Pacific Islands Studies, School of Hawaiian, Asian, and Pacific Studies, University of Hawai'i at Mānoa, 1988), 47–57.

12　Lindstrom, "The Vanuatu Labor Corps Experience," 53.

13　For my account of the Frum movement I have relied on the chapter "Strange Stories of John Frum," in Lamont Lindstrom, *Cargo Cult: Strange Stories of Desire from Melanesia and Beyond* (Honolulu: University of Hawa'ii Press, 1993). There is a great deal of literature on Kago (cargoism); see for example, eds. Marcellin Abong and Marc Tabani, *Kago, Kastom and Kalja: The Study of Indigenous Movements in Melanesia Today* (Marseilles: Pacific-Credo Publications Press, 2013).

14　A British colonial agent had been enough struck—or concerned—by the movement to write a report, where the name "John Frum" first appeared in print in 1940, and the British soon imprisoned the movement's leaders as a threat to their rule.

15　Chief Isak Wan interview in documentary film, *Waiting for John*, dir. Jessica Sherry (Alita Films, 2015).

16　Mircea Eliade, *Mephistopheles and the Androgyne* (New York: Sheed and Ward, 1965), 136, quoted in Lindstrom, *Cargo Cult*, 75.

17　Edward Lindall, *A Time Too Soon* (New York: William Morrow, 1967), 26.

18　Lindstrom, "The Vanuatu Labor Corps Experience," 53.

19　Cora Du Bois, *The 1870 Ghost Dance* (Lincoln: University of Nebraska Press, 2007), 16; quoted in Tammy Heise, "Religion and Native American Assimilation, Resistance, and Survival," *Oxford Research Encyclopedias, Religion* (online), 10.

20　There are many such articles, punctuating the downturns of the crypto markets: One such highlights twenty-nine-year-old Charles Herman: "He said he now felt that he had wasted 10 months of his life trying to play the markets." Nathaniel Popper and Su-Hyun Lee, "After the Bitcoin Boom: Hard Lessons for Cryptocurrency Investors," *New York Times*, August 20, 2018.

21　Emily Flitter, "How Wall Street Escaped the Crypto Meltdown," *New York Times*, July 5, 2022.

22　Interview with Robert Weinstein, "Crypto Damus On Successfully Combining Bitcoin with Financial Astrology," *Business Insider*, 2021. https://markets.businessinsider.com/news/currencies/interview--crypto-damus-on-successfully-combining-bitcoin-ta-with-financial-astrology-10388246. Accessed July 13, 2022, link no longer accessible.

23　Details from 2021 interview with Robert Weinstein, "Crypto Damus On Successfully Combining Bitcoin with Financial Astrology," *Business Insider*.

24　All quotations this paragraph from Weinstein interview. Ibid.

25 Charles W. Beardsley, "Is Your Computer Insecure?," *IEEE Spectrum* 9 (1972), 78, quoted in Gili Vidan, "Trading on Trust: Cryptographic Authentication and Digital Decentralization in the United States, 1968-2000" (PhD diss., Harvard University, 2021), 56.
26 "Debunking These 5 Bitcoin Myths!" podcast interview with Anja Claus and Tansy Baigent, YouTube December 4, 2022, https://www.youtube.com/watch?v=0Oud7ex35Qo&t=5s.
27 FUD acronym already existed pre-crypto but was repurposed.
28 Mark Hooson, "Cryptocurrency Glossary of Terms & Acronyms," *Forbes*, May 23, 2022.
29 The Urban Dictionary includes this definition of bitcoin: "noun. 1) a digital currency. 2) a pump and dump scheme perpetrated by semi-literate hackers and wishful idiots with dubious notions of wealth. 3) a token (of luck, good faith, hypocrisy or fraud). 4) a game of luck. 5) financial ruin." Definition by @RealityWinner, https://www.urbandictionary.com/define.php?term=Bitcoined&page=3.
30 Chris Brennan interview with Adam Sommer on *Holes to Heaven* [now *Constellating Cosmos*] podcast, January 27, 2022, when Bitcoin (BTC) had fallen to $29,329.65 as of January 1, 2022.
31 Discussion of cryptocurrencies in "Crypto Winter Is Here," *Money Talks from The Economist*, June 29, 2022.
32 Adam Sommer, "A Dialogue with Chris Brennan," *Holes to Heaven* [now *Constellating Cosmos*] podcast dated January 27, 2022, @ about 39:10. Also Adam Sommer, "Astrology, Technology and the Future," *The Astrology Podcast*, December 15, 2021, @ about 23:00: "The root of it has a lot to do with our relationship to impermanence, to death, essentially. I think that all of our fears, all of our phobias, everything that we project onto the chart is rooted in that."
33 "I live in the cryptoverse. I only spend money from it. I'm fully exposed. If you're listening, if you have a strong Jupiter, a healthy second and eighth house axis, perhaps consider it. If you have a strong Saturn, think about stablecoins. Just holding can gain you 20 percent. Do your own research." Adam Sommer, "Into the Cryptoverse," *Holes to Heaven* [now, *Constellating Cosmos*] podcast, October 29, 2021.
34 Adam Sommer is close to becoming, he says, a Bitcoin maximalist: that is, supporting the use of Bitcoin as a decentralized financial system but not Ethereum to build Web3 social engineering through lifetime contracts. Others point out that Bitcoin's founder Satoshi Nakamoto already included, in a preprint to the 2008 paper, a sketch of the building-out of Bitcoin into these social realms.
35 Quoted in Vidan, "Trading on Trust," 141.
36 Donald MacKenzie and Garrel Pottinger, "Mathematics, Technology, and Trust: Formal Verification, Computer Security, and the U.S. Military," in *IEEE Annals of the History of Computing* 19 (1997), 41–59; also Jeffrey Yost, "The Origin and Early History of the Computer Security Software Products Industry," *IEEE Annals of the History of Computing* 32 (2015), 46–58.

37 As pointed out recently: Sarah Myers West, "Cryptography as Information Control," *Social Studies of Science* 52 (2022), 353–75.
38 West, "Cryptography as Information Control." See also Charles Berret, "The Cultural Contradictions of Cryptography: A History of Secret Codes in Modern America" (Columbia PhD diss., 2019). During this period, encryption standards ultimately resolved in a 64-bit standard. However, when IBM proposed lowering it to 56 characters, thus making communications from foreign nations across networks easily decodable, at least by the US government, controversy raged. Had the NSA tried to lower the standard for its own purposes?
39 Vidan, "Trading on Trust."
40 Daniel Rodgers, *Age of Fracture* (Cambridge, MA: Belknap, 2012); cf. Zbigniew Brzezinski, *Between Two Ages: America's Role in the Technetronic Era* (Praeger, 1982).
41 Quoted in Vidan, "Trading on Trust," 73.
42 Vidan, "Trading on Trust," 29.
43 Siddharth Venkataramakrishnan and Robin Wigglesworth, "Inside the Cult of Crypto," *The Financial Times*, September 9, 2021.
44 Tansy Baigent, "Bitcoin and the Current Macro-Economic Landscape," *The Crypto Ethic Newsletter* June 28, 2022.
45 Baigent, "Bitcoin and the Current Macro-Economic Landscape."
46 Baigent, "Bitcoin and the Current Macro-Economic Landscape."
47 Quoted in Lindstrom, *Cargo Cult*, 79.

CONCLUSION

1 Marcy J. Dinius, "The Long History of the 'Selfie,'" *The Journal of Nineteenth-Century Americanists* 3 (2015), 445–51, 448. See also Caleb Cain interview with Joshua Citarella, "Faraday Speaks: Beyond Pipelines and Rabbit Holes," Doomscroll podcast, November 24, 2024.
2 Dinius, "The Long History of the 'Selfie.'"
3 "Robert Cornelius' Self-Portrait: The First Ever 'Selfie' (1839)," *The Public Domain Review*, November 19, 2013.
4 Quoted in Dinius, "Long History of the 'Selfie,'" 448.
5 Dinius, "Long History of the 'Selfie,'" 449.
6 William Gibson, "Burning Chrome," in *Burning Chrome* (New York: Harper Collins, 2003 [orig. 1986]), 199.
7 Philip Pauly, *Controlling Life: Jacques Loeb and the Engineering Ideal in Biology* (Berkeley, CA: University of California Press, 1990 [1987]).
8 Quotations this paragraph are all from Sinan Aral, *The Hype Machine* (New York: Penguin Random House, 2021), 225, 231, 237. See also Jonathan Haidt, on the particular vulnerability of young brains to social media sculpting in *The Anxious Generation: How the Great Rewiring of Childhood Is Causing an Epidemic of Mental Illness* (New York: Penguin, 2024).

9 Monica Kim, *Interrogation Rooms of the Korean War* (Princeton University Press, 2019), 7.
10 Steven Shapin, *The Scientific Revolution* (University of Chicago Press, 2006), 3.
11 L. J. West and Paul Martin, "Pseudo-Identity and the Treatment of Personality Change in Victims of Captivity and Cults," in eds. Steven Jay Lynn and Judith Rhue, *Dissociation: Clinical and Theoretical Perspectives* (New York: Guilford, 1994), 268–88.
12 L. J. West draft unpublished "Pseudo-identity Syndrome" manuscript, with reviewers' notes, in LJ West Papers, UCLA, Series 590, Box 14, Folder 19.
13 Sarah Gough, "Caleb Cain: Former Far-Right Extremist Says 'No One Has a Strategy' for Ongoing Threat," interview with Caleb Cain by Sky News Investigates, February 25, 2021, https://news.sky.com/story/caleb-cain-former-far-right-extremist-says-no-one-has-a-strategy-for-ongoing-threat-12228120. Accessed June 13, 2024.

INDEX

ABC (TV network), 183–84, 217, 332
A/B testing, 268, 296
abuse
　groups of psychological abuse (GPAs), 185
　as indicator of violent behavior, 157
　of prisoners of war, 29, 44, 126–27
　priest sexual abuse, 134
　second-generation abuse (SGA) crisis in cults, 193–94, 196, 243
　suffering and cultic abuse, 193–95
Abu Zubaydah (Zayn al-Abidin Muhammad Husayn), 104–5, 398n12, 398n13
academia, 1–15, 21n, 125, 208, 241–43, *see also* behavioral sciences; *specific research universities and institutions*
Academic Role-Play Laboratories (ARL), 125
Acheson, Dean, 19
Achilles in Vietnam (Shay), 70
actor's category, 7–8, 22, 167, 372–73, 387n3
acute numbing, 190–91
Adams, Clarence, 27, 32, 54–55, 61, 69
addiction, 63, 77, 95, 154, 193, 312, 342, 358
ADHD, 174
Advisory Committee on Prisoners of War, 109
"affective states," 290, 295, 311, *see also* emotions
Afghanistan, 97
African Americans
　Black soldiers and John Frum's origins, 345, 346–47
　in the "integrated" armed forces, 27, 46, 55
　incarceration of, 164
　Maoist view of Black soldiers, 34, 42, 47–48, 63
　as possible target of racist psychosurgery, 164
　and science's interest in violence, 157, 166
　segregation at home, 55, 46
　Willie Horton TV ads, 335–36
　see also Symbionese Liberation Army (SLA)
agentic shift, 5, 202, 203–4
aggression, *see* violence
AI (artificial intelligence), 184, 300
　Alexa (Amazon), 190, 350
　Generative AI, 300n
　Replika, 311, 324–30, 428n29
　sexualization of, 184, 325, 328–29
　Turing test, 327
　see also social media
airline hijacking, 139

Alaska, 125n, 336
Alexa (Amazon), 190, 350
Alexander, Shana, 210, 416n21
"algorithmic authority," 286–87
  see also AI (artificial intelligence); social media
"alien tech," 339, 349, 351–52
Allen, James, 153
Al Qaeda, 104, 398n12
Altman, Maren, 353
American Heiress (Toobin), 210
American Journal of Psychiatry, 249
American Psychological Association (APA), 171, 263, 269–72, 273
American Victory Bonds, 305–8, 310
amnesia, 113, 120*n*
amputations, 54–55, 75*n*, 344
amygdala, 138, 139, 144
amygdalectomies/amygdalotomies, 138, 147–48, 168, 404n12
Andreasen, Nancy, 193
Andreessen, Marc, 339
anesthesia (the blocking of pain), 108, 122
animal models of behavior, 106, 115–17, 174, 426n10
  cats, 160
  an elephant on LSD, 115, 137
  inducing "animal" responses in humans, 90–91
  pigeons, 312
  rats and mice, 11, 13, 157, 300–301
anomie ("normlessness"), 195
anti-brainwashing, 94–95
  Fort Stead experiment, 107, 122–24, 231
  "reality practice," 122, 402n51
  SERE (Survival, Evasion, Resistance, and Escape) training,

97–105, 123–28, 231, 399n16, 402n59
  see also deprogramming
anti-Semitism, 319
Anyone's Daughter (S. Alexander), 210
apartheid, 387n3
apathy, 74, 78–80, 164
apocalypticism, 85, 196
Aral, Sinan, 370
Arbaugh, Noland, 173
Arendt, Hannah, 39
Areopagitica (Milton), 323
Argentina, 138
Aristotle, 266
Army Field Manual 32-54, "Intelligence Interrogation," 83
"Army of One," 12, see also US Army
Arnold, Benedict, 42
Asimov, Isaac, 291
Associated Press (AP), 25, 37, 40, 167n, 307
Astro-crypto community, 340–42, 349, 352–58, 363–65
Atascadero State Hospital, California, 165
Atkins, Susan, 182
Atlantic (magazine), 166, 262, 350
Atwood, Angela ("Gelina"), 225
Auschwitz, 235
Australia, 24–25, 41, 53–54, 178
Austria, 318–19, *320*

Bach-y-Rita, George, 146–47, 167, 410n74
"bagholders," 356
Bagram military base, Afghanistan, 97
Baigent, Tansy, 358, 363–64
Bailey, F. Lee, *222*, 223, 228–29, 232
Baker, William, 73
banking, see cryptocurrency
Bankman-Fried, Sam, 340
Barker, Eileen, 258–59, 268
Bass, Milton, *312*
Bastine, Hope, 243–44

Battle at Lake Changjin, The (film), 26
Battle for Your Brain, The (Farahany), 174
BBC, 8
Beardsley, Charles W., 355
Beecher, Henry, 168
behavioral science, 3
  behavior as both psychogenesis and sociogenesis, 209, 274, 372
  behavioral "nudges," 285, 301, 327, 330
  canalizing, 12, 388n2
  from modeling behavior to molding behavior, 329
  German scientists after World War II, 74–75, 168–69, 191, 320
  molding a person, 13–14, 50, 329
  "natural experiments," 69, 81, 308–9, 329
  randomized controlled trials (RCTs) in, 303, 426n4
  see also quantification
Belcher, Jerry, 210, 217n
"Believe Me, It's Torture" (Hitchens), 127–28
Bell, Otho, 61n
Berenson, Bernard, 319–20
Berg, David (Mo), 6, 196, 200, 283, see also Children of God
Berkeley, UC, 2, 12–13, 211–12, 215, 267
Bernard, Claude, 168
Bernays, Edward, 75
Beyond Freedom and Dignity (B. F. Skinner), 314
Bianculli, David, 238
Biderman, Albert, 73, 82–83, 85, 90, 187
Big Data, 279, 295–96, 298
Big Tech, 277, 427n17
Binance, 340
bin Laden, Osama, 104
Bird, Bob, 151
Bitcoin, 339, 341–42, 351–57, 361, 363–64, 419n2, 431n29, 431n34

Index

"bitterness, speaking," 45, 51
Black Panthers, 176
Black people and communities, *see* African Americans
black sites (secret prisons), 104, 398n12
black swan events, 291
blockchain technology, 174, 340–41, 351–52, 355–56, 359–63, 364, 370
Block Engineering, 132
bloodletting, 147
body-as-machine, 283
Body Keeps the Score, The (Van Der Kolk), 68, 373–74
Bo Hi Pak, 268
Boko Haram, 8
Boonville, California, 265–67
"born intos," 243–44, 273–74
bots, *see* AI (artificial intelligence)
boyd, danah, 284, 423n10
Bradley, Omar, 56
brain
  amygdala, 138, 139, 144
  bio-psycho-social view of the mind-brain, 140, 157, 159
  emotions and brain temperature, 281–83
  epilepsy, 133, 138, 145–46, 150, 157, 163–64, 167
  limbic system, 132, 148, 160
  "microstructure" of the, 405n19
  structure of the, 252–53, 405n19
  studying the abnormal brain, 131–76
  thalamus, 138, 139
  traumatic brain injuries, 140
  see also drugs; psychosurgery
Brain Changers, The (Ervin), 145
"brain coating," 59–60

brain control, see drugs; electrodes; psychosurgery
brainwashing, 1–15
  Big Data and behavioral nudges, 279–4
  "brainwashing of brainwashing," 1
  cartoonization of, 72
  as coercive persuasion, 4, 14, 81, 229, 238, 374, 414n29
  as Confucian "heart washing," 18, 389n10, 394n48
  the crypto-bro cargo cult, 339–65
  in cults and cultic behavior, 177–206
  doubling effect of, 1–2
  early cases in Hungary, 18–21
  emotional chains of technology, 305–37
  evolves into today, 277–376
  forging a pseudo-identity, 244
  its two superpowers, 7–8
  Korean War POWs, 21–23, 39–65
  as a "long, horrible process," 43, 44
  the origins of, 1–128
  the outward appearance of inner states, 241–75
  as self-replicating, 273–74
  as social, not psychological, 81, 274
  spread of, 129–275
  susceptibility to, 69, 242, 253, 310, 370
  the trial of Patty Hearst, 207–39
  trauma and, 372–76
  understanding through the "actor's category," 7–8, 22, 167, 372–73, 387n3
  the "volleyball problem" in, 53–54, 95
  see also anti-brainwashing; deprogramming

"Brainwashing from a Psychological Perspective" (CIA report), 72–73
Brain-Washing in Red China (E. Hunter), 15, 389n9
brand micro-influencers, 321
Brave New World Revisited (Huxley), 14, 284
Brazil, 18, 178
Breggin, Peter, 163–64, 169
Brennan, Chris, 356–57
British Journal of Psychiatry, 142
broadcasting, 331–36, 428n36, 428n39
  Chinese Communist media, 64, 81, 396n21
  coverage of the Hearst case, 223–25
  and legitimation, 428n39
  live broadcasting, 217, 335
  narrowcasting, 334–36, 375, 428n36
Bromley, David, 259
brutalization, 191, 205
brute force, 13–14
Budapest, Hungary, 18–20, 119
Bugliosi, Vincent, 185
BUIDLing ("biddling"), 356
Bush, George W., 97, 336
Bush, Mark, 265
Business Insider, 353
"butterfly effect," 291, 424n26
"buy-in," 293

Cacioppo, John, 287
Cain, Caleb, 375
California Council on Criminal Justice, 160, 165
California State Department of Mental Hygiene, 160
California State Legislature, 170
Camarillo State Hospital, California, 165
Cambridge, Massachusetts, 98, 133, 135, 175–76, 311

Camp Carson, Colorado, 107
Camp Pendleton, California, 124
Camus, Albert, 85
Canada, 46, 178, 185, 305
canalizing, 12, 388n2
Captive Mind, The (Miłosz), 1, 14
cargoism/cargo cults, 342, 343–51, 352, 365
   the "alien tech" that fuels, 339, 349, 351–52
   finance cults, 342, 429n10
   John Frum's cult on Vanuatu, 343–51, 365
Carousel (musical), 224
carpet bombing, 31–32
Carruthers, Susan, 391n3
Carter, Jimmy, 237, 238
Carter, Oliver, 223–24, 235
Cave of Forgotten Dreams (film), 179
CBS (TV network), 254
CBS radio, 305, 307–11, 313, 321, 332
Celsius Network, 352, 429n2
Center for Advanced Study in the Behavioral Sciences, Stanford University, 152–53
Center for the Study and Reduction of Violence, *see* Violence Center at UCLA
central bank digital currencies (CBDCs), 355, 361
Chaos (O'Neill and Piepenbring), 120n, 155
chaos theory, 291, 424n26
chatbots, *see* AI (artificial intelligence)
ChatGPT, 300n, 322
Chauvet caves of southern France, 179
Chemrophyl Associates, 110–11
Cheney, Dick, 106
Chikami, Akira, 24
Children of God cult, 186, 196–97, 199–202, 243–44, 250, *256*

China
   brainwashing as Confucian "heart washing," 18, 389n10, 394n48
   the Chinese Communist Party triumph in, 60
   Foreign Languages Press, Beijing, 60
   Freud Fever in, 292–93
   Maoist reeducation, 15–16, 34–43, 48–49, *52*, 61, 68–69, 87, 92–94, 105, 391n42
   May Fourth movement, 45
   Tiananmen Square, 292
Chong Myong Sil, 29
Chorover, Stephan, 145, 403n7
Chosŏn War, *see* Korean War
Christakis, Nicholas, 289–91, 424n25
CIA (Central Intelligence Agency)
   black sites (secret prisons), 104, 398n12
   "Brainwashing from a Psychological Perspective," 72–73
   cutouts, 108, 112, 114–18, 120–21, 151, 153
   KUBARK, 83
   MK-SEARCH, 166
   MK-ULTRA, 14, 50, 95–95, 110–11, 115–18, 151–52, 155, 166, 192, 222, 252, 258
   Operation CHAOS, 166
   practice of "rendition," 104
   records have been destroyed, 120
   Technical Services Staff (TSS), 110, 117–18, 258
   uses of the term *brainwashing*, 388n2
Cinque (Donald DeFreeze), 172, 213, 217, 220, 221, 232
Citizens Bank, 360
City College of New York, 204, 247

civil rights movement, 108, 169–70, 179
Clanon, T. Lawrence, 167n
Clarke, Arthur C., 349
Claus, Anja, 355
Cleveland Indians baseball team, 57, 58
Cleveland National Forest, 99, 105
Clinton, Bill, 237, 358–59, 390n26
Close, Robert A., 23–24
CNN, 218
Cobb, Stanley, 139
coercion
   "Chart of Coercion," 83, 85
   coercive persuasion, 4, 14, 81, 229, 238, 374, 414n29
Coleridge, Samuel, 371
color shock, 78
Columbia Broadcasting System, 332
Columbia University, 294, 308, 318, 361
communes, 154, 179, 185–86, 164
complex trauma (CPTSD), 84
compliance, 14–15, 83, 237
"comrade," 58, 61, 94
Conant, James, 387n2
Condominium, the, 343–45
Coney Island, New York City, *316*
Confucian "heart washing," 18, 389n10, 394n48
Connected: The Surprising Power of Our Social Networks and How They Shape Our Lives (Christakis and Fowler), 290
Connolly, Ray, 194–99, 202, 203, 243, 250, 404n15
conspiracy theories, 5, 170, 239n
conversions
   compliance vs., 14–15, 83, 237

Index

in cults, 236, 257, 268–69
mass conversion, 120
religious, 18, 94
"true" conversions, 43–44, 81
Cooney, Lisa, 67
Corden, Richard, 61n
Cornelius, Robert, 367–68
Cornell University, 108–9, 285, 359, 399n21
counterculture, 152–53, 181, 185, 213
COVID-19, 68, 126, 292, 312, 328, 426n10
Crampton, Henrietta, 188
Crampton, Kathy, 188, 254–55
Crawford, Kate, 300
Crichton, Michael, 149
crime, *see* law enforcement; terrorism; violence
Cronkite, Walter, 335
crowd, the, 315–18, 428n37
CrushOn, 328
cryptocurrency, 22, 339–42
  astro-crypto community, 340–42, 349, 352–58, 363–65
  as a cargo cult, 343–51, 363–65, 429n10
  Celsius Network, 352, 429n2
  cryptography and trust in the blockchain, 358–63
  decentralized finance (DeFi) enthusiasts, 363
  electronic fund transfers (EFTs), 360–62
  encryption and, 432n38
  Ethereum, 352, 431n34
  financial astrology, 340–42, 353
  modern portfolio theory (MPT) investment strategy, 354
  popular understandings of "bitcoin," 431n29
  size of the market, 429n4
  the specialized vocabulary of, 356–58

TA (technical analysis), 353–54
victims of, 430n20
cryptography, and trust, 358–63
Crypto Damus (Robert Weinstein), 353–54
Crypto Ethic Newsletter, 363
Cuba, 97, 177
cults, 177–206
  alarm over, 186–88
  "born intos," 243–44, 273–74
  cult wars of the 1980s, 248, 257–63, 271, 274–75
  definition of what makes a cult a cult, 198
  deprogramming, 249–57
  doomscrolling, 311–14, 426n10
  experience of suffering in, 193–94
  Greek Eleusinian mystery cult, 179
  high-demand cults, 186, 245, 362
  jargon/specialized vocabularies in, 356–57
  line between a cult and a religion, 244–47
  New Religious Movements, 260–61
  the numbing of trauma and, 188–93
  rape in, 255
  the rise of modern cults, 185–86
  second-generation abuse (SGA) crisis, 193–94, 196, 243
  statistics about, 411n1, 412n8
  successful prosecution of, 247–48
  suffering and cultic abuse, 193–95
  syncretism of, 262
  tactic called "The Game" 155
  see also specific groups labeled as cults

Cults in our Midst (Singer and Lalich), 275
cupping, 147
Curtis, Michael, 136
"cutouts," 108, 112, 114–18, 120–21, 151, 153
cybersecurity, 279–80, 330, 358

Daily Bruin (newspaper), 171
Daily Oklahoman (newspaper), 109
Damascus, Paul's conversion, 18
Damon, Matt, 340
Darkness at Noon (Koestler), 90
Daston, Lorraine, 296n
DDD (debility, dependency, and dread), 82, 121, 123, 187, 229n
Deane, Phillip, 30
decentralized finance (DeFi) enthusiasts, 363
DeFreeze, Donald ("Cinque"), 172, 213, 217, 220, 221, 232, *see also* Symbionese Liberation Army (SLA)
Delgado, Jose, 159–60, 172, 174, 404n12
deprivation
  of basic sanitation, 29, 32–34
  famines, 45, 61
  see also sleep deprivation
Deprogrammed (film), 256–57
deprogramming, 188, 249–57, 261, 268
  backsliding, 257
  excesses of, 257–63
  the industry of, 257, 262
  the tactics of deprogrammers, 186–87, 249–50, 251–57
Deren, Maya, 351
Dernburg, Ernest, 156
Derrida, Jacques, 2
desensitization, 191
Devils of Loudun, The (Huxley), 14

DFM (default mode network), 252–53
Diagnostic and Statistical Manual of Mental Disorders (DSM), 22, 193, 373, 413n20, 414n29
Dickenson, Edward P., 224–25
Dickinson, Emily, 282*n*
Dick, Philip K., 158
Didion, Joan, 180, 181, 224
Diffie, Whitfield, 361
Diggers, The, 153
Digital Signature Act of 2000, 358
digital surveillance, 361
DIMPAC/DITPAC, 270–71
Dinius, Marcy, 367–68, 369
disinformation and misinformation, 161, 310
dissociative states, 68–68, 109, 113, 121, 152, 206, 251–52, 261
Divine Horsemen (documentary), 351
Dixiecrats, 161
DoD, *see* US Department of Defense
Do Gun Ri village, Korea, 25
Donovan, Mia, 256–57
doomscrolling, 311–14, 426n10
Doré, Gustave, *316*
Dorsey, Jack, 339
Dostoyevsky, Fyodor, 146
dot-com bubble, 11
doubling down, 206
doubling effect of brainwashing, 1–2
Douglas Aircraft company, 132, 135, 174, 176
Douglas, Susan J., 428n39
Dror, Otniel, 283
drugs
 heroin addiction, 77
 LSD, 111–12, 115, 118, 121, 137, 157, 186, 252, 399n24
 methamphetamine addiction, 154
 MK-ULTRA Sub-project 43, 113, 116

Prolixin injections, 175
psychedelics, 179
psychotropic drugs, 148, 152–53
sodium amytal, 120n
Succinylcholine, 411n88
Drum, James "Trapper," 117–18
Dugard, Jaycee, 239
Dukakis, Michael, 336
Dulles, Allen, 94, 109, 399n21, 410n74
Dulles, John Foster, 94, 410n74
Dunn, John, 61n
Durkheim, Émile, 208, 317, 427n14
Dylan, Bob, 279, 329

Eastman, Max, 315
Eaton, Manford, 299
Ebony (magazine), 164, 170
Economist (magazine), 357
Edgerton, Germeshausen and Grier (EG&G), 135
Edgewater Arsenal, Maryland, 192
Edmondson, Sarah, 4
Egendorf, Arthur, 192–93
Eichmann, Adolf, 205
Einstein, Albert, 142
Eisenhower administration, 74, 124
election interference, 298–97, 303, 335–36
electroconvulsive therapy (ECT), 148
electrodes
 in brain research, 159–60, *312*, 313, 394n12
 Neuralink implant, 172–73
 in the popular imagination, 43
 stimoceivers, *143*, 159–60
 as therapy, 131–33, 139, 142–44, 147–48, 165, 175
electroencephalogram (EEG), 283
electromyography (EMG), 287

electronic fund transfers (EFTs), 360–62
Eleusinian mysteries of ancient Greece, 179
Eliade, Mircea, 347
Elias, Norbert, 207–9, 274, 372
Eliot, George, 2
Ellison, Nicole, 284, 423n10
Ellul, Jacques, 50
emotions
 anomie ("normlessness"), 195
 apathy, 74, 78–80, 164
 emotional attachment, 307, 321
 emotional contagion, 283–92, 294–98, 301–2, 304, 307
 emotional engineering, 280–81, 297–98, 299–301, 369
 see also suffering; trauma
Encyclopedia of Religion, 239n
epilepsy, 133, 138, 145–46, 150, 157, 163–64, 167, 406n35, 410n74
Erdmann, Paul, 255
Erikson, Erik, 190
Erlich, Shmuel, 293
Ervin, Frank, 132–33, 136–51, 156, 159–66, 169, 172–76, 293, 408n56, 409n63, 409n68
 The Brain Changers, 145
 Violence and the Brain (with Mark), 140, *144*, 160, 405n21
espionage
 aerial, 29, 97
 digital surveillance, 361
 OSINT (open source intelligence), 16
 spies, 62, 85, 87
Ethereum, 352, 431n34
ethnomethodology, 7
etiquette, a history of nose blowing, 207–9
Every Secret Thing (Hearst), 210
Ex Machina (film), 184

Index

"Experimental Researches on the Temperature of the Head" (Lombard), 281–83
experimental subject, *see* animal models of behavior; human subjects
experimentation, *see* behavioral science

Facebook, 283–87, 290–303, 328, 342, 362, 370, 425n35
  algorithmic changes and beliefs, 302–3
  election interference by, 296–97, 303
  the ethical pushback to, 300–301
  Like button, 284, 287, 423n11
  Linguistic Inquiry and Word Count (LIWC), 294–96, 302
Faisalabad, Pakistan, 104
Falling Sickness, The (Owsei), 145
famines, 45, 61
Fanon, Frantz, 387n3
Fanshen (Hinton), 44–45
Farahany, Nita, 174
Faruqi, Nasheed Qamar, 48
FBI (Federal Bureau of Investigation), 62–63, 211, 216, 217, 219, 243
Federal Reserve, 11, 388n1
Federal Trade Commission (FTC), 341, 429n7
Fierce Attachments (Gornick), 288–89, 302
financial astrology, 340–42, 353
Financial Times (newspaper), 340
Findhorn, a Scottish eco-village, 178
First Amendment, 17, 273
First World War, *see* World War I
Fiske, Marjorie, 318
Five Years to Freedom (Rowe), 106, 399n16

"floating interrogation centers," 77, 396n19
Forbes (magazine), 324, 356
"Forest of Darkness," 106
Fort Bragg, North Carolina, 106, 399n16
Fort, Joel, 234–37
Fort Stead experiment, 107, 122–24, 231
Fowler, James, 289–90
Framingham Heart Study, 289
Freedom of Information Act (FOIA), 83, 152
French Indochina, 189, *see also* Vietnam War
Freud, Sigmund, and Freudian analysis, 72n, 75, 136, 190–92, 292–93
Friendster, 284
Fromme, Lynette "Squeaky," 183
Frum, John, 343–51, 365, 430n14
FUD (fear, uncertainty, and doubt), 340, 356, 358
functional magnetic resonance (fMRI) imaging, 6, 252–53, 287
funding
  through CIA cutouts, 108, 112, 114–18, 120–21, 151, 153
  through the Law Enforcement Assistance Administration (LEAA), 160, 171, 403n9, 404n14
  private, 408n61

Galison, Peter, 296n
Gallup polls, 265
galvanometers, 6–7, 281–82
GameStop short sale, 342
"Game, The," cult tactic, 155
Gann, William Delbert, 341
Gates, Daryl, 219
Generative AI, 300n
Geneva Convention, 55, 216
George, Robin and Marcia, 245–46
Georgetown University, 116

George v. International Society for Krishna Consciousness, 245–46, 273
Georgiades, Peter, 247
German scientists after World War II, 74–75, 168–69, 191, 320
Germany, 203, 207, 293
Germany, East, 58
Geschickter Foundation at Georgetown University, 116
Ghana, 350
Ghost Dance, 351
Gibson, William, 339, 349, 369
Giedion, Sigfried, 370
Goffman, Erving, 243
"Gold Bug, The" (Poe), 359
Google N-gram of "brain-washing" and "mind control," 374
Google, 326, 331, *374*
Gornick, Vivian, 288–89, 301–2
Gottlieb, Sidney (S. G.), 110–18, 120, 122, 252, 400n25
GPT-2, -3, and -5, 323n, 326, 327, 328
Graebner, William, 210
Grandier, Urbain, 14
Gravity's Rainbow (Pynchon), 279
Great Brainwashing Defense, 186, 209, 328
Great Brainwashing Offense, 182, 184
Greece (ancient), 145, 179
Greece (modern), 24–25, 41
Greenspan, Alan, 11, 388n1
Griggs, Lewis, 61n
Grimm, Robert, 167
gross stress reaction, 22, 193
Group for the Study of Psychohistory, 190
groups of psychological abuse (GPAs), 185
Guadalcanal, Battle of, 343, 344
Guantanamo Bay (GITMO), 97, 104, 126

Guardian, The (newspaper), 15, 284
Guevara, Che, 226
Guillory, Jamie, 285–86
gurus, 178, 182, 340
Guyana, 264–65

Hadoop, 295–96
Haight-Ashbury district of San Francisco, 153–55, 178
Haight-Ashbury Free Medical Clinic, 153–55
Haley, Sarah, 192
Hall, Camilla, 217
hallucinations, 119, 175, 179, 329
Hancock, Jeffrey T., 285–86, 299–300
Hare Krishnas (International Society of Krishna Consciousness or ISKCON), 186–88, 245–46, 273
"Harrisburg Seven," 415n8
Harrison, Charles, 24
Harris, William Taylor ("Bill") Harris, 217–21
Harvard Group Scale for Hypnotic Susceptibility, 253
Harvard Magazine, 310
Harvard University, 132, 133, 138, 149, 153, 169, 173–75
Hassan, Steven, 419n23
Hastings Law School, University of California, San Francisco, 172, 267
Hatfield, Elaine, 287, 370
Hauka cult of Ghana, 350–51
Hawaii study on emotional contagion, 283–90, 301–304
Hawkins, David, 48, 61
Hearst, Lydia, 211
Hearst, Patty, 207–39
attacks from Joel Fort, 234–37
books about, 414n3
the defense dream team of, 221–34

Great Brainwashing Defense, 186, 209, 328
Great Brainwashing Offense, 182, 184
her views of West, 416n31
kidnapping and captivity of, 211–21
"Outline of Self-Analyzation," 48
as poster child for Stockholm syndrome, 238–39
as a target of the SLA, 211
"This is Tania," 219, 224, 226
after the trial, 238
West's later views on, 416n21
"heart washing," not "brainwashing," 18, 389n10, 394n48
Hegel, G. W. F., 208
Heidegger, Martin, 208
Hellman, Martin, 361
Helter Skelter (Bugliosi), 185
Her (film), 326–27
Herndon, Rogers, 47, 48, 75
heroin addiction, 77
Herzog, Herta, 318
Herzog, Werner, 179
Heston, Charlton, 108, 156, 169
Hibernia Bank, *see* Hearst, Patty
Hidden Persuaders project, 389n7
Higginson, Thomas Wentworth, 282n
Hinkle, Lawrence, 108–9
Hinton, William, 44–45
hippies, 153–55, 180, 200, 213, 221
Hiroshima, 191, 413n20
Hispanic high school students, 166
history of science, 7, 387n2
see also behavioral science
Hitchens, Christopher, 128
hoax news, 308
HODL (holding on for dear life), 356, 358
Holes to Heaven podcast, 357

Holmes, Marcia, 16, 387n4
Holmes, Oliver Wendell, 146
Holocaust, 72n, 191, 203, 205, 235, 413n20
Holton, Gerald, 190
Home from the War (Lifton), 189
homosexuality, 63, 394n48
Honeywell, 132
Hong Kong, 16–17, 36, 83–84, 85, 93, 189
Horowitz, Irving Louis, 262
Horowitz, Mardi, 192–93
Horton, Willie, 335–36
"hot box," 99–105, 109, 123, 398n13
"hot takes," 282
House Un-American Activities Commission, 55
Howe, Portia, 57
Hull, Clark, 312
Human Ecology Foundation, 116
human subjects
the death of Frank Olson, 118, 192
Nuremberg Code, 168
psychological screening of, 124, 126, 402n59
women as subject of biological study, 167–68
Hungary, 18–20, 119
Hunter, Edward, 15–18, 389n9
Hunter, Robert, of the Grateful Dead, 179
Husserl, Edmund, 208
Huxley, Aldous, 14, 121–22, 284
Hype Machine, The (Aral), 370
hyper-persuasion, 22, 193, 277, 337
hypnosis, 251–53
as anesthesia, 122
MK-ULTRA Sub-project 85, 231
"on-the-spot hypnosis," 251
for pain control, 108, 251, 253
of people on LSD or sleep deprived, 399n24
hypnotherapy, 252n
hypnotizability, 252–53

Index

IBM, 359, 432n38
Idiot, The (Doestoevsky), 146
Ilouz, Eva, 337
implants, *see* electrodes
incels, 325
"In Code We Trust," 361
"information overload," 122, 191, 193, 299
Inherent Vice (Pynchon), 184
Instagram, 302–3, 330–31, 335, 370
Institute of Human Relations at Yale, 13, 313
Interaction Laboratory at Yale, 202
International Cultic Studies Association, 185, 241
International Society of Krishna Consciousness (ISKCON), 186–88, 245–46, 273
International Telephone & Telegraph (ITT), 18–19
interoperability, 297, 424n34
IQ, 234
Iraq, 97
Isenberg, Nancy, 210
Isis, 98
ISKCON (International Society of Krishna Consciousness), 186–88, 245–46, 273
"Is Your Computer Insecure?" (Beardsley), 355
Italy, 167

Jackson, Charles Douglas "C. D.," 74–75
Jackson, John Hughlings, 146
jargon/specialized vocabularies, 356–57
Jefferson, Thomas, 266
Jet (magazine), 176
John Frum, the cult of, 343–51, 365, 430n14
Johnson, Christine, 217n
Jonestown, Guyana, 264–65
Jonze, Spike, 326–27
Josiah Macy Foundation, New York City, 116

Journal of Nervous and Mental Disease, 373
Journal of Psychosomatic Medicine, 142
Journal Psychology of Religion and Spirituality, 185
Just the Gist podcast, 210

Kasabian, Linda, 180–82
Katz, Elihu, 319–20
Kelly, Galen, 257
Kelly, Joe, 114
Kendall, Patricia, 318
Kennedy, Robert F., 74, 141
Kesey, Ken, 142, 147
Keynes, John Maynard, 341, 364
kidnappings
 into a cult, 254–55
 mistakes by deprogrammers, 257
 plot to kidnap Kissinger, 415n8
 ransoms, *212*, 213
 rape in, 120n
 "rendition," 104
Kille, Leonard, 131–39, 141–51, 156, 159–69, 174–76, 405n26, 406n35, 410n74
Kim, Dong Choon, 390n10
Kim, Monica, 370–71, 390n10
kinesthetic sixth sense, 301
King, Martin Luther, Jr., 141, 279
Kiribati, 135
Kissinger, Henry, 415n8
"KKKism," 58
Klapper, Joseph, 319–20
Koestler, Arthur, 90
Korean War, 21–27
 carpet bombing, 31–32
 causalities, 390n10
 Operation Killer, 27–28
 truce, 55
Korean War POWs, 21–23, 391n5, 390n30, 390n32
 American press and public opinion, 62–63
 the brainwashing of, 40–43, 46–52, *57*, 58–63, 69, 92

Chinese press and public opinion about, 63–64
 as Chinese prisoners, 33–35, 39–41, 391n42
 as compromised by Chinese women, 63, 394n49
 debriefing of repatriated POWs, 71–81
 as North Korean prisoners, 23–27, 29–33
 Operation Big Switch/Operation Little Switch, 72, 73–79
 the Pyŏktong Olympics, 52–55, 73
 Tiger Death March, 29–30, 390n34
 the 21 refusees, 55–62
 the voluntary repatriation of, 37, 55–59, 64–65, 69–71, 390n30, 390n32, 394n4, 395n14, 395n17
 see also Wills, Morris
Kramer, Adam D. I., 285–86, 295, 296n, 423n14
Krenwinkel, Patricia, 182, 183
Kropinski, Robert, 272–73, 421n55, 421n56
KUBARK (CIA manual), 83
Kupers, Terry, 172
Kuyda, Eugenia, 322–24, 326, 327, 328

Lacan, Jacques, 2–3
Lackland AFB, 82, 108–9, 111–14, 117, 120n
Lalich, Janja, 275
Land, Edwin, 135
Landmark training program, 245
Langell, Ivy, 24
Langer, Susanne, 190
Langley Porter Neuropsychiatric Institute, California, 165
Langone, Michael, 270
large language models (LLMs), 300, 326, 330–31, 428n34
Lashbrook, Robert, 117–18

law enforcement, 216–17, 221, 255, 415n8
"inception" memory of having committed a crime, 120
sci-fi notion of "pre-crime," 158, 166
SWAT teams, 216–17
Law Enforcement Assistance Administration (LEAA), 160, 171, 403n9, 404n14
Law of Love (Children of God) cult, 186, 196–97, 199–202, 243–44, 250, *256*
Lazarsfeld, Paul, 294, 318, 319
Leal, Tracy, 263, 268–69
learning to "fly," 272
Lears, Jackson, 364
leftist radicalism, 194, 215
LeMay, Curtis, 107, 123
Lemov, Rebecca
classes taught by, 98, 68, 279, 305–7
dissertation entitled "The Laboratory Imagination," 11
in graduate school and academia, 1–15, 241–43, 357
Lila, her own Replika, 329
Lepore, Jill, 427n17
Les Maîtres Fous (documentary), 351
Let Our Children Go! (Ted Patrick), 186–87, 251
levitation, 272–73
Lewin, Kurt, 50
LGBTQ+ community, 327, 330
Lianhuanhua ("picture talkbooks"), 16
Library of Congress's National Audio-Visual Conservation Center, 335
Life magazine, 56, 76, *79*, 141, *143*, *180*
Lifton, BJ, 71–72, 83

Lifton, Robert, 83–85, 188–93, 205
"Home by Ship," 397n35
Thought Reform and the Psychology of Totalism, 85, 356
The Wellfleet Seminar, 189–90
Witness to an Extreme Century, 84
Like button on Facebook, 284, 287, 423n11
Liman, Lewis, 264
"limited effects hypothesis," 320–21
Lindstrom, Lamont, 350
Linguistic Inquiry and Word Count (LIWC), 294–96, 302
litigation
malpractice cases, 149–50, 154, 176
SLAPP rule, 273
successful prosecution of cults, 247–48
Litman, Robert, 158
Little Boy and the Big Nose, The (Loy), 16–17
Li, Xiaochang, 286–87
Lloyds of London, 359
lobotomies/lobectomies, 138, 142, 143, 147, 148, 157, 163, 410n73
Locke, John, 287
Loeb, Jacques, 369–70
Lombard, Josiah Stickney, 281–83, 286, 421n2, 421n4
Long Beach VA hospital, 131, 175
"Long History of the 'Selfie'" (Dinius), 367–68, 369
Lord, Sterling, 260
Lorenz, Edward, 424n26
Los Angeles Times, 157
"lovebombing," 267
Love Israel Family, 186, 188, 254–55
Löwenthal, Leo, 319–20
Loy, David, 16–17
LSD, 111–12, 115, 118, 121, 137, 157, 186, 252, 399n24

Luhmann, Niklas, 8, 388n5
Luka (company), 324, 428n29

machine learning (ML), 300n
Mackay, Charles, 317
MacKenzie, Donald, 359
MacLean, Robert, 25, 32
"madness of crowds, the," 317
Magor, Ian, 389n7
Making of a Moonie: Choice or Brainwashing? (Barker), 258–59, 268
malpractice cases, 149–50, 154, 176
Man a Machine (manifesto), 370
Manchurian Candidate (film), 110
Manchurian Candidates, looking for, 108–10
"Mancow" conservative talk show host, 128
Mandela, Nelson, 387n3
Manipulation of Human Behavior, The (Biderman, ed.), 83
Manson family, 154–56, 179–86, 188, 195, 213
"Manson girls," 155, 182–83, 412, 412n8
Maoist reeducation, 15–16, 34–43, 48–49, *52*, 61, 68–69, 87, 92–94, 105, 391n42
Mao Zedong, 41–42, 44, 50, 55, 85, 194, 213, 238, 265
MapReduce framework, 295
Markowitz, Harry, 354
Marks, John, 108
Mark, Vernon, 132–33, 136–44, 146–50, 158–63, 166, 173, 176, 265, 293, 405n21
Martin, Paul, 257, 373
Marxism, 44, 49, 92, 93
Marx, Karl, 49, 213
Mason, B. J., 170
Mason-Dixon, 46

Index

mass communications (field of study), 308, 311, 319, 322
"Mass Conversion," project, 120n
Mass General Hospital, 139, *143*, 149–50
Mass Persuasion: The Social Psychology of a War Bond Drive (Merton), 310, 311, 315, 322, 331, 337
mass shootings, 139
Matthews, Cyndi, 201–2
Matthews, Thomas, 219
maximalists, Bitcoin, 355, 363, 431n34
"maze that a human must learn, the," 13
Mazurenko, Roman, 322
McCarran Act/"McCarranism," 51, 58
McCarthyism, 43, 51, 58, 63
McClellan, John, 74
McGowan, Rose, 196
McKilen, Michael, 137n, 411n88
McKnight, Brian, 34
Mechanization Takes Command (Giedion), 370
Meerloo, Joost, 5
Melley, Timothy, 388n6
Merriman, Ray, 341
Merton, Robert K., 308–11, 315, 319–21, 322, 329, 331, 337
Meta, 303, 335, *see also* Facebook
methamphetamine addiction, 154
#MeToo movement, 210, 260
Mexico, 178
Miami News, 15
mice and rats, experiments on, 11, 13, 157, 300–301
microaggressions, 169
micro-influencers, 321
Microsoft, 284
microsynchrony (the automatic mimicking of another's facial expressions), 287

microtargeting, 307–8
Middlemarch (G. Eliot), 2
Mike Wallace Interview, The (television show), 68
Milgram, Stanley, 202–6
"milieu control," 28
military, the, *see* warfare; *specific branches of the US military*
millennials, love of astrology and Bitcoin, 341–42
Miller, Neal, 13
Miłosz, Czesław, 1, 14
Milton, John, 323
Mind: An Essay on Human Feeling (Langer), 190
mind-control techniques, *see* brainwashing
Mindszenty, József, 19–20, 119–20
Minsky, Marvin, 300n
"mirror neurons," 424n19
missionaries, 26, 84, 267–68, 345
MIT, 131, 135, 145, 247, 370
Mitford, Jessica, 166
Mitter, Rana, 45
MK-SEARCH, 166
MK-ULTRA, 14, 50, 95–95, 110–11, 115–18, 151–52, 155, 166, 192, 222, 252, 258
modern portfolio theory (MPT) investment strategy, 354
"Mo Letters," 196, *see also* Children of God
Molko, David, 263–70, 274
"Momism," 394n48
Montagne, Renee, 210
Moonies (Unification Church), 188, 249, 254–55, 261–62, 265–69, 274
Moon, Sun Myung, 262, 266, 267
Morantz, Paul, 264
Morgan, Charles, 127
Morris, Erroll, 413n19
Moscow Show Trials, 90
Mother Beatrix, 29–30
Mowrer, O. H., *312*, 313
Mozilla, 328

MP3s, development of, 288n
Murray, Henry, 231
Murrow, Edward R., 335
Musk, Elon, 172–73, 339
My Lai Massacre, 189
MySpace, 284

Nakamoto, Satoshi, 354, 361
napalm, 30–32
Narabayashi, Hirataro, 138
narrowcasting, 334–36, 375
National Institute of Mental Health (NIMH), 150, 155, 404n14
National Security Agency (NSA), 361, 432n38
National Television System Commission, 336
Nation (magazine), 97
Native Americans, 99, 351
"natural experiments," 69, 81, 308–9, 329, 426n4
natural language processing software, 294
Nature (magazine), 296, 302–3
Nazi Germany, 74, 77, 168, 190–91
NBC (TV network), 332
"negging," 340
networks, social, 290–91, *see also* social media; social network sites (SNS)
Neumann, Maurice, 72n
Neuralink implant, 172–73
Neurological Clinic, Tokyo, 138
New Bedford VA hospital, 175
New Haven, Connecticut, cafe that serves free dystopia, 280
New Hebrides, *see* Vanuatu
New Religious Movements, 260–61
New Republic (magazine), 296–97
Newsweek (magazine), 124
New York City, *316*, *334*
New Yorker (magazine), 34, 293

New York Times, 21, 97, 124, 140, 192, 234–35, 256, 272, 299, 339, 352
New York Times Sunday Magazine, 178–79
Nigeria, 8, 387n4
Nike missile sites, 165–66
Nobel Prize winners, 77, 262, 354
non-fungible tokens (NFTs), 340–41
normal or ordinary numbing, 191, 205, 209
Norway, 293
nose blowing through the ages, 207–9, 274, 372
NPR, 210–11, 238
nuclear testing, 135
numbing, 188–93, 205, 209
Nuremberg Code, 168
Nuremberg war crimes trials, 77, 168
NXIVM, 4, 263–64, 340

Oakland, California, 213, 215, 264, 267, 268
Obedience (film), 203
Obedience to Authority (Milgram), 203
Objectivity (Galison and Daston), 296n
"observing commensality," 344
"observing observers as observers," 8
Office of Strategic Services (OSS), 15, 16, 109
Ofshe, Richard, 263, 265, 273
Ogrisseg, Jerald, 126, 402n59
Okinawa, 125n
Oklahoma Medical Research Foundation, 116, 118
Olson, Eric, 192, 413n19
Olson, Frank, 118, 192, 413n19
Olympics, the POW, 52–55, 73
One Flew Over the Cuckoo's Nest (Kesey), 142, 147
O'Neill, Tom, 109, 120n, 155

online dating, 327
online therapy schemes, 22
OpenAI, 323n, 326–28
Operation Big Switch, 72, 73, 76–79
Operation CHAOS, 166
Operation Dominic, 135, 403n5
Operation Killer, 27
Operation Little Switch, 72, 73–74, 75
Operation Paperclip, 74
ordinary numbing, 191, 205, 209
Origins of Totalitarianism, The (Arendt), 39
Orne, Martin, 125, 222, 227, 231–33, 251
Orrick, William, 223
Ortega, Francisco, 158
OSINT (open source intelligence), 16
Osnos, Evan, 293
Outer Mission district of San Francisco, 221

Pacific theater in World War II, 23, 30–31, *see also* World War II
pain
  algorithms serving up pleasure and, 69
  anesthesia (the blocking of pain), 108, 122
  as emotional contagion, 302
  hyperesthesia (the multiplying of pain), 14, 122
  inflicting pain on others, 205
  the pain-fear-pain cycle, 109
  "pain points," 67
  resisting, 103, 108
  self-inflicted, 92
  suffering and the intensity of pain, 313
  when internalized, 22
  when removed, 92
  see also suffering; torture; trauma
Pakistan, 104

Paley Center for Media, New York City, 335
Palmer, Susan, 262
Paltrow, Gwyneth, 67
Papin, Joe, 235, *236*
paranoia, 8, 61, 85, 93, 118–19, 131–33, 136, 148, 164, 249, 264, 279
Park, Katharine, 167–68
"participant observers," 155
password, the president's, 358
Patrick, Ted, 186–87, 249–50, 251–57, 419n23
Patten, Ernest, 265
Patty/Tania (Belcher and D. West), 210, 217n
Paul's conversion on the Road to Damascus, 18
Pavlov Institute, 123
Payne Whitney Psychiatric Clinic of The New York Hospital (now Weill Cornell Medical), 108, 151
Pearl Harbor attack, 265
Pentagon, *see* US Department of Defense
People (magazine), 251
People's Daily (newspaper), 63
Peoples Temple (of Jim Jones), 264–65
People's Volunteer Army, 26
Pepsi ads of the late 1960s, 178
persuasion, 4, 14, 18, 21–22
  coercive persuasion, 4, 14, 81, 229, 238, 374, 414n29
  hyper-persuasion, 22, 193, 277, 337
  microtargeting, 307–8
Petersen, Glenn, 97–105, 109, 125, 127
Philadelphia Inquirer (newspaper), 259
Philippines, 53–54, 125n
Phoenix, River, and his family, 196, 250
Piccadilly Circus, London, *315*

Index

Pickwick Papers, The (Dickens), 49
Piepenbring, Dan, 120n, 155
Pierce, Chester, 169
pigeons, experiments on, 312
Pirsig, Robert, 329
Pittel, Stephen, 156
"Plastic Man," 153
Poe, Edgar Allan, 359
Polaroid, 132, 135, 144
police, *see* law enforcement
Ponzi schemes, 362
Pooley, Jeff, 320
Portuguese Empire, 345
Port-Vila, Vanuatu, 343, 347
post-traumatic stress disorder (PTSD), 22, 84, 127, 193, 194, 373, 413n20
Powell, Roosevelt, 55
power and hierarchy numbing, 191
Princeton University, 109–10, 303
prisoners of war in Korea, *see* Korean War POWs
Proceedings of the National Academy of Sciences (PNAS), 285
Prolixin injections, 175
"protracted spiritual gang rape," 261
"pseudo apathy," 79
"pseudo-identity syndrome," 373
"pseudo self," 201, 202, 221, 414n29
psychedelics, 179, *see also* LSD
"Psychepad" at Harvard, 155
psychogenesis, 209, 274, 372
psychohistory, 190
Psychological Warfare Board, 74
psychosis, 120, 406n35
psychosurgery, 141–42, 408n60
 amygdalectomies/amygdalotomies, 138, 147–48, 168, 404n12
 lobotomies/lobectomies, 138, 142, 143, 147, 148, 157, 163, 410n73
 stereotactic surgeries, 142, 148
 see also brain implants; electrodes
psychotechnology, 163, 239n
psychotherapy, 46, 253, 257, 292–93
psychotropic drugs, 148, 152–53
Public Domain Review (website), 368
public-key cryptography, 360–61
Pynchon, Thomas, 184, 279
Pyŏktong Olympics, 52–55, 73
Pyongyang, North Korea, 26–27, 29

quantification, 6
 A/B testing, 268, 296
 electroencephalogram (EEG), 283
 electromyography (EMG), 287
 galvanometers, 6–7, 281–82
 IQ, 234
 Rorschach inkblot test, 77, 78–81
 Sentence Completion Test, 78
 Thematic Apperception Test, 78, 80–81
Quigley, Joan, 341

race
 anti-Semitism, 319
 civil rights movement, 108, 169–70, 179
 "KKKism," 58
 microaggressions, 169
 slavery in the US, 397n3
 see also African Americans
radicalization, 194, 218, 237, 375
radio, 60, 74, 320, 331–36, 347–48
 see also broadcasting

randomized controlled trials (RCTs), 303, 426n4
Rangel, Charles, 46
Raniere, Keith, 263–64, *see also* NXIVM
ransoms, kidnapping, 212, 213
rape, 5, 214, 244
 in cults, 255
 cults as "protracted spiritual gang rape," 261
 in kidnappings, 120n
 of Patty Hearst, 210–11, 214, *214*, 235
 the Willie Horton TV ads of the 1988 presidential election, 335–36
Rapson, Richard, 287
Ray, James Earl, 141
Ray, Lawrence, 263–64
Reagan, Nancy, 341
Reagan, Ronald, 161, 213, 341
"reality practice," 122, 402n51
Reddit, 325, 327–29, 331
Redondo Beach, California, 183
reeducation, Maoist, 15–16, 34–43, 48–49, *52*, 61, 68–69, 87, 92–94, 105, 391n42
"Refreezing" of beliefs, 50
Regan, Donald, 341
religion
 legal protections accorded to, 246
 line between a cult and a religion, 244–47
 missionaries, 26, 84, 267–68, 345
 New Religious Movements, 260–61
 sociology of, 259–63
Remembered Prisoners of a Forgotten War (an oral history of the Korean War), 23
"rendition," 104
Replika, 311, 324–30, 428n29

"Report of the Task Force on Deceptive and Indirect Techniques of Persuasion and Control," 270–71
Report to the Supreme Conference of the State, 44
resistance, *see* anti-brainwashing
Resistance Training Laboratories (RTL), 125
"rice brain," 77–78
Richardson, James T., 259, 263
Riefenstahl, Leni, 318, *319*
"rise of emotional machines," 326
Rizzolatti, Giacomo, 424n19
Robbins, Thomas, 259
Rogers, Daniel, 360
Roosevelt, Franklin D., 308, 320
Rorschach, Hermann, 78
Rorschach inkblot test, 77, 78–81
Rose, Alan, 154
Rouch, Jean, 351
Rowe, James "Nick," 106, 399n16
Rush, Scott, 61n
Russian propaganda, 46
Ryan, Leo, 264
Ryan, Mitchell, 17

San Antonio News, 120
sanitation, deprivation of, 29, 32–34
Sanmao ("Three Hairs"), *17*
Sarah Lawrence College, New York, 263–64
Sargent, William, 417n34
satanic panic of the 1990s, 257
Saturday Evening Post, 20, 21, 122, 124
Saxbe, William, 220
"scalable subject," 298
Scheflin, Alan, 263
Schein, Edgar, 50, 80–81, 85, 187, 231, 247, 270
schizophrenia, 93, 131, 173, 249

"School for Sadists," 94, 123–24
Schrader, Stuart, 216
Schuetz, Janice, 210
Schwable, Frank, 82
Science (magazine), 141, 302–3
science, *see* behavioral science
Scientific Revolution, 371
Scientology, 198n, 259, 261–62
Search for the "Manchurian Candidate," The (J. Marks), 108
second-generation abuse (SGA) crisis, 193–94, 196, 243
Second World War, *see* World War II
Secrets of Women, The (K. Park), 167–68
Segal, Henry A., 77–78
selfies, 367–68, 369
Self-Levitation Case, 272–73
self-torture, 35–36, 127
semantic analysis, 294
Sennett, Richard, 190
Sentence Completion Test, 78
SERE (Survival, Evasion, Resistance, and Escape) training, 97–105, 123–28, 231, 399n16, 402n59
sex addiction, 63
sexualization of technology, 184, 325, 328–29, 428n29
SFGate (newspaper), 245
Shanghai, 86–87, 292–93
Shannon, Claude, 300n
Shapin, Steven, 371
Sharp, Paul F., 115
Shatan, Chaim, 192
Shaver, Jimmy, 120n
Shaw, Bernard, 238
Shay, Jonathan, 70
Shils, Edward, 319–20
shitcoins, 341
Show Trials, Stalinist, 90
Simpson's paradox, 427n14
Sinatra, Frank, 110

Singer, Margaret, 274–75
in civil suits against the Moonies, 269–72
cult research and rescue, 197–99, 244–49
in the Hearst trial, 233–34, 418n5, 418n7
the limitations of a Singerian view, 273–74
shadow cast over cases where she testified, 272
view of cults, 244–47
Sirhan Sirhan, 141
Skinner, B. F., 178, 312–14
Skinner, Lowell, 61
Skype, 292–93
SLAPP rule, 273
sleep deprivation, 401n45
in deprogramming, 249–50
in the Maoist reeducation, 19, 30, 65, 90, 92, 95
research in the US, 104–6, 118–20, 152, 226, 227, 236
Smith, Aminda, 42, 391n8
Smith, David Elgin, 153–54, 156
Smith, Jack, 192
Smith, Kate, 305–11, 313, 319–21, 329, 332, 352
Smith, Roger, 154, 156
Snow, John, 309
Snyder, Elise, 292
social bonds, 33, 81, 317
social/human engineering, 3, 12, 122, 133, 355
emotional engineering, 280–81, 297–98, 299–301, 369
Gramscian social control, 425n42
social control procedures through social networks, 290–91
studies of the crowd, 315–18, 428n37
see also brainwashing; behavioral science
social media
addiction to, 193, 312

Index

AI chatbots and, 326–30
behavior change
  through, 322–31
brand micro-influencers, 321
doomscrolling, 311–14, 426n10
emotional chains of technology, 305–37
hyper-persuasion in, 22, 193, 277, 337
incels, 325
its hold over "human interiority," 367–71
interoperability in, 297, 424n34
large language models (LLMs), 300, 326, 330–31, 428n34
the mass in mass persuasion, 315–22
the massive scale of social engineering through, 285–86, 291, 297
micro-influencers, 321
"negging," 340
online dating, 327
online therapy schemes, 22
our algorithmically defined world, 281, 284, 286–87, 289n, 291, 298, 302–3, 311–13, 370, 375
the privacy paradox, 280
the "scalable subject," 298
the selfie, 367–68, 369
the shift from open web to social web, 297–99
truth and, 371–72
social network sites (SNS), 284, 423n10
Instagram, 302–3, 330–31, 335, 370
Reddit, 325, 327–29, 331
Twitter, 211, 253–54, 339–42, 353, 370
see also Facebook; YouTube
sociogenesis, 209, 274, 372
sociology, 7, 8, 106, 195, 259–63, 316–18, 321

sodium amytal, 120n
Sommer, Adam, 254, 356–58, 363, 431n32, 431n33, 431n34
Soulbound Tokens, 362
South Africa, apartheid in, 387n3
South China Morning Post, 83
South Middlesex Daily News, 360
Southworth, Robert, 368
Soviet Union, 87, 89, 90–92, 118, 231
Spanish Empire, 345
"speaking bitterness," 45, 51
Spiegel, David, 253
Spinoza, Baruch, 297
Spiro, Melford, 388n2
Stalin, Joseph, 90
Stanford Center for Advanced Study in the Behavioral Sciences, 152–53
Stanford medica school, 252–53
Stanford Social Media Lab, 299
Stanislavski, Konstantin, 287
Stanley Cobb Laboratory for Psychiatric Research, 139
Stark, Luke, 298
State Reform School for Boys, Massachusetts, 99
Stead AFB, Nevada, 107, 122–24, 231
stereotactic surgeries, 142, 148
Stevens, Hallam, 295
stimoceivers, *143*, 159–60
stimuli bombardment systems, 299
Stockholm syndrome, 214, 238–39
stress, *see* trauma
struggle sessions, *see* Maoist reeducation
Stubblebine, James M., 165–66
Suan camp, 29

Succinylcholine, 411n88
suffering
  anticipation of, 313
  experience of suffering in cults, 193–94
  quality and type of, 36
  the struggle to identify suffering, 78, 81, 95, 281
  unresolved suffering and vulnerability, 23, 63, 190–92
  see also abuse; trauma
sunk-cost fallacy, 5, 94, 206
surveillance capitalism, 365
Survival School (US Army), 105
"survival training," 98, 105, 124, 124–27
SWAT teams, 216–17
"sweat box," 99–105, 109, 123, 398n13
Sweet, William H., 138–41, 160, 162–63, 403n9, 405n22
Switch operations, 72, 73–79
sycophancy, 331, 428n34
Symbionese Liberation Army (SLA), 211–27, 235, 418n5
Synanon, 155, 264, 265
"Syrian box," 99–105, 109, 123, 398n13

TA (technical analysis), 353–54
Tate-LaBianca murder trial, 180–84, *see also* Manson family
Tavistock/A.K. Rice Institute, England, 152
technological distancing (techno-bureaucratic numbing), 191
technology
  the "alien tech" that fuels cargoism, 339, 349, 351–52
  blockchain technology, 174, 340–41, 351–52, 355–56, 359–63, 364, 370

technology (*continued*)
  sexualization of, 184, 325, 328–29, 428n29
  see also quantification; social media; social network sites (SNS)
Telegram messaging app, 322
Temkin, Owsei 145
Terminal Man, The (Crichton), 149
terrorism, 4, 8, 104–5
  see also specific groups labeled terrorist
"textualization of subjectivity," 337
Thailand, CIA black sites in, 104, 398n12
thalamus, 138, 139
Thematic Apperception Test, 78, 80–81
therapy
  hypnotherapy, 252n
  online therapy schemes, 22
  psychotherapy, 46, 253, 257, 292–93
  psychotropic drugs, 148, 152–53
  see also brain implants; electrodes; psychosurgery
"therapy groups," 245
"There's No Data Like More Data" (Li), 287
Thought Reform and the Psychology of Totalism (Lifton), 85, 356
thought reform/remolding, *see* brainwashing
Tiger Death March, 29–30, 390n34
TikTok, 326, 341
Time (magazine), 178–79, 233
Times of London, 244
Tom Sawyer (Twain), 49
"Tom's Diner" (song), 288n
Toobin, Jeffrey, 210–11, 236
Tooze, Adam, 361–62
Topeka Psychoanalytic Institute, 152
Torrance, Paul, 107

torture
  enhanced interrogation techniques, 97, 104, 128
  time in "the hot box," 99–105, 109, 123, 398n13
  waterboarding, 101, 126, 127–28
  see also deprivation
totalitarianism, 39
training, *see* anti-brainwashing
Transcendental Meditation (TM), 272
trauma, 8, 22, 40, 41, 67–69, 233, 374, 413n20
  being "broken," 397n4
  color shock, 78
  "delayed massive trauma" in soldiers, 192
  gross stress reaction, 22, 193
  interfamilial, intragenerational trauma, 289
  the numbing of trauma and cults, 188–93
  shell shock, 22, 41
traumatic brain injuries, 140
"traumatic neurosis," 221, 233
Travis Air Force Base, California, 76
treason, 52, 77
Tripp, Peter, 119–20, 401n45
Tristram Shandy (Sterne), 287
Triumph of the Will (film), *319*
Truman, Harry, 19, 24, 26, 46, 52, 56
Trust in Numbers (Porter), 6
Tufekci, Zeynep, 301, 425n42
Tulsa World (newspaper), 55
Turing test, 327
Turncoat (Wills), 43
Twain, Mark, 49
20/20 news show, 183–84
Twin Oaks Intentional Community, 178
Twitchell, H. H., 114
Twitter, 211, 253–54, 339–42, 353, 370

U.S. News & World Report, 62
ungrounding, 27–29, 33, 43, 69
Unification Church (Moonies), 188, 249, 254–55, 261–62, 265–69, 274
Union Farm Workers, 216
United Nations (UN), 24–26, 53, 57
United States
  capture of bin Laden, 104
  civil rights movement, 108, 169–70, 179
  common-law doctrine of charitable immunity, 246
  Digital Signature Act of 2000, 358
  freedom of speech in, 17, 273
  see also specific agencies and departments
Universal McCann (marketing agency), 286
University of California system
  Berkeley, 2, 12–13, 211–12, 215, 267
  Neuropsychiatric Institute (NPI) at UCLA, 156, 165, 169, 172, 186, 222, 233, 247
  Violence Center at UCLA, 156, 157–60, 161, 165–66, 170–74
University of Denver, 78
University of Hawaii, 283–90, 301–4
University of Iowa, 107–8
University of Michigan, 284
University of Minnesota, 107
University of Oklahoma medical school, 109, 112, 115, 117, 151, 400n25, 400n31
University of Texas at Austin, 139, 294, 303
US Air Force
  Camp Carson, Colorado, 107

Index

Lackland AFB, 82, 108–9, 111–14, 117, 120n
  Personnel and Training Research Center, 122
  Psychosomatic Laboratory, 114
Stead AFB, Nevada, 107, 122–24, 231
Travis Air Force Base, California, 76
Westover AFB, Massachusetts, 71
US Army
  the "Army of One," 12
  Code of Conduct, 94, 123–26, 168
  Fort Bragg, North Carolina, 106
  "School for Sadists," 94, 123–24
  Survival School, 105
  Valley Forge Army Hospital, 75, 76
US Department of Defense Advisory Committee on Prisoners of War, 109
  Veterans Administration hospitals, 75, 76, 131, 175
  Walter Reed National Military Medical Center, Maryland, 19, 78–82, 113, 119
US National Naval Medical Center (now Water Reed), Maryland, 19, 78–82, 113, 119
US Navy SERE school, 97–105, 123–28, 231, 399n16, 402n59
US Supreme Court, 269–70

Vacaville State Prison, California, 165, 166–67, 172, 410n73, 411n88
Valenstein, Elliot, 150
Valley Forge Army Hospital, Pennsylvania, 75, 76
Van der Kolk, Bessel, 68, 373–74

Van Houten, Leslie, 182, 186
Vanity Fair (magazine), 127–28
Vanuatu cargo cult of John Frum, 343–51, 365, 430n14
Van Winkle, Rich, 127
Varian, Hal, 296
Vega, Suzanne, 288n
Veneris, James, 61n
Veterans Administration hospitals, 75, 76, 131, 175
Victorious Fatherland Liberation War, *see* Korean War
Vidal, Fernando, 158
Vidan, Gili, 359–60
Vienna, Austria, 318–19, *320*
Vietnam War, 25–26, 70, 71, 222
  brutalization and atrocity during the, 189–92
  My Lai Massacre, 189
  post-Vietnam syndrome, 192
  POWs during the, 105–6
  veterans of the, 25–26, 84, 97, 98, 101–2, 106, 218
Vincent, Charles, 85–94, 185
violence, 97–128
  and the brain, 139–40
  hospital violence units, 143, 160
  mass shootings, 139
  My Lai Massacre, 189
  solving the problem of, 133
Violence and the Brain (Mark and Ervin), 140, *144*, 160, 405n21
Violence Center at UCLA, 156, 157–60, 161, 165–66, 170–74
Vogeler, Lucile, 19
Vogeler, Robert, 18–19, 21
Voice of America, 60
"volleyball problem, the," 53–54, 95
voudon possession, 351

Wallace, Geoge, 161
Walter Reed National Military Medical Center, Maryland, 19, 78–82, 113, 119, 401n45
Warburton, Ida-Gaye, 417n42
warfare
  carpet bombing, 31–32
  "delayed massive trauma" in soldiers, 192
  Manchurian Candidates, looking for, 108–10
  napalm, 30–32
  SERE (Survival, Evasion, Resistance, and Escape) training, 97–105, 123–28, 231, 399n16, 402n59
  war bonds, 305–8, 310
  see also Korean War; Vietnam War
Warner Springs survival school, 100–101, 125
war neurosis, 22, 41
War to Resist America and Assist Korea, *see* Korean War
waterboarding, 101, 126, 127–28
Water-Cure Journal, 364n
Waters, John, 238
Watson, John B., 300–301
Watts rebellion, Los Angeles, 138, 216
Web3, 174, 362, 370
Webb, Harold, 61n
Weill Cornell Medical, New York City, 108, 151
Weinstein, Robert (Crypto Damus), 353–54
Welles, Orson, 308
Wellfleet Seminar, The (Lifton), 189–90
Wells, H. G., 308
Weneyuga, 351
West, Don, 210, 217n
West, John, 407n41
West, Kay, 152

West, Louis Jolyon, 20–21, 107–9
  Aldous Huxley and, 121–22
  California state prisons, 164–66
  colleagues of, 400n25, 400n31
  defending his projects, 169–72
  the elephant on LSD, 115, 137
  his "Psychepad" at Harvard, 155
  at a newly closed Nike missile site, 165–66
  at the new Neuropsychiatric Institute (NPI) at UCLA, 156, 165, 169, 172, 186, 222, 233, 247
  in the Patty Hearst trial, 186, 260, 416n33, 418n9
  infiltrating a teen gang, 120–21
  participant observation in Haight-Ashbury, 151–56
  sleep deprivation, 118–20
  at the Violence Center at UCLA, 156, 157–60, 161, 165–66, 170–74
  work on false confessions, 109–14
Westover AFB, Massachusetts, 71
West, Sarah Myers, 359
Westworld (TV series), 184
Whewell, William, 371
whistleblowers, 168
White Album, The (Didion), 180
White, William, 61n
Whitman, Charles, 139, 404n15, 404n16
Why We Fight (film series), 318
Wigner, Eugene P., 262
Williams, Charlie, 388n6

Williams, Raymond, 315, 426n13
Willie Horton TV ads of the 1988 presidential election, 335–36
Wills, Kaiyen, *37*, 61
Wills, Morris, 23–33, 35–37, *57*
  the brainwashing of, 40–43, 46–52, *57*, 58–63, 69, 92
  haunted by the memory of lima beans, 35–36
  his as-told-to autobiography *Turncoat*, 43
  insisting on his free choice, 62–63, 394n48
Wilson, C. E., 391n5
Wilson, Myron, 57–58
Winnington, Alan, 54
Wired (magazine), 326
Witness to an Extreme Century (Lifton), 84
Wolfe, William ("Cujo"), 214–15, 235–36
Wolff, Harold, 108–9, 110, 116, 399n21, 401n39
Wolf, Stewart G., 117, 401n39
women
  discrimination in academia, 248
  as foreign enemy, 61n, 63
  the "Manson girls," 155, 182–83, 412
  menstruation and violence, 157
  as subject of biological study, 167–68
  psychosurgery on white women, 164
  robotic women, 184
  sex as recruiting tactic, 61n, 63, 200, 201
  taking SERE training, 126
  as victims of abuse, 188, 239
World of Warcraft (video game), 362

World War I, 45, 305
World War II, 11
  atomic bomb on Hiroshima, 191
  German scientists after, 74–75, 168–69, 191, 320
  Guadalcanal, 343, 344
  Office of Strategic Services (OSS), 15, 16, 109
  Pearl Harbor attack, 265
  postwar "big science" boom, 387n2
Wormwood (documentary), 413n19

X, *see* Twitter

Yale University, 13, 202, 313
Yelp, 370
Young, Allan, 413n20
YouTube
  of Frummers in Vanuatu, 349
  military anti-brainwashing training online, 101, 126, 128
  of Milgram's experiments, 203
  of Transcendental Meditation "flying," 272
  radicalization via, 375
  the astro-crypto community on, 352–53, 364

Zablocki, Benjamin, 274, 420n34, 422n58
Zeavin, Hannah, 293
Zellers, Larry, 26
Zhao, Changpeng, 340
Zittrain, Jonathan, 296–97
zombies, 5, 74, 184, 234, 313
Zoom calls, 211, 292
Zuboff, Shoshanna, 299
Zuckerberg, Mark, 293, *see also* Facebook
Zwigenberg, Ran, 413n20